SLAVERY *in the Age of* REASON

Alexandra A. Chan

SLAVERY
in the Age of
REASON

Archaeology at a
New England Farm

The University of Tennessee Press / Knoxville

Copyright © 2007 by The University of Tennessee Press / Knoxville.
All Rights Reserved.
Cloth: First printing, 2007.
Paper: First printing, 2015.

Library of Congress Cataloging-in-Publication Data

Chan, Alexandra A., 1973–
Slavery in the age of reason : archaeology at a New England farm /
Alexandra A. Chan. — 1st ed.
      p. cm.
Includes bibliographical references and index.
ISBN-13: 978-1-62190-192-1

1. Isaac Royall House (Medford, Mass.) 2. Medford (Mass.)—Antiquities. 3. Medford
(Mass.)—Buildings, structures, etc. 4. Royall, Isaac, 1677–1739—Family. 5. Medford
(Mass.)—Biography. 6. Slavery—Massachusetts—Medford—History. 7. Slaves—
Massachusetts—Medford—Social conditions. 8. Farm life—Massachusetts—Medford—
History. 9. Landscape—Social aspects—Massachusetts—Medford—History.
10. Medford (Mass.)—Race relations. I. Title.

F74.M5C48 2007
305.8009744'4—dc22   2006101989

To my husband

CONTENTS

Illustrations

Figures

Tables

Acknowledgments

Exploring the world that the people at Ten Hills Farm made together—both black and white—has been in part a labor of love for me, but one that would never have seen the light of day without the financial, intellectual, and emotional support I have received from various quarters. I owe a great debt of gratitude to all of the following.

The intellectual support and guidance of my advisers and mentors have been formative in my development as a historical archaeologist. Dr. Mary Beaudry and Dr. Ricardo Elia, both of the Boston University Department of Archaeology, have opened my eyes to approaches, methods, and styles that have kept me passionate about the discipline, and they gave me the autonomy to run these excavations as I saw fit, for better or for worse. Converting a dissertation into a book, and one intended to reach a wider audience, is naturally a difficult undertaking and the help and guidance of my editor at the University of Tennessee Press, Scot Danforth, and the constructive, as well as challenging, comments of my various reviewers have been invaluable in that process.

Of course, the Royall House Association's dedication to creating a new history for the site lies at the base of all work conducted there. My thanks go to Peter Gittelman, then-president of the association, for his vision and interest and commitment; Jay Griffin, the curator, for his fount of knowledge and local connections; and Fred Schlicher and Leslie Spieth, the two-person public relations office, for facilitating work at the site and for drumming up interest and providing a venue for sharing the finds over the years. Thanks, too, are owed to the City of Medford for granting access to the park and for contributing the original topographical site plan and to the Ladies' Gardening Club of Medford, who forgave the mincemeat our teams made of its lovely grounds.

I also wish to say thank you to the Boston University Graduate School of Arts and Sciences, Tufts University, the Medford Historical Society, the Royall House Association, and the Ford Foundation for providing financial support during the first and second seasons of excavation. And then my heartfelt gratitude must also go to Dr. Julie Hansen, of Boston University, who was unflaggingly jovial and accommodating about conserving artifacts and floating and analyzing numerous soil samples when the funds had finally run out. Who says you cannot get something for nothing?

Dr. Kenneth Kvamme, Meg Watters, and Daniel Welch, all then of Boston University, also volunteered their time as consulting experts in the field of remote sensing, helping us by locating important subsurface features before shovel ever went to earth. Not to be forgotten are the many excellent student volunteers as well, particularly Trent Bingham, Karen Mansfield, and Matt Tennyson, whose grunt work in the field and lab for three years made this analysis possible.

Finally, I would like to thank my parents, Robert and Karen Chan, for instilling in me their own natural curiosity about the world and the untold millions who called it home before we did.

A Note on Permissions

Parts of chapter 6 appear in different form in "Bringing the Out Kitchen In? Experiential Landscapes of Black and White New England," in *Archaeology of Atlantic Africa and African Diaspora,* ed. Akinwumi Ogundiran and Toyin Falola (Bloomington: Indiana University Press, forthcoming).

Also, I gratefully acknowledge permission of the museums named below to reproduce the following images:

Figure 23 (left): John Singleton Copley (American, 1738–1815), *Isaac Royall,* 1769. Oil on canvas, 127 x 101.6 cm (50 x 40 in.). Museum of Fine Arts, Boston. The M. and M. Karolik Collection of Eighteenth-Century American Arts, 39.247.

Figure 23 (right): John Singleton Copley (American, ca. 1738–1815. *Mrs. Isaac Royall (née Elizabeth McIntosh),* ca. 1769. Oil on cavas. Unframed, 50" H x 40", 127 cm x 101.6 cm; framed, 58" H x 47" W, 147.3 cm x 120.6 cm. Virginia Museum of Fine Arts, Richmond. Gift of Mrs. A. D. Williams.

Figure 28: John Singleton Copley (American, 1738–1815), *Mary and Elizabeth Royall,* about 1758. Oil on canvas, 145.73 x 122.24 cm (57³/8 x 48 in.). Museum of Fine Arts, Boston. John Knight Fox Fund, 25.49.

ABBREVIATIONS

AHS	Antigua Historical Society
MAR	Massachusetts Acts and Resolves
MHC	Massachusetts Historical Commission
MHS	Massachusetts Historical Society
NEHGS	New England Historical and Genealogical Society
NPS	National Park Service
RHA	Royall House Association
RHS	Rhode Island Historical Society

Introduction

I must ask your Pardon for the Trouble of Sending me one more [Negro Boy], not less than 16; & not exceeding 20 years of Age. Let him be a likely one, altho' he should cost five Pounds extraordinary.

—Jonathan Belcher, governor of Massachusetts, to Isaac Royall, Sr., 1732

. . . nothing should inhibit the impulse that causes a writer to render experience which may be essentially foreign to his own world; it is a formidable challenge and among an artist's most valuable privileges.

—William Styron, 1992

Overview

In 1783 an angry, illiterate, and elderly African woman, known simply as Belinda, dramatically entered Boston's historical stage when she recalled for her transcriber, thought to be Prince Hall, how she had been kidnapped at age 12 from her home on the banks of the Rio de Volta, by men "whose faces were like the moon" (RHA files; fig. 1). She is of interest not just because she belonged to the Isaac Royall family and would have spent nearly 50 years of her life on its Medford, Massachusetts, estate, which is the topic of this book, and not just because her story, as recounted in the petition, is dramatic, tragic, and consummately human. She is also of interest because she managed to break the bonds of anonymity that held the vast majority of her comrades in suffering—the thousands of African and Creole slaves who lived and labored and died in colonial New England—and causes us to focus our intellectual curiosity and academic inquiry on the African and African American experience in bondage there. But Belinda's plight can do little more than pique our curiosity. The details of her life are painted in a single document in broad brush strokes, and her ultimate fate is completely unknown. Even less can be said about her fellow slaves who had labored beside her for the Royalls during their tenure in Medford from 1737 to 1775. For 50 years, Belinda told her transcriber, "her faithful hands" had been

> Compelled to ignoble servitude for the benefit of an Isaac Royall, untill, as if Nations must be agitated, and the world convulsed for the preservation of that freedom which the Almighty Father intended for all the human Race, the present war was Commenced. (1783; RHA files)

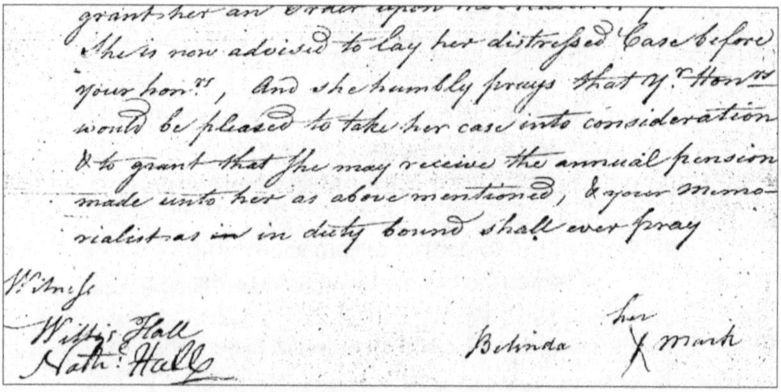

grant her an Order upon the
She is now advised to lay her distressed Case before
your hon.rs, And she humbly prays that Y.r Hon.rs
would be pleased to take her case into consideration
& to grant that she may receive the annual pension
made unto her as above mentioned, & your Memo-
rialist as in in duty bound shall ever pray

Willis Hall
Nath.l Hall
Belinda her X mark

Fig. 1. "The Memorial of Belinda, an African, formerly a Servant to the late Isaac Royal Esq an Absentee." Massachusetts Archives, *Acts and Resolves,* October Session, 1787, chapter 142. (Courtesy of the Massachusetts State Archives.)

And the writer of the petition went on to say that

> The face of your Petitioner is now marked with the furrows of time, and her frame feebly bending under the oppression of years, while she, by the Laws of the Land, is denied the enjoyment of one morsel of that immense wealth, apart [*sic*] whereof hath been accumilated [*sic*] by her own industry, and the whole ugmented [*sic*] by her servitude. (1783; RHA files)

The Royalls, as Loyalists to the Crown, had by this time been in exile in England for eight years, and Isaac Royall had been dead for two. Belinda, one of the women whom they had held in slavery and who had been left behind in Massachusetts, was petitioning the General Court for an annual pension paid out of Isaac Royall's estate to sustain her and her infirm daughter in their newfound and impoverished state of freedom. Massachusetts had freed all of its slaves that very year. Her petition was granted—once. She returned to court in 1787, stating that she

> afterwards received out of the Treasury £15.12 for one year's allowance, & no
> more & that she never could obtain any more to this day tho she often applied to
> the Governour & Council to grant her an Order upon the Treasurer for the same.
> (House of Representatives 1787)

Once again her petition was granted, but what became of Belinda or her daughter after 1787, the documents do not tell (House of Representatives 1787). From a modern perspective, they can be said to have ended their lives mostly the way they had lived them—anonymously. The fact that Belinda was enslaved for most of her life, the fact that she had to petition the court to get any kind of compensation for her years of forced labor and oppression, the fact that she had to fight to get the pension even after it had been granted, and the fact that this episode provides the most information we have on any enslaved African or Creole at the Royalls' estate, all attest the racist attitudes and racial discrimination born of slavery that have plagued this country—North and South—from its inception. Not only does the incident raise questions about what it might have been like to be enslaved in New England and the ways it might have been different from or similar to plantation slavery in the South or Caribbean, but it reminds us of how our country's history has made addressing these questions from the documentary evidence alone a difficult undertaking.

This book attempts to partially fill that lacuna by providing a historical archaeological investigation of colonial New England slavery. The legacy of colonialism continues to pervade societies throughout the Western Hemisphere, shaping their histories as well as their modern national consciousness. Its study therefore remains both vital and relevant but has been dominated by historians (McEwan and Waselkov 2003:1). Historical archaeology has long counted among its key contributions to our understanding of colonial encounters in the Americas, however, the "value of archaeological sources in exploring the *materiality* of those encounters" (Stahl, Mann, and Loren 2004:83, emphasis added). One great advantage that archaeologists have, for example, is that their principal objects of study—artifacts—serve as primary evidence (much like primary documents for the historian) of people forgotten or represented only indirectly in the written record. Artifacts are also "historical events" unlike any other in that they can effectively be reexperienced in the present (Prown 1993:3). They allow us to empathize with, and engage, past people not just intellectually, or academically, as historical documents do, but actually sensorally.

This materiality provides another advantage to archaeologists as well, for "by its very three-dimensionality," material culture lends itself to all kinds of analyses not possible with historical documents—physical, spatial, stylistic (McEwan and Waselkov 2003:1; see also Csikszentmihalyi 1993).

Those who study material culture by trade know that artifacts are not just inanimate objects, used and discarded, cultural leftovers. They are *metaphorical expressions of* culture (Prown 1993:11). Objects, architecture, or landscapes can in many ways be seen as physical embodiments of the assumptions, attitudes, and values of the people who built, shaped, or used them. As such they contain deep structural meaning that can be studied anthropologically. They can also communicate messages—both among the actors in the past who used them and between them and us. Quite simply artifacts open a portal into the mindset of people long gone.

This is heady stuff for archaeologists, for it means that in the mundane refuse of daily life, the historically invisible can come vibrantly to life. Belinda and the people she labored with at Ten Hills Farm were not people "without history" (see Wolf 1982); their histories were simply inscribed in often-overlooked places: in mended vessels from the great house, in the smooth surface of a stone bead, in the seed remains of berry picking, or in the butchered remains of animals. Artifacts lend heft, depth, and texture to historical narratives; they document the past as much as any deed, letter, or newspaper can. But of course documents are also artifacts, and if approached as such, they can provide a richness of detail that the archaeological record cannot about the world in which these people lived. Documents as artifacts—artifacts as documents—the best histories pass easily between them. Used in conjunction, they present a compelling and often poignant means of knowing the past.

Setting the Scene

The Royalls' estate was first known as Ten Hills Farm and was part of the original land grant from the Crown to Governor John Winthrop in 1637. Eventually, however, Isaac Royall, Jr., dubbed it "Royallville," and even made stipulations in his will to see to it that the estate would continue to go by that name after his death (Harvard Law Library Special Collections 1778). The Royall House, as it stands today, has been owned and managed as a historic house museum by the Royall House Association since 1908. It was designated a National Historic Landmark in 1962 for its mid-Georgian architecture and because, despite the shopworn claim among so many old New England homes that "George Washington slept here," at the Royall House it is actually true. George Washington strategized there with Generals Stark and Lee, who had turned the house into a temporary headquarters, during the Siege of Boston in 1775.

Only a small fraction of "Royallville's" original 600 acres remains, the estate having long since been divided and subdivided into commercial and residential plots. The property currently owned by the Royall House Association comprises about 0.8 acres and includes the mansion house, out kitchen/slave quarters, and a bit of landscaped lawn east and west of the mansion and south of the slave quarters (fig. 2). Adjacent to this property, to the northeast, is Royall House Park, now owned by the City of Medford, but originally part of the Royall mansion's frontage on the main highway to Medford Square. In these verdant flecks, amid a sprawling concrete suburbia, visitors stroll and sit and find their centers again.

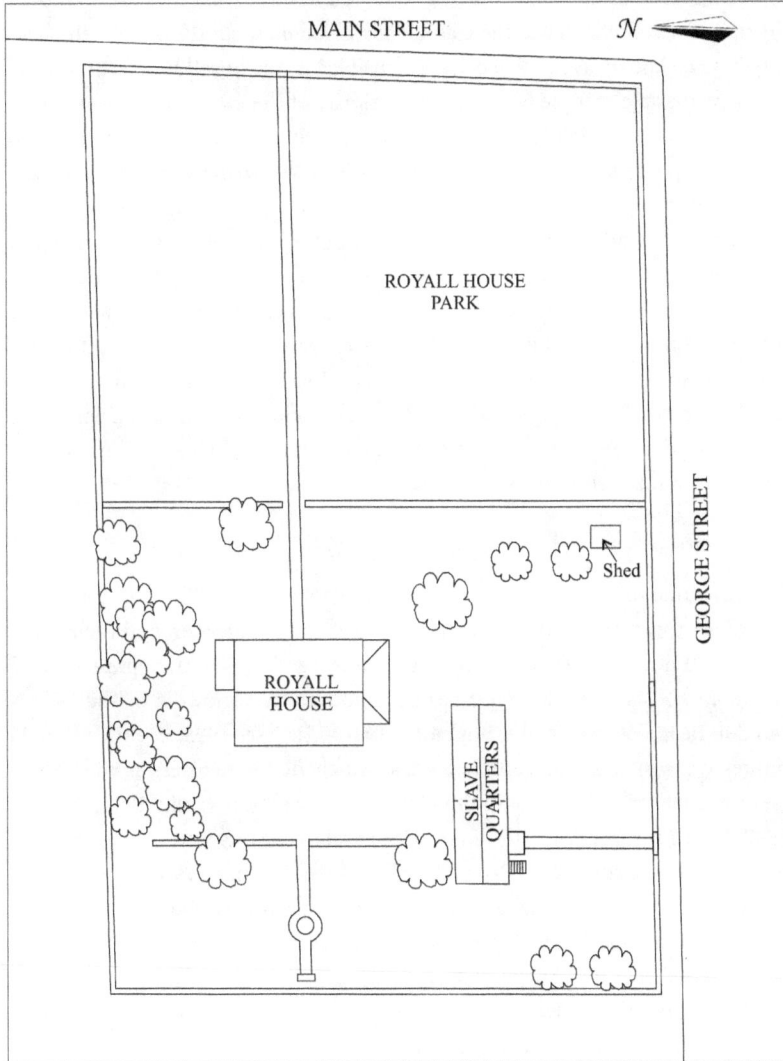

FIG. 2. Plan of the current extent of the Royall House site.

A more curmudgeonly observer would snipe that they were really just waiting for the 96 bus to Harvard Station. Here too archaeologists actively probed the earth with remote sensing and subsurface test excavations during the summers of 1999, 2000, and 2001. The features, artifacts, ecofacts, and evidence for landscaping activities discovered in the park and in the yards surrounding the mansion and slave quarters provide the physical data for this venture.

The Royall House and its slave quarters are one of the last relics of slavery in New England. In some ways, then, the most obvious contribution of archaeology to our understanding of this site might be seen to lie in what it can reveal about the daily lives of what has come colloquially (though, as stated, not strictly accurately) to be known as the "historically invisible." At the Royall House, these "historically invisible" people represent the majority of the inhabitants at the site: at the very least, some 64 black men, women, and children who lived, labored, and died to support a lavish lifestyle for the Royalls, who owned them. One can easily imagine that archaeology would have much to tell us about these people.

That being said, this is not just a book about the cruelties of enslavement; nor is it even just about black people. The Royalls and the people they held as slaves led vastly different lives, occupying the very highest and the very lowest strata of the social spectrum. And yet they were inextricably linked, partners in the same dance. By studying them together we come to the richest understanding of who they were on their own, as well as how they all contributed—black *and* white—to the forging of a new nation, as indebted to the drama and tragedy, triumphs and individual human episodes, of their lives as to those of any other.

Lines of Inquiry

Although one of the most exponentially burgeoning subfields of historical archaeology today, the study of the African diaspora, its peoples, and their experiences, continues to have a relatively "limited archaeological representation" (Franklin and McKee 2004:3). It has been dominated regionally by the American Southeast (Singleton and Bograd 1995:14–15; Orser 1998:65–66), although impressive work has been completed in as widely disparate places as West Africa (see DeCorse 1999, 2001; Ogundiran 2002), the Caribbean (Delle 1999; Handler 1997), and Latin America (see Orser 1994; Weik 2004), as well as other regions of North America itself (see Deetz 1988; Fitts 1996; Garman 1998; Yentsch 1994). Topically the plantation has dominated, despite a recognized diversity of slaveholding operations. Wilkie (2004) claims that the latter phenomenon, at least, can be attributed to a number of factors. First, most Africans brought to the New World did find themselves enslaved within a plantation setting. Second, plantations have offered an "attractive unit" of study because they are spatially circumscribed and are sometimes thought to present a microcosmic view of slaveholding society at large (Wilkie 2004:110). Third, plantations were central to the development of race relations in this country as an economic, social, and political unit, as well as an arena for cultural discourse and contestation. All this notwithstanding, however, the historical archaeological focus on the plantation setting is also partly the result of the way historic preservation has typically been carried out in this country. Archaeology is often mustered to support interpretations of sites associated with famous "dead white men" (Wilkie 2004:110): Thomas Jefferson at Monticello, George Washington at Mount Vernon, Andrew Jackson at the Hermitage.

Ultimately, then, and without criticizing or dismissing the importance and value of the pioneering work done on plantations, one can maintain that archaeology has inadvertently reinforced stereotypes in public consciousness that link African Americans *only* with plantations and slavery, and systems of forced servitude *only* with the American South or the Caribbean (Wilkie 2004:110). As such, it is especially worthwhile to seek understanding of a wider cross-section of the African diaspora experience, which was incredibly diverse. What is more, it is important to make that research interesting and accessible to a range of different publics, including, and perhaps even especially, to nonarchaeologists. This book uses a historical archaeological perspective and a style of writing that attempts to remain as accessible as possible to focus on the experiences of master and slave at a large 18th-century estate in eastern Massachusetts—far distant from the cane and cotton fields of popular imagery of American slavery.

It may come as a surprise to some that, among the archaeological investigations of 18th-century colonial populations of South Carolina, the chances are two to one that enslaved Africans, as opposed to Euro-Americans or Native Americans, created an archaeological site (Ferguson 1979:15). African Americans have gone unrecognized for so long in the archaeological record, scholarly works, and popular imagination, that many Americans are unaware of the fact that the majority of sites we excavate in this country are tied in some way to this historically invisible minority (Ferguson 1979:15). Though the slave populations in New England were never as numerous as in plantation America, slaves and free blacks have been a significant part of the population, economy, and society of the North as well, and that since the end of the 17th century.

Massachusetts was the first colony legally to sanction the institution of slavery, incorporating it into its Body of Liberties of 1641, and the slave trade was one of the foundations of the colonial economy. Africans had been present in the colony at least since 1638 and were found in all walks of life. In the century and a half between colonization and the War for Independence, African and Creole slaves were brought to New England in relatively small numbers, never reaching more than 2–3 percent of the total population (Piersen 1988:166–69). Nevertheless a focus on numbers in this situation obscures the real issue: the entrenchment of slavery and the slave trade in the New England economy and the profitability of the labor and products of slaves (Bailey 1992:207–8). Their importance in relieving the generalized labor shortage in New England—working in everything from domestic service, to industry, to agricultural production—made it inevitable that they would leave a large mark on the "economic, political, social and religious institutions of their masters" (Greene 1942:316; Bailey 1992:209). And yet one of the most neglected aspects of New England history and development is the role played by the transatlantic slave trade and the institution of slavery in that region, a role that persisted into the 19th century.

Economic ties between South and North were characterized by Charles Sumner as late as 1848—in reference to the enormous textile mills of New England such as Lowell, Massachusetts, and Manchester, New Hampshire—as a diabolical covenant between the "Lords of the Lash" and the "Lords of the Loom" (Bailey 1998:43). The effect of African Americans on New England history and culture, then, must be considered beyond mere "numerical considerations," for their influence belied their numbers (Greene 1942:320).

Beginning in the 18th century, African slaves in New England increasingly became the sole source of cheap or free labor in all sectors of a complex economy, as Native Americans and white indentured servants were gradually phased out as appropriate or efficient candidates for servitude. Enslaved people often followed their masters' calling and even assumed high-level positions from time to time under their masters' tutelage. Indeed enslaved people in colonial New England were likely to be highly skilled, either in a particular craft or in carrying out a variety of tasks—as jacks-of-all-trades—that were critical to the running of a business, farm, or household (see Bailey 1992, 1998; Berlin 1998; Greene 1942; Kolchin 1993; McManus 1973; Piersen 1988). These were not "extenuating" circumstances of slavery, but alternative incarnations of it. Bondage was a bitter fate whatever the circumstances or setting of its existence.

Paynter (1990) has said that the Massachusetts landscape has made the presence of African Americans, beyond the great figures of history such as W. E. B. Du Bois, Frederick Douglass, or Phillis Wheatley, invisible. In 1990 there were 30,000 sites in Massachusetts that had been listed on the National Register, but no more than thirty had been dedicated to African Americans (Paynter 1990:51). The result has given the distinct impression that there simply were not any black Americans in colonial New England and that their role in the economy and society was negligible.

This raises another important point. American slavery is not really a story about black people in America; it is a story about black people as Americans—a difference perhaps of semantic subtlety, but one of great conceptual importance. One cannot understand the process of colonization and ethnogenesis in the Americas without taking into consideration the profound impact that Africans, imported as slaves, had on the emergence of a uniquely American culture (Armstrong 1990). With the exception of a few uncommon individuals, however, African slaves did not generally write about themselves; rather, they were written about by people with significant cultural biases or political agendas of their own. As such, material culture pertaining to the life and culture of the enslaved is invaluable as a supplement—and complement—to documentary lines of evidence.

Studying the process of racialization (how white became "white" and black became "black"), sociocultural change, and exchange in New England will necessarily rely much on archaeological remains, but it promises to contradict the popular perception that "the master class called the tunes and slaves danced the beat" (Piersen 1988:ix). Indeed the reining in of black autonomy in New England law, ideology, and practice was formidable, but African Americans in the whole of the western hemisphere managed, in spite of this, to create folk cultures all their own that were unique both from their African roots and their new American surroundings. They would also become an integral and organic component of regional American cultural traditions. Religion, work, crafts, foodways, music, dress, medicine, and speech all ensured that enslaved people led a "double identity" in this country, on the one hand as an invisible and discounted minority, and on the other as rich and creative negotiators of their own subcultures (see, among others, Ferguson 1992; McKee 1987; Wilkie 1995, 1996, 1997, 2000; Yentsch 1992, 1994, 1995).

This book is the result of three seasons of archaeological investigation at the Royall House and its slave quarters in Medford, Massachusetts. It has been a multidisciplinary, multistage project aimed at interpreting the daily existence and modes of cultural creation and expression among enslaved African Americans on the Royall estate, as well as the nature of their interactions with the Royall family who owned them. It is about discourses of colonialism in the Age of Empires (see Hall 2000). It examines how social action transformed material objects into dynamic and creative expressions of self and group belonging and how that self was continually reinvented in response to the Other, within a particular social and historical context of exploration, colonization, secularization, and burgeoning capitalism.

It is also concerned with the process by which *racial* boundaries arose between African and European Americans. Orser (2007) has called this process "racialization," and the term refers to the way in which "whiteness" and "blackness" were constructed in a particular time and place. Race, of course, has no biological or scientific validity, but it remains an appropriate framework for understanding social phenomena and can in fact be engaged archaeologically, because even though race is not real, *racism* is. The actions of those who operate within its paradigm have tangible consequences for the world, the landscape, and the people who lived— and live—within it. This, says Orser (2007:115), is at the heart of archaeologists' ability to contribute relevant insight about it. Racism, he claims, "creates action and affects practice." As such, it is a cognitive phenomenon, like ideology, which nevertheless leaves material traces of itself in the archaeological record.

Several scholars have attempted to explore the ways in which artifacts and other elements of the material world reflect how race could be structurally connected to material manipulation and consumption (see Babson 1990; Epperson 1990, 2001; Fitts 1996; Garman 1998; Hall 1999; Mullins 1999a, 1999b; Orser 2001, 2007). On consideration of the various lines of evidence available at the Royall House too—documentary, material, and otherwise—it does seem that *race* and discourses of colonialism are the proper interpretive frameworks for making sense of the data at this site.

Of course, using race to understand the material world of the Royalls and the people they held as slaves is very far from making any essentialist claims about the "material nature" of "blackness" and "whiteness." Rather, it is meant to stand in opposition to what anthropologists might call a "culturalist viewpoint" (Orser 2001:5), where material culture associated with the enslaved people at the Royall House would be cast as part of, say, an emergent African American *ethnicity*.

Ethnicity has been popular in the archaeology of minority groups and widely gained acceptance over race in this country—particularly in the 1980s and 1990s—as part of a cross-over phenomenon from other, albeit related, disciplines (see McGuire 1982; Jones 1997, 1999). As anthropologists and ethnographers more rigorously developed understandings of the nature and role of ethnicity in social groups (see Barth 1969; Sarna 1978; Stern 1991), archaeologists began to see a way to avoid the troubling implications of social scientists' construction and use of race in the past (Orser 2007:75ff).

To be specific, the history of the relationship between anthropologists and "hard scientific" understandings of human diversity is a long and unsavory one. The collusion of early anthropologists in the construction of concepts of "race" and the "scientific" underpinnings of the "white man's burden" runs deep (Gould 1996). It is understandable that more recent practitioners would be loath to be associated in any way with this early history. "Ethnicity is cultural," the argument implicitly ran. "Race is biological. And everyone knows today that there is no link between biology and culture." The anthropological ancestry of New World archaeology has legitimated the approach, as well, for it has cast the discipline first and foremost as the study of cultures and humanity. And, indeed, as advances in genetics began to show that race could not even be said to be biological anymore—and was in fact nothing more than a troubling figment of our collective imagination—race as a viable explanatory framework seemed consigned to oblivion (see Marks 1994; Rensberger 1981).

"Ethnicity," on the other hand, was certainly real. And as a fluid and flexible entity—manipulable and, on some level, voluntary—it bolstered scholarship that sought to counter traditional, and often bleak, interpretations of disenfranchised groups by focusing on things such as resistance and everyday empowerment (see Babson 1990; Jones 1999; Sarna 1978). The idea of ethnicity being wielded as a strategic weapon against social, cultural, or economic adversity or discrimination was, and is, a popular one (Stern 1991:xiv). Choosing what traditions, styles, and meanings to combine into expressions of ethnicity—what aspects to emphasize and what to keep clandestine—was seen to give oppressed people a measure of active control in their own lives.

Within this framework the establishment of regional or local African American subcultures would not have been a passive inevitability. African Americans would have had an active part to play in the *creation* of their own ethnic identities, thereby providing a well of communal strength and group solidarity for themselves, founded on a mutual commitment to the resistance (advertent and inadvertent) of the harsh impositions of American racist ideology.

The message is a positive one, but, unfortunately, determining which social dimensions were most at work in the occurrence of a set of artifacts is hard to sort out (McGuire 1982). What forms "ethnic" expression may take are as equally determined by social and economic factors as they are by any essentialist "cultural" ones of, for example, "African" or "European," or even "Akan" or "English." People began to wonder whether it would be appropriate, for instance, to characterize African American subcultures in terms of their ethnic African origins without taking into consideration the social status of "slave," the racial status of "black," or the economic status of "poor" (see Howson 1990). Suddenly the use of the word "ethnicity" began to seem problematic because it smacked of a self-determinism that was inspirational, to be sure, but not necessarily reflective of the reality of these people's lives.

This is in fact an issue with which all scholars of slavery must continually struggle: how to simultaneously—and explicitly—recognize the creativity and resilience of the enslaved, without disregarding or downplaying the dehumanizing social and economic impositions of slavery and American racialization within which such creativity was negotiated. These notions are not necessarily at odds, but it requires continual effort on the part of scholars not to appear to have replaced "a mythical world in which slaves were objects of total control" with an "equally mythical world in which slaves were hardly slaves at all" (Kolchin 1993:148–49).

Talking about ethnicity in the case of a racially distinct minority that was institutionally excluded from the mainstream presents an interpretive obstacle to students of culture because a significant element of the voluntary has been removed by the rigid societal strictures of the day. If scholars are to talk about the creation of minority ethnicities in a historically racist society at all, it must be with an understanding of the *involuntary* social, cultural, and economic constraints imposed by race (Harrison 1995)—or, at the very least, by racialization.

The truth, though, is that the relationship between race and ethnicity is a complicated one, and the two are not mutually exclusive. They work in tandem. It is possible, for instance, for expressions of ethnicity to be "racially motivated" (Orser 2007:81; see also Liu 1998), the product equally of being nonwhite in a white-dominated society as of anything specifically tied to cultural practices learned from parents and grandparents.

It is also possible that neither race nor ethnicity is the primary factor at work and that the actions of a person who belongs to both a racial and an ethnic minority may in spite of this be most governed by sociohistorical context. Praetzellis, Praetzellis, and Brown's (1987) fascinating study about Chinese merchants on I Street, once part of Sacramento's Chinese District during the Gold Rush of the mid 19th century, is a case in point. There archaeology suggested or detected a mixture of a distinctly Chinese-built environment, governed by geomantic principles; Chinese food-storage vessels and tableware; non-European methods of butchery on food remains; but also a significant presence of European utensils and tablewares. Rather than reading this mixed material record as a sign of acculturation or assimilation of Chinese immigrants into Anglo-American cultural forms, however, Praetzellis, Praetzellis, and Brown (1987:46) position the artifacts in relation to these people's role as merchants and cultural arbiters between the Chinese community and "influential outsiders."

Here was an example of Chinese merchants asserting themselves as a breed apart—from the vast undifferentiated sea of Chinese laborers on the one hand, but also from Euro-American clients and associates whom they entertained on the other. They used material statements to manipulate their image as an exotic and alluring but refined and ultimately nonthreatening presence to achieve certain social and economic goals for themselves and their families. Expressions of ethnicity in this case would have been drawn from Chinese cultural norms and influenced by the racial climate of the day, which made these merchants not just Chinese, but quintessentially Other. The point is, though, that neither race nor ethnicity might have been as important in the patterns of material culture observed at this site as the particular sociohistorical context of the Chinese merchants' relationship to Euro-American clients, associates, and sponsors.

In just the same way, the African American expressions of identity at the Royall House cannot be understood simply as a cultural phenomenon—even a dynamic one (Stern 1991)—but must take into consideration the social and economic roles and relationships that slavery, emergent notions of race, and poverty imposed. Thus the material culture at this site should be read in terms of what it can tell us about the respective roles of African heritage, American resources, social relationships of slavery, and real-world consequences of racialization in the forms of self-expression present there.

The question now may arise of whether the archaeology at the Royall House has any broader social application beyond telling an interesting story about the past. At the base of all archaeological undertakings is the assumption, implicit or explicit, that somehow the past contains the seeds of the present; that it can, in effect, explain *why* things are the way they are. For example, why are there white people and nonwhite people in this country today? Why are there rich and poor, upper class and lower class? Understanding and studying race and class as American ideologies brings us far toward answering the question of why they exist, as well as establishing them as cultural, *learned* phenomena.

For example, the ideology of race makes race appear to be an "innate attribute of the human condition" (Epperson 1999b:103). It provides the rationale for social and economic distinctions and inequities, and it allows the creation and exploitation of huge labor forces. The question that Leone (1999:6) asks is how is this possible without having to resort to "continual violence"? The answer in part is that race as ideology is paradoxically not only harmful, but also pacifying. Ideology masks the arbitrariness of a social order and makes it acceptable—not in the sense of being desirable, but insofar as making it make sense—to everyone within that order, regardless of whether they stand to gain or lose by adhering to it. In some ways, then, the ideology of race is at the very beating heart and soul of a capitalist society, and at its broadest level archaeology at the Royall House offers us an opportunity to see how these categories of black and white, laborer and gentry, were originally constructed. It also reveals them as constructions in the first place.

Leone (1999:9) argues that by bringing to light "places and time periods in which entrenched categories were still in flux," archaeology can raise consciousness about the arbitrariness of the constructs that govern our lives today. Recognizing these essentialisms as random and as having specific historical origins is the first step in challenging them and maybe one day getting rid of them altogether.

The Practice of Writing

Having now outlined the theoretical underpinnings of the project, we find that what remains are a few finer points about the practice of writing and just whom archaeologists are writing for.

While no scholar today would actually try to claim that northern slaves were happy slaves, substantial differences in population structure and economy as well as in religion and law have led some to conclude that slavery in the North could be gentler than in plantation settings (see Berlin 1998:57; Greene 1942:219). Some have also argued that the close working and living conditions of New England masters and their slaves made relations in the region more incorporative or familial in nature than elsewhere (Piersen 1988:26). And it has been implied that northern blacks, vastly outnumbered in a region that was at least 95 percent white throughout the colonial era, might have been more quickly and completely assimilated into European cultural forms than in the predominantly black regions of the South and Caribbean (see, for example, Twombly and Moore 1982; Berlin 1998; Piersen 1988:22).

Such studies have attempted to explore the various differences in systems of slavery that fell outside the geographic regions traditionally associated with enslavement. The research is pioneering but does leave room for dialogue. Among historical archaeologists, there has been an increasing awareness of, and a desire to make archaeological research both relevant and useful to, a multiplicity of publics that goes far beyond other members of the academy (Franklin and McKee 2004; McKee 1994; Potter 1991; Potter 1997; Stahl, Mann, and Loren 2004).

There has also been a recognition of the past as a public heritage, which has underscored the educational importance of making the past accessible to more than just students and colleagues (Stone 1997:23; see also Gathercole and Lowenthal 1990; Vitelli 1996). Many scholars find themselves publishing and presenting in a variety of venues, for diverse audiences, which may include historians, anthropologists, archaeologists, museum professionals, and educators, but also lay people of varying degrees of interest and informedness. As such one cannot assume the knowledge base of the consumers and must undertake to become more self-aware of the ways in which one communicates the results of research, as well as anticipate how these might affect the way results are read and understood by a variety of different audiences (Potter 1991). Other authors using comparative frameworks for addressing various aspects of slave life in the Americas have successfully explored social, economic, demographic, and geographic differences while still managing to be explicit about locating material conditions within a system that was ultimately oppressive and set the outer limits (see, for example, Fitts 1996; Garman 1998; McManus 1973; Morgan 1998).

History or Anthropology?

Debates about whether archaeology's true allegiance is to history or anthropology and whether what it is we engage in, what drives us to endure insects, weather extremes, and innumerable other emotional and physical discomforts of our profession, is more rightly seen to be science or art are not discussed here. In some ways, I have thought of myself as using science in the pursuit of art.

There are constraints now, certain standardized, formalized ways of unlocking secrets that artifacts contain, of keeping our heads out of the clouds and our feet firmly on the ground. But imagination is still the element that binds (see Schrire 1995:11). Imagination is what presses us forward, what keeps us digging. While there is rigor involved in the ordering of thousands of artifacts into discernible patterns of date, frequency distribution, decoration, ware types, production methods, market availability, or cost, the most critical informational value that artifacts have lies not just in what they can tell us about dates and purchasing power, but in what they might have meant to the people who made and used them. As scientists we of course want to characterize the nature of our collections as accurately as possible, but as humanists we want our stories to have depth, color, taste, and texture. I have written here as scientist and humanist. As a result, this book has derived its inspiration from the disciplines of both history and anthropology; it seeks out a balance between the general and the particular, tries to uncover broad cultural processes as well as individual histories and, most important, to address the relationship between the two.

I use the concepts of *habitus, praxis,* performative social discourse, multi-locality, and implication to integrate meaning and agency into the analytical approaches and methods at the Royall House. I have utilized an ethnographic approach and analysis on documents, architecture, landscape, and artifacts to focus on the diverse experiences of the many individuals from that site—white and black—and offer possible interpretations of how those different experiences were negotiated through material symbols. In fact it is in the material—in document, artifact, landscape, and architecture—that I have seen some of the most poignant contestations between master and slave as they struggled to define themselves and each other in a world that was violent and shifting and anything but fixed.

Telling Stories

Traditional academic rigor aside, I am also someone who from earliest childhood has been most interested in finding out what it was like to live in the past, and I have grappled with the style of presentation I would employ here as a result. It has, for me, always been important to maintain a human element in the presentation of "data," for what child ever wanted to be an archaeologist because she was fascinated by "energy-capturing systems" or the graphic relationship between "storage dependence and effective temperature" (Binford 1980 [1996]: 50, 55)? I hope I have succeeded in capturing something of the ethos of the times here—some of the drama and tragedy and individual human episodes that both resulted from and contributed to the sweeping, global tides of imperial expansion, colonialism, and the birth of a new nation.

To this end, I have tried to maintain a narrative style as much as possible. To make the Royalls, their slaves, and the world they made together at Ten Hills Farm accessible, I have in a few instances presumed to describe scenarios, or even write fictional vignettes (italicized pages), ascribing thought, emotion, and motive to people I never knew. The danger, of course, is that my stories are more about myself and my own interests and biases, than about the Royalls or those they held in bondage, and I have often wondered what Isaac Royall, Jr., would have made of my psychoanalysis of his life. I imagine that as someone who was very much a man of his times and concerned with appearances, he is rolling in his grave even as I write. But here again, I make attributions. More troubling to me is the question of what Jemmy or the boatman would have said about my feeble attempts to describe their lives or their pain (in chapters 6 and 7). Perhaps a more tangible concern, as an author, would be the question of how my audiences, intended and otherwise, will respond to these somewhat experimental, although by no means unprecedented, forms of interpretation and representation (see, for example, Joyce 2006 for an outstanding critical synopsis of the sustained experiments in writing to be found in the historical archaeological discipline). I imagine that some will take issue, if not downright offense, at my willingness to take the voice of enslaved people, although I have refrained from using the first person in any of the narratives presented here, including the ones involving Isaac Royall.

If we are irrevocably imprisoned by the walls of our own immediate experience, we might as well all pack our things and go home. The social sciences as a whole would become impracticable. As a young, biracial, Chinese-American woman of the 21st century, I suppose I have as much in common with a wealthy white slave trader of the 18th century as I do with an enslaved African of the same period. I therefore knowingly take on the "alluring challenge of alien worlds" equally with my representations of each (Styron 1992:455).

Empathetic thinking is something we all do, as archaeologists, whether we want to admit it or not (Johnson 1999:104). Ethnographers know that to render the experience of others responsibly, however, one must not assume "too broad an authority" (Joyce 2006:2; Clifford and Marcus 1986). Traditional academic writing will seek to use objective, "scientific" language to render the writer herself transparent, invisible, and therefore, the process by which he or she produces knowledge opaque and beyond reproach. By contrast an explicit reflexivity in the text, which acknowledges not only the presence of the author-narrator, but also a situatedness in relation to the past human subjects commented on, breaks the wall of silence. I have inserted myself here as a speaking subject "who sees as well as is seen," and who can therefore be questioned, probed, and argued with (Clifford 1986:14). Stahl, Mann, and Loren (2004:84) have called this an "embedded model" of writing; it works to bring the mechanics of knowledge production into view by breaking up the inexorable flow of the traditional scientific narrative. It reminds readers that the truths presented in this book are grounded in evidence but are still interpretations of an author, a person—incomplete, open to criticism, debate, and reinterpretation.*

A convergence of interest and occupation among historians, anthropologists, and archaeologists has also required experts in each discipline to meet the challenge of interdisciplinary communication. This may mean acknowledging and responding to the fact that the traditional basis for our knowledge claims may not be obvious to people from other disciplines. It may also require amendments to discipline-specific jargon and rhetoric that obfuscate rather than illuminate our discussions for nonexperts. In any case it seems clear that "no one can pursue the business of writing as usual" anymore (Stahl, Mann, and Loren 2004:94; see also Greenblatt and Gunn 1992).

The ever-widening arc of audiences we can expect the results of our research to reach today is encouraging, and as it grows to encompass various sectors of the lay public as well, historical archaeologists have been more explicitly engaged with "problems of narrative and representation" than practitioners of any other tradition in archaeology (Joyce 2006:1). Many historical archaeologists are beginning to believe that we should really "*strive* to create personal connections between the consumer and the people of the past" (Wilkie 2004:114, emphasis added). Indeed, with our ability to connect with the past sensorally, as well as intellectually, and academically, archaeologists are in a unique position to make dialogues of race, ethnicity, or culture accessible and interesting to a wider set of people than ever before. An embedded model of writing, for example, also invites nonexperts to engage in the debate, for it exposes knowledge as contingent, subjective, and open to challenge. This is a gift that should not be squandered because the notion of "rigorous partiality" is wrongly assumed to be a contradiction in terms (Clifford 1986:25).

A number of scholars have been exploring alternative ways of interpreting their sites for their readers, through the use of narrative styles or fictional vignettes (see Ferguson 1992; Gibb 2000; Michael 1998; Praetzellis 1998; Spector 1991). These authors use stories not as a substitute for practical archaeology or even as something intending to represent actual events, but as a heuristic device, "an additional way of explaining what their sites are about" (Praetzellis 1998:2). Such stories can have value in their ability to "create understanding as well as knowledge" (Gibb 2000:3).

---

*Although historical archaeology has seen the most explicit and sustained engagement with these issues, one prominent prehistorian, Hodder (1989), has also called for the return of the narrator's voice to the daily grind of archaeological writing and representation.

They also serve to democratize our interpretive capabilities. The color and grain we have regained from historical records about the lives of the Royall family seem almost riotous when compared with the merely drab and shadowy hues we seem able to conjure of the people they held as slaves. To speak in great depth about the fabric and texture of Isaac Royall's life, aspirations, and motives, but then to speak only categorically of slaves, bondsmen, or blacks as counterpoint, gives African Americans the kind of bleak, dehumanized, anonymity that forces precisely no one to grapple with the reality of American slavery in any near or painful way. As a result they who were silently disregarded in life can be silently disregarded in death through their scholarly relegation to the more comfortable distance of the abstract (see Wilkie 2004:115).

The stories I have told in this book strive to bring the Royalls *and* their slaves more to life, but by establishing my presence as an author and a narrator, I try to diffuse criticisms of simply putting myself in another's place. The stories are all tied in some way to hard data recovered from or pertaining to the site (that is, the Royalls did have a New Year's Eve Party in 1737; handmade artifacts of leisure were recovered from the grounds; and there would have been one or more boatmen to take produce from Ten Hills Farm to Boston), but they are not supposed to be a true representation of real events. While recognizing that Isaac, Sr., Isaac, Jr., Jemmy, and the boatman were unique as individuals, I have also abstracted them, within a contextualized historical ethnographic framework, into figures whose particular stories, speculative though they may be, are grounded enough to perhaps shed light on the wider human experience of master and slave in the colonial era. As such they *are* intended to provide some small clue as to what it was like to live as master or slave at Ten Hills Farm but certainly do not purport to tell what happened there.

A former student, David Singer, from Vassar College, during a class discussion about telling stories one day in the Archaeology of Early African America course I taught in the fall of 2001, summed it up as follows: "It might not be true, but I feel like . . . it could have been. And, I don't know. To me that's enough." I agree with David, that not only is it enough, but telling stories that could have been true, whether they are in short story or field report format, is the best an archaeologist has to offer.

Chapter 1
BEGINNING THE RESEARCH

It goes without saying that we can never be completely
explicit about our biases and preconceptions. This should
not stop us trying.

—MATTHEW JOHNSON, 1999

Constructing History

Who was Isaac Royall, Sr.? The answer to that question seems at first to be quite
simple. Much of his life as a wealthy freeman was a matter of public record. He
was born in North Yarmouth, Maine, in 1677 and died in Charlestown, Massachusetts, in 1739. He was white and a son of a carpenter, merchant mariner,
slave trader, sugar planter, husband, father, and self-made man. Another, and
perhaps more contentious, way to answer that question, however, is to say that
Isaac Royall is who we want him to be. While researching the Royalls for this
study, I was confronted with that impression repeatedly. I could use a variety of
primary documents to reconstruct a timeline of events for his life, but alone they
did not really convey the essence of him. To give isolated events flow, coherence,
and meaning, one has to provide a narrative framework, and, depending on the
framework one chooses, one can come up with a variety of different portraits.

To date the only narrative context for this timeline of events is to be found
in antiquarian interpretations of the late 19th and 20th centuries (see Brooks
and Usher 1886; Drake 1906; Hooper 1900; Hoover 1974; Jackson 1907; Oliver
1894, 1896, 1899; Wild 1908). Although they stand alone as the only published
accounts of Isaac Royall, they bring us no closer to any understanding of the man
or his times. Antiquarian writing helped to "fix" and perpetuate the Royalls' narrative within a colonial revivalist framework that persists to this day, aimed at the

romantic glorification of the benevolent patriarch and the self-made man. The result is a descriptive but static portrait of a man, which uncritically embodies many of the modern ideologies of American male-oriented individualism, but which is completely divorced from the social context of the portrait's construction, as well as from the context of the man's own existence.

Fɪɢ. 3. A pageant produced by the Royall House Association in 1905, depicting the English tea ceremony in the Royall House courtyard. (Photograph courtesy of the Medford Public Library.) The emphasis is on period finery and the wealth, status, and elegant hospitality of the Royalls during the house's golden age. A servant in blackface, standing in the background, is the sole visual referent to the Royalls' role as merchants and slave traders.

Fɪɢ. 4. In 1915 the Royall House Association produced *The Pageant of the Royall House*, which was meant to bring the "history of the house . . . to life" (Sammarco 1999: 32). Here the Spirits of Hearth and Home are chasing away the Spirits of Snow, Wind, and Rain. (Photograph courtesy of the Medford Public Library.) In this portrayal, the Royalls do not figure at all, either with or without the people they enslaved, and the house itself becomes the subject of Classical Revival adulation.

The Royalls lived and died in the Age of Empires, within a social context of uneasy and often violent colonial discourses of conquest, subjugation, power, status, assertions, and contestations between those who ruled and those who served. To portray Isaac Royall and his peers in isolation from these circumstances—simply as wealthy merchants, peaceful farmers, or benevolent aristocrats, for example—is to tell only part of the story at best and to misrepresent it at worst (figs. 3, 4, 5, and 6). In either case such a portrait must of necessity obscure the answer to our question: who was Isaac Royall? Among the many other goals of this research, I wanted to paint a more essential portrait of the Royalls than can be found in antiquarian literature: one that did more than just adore them, or—as it would be so easy to do—deplore them. As people interested in anthropology, we should be trying to understand them. Times were different then. Culture was different then. We cannot impose 21st-century understanding and morality, or even ideas about "common sense" or "logic," on 18th-century minds because these ideas have historicity. They change and evolve. Thus the

FIG. 5. Another segment of the 1905 pageant "A Visit from George Washington" depicts George Washington kissing the hand of Molly Stark, wife of General Stark, who was headquartered at the Royall House during the Revolution. (Photograph courtesy of the Medford Public Library.) This reflects that George Washington in fact did sleep here. The house's use as a headquarters for Generals Stark and Lee and the visit from George Washington were among the principal criteria for nominating the house to the National Register of Historic Places.

Fig. 6. A more recent pageant put on at the Royall House by the Colored Ladies' Theater Group, led by Pam Goncalves (far right), 2001. In this scene African American reenactors portray the old African American folk tradition that it was the promise of red cloth that first lured Africans aboard European slave ships. This pageant was put on as part of the Royall House Association's contemporary revisionist approach to the site. This family/community day was entitled "The Forgotten Royalls." (Photograph by Karen Chan.)

unquestioned assumptions of race, class, sex, and privilege that cast these things in the 18th century as manifestations of a natural hierarchy, rather than a cultural one, essentially—fundamentally—distance us from our subjects and present an obstacle to our understanding of their world. It is an obstacle that, while unavoidable, however, is not necessarily insurmountable.

The social construction of "the past" is one issue that should continue to concern us, though. What do archaeologists know? How do they know it? Is there ever knowledge that is both objective and universal, independent of the mind who seeks it? Or is all "truth" perception? In short, to what degree do we inadvertently create the past in our own image (see Handsman and Leone 1989)? Fortunately scholars seem largely to agree that by fitting propositions against a variety of different data sources and seeing what these sources reveal not only about the topic at hand but also about each other, and then by using these revelations to further modify one's propositions, an archaeologist can in fact delineate a range of "plausible interpretive options" (Wylie 1989:26) and, in so doing, come to a better understanding of "what really happened" in the past.

Strictly speaking, then, while recognizing that all knowledge is an inherently social enterprise, to say that Isaac Royall is who we want him to be may exaggerate the situation. It does draw our attention, however, to an important interpretive dilemma. "In historical archaeology," writes Martin Hall, the agency of historical actors is "triply inscribed":

> First, there is the original actor, whether slave or governor, whose material and verbal expression has created the archaeological record. Secondly, there is the witness to such acts of historical production, whether court or scribe, enumerator, diarist, or travel writer.... And thirdly, there are the interpreters—the authors of theoretical works, precedent archaeological historical texts, and myself. (Hall 2000:9)

Much of the Royalls' own agency comes to us through second- or third-degree filters—from witnesses and interpreters. The original actors—Isaac Royall, Sr. and Jr., and their family—have left us a relatively rich archaeological record, but a heavily male-dominated and fragmentary documentary record that includes a handful of letters, wills, and inventories and an account book ledger that records accounts payable and receivable from 1724 to 1749. Town, vital, and court records from Medford, Stoughton, and Antigua provide genealogical information and much of what we know about the male Royalls' public lives. Contemporary newspapers recount important political and social events of the day; they are informative but betray profound prejudices and must be recognized for the "enthusiastic agents of oppressive regimes" that they were (Hall 2000:10). The rest of what we know about the Royalls comes from interpretations of antiquarian writers (local historians mostly) of the late 19th and early 20th centuries, enthusiastic agents of their own genealogies and cultural legacies. These documents should be recognized as artifacts themselves and should be interpreted as such—etically as well as emically (see glossary).

With our sources arranged before us, we must select a framework for their narrative, and it does seem that discourses of colonialism is the proper one for making sense of the Royalls. Both father and son—as merchants, slave traders, and colonial elite—were intimately involved in the commercial acquisition and redistribution of commodities that drove Europe's colonial expansion from the 15th to the 19th centuries. Their actions and the course that their lives took must be interpreted within that context. What is more, as archaeologists, we have the additional task of identifying the ways in which these discourses of power were made manifest through physical objects, or we risk the threat of being merely illustrative.

Our challenge then is clear, though perhaps not easily met. We see the Royalls now as dimly visible beneath multiple layers of agency—and we must somehow contrive to construct their history again, our own agency in that process, of course, only adding to the number of filters through which we must direct our gaze. The framework we choose to employ, the questions we choose to ask, may be influenced by our own research interests and sociopolitical environment, both within the discipline of archaeology and in society at large. These will necessarily affect the color, light, and shadows of the portrait—their placement and intensity. And in the end the portrait will still be but an interpretation and a work in progress. In addition pre- and postdepositional factors have affected what physical remains first entered and then were preserved in the archaeological record. Archaeological methods and sampling techniques affected their recovery. Meanwhile colonial documents generally ignore or distort the voices of the "silent" majority— women, working poor, Native Americans, and enslaved Africans—to project a male, hierarchical, and orderly society that was more ideal than real. Amateur historians have sought, through the Royalls, to give themselves and their society time depth and legitimacy in their constructed narratives of their ancestors. All of these sources tend to obscure rather than illuminate "our understanding of *how* the dispossessed *became* powerless and *how* ruling classes *legitimated* the world they built" (Handsman and Leone 1989:120, emphasis added).

In the end, what we want to accomplish is to transcend some of these setbacks through an acute awareness of our own biases and those of the original actors, witnesses, and interpreters we study. We want to achieve the distillation of an essence that stands up to multiple levels of scrutiny and come to some understanding of how specific events in the lives of specific people fit within, and thus derived meaning from, a global discourse of colonialism. But first we need a little background.

Finding the Site

I began this study fresh out of college and with what Theresa Singleton (1999:1) might have called a "moral mission": to "tell the story of Americans—poor, powerless, and 'inarticulate'—who had been forgotten in the written record." Sitting in a graduate seminar at Boston University in 1996, when the tips of the leaves were just bleeding to yellow, and when I still had much to learn, I was electrified at the possibility of using archaeology to address the lives of early African and African American bondsmen in the North. The Royall family, who purported to own these people, was of little interest to me at that time. Have we not heard enough for the time being about our Great White Forefathers, I asked myself. Does anyone really ever need to hear another narrative again about rich, white, dead men? I was only 23 years old and had just graduated from Vassar College, where it was distinctly unfashionable to be rich and white, let alone male.

Despite these beginnings, the current of my research was powerful. It carried me where it would, and it was not long before I realized that any thorough study of the black men, women, and children enslaved at the Royall House was going to have to be as much about the people who enslaved them as about the enslaved individuals themselves. The fact that Isaac Royall was a wealthy white man, much of whose life and accomplishments was a matter of public record, should not seduce us into thinking that we already know his story or that it is less interesting in comparison with the stories of those he held in servitude. As anthropologists we should be trying to reconstruct a cultural environment where to be a philanthropist as well as a slave trader and slaveholder did not constitute a contradiction in terms.

I did not find the Royall House so much as it found me. The Royall House Association (RHA) had approached one of its members, Professor Ricardo Elia, of the Boston University Department of Archaeology, to embark on an archaeological investigation of the Royall House that would allow the association to implement a more contemporary, revisionist interpretation of the site. The association's vision was to steer the tours and exhibits more to the African and Creole experiences there, as well as to situate the Royalls within the proper cultural framework of colonial mercantilism and slave trading. Professor Elia was one of my advisers at the time and was teaching a seminar called Archaeological Ethics and the Law in which I had enrolled; it was in this seminar that I became fascinated by the possibilities I perceived in a collaborative effort with the RHA. At the time, and indeed to this day, it is rare to find such a small museum with few resources making archaeology a priority. The goals of the archaeological investigation, as outlined in the permit application written and submitted to the Massachusetts Historical Commission by Elia, were as follows:

1. To conduct a limited program of subsurface testing in order to identify and assess buried archaeological resources at the Royall House site.
2. To identify which areas of the site contain potentially significant archaeological deposits.
3. To assess the potential of archaeology to contribute significant research information about the site and its occupants.
4. To assess the potential of archaeology to enhance the interpretation program of the Royall House Association.
5. To make recommendations for the future preservation and management of the site's archaeological resources.

We opted to make remote sensing an essential component of the survey. The size of the site and the general lack of surface clues as to the placement of subsurface features, as well as conservation considerations and the RHA's desire to maintain the grounds in a way that did not interfere with public visitation and use, also dictated the necessity of incorporating remote sensing techniques into the project plan. Dr. Kenneth Kvamme's and Margaret Watters's interpretations of several distinct anomalies in their respective resistivity and ground-penetrating radar (GPR) surveys of the Royall House grounds were used to guide the exploratory phase of excavation directed by Elia in June 1999 (see figs. 9 and 10, below). When I took over direction of the excavations in 2000 and 2001, GPR surveys conducted by Daniel Welch in the east, west, and south yards of the slave quarters, guided the efforts there (see fig. 11, below).

As most archaeologists who have done work in places with high visibility will agree (in urban or suburban contexts, for example, where there is much foot and vehicular traffic), talking with curious onlookers is part of the job. One of the most frequently asked questions, besides "Finding any bones?" (which is sometimes just the case), would surely have to be "Finding any gold?" (which, for me at least, has never yet been the case). To such a question I am apt to reply, "No, something better," and then go on to share with the onlooker this little pearl of wisdom: archaeologists do not dig for things; they dig for information.

Anne E. Yentsch (1994:36) says that a site can "be described as rich when it contains many artifacts and features or when its artifact assemblages speak of wealth within the community." Another way a site can be characterized as rich is

FIG. 7. View north from the interior of an unidentified outbuilding in the slave quarter's west yard. Artifacts, such as the ones tumbling out of the excavation sidewall to the left of the picture, numbered in the thousands and dated to the second and third quarters of the 18th century.

when "it stretches the imagination" (Yentsch 1994:36). The Royall House site, by either definition, was rich. It was rich because it yielded more than 65,000 artifacts and numerous features indicative of an 18th-century way of life (historic walkways and garden features, a cobbled courtyard, a drywell, a well, and a small outbuilding foundation filled to the brim with the remnants of the Royall household assemblage after they had fled the colony during the Battle of Lexington; see figs. 7 and 8). It was also rich because it stretched the imagination. It contained archaeological evidence about the nature of northern bondage and the relationships that existed between northern masters and their slaves. Better yet, some of the evidence ran contrary to archaeological expectations, which were based on observations of material culture patterns at slave sites across the South and in the

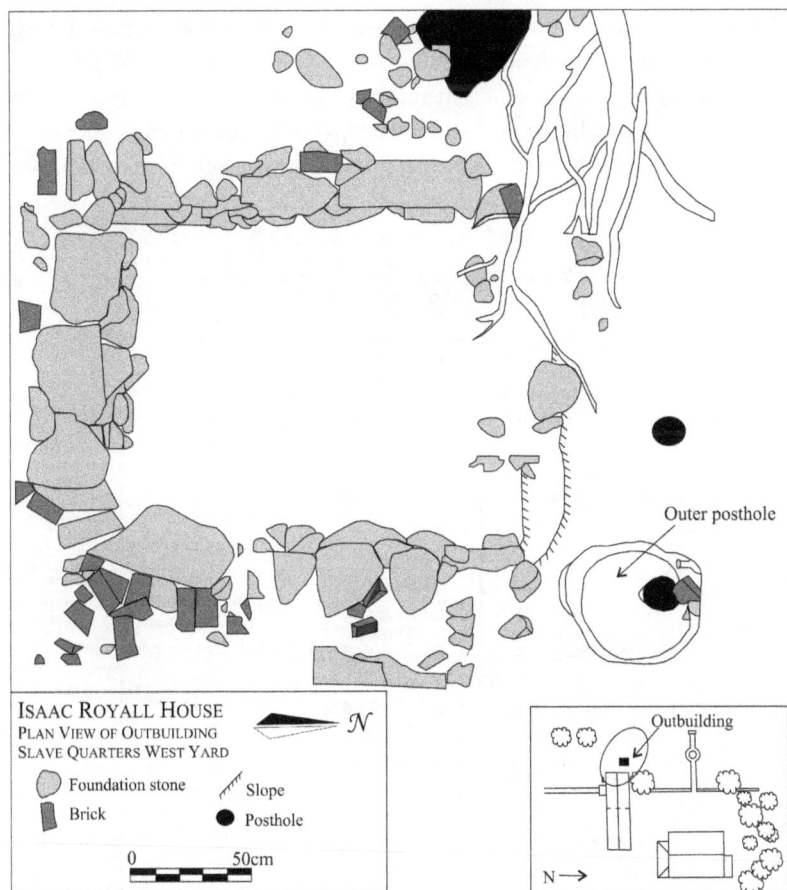

ISAAC ROYALL HOUSE
PLAN VIEW OF OUTBUILDING
SLAVE QUARTERS WEST YARD

Foundation stone   Slope
Brick   Posthole

Outer posthole

Outbuilding

0   50cm

FIG. 8. Plan view of the west yard outbuilding once it had been fully exposed in 2001. This feature yielded tens of thousands of artifacts dating to the period of the Royalls' and their enslaved people's occupation of the site.

Caribbean. The excavations at the Royall House therefore beg the question: are the differences in the physical manifestations of slavery at the Royall House merely idiosyncratic, or are they reflective of some deeper-lying systemic differences between northern and plantation slavery? Finally, the Royall House stretches the imagination by forcing us to think about how the physical world is manipulated to negotiate culture, identity, or power. It asks us to step outside the realm of our own experience and to think about what it was like when the "self-made man" was still a new idea and not yet assured of becoming an ideal; what it was like to be philanthropist as well as slave trader; and what it was like to be African and enslaved in colonial New England.

Royall's Medford Estate

The property, once a sprawling plantation of more than 500 acres, now consists of the ca. 0.8 acres acquired by the Royall House Association in 1908 and has since then served as a historic house museum. The still-commanding house sits on elevated ground, but amidst vinyl-sided homes and swimming pools; overlooking a flashing red light and a bus stop, the house has lost much of its power. And power it was indeed meant to invoke.

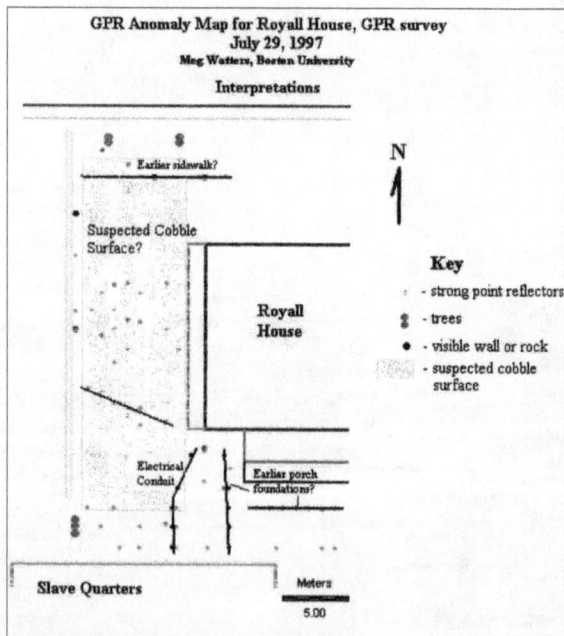

FIG. 9. Ground-penetrating radar image from the courtyard, showing extent of the cobbles beneath the grass, some possible earlier porch construction lines, and the location of several utility lines. (Image by Margaret Watters.)

In 1736, the year before the Royalls took up residence there, Medford was what one might almost call a hamlet, with only 665 inhabitants (Seaburg and Seaburg 1980:100). It is located along the banks of the tidal Mystic River, which at the time, lazily curled through a plain of open marshes and wetlands. Its steep banks and deep waters made the river navigable by ships and soon established it as a principal thoroughfare to the interior and back again from Boston markets. Although this assured that the town would not be unconnected from the rest of the world, there were never more than 1,000 people for as long as the Royalls lived there, and it remained provincial in essence.

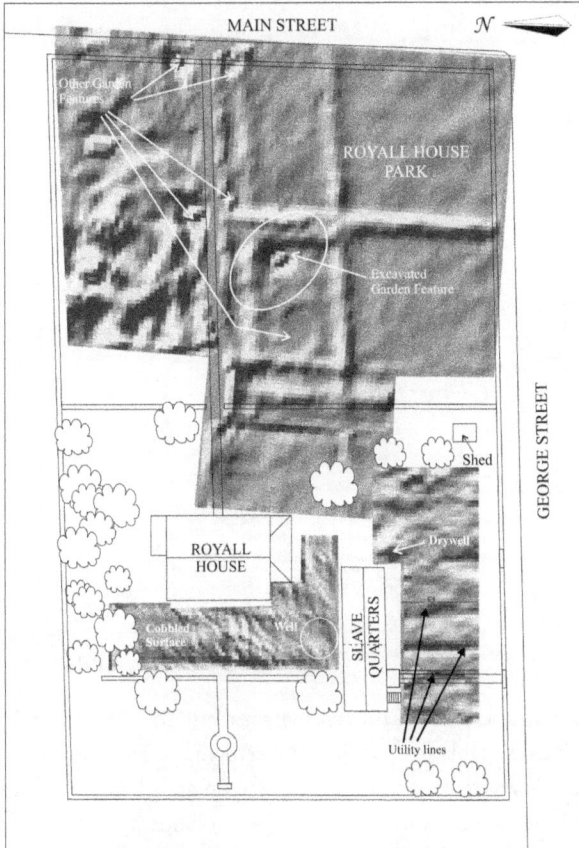

FIG. 10. Analytical hillshading of the three resistivity survey areas: the park, the courtyard, and the slave quarters' south yard. (Resistance imagery by Kenneth Kvamme and Marni Blake.) Anomalies in the park were interpreted as historic walkways and garden features meant to present an imposing facade to passersby in the 18th century. The linear anomalies behind the slave quarters were interpreted as modern utility lines and trenches. The stippled anomaly in the now-grassy courtyard was interpreted as a cobble-paved driving surface and receiving area. The interpretations of all of these anomalies were confirmed through excavation.

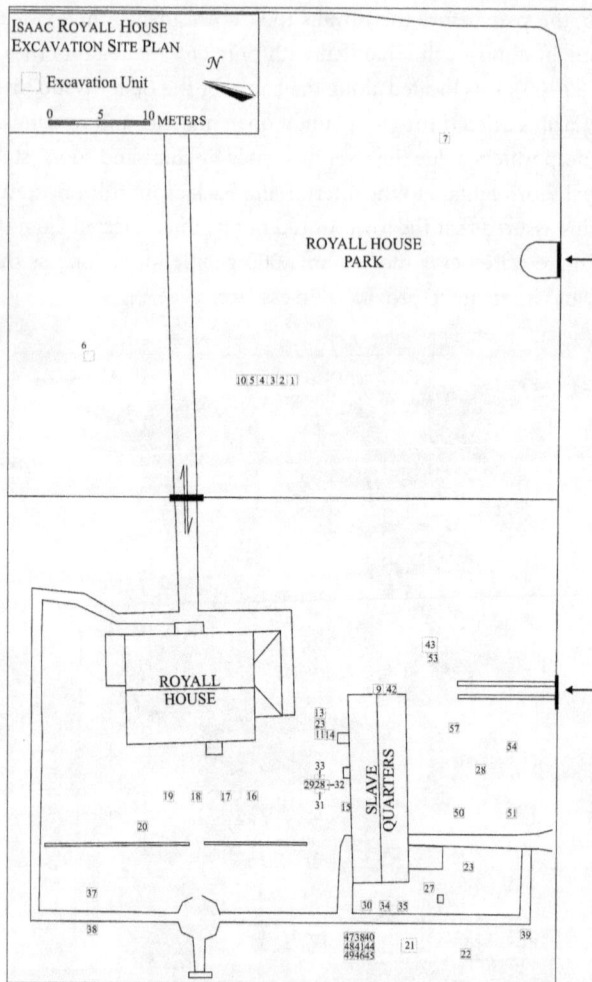

FIG. 11. Plan view of excavations on the Royall House grounds.

Beyond the flood plain of the salt marshes, one could find wooded uplands and rolling hills, suitable for farming and settlement. Founded in 1630, by the time the Royalls arrived a century later, these uplands had been largely cleared of forest and tamed into a neat, mixed agrarian landscape of farms and fields, fences, bridges, and roads. The woods were not so very far away, though, and wolves, wild cats, boars, bears, and deer might be seen from a distance. A tiny, circumscribed town center of shops and small industries sprang up at Medford Square, perhaps a mile down the road from the Royalls' new home. In this industrious little landscape, sparsely settled, and modestly profitable, the grandeur of the Royalls' seat, while not unheard of, would have been startling and undeniable—from its size, to the quality and sturdiness of the building materials and craftsmanship, to the trend-setting fashion in architecture that it represented.

The house is of a neoclassical architectural design that implicated the villas of ancient Rome and thus incorporated their antiquity and cultural legitimacy into its own. The phenomenon of cultural "implication," as developed by Robert St. George (1998:2), is a pertinent one in the study of material things. It refers to the way in which thoughts or ideas can be conveyed through material symbols without specifically referencing them. By taking things, places, ideas, or (as in the case of language) words from another time and place and putting them into a new and sometimes unexpected context, associations and evocations of other cultural milieus can be brought to mind; perceptions, and even actions, can be manipulated.

Using such material symbols as architecture and landscape, the Royalls brought the grace and opulence of the Caribbean and the novelty of modernity to this tiny corner of New England. Meanwhile the "implicated" places of their estate and grounds appeared to give a temporal depth to the family's influence that was not real. Not even a generation removed from the stain of fortunes made in trade, the Royalls were in today's terms nouveau riche. That they were nevertheless able to make a complete ascendancy is testament to their adept engagement in social discourses of identity and power. Archaeologists might argue that many of these discourses, or "conversations," can be overheard 250 years after they took place because they were conducted in part within the realm of material things.

The core of the house was not originally so grand. A farmer driving his cart from town in 1732 would have seen a rather unremarkable saltbox structure belonging to the Usher family, built sometime in the 17th century on the parcel of land known as the Ten Hills Farm, granted to Massachusetts's first governor, John Winthrop, in 1637 (fig. 12).* It would have been a respectable house, but when Isaac first bought the property from Antigua through one of his agents, he found his close personal friend, Massachusetts governor Jonathan Belcher, was skeptical about the prudence of the purchase. "If you were here," he wrote, "I am perswaded you would not be so fond as you have been of [it]," and went on to describe how the land, buildings, and fences were in a "ruinous" condition (Royall Correspondence: Aug. 15, 1732).

---

*Governor Winthrop was only the first in a parade of illustrious personages, however, to inhabit or visit the house over the next three centuries. The house was listed as a National Historic Landmark in 1962 for its exemplary mid-Georgian architecture, its origins as part of the Ten Hills Farm grant from the English Crown to Governor John Winthrop, and its role as military headquarters for General Stark during the siege of Boston in the American Revolution (*Royall House Reporter* 1962). The house has been restored to the style of its eighteenth-century occupancy by the Royall family.

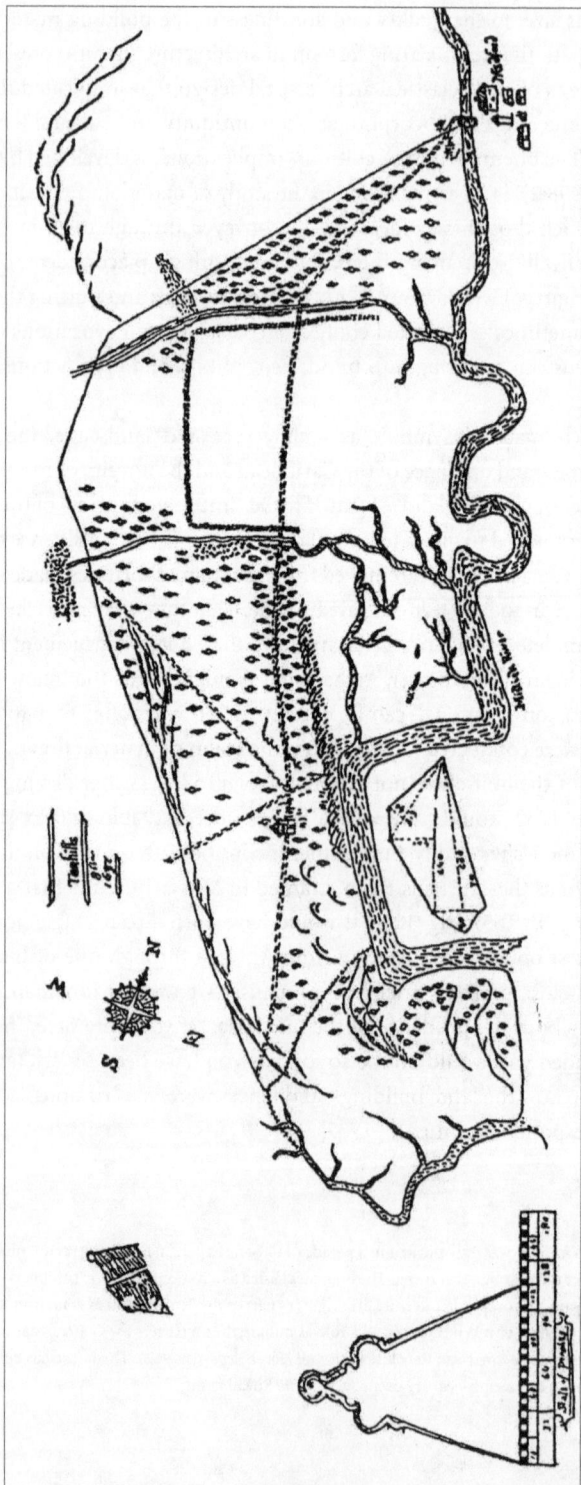

FIG. 12. Plan of the original Ten Hills Farm land grant given by the Crown to the Massachusetts Bay Colony's first governor, John Winthrop, in 1637. (Courtesy of the Royall House Association.)

The house at the time of purchase was two and one-half stories high and one room deep, with a chimney on each end. It is thought to have been built either by Mrs. Peter Lidgett, who acquired the property in 1677, or Lieutenant Governor John Usher, who bought it in the 1690s (Finney 1974:23).

Archaeological testing and historical maps seem to confirm that, although it was on Winthrop's land, this was not the original Winthrop structure, and it has been dated instead to the late 17th century (Chan 2003:155–67). In 1677 the Winthrops had sold the property to Elizabeth Lidgett. In 1700 she bequeathed the house and lands to her son, Charles, though her daughter was married to Usher and lived at the property with him from the 1690s to 1732. It was the Ushers who are supposed to have built on to the original structure in order to enlarge the first floor to its current two-room depth. They dug a cellar and built a lean-to structure to the west side of the house, the outline of which is visible to this day in the brickwork of the western elevation of the house (fig. 13). It was Elizabeth Usher who sold the property to Isaac Royall, Sr., in whose family it remained until 1775, after which the patriot government seized the property indefinitely (fig. 17).

Back in 1732, however, construction and renovation had only just begun, and as it continued over the next several years in anticipation of the new neighbors' arrival from exotic lands, Medford might have looked on in curiosity, envy, and suspense. The more affluent of the townspeople might have wondered on street corners, in taverns, and in drawing rooms just what sort of man this Isaac Royall might be, what accomplishments his wife and daughter could boast, or whether his son might be in need of a wife. They would have recognized the Royalls as one of their own before ever a Morocco slipper alighted doorstep. The improvements the Royalls were making to their new home declared them to be well-to-do.

But the meanings the Royalls' and their peers imbued in this Medford country seat were arbitrary, not fixed, and as such, represented only one side of an on-going social discourse—a statement made by the Royalls about who they thought they were and understood by their peers to be evidence of their mutual belonging to a group apart (Cook, Yamin, and McCarthy 1991; Hall 1992; Shackel 1992). How others interpreted and thus responded or replied to these statements of power and legitimacy, however, will be a major theme throughout the discussions in this book, as will the linguistic metaphor of "discourse" with material things in general.

For instance, it was not just where one's house was or what it looked like that helped to define one's status, but also how one dressed, walked, and talked and who one's friends and family were. These things informed a person's perception of the landscape and the figures who inhabited it on a more intimate, detailed level (Isaac 1982). A wig, for example, or lace cuffs, silver buttons, or gold shoe buckles were sure signs of a gentleman, and they were worn self-consciously as such.

Reverend Devereux Jarratt, writing of his boyhood in the 1730s and 1740s, observed that

> We were accustomed to look upon, what were called *gentle folks,* as beings of a superior order. For my part I was quite shy of *them,* and kept off at a humble distance. A *periwig,* in those days, was a distinguishing badge of *gentle folk*—and when I saw a man riding the road, near our house, with a wig on, it would so alarm my fears, and give me such a disagreeable feeling, that, I dare say, I would run off, as for my life. (1806:14; emphasis in the original)

We may imagine, then, that when the Royalls arrived, they were held in something close to awe in the still rather provincial Medford landscape. Isaac, Jr.,

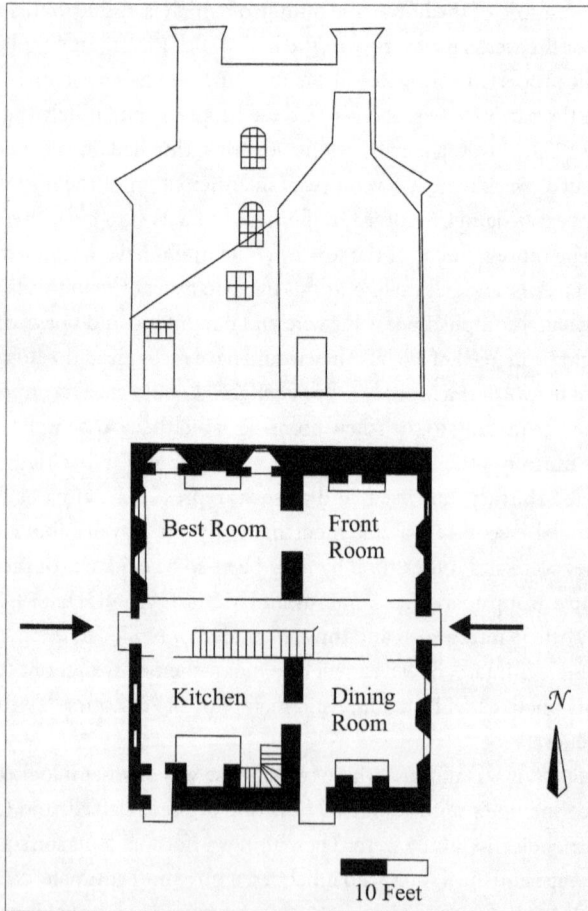

FIG. 13. Diagrams showing the construction phases and floor plan of the Royall House. (After *Colonial Homes* 1989 15 [5]: 101.)

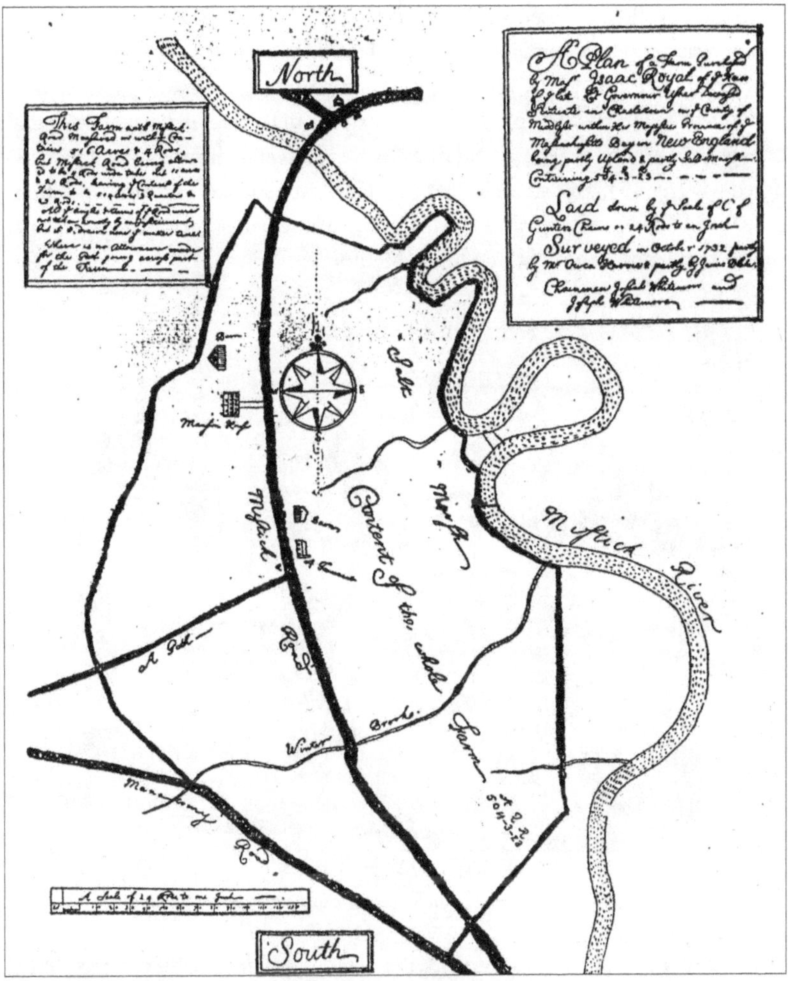

FIG. 14. Deed plan of the Royall Estate in 1732. (Courtesy of the Royall House Association.)

received a magnificent wig from his father shortly after their arrival, bought for the rather extravagant price of £14 (Account Book: Sept. 12, 1737). Though he was but 18 years of age at the time, this was about the price a common farmer might pay for two heifers, a cart horse, a mare and a colt, or a half-dozen swine (Middlesex County Probate 1739). Isaac Royall, Sr., could—and did—spend the same amount on a large mahogany table with a parcel of china, two fowling pieces, and beds and bedding for five of his "Negroes" (Middlesex County Probate 1739). The wig was a luxury, but incorporated as a matter of course into the Royalls' construction and presentation of self, it declared them to be a breed apart.

Isaac Royall, Sr., presents an interesting foil to Reverend Jarratt. He was the son of a carpenter too, and it may be that Isaac himself had once harbored similar feelings as a boy to the reverend's, with regard to "gentle folk." Rather than run in fear as Jarratt had done, however, it seems that Isaac had determined that one day it would be *he* who would ride down the street on horseback with a powdered wig (fig. 15). This small insight into his personality and private aspirations may foreshadow, and explain in a way, many of the patterns of material culture we find evidenced from his later life in Medford.

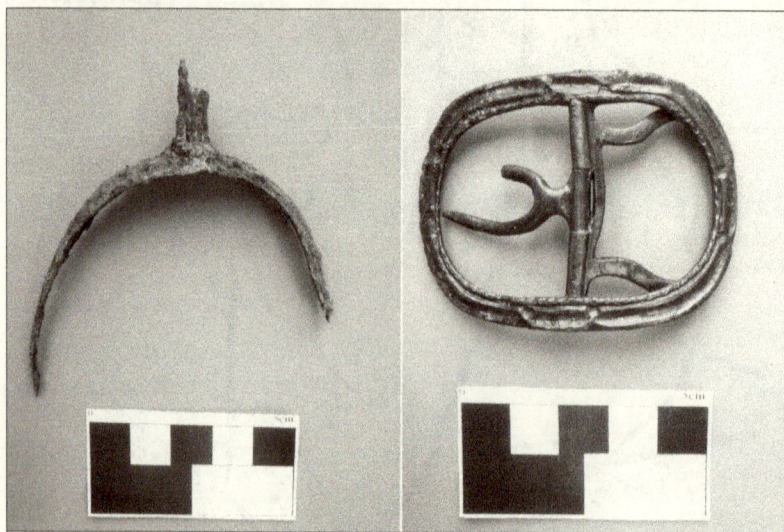

FIG. 15. Marks of a gentleman. An iron boot spur from the courtyard, top, and a brass shoe buckle from the outbuilding foundation in the slave quarters' west yard, bottom.

Indeed, under Royall ownership, the house and lands achieved their most glorious state, which Finney (1974:26) has characterized as "remarkable examples of the Georgian style." The 1732–37 remodeling period before the family moved into the house raised it to its current three-story height and gave the house its modern eastern and western facades (Finney 1974:30; figs. 16 and 17). Royall encased the old brick structure in wooden clapboards, which were more amenable to economical architectural elaboration than stone or brick (Morrison 1952:485).

Archaeological excavations around the house and grounds have revealed good evidence of the various construction and refurbishment activities that were undertaken when the Royalls first bought the property. For example, oral tradition at the Royall House has always attributed the intact cobbled surface beneath the west lawn of the mansion to the Royalls, but there was no documentation of it as such. A rich midden of sheet refuse in a hard-packed soil recovered from directly beneath the cobbles contained Buckley ware, white salt-glazed stoneware, and Westerwald stoneware, while later temporal indicators such as creamware or pearlware were conspicuously absent, so that excavations were consistent with the oral tradition (see Hume 1969; Miller et al. 2000).

FIG. 16. The modern eastern facade of the mansion house, facing Main St., part of Isaac, Sr.'s initial enlargement and beautification of the house between 1732 and 1737. (Photograph by the author.)

FIG. 17. Modern western facade of the mansion house, thought to stem from Isaac, Jr.'s continuing beautification efforts after the death of his father. (Photograph by the author.)

The cobbled surface seems to mark a temporal delineation between the first and second halves of the century, as well as a functional transition from work yard to formal receiving area, which allows us to interpret it as the result of one of the Royalls' many beautification efforts in the first years of their ownership. Indeed this was no slapdash pavement done for expediency. The cobbles were skillfully laid and perfectly fitted to create a smooth and comfortable walking and driving surface. They are quite in keeping with the accounts of the Royalls' having hired only the finest artisans, craftsmen, and carpenters in Medford during the five-year preparation of the estate for habitation (Hoover 1974). The townspeople would have known that something very grand was happening.

It was also at this point that brick slave quarters and other outbuildings are supposed to have been erected. Indeed a thick layer of construction debris sprinkled with 18th-century artifacts that date the deposit approximately to the first half of the century, including tin-glazed earthenware, Buckley ware, buff-bodied combed and dotted slipware, and hand-wrought nails was discovered 1.5 meters south of the of the brick half of the slave quarters. The artifacts that help date the deposit suggest that the debris was part of an expansion of the original one-story brick out kitchen into something that would be large enough to house several slaves that would be arriving with their master. This deposit is located immediately atop subsoil. In fact absence of historical topsoil in most of the slave quarters' south (back) yard has led us to speculate that the Royalls might have borrowed soil from this area for use in their many landscaping activities around the property, leaving the area behind the quarters stripped bare. A large, oval stone-and-pebble feature discovered in the park, for example, has been tentatively identified as a garden bed that decoratively flanked the wide gravel walk that led to the front door of the mansion (Chan 2003:167ff.). Our resistivity survey further suggests that it was but one of several (see fig. 10).

What these discoveries also betray is a cognitive separation in the use of space that was being built into the very landscape of the estate before its occupants had even arrived. They are significant because the Royalls' social construction of space presents one of our first clues about how the process of racialization at the Royall House might actually have begun. Like ripples on the surface of a pond, they also show the Royalls' statements of power reaching far beyond their own inner circle, or social set, and extending to the vast sea of their social underlings—laborers, tenants, and, of course, slaves.

Most particularly, in the efforts expended on the house and slave quarters and the visible areas of the property (and in the lack of effort shown in the domain of the enslaved), we begin to see how *ideas* about social differences were made tangible and thus perhaps more apparently "real." The Royalls' own notions of the difference between work and leisure, clean and unclean, master and slave, and ultimately white and black were being structurally embedded into the environment itself. It was precisely through such material mechanisms—archaeologically accessible on a small, local scale—that these ideas could gain currency across American colonial society at large. As part of the very landscape, entering perception in a sensory, subliminal fashion, these ideas were able to gain power by becoming "common sense," "natural," or "obvious" (Leone 1999:8).

Such structural segregation may have underscored the social differences of race and class, as they were understood at this estate, but it also ensured that those who were being segregated would have space and time to themselves (Garman 1998; Jones 1990). While the Royalls strolled through immaculate gardens and took in the stunning vistas of their house and lands, the slave quarters' back and side yards were stripped bare and left strewn with garbage, rubbish, and rubble. They would have been left that way because the principal inhabitants there were black and enslaved and thought to be deserving of nothing more. But these yards would also have been a space belonging to (or at least left to) precisely those people as a place of their own.

As such the meanings given to the Royall House landscape were variable and contingent and represented a crack in the facade of total domination that slaveholders sought to project through the manipulation of landscape (see Delle 1999; Epperson 1999a). In fact Garman (1998:134) has proposed that New England slaveholding estates comprised a variety of such "shared but contested" spaces. It is a phenomenon that Rodman (1992:651) has called "multilocality": the way in which place can be multiply inscribed with meaning, depending on one's rank, social position, or physical experience of it. The archaeological visibility of alternative social constructions of place is well worth examining.

Isaac Sr.'s 1739 probate inventory lists an "Out Kitching" on the property, as well as several barns, a coach house, a stable, a corn house, and a pigeon house (see fig. 19, below). At the time of Isaac Royall, Sr.'s death, the house and lands were appraised at £50,000 and £37,000, respectively (Morrison 1952:485)—nearly eight times what he had paid for it. This no doubt partly reflected inflation and a strong colonial economy, but it must also have reflected the extent of his beautification and improvement of the property.

Isaac Royall, Jr., by this time a colonel, was even more fashion conscious than his father and enjoyed spending his money on the various accoutrements of a wealthy Bostonian. The interior rooms were redecorated to keep Colonel Royall abreast of elite Bostonian fashion, a standard said to have been set by Thomas Hancock in town (Morrison 1952:486). Isaac, Jr., also had the western facade redone to imitate the look of masonry blocks. The RHA's restoration efforts of 2002 revealed some of Isaac, Sr.'s old clapboarding beneath the new veneer. The grounds were a landscape of fruit trees, shrubs, a back courtyard paved with large cobblestones, and gardens. An octagonal summer gazebo and small garden, represented on contemporary maps (fig. 18), stood on an artificial hillock at some distance from the house. Later photographs of the structure, before it was demolished, show a bell-shaped roof with a statue of winged Mercury at its peak, the remains of which are stored in the Royall House attic, and we are told that it also housed a "walled cellar entered by a trap door" (Wild 1908:171). The house could be approached on foot or horse through a gate on Main Street (then Mystic Street) flanked by wooden posts and opening onto a "broad graveled walk, bordered with box," that led visitors in 70 paces to the door (Hooper 1900:4). Farther to the north were massive stone gateposts that marked the entrance to the carriage drive that also turned off of Main Street and led around to the courtyard in back, under the "shade of magnificent old elms . . . and paved with large round beach pebbles" (Drake 1906:121; fig. 19). Wild (1908:170) also states that the Royalls' landscaped center of the estate was separated from the main highway by a high wall, which was in turn broken by a low wall and fence directly in front of the mansion.

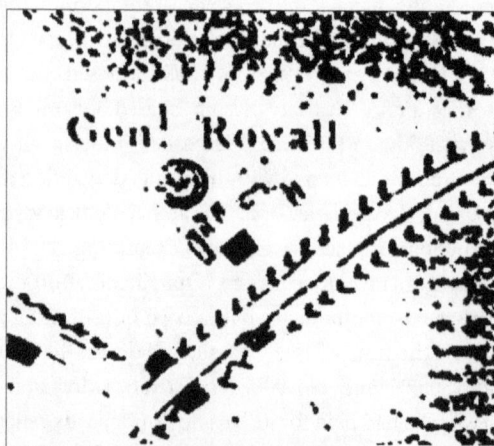

Fig. 18. Detail of the 1777 Henry Pellham map of Medford, showing house, slave quarters, a variety of outbuildings, and the summer house on a hill in back, represented by the large circle. (Courtesy of the Royall House Association.)

The house, abandoned by the Royalls, who fled after the Battle of Lexington, was used by Generals Stark, Lee, and Sullivan as a military headquarters during the siege of Boston in 1775 and visited by General Washington for consultations with these men (Finney 1974:31). The fledgling republican government eventually confiscated the property for having belonged to a loyalist (Blake 1998:15), and Washington's secretary, Colonel Cary, is said to have bought the property and

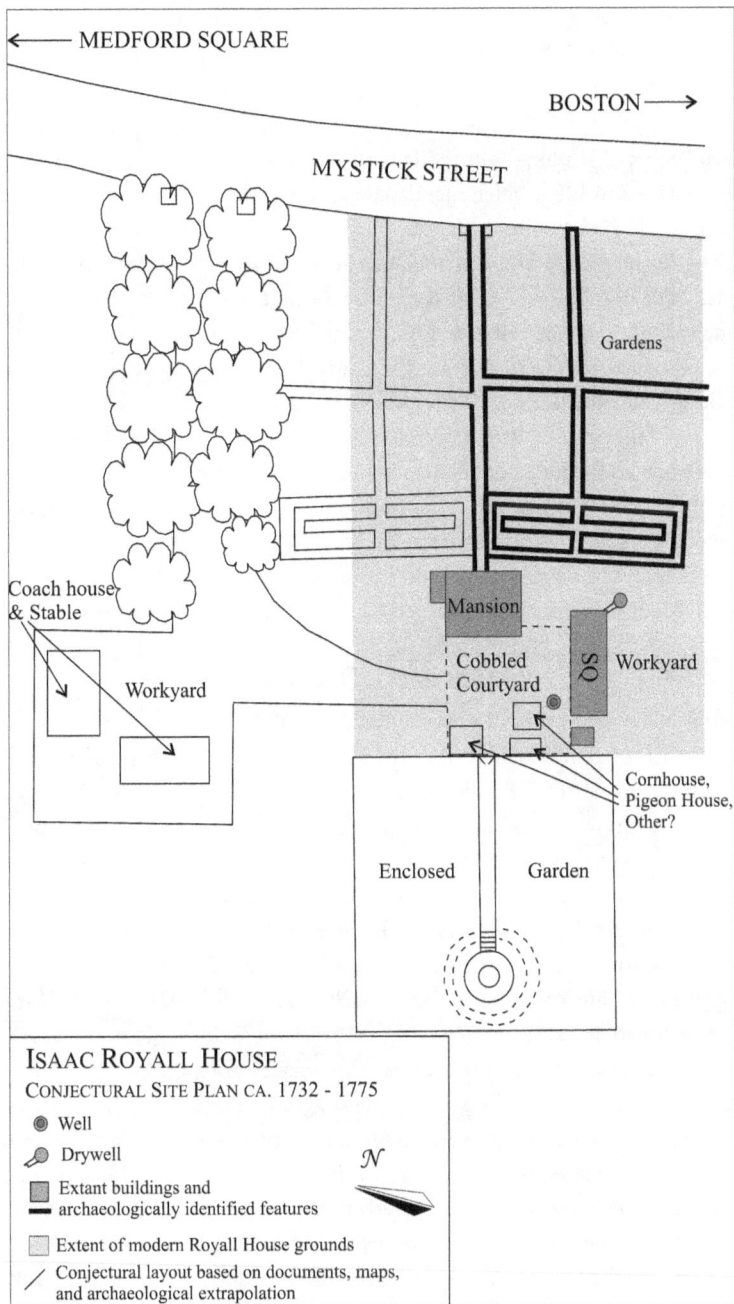

FIG. 19. Reconstruction of the Royall House site, ca. 1732–75. (After Lamar [n.d.], the 1777 Pellham map of Medford, and archaeologically identified features.) In addition Isaac, Sr.'s probate inventory lists four barns, three old and one new, in the vicinity of the mansion house, as well as a pigeon house, corn house, coach house, and stable. The exact location and size of these structures are not indicated, but presumably the coach house and stable are the structures shown to the northwest of the house in the Pellham map, while the pigeon house and corn house are among the small outbuildings depicted north-northwest of the slave quarters.

lived in it for two years after the Revolution (Finney 1974:31). At that point the trail of ownership fades until 1806, when deeds show Samuel Dexter, Benjamin Hall, and William Sumner selling off parts of the estate to William Welch. One source states that in 1792 the new government ceded the title back to Elizabeth Royall Pepperell Hutton—a granddaughter of Isaac Royall, Jr.—as a result of the Treaty of Paris in 1783, which mandated the return of Tory property confiscated during the war (Blake 1998:17).

The Royall House property today, as acquired in 1908, is defined by Royall House Park to the northeast of the house, George Street to the southeast, and residential plots to the northwest and southwest. The Royall House Park, 0.76 acres, is owned by the city of Medford, which is a good example of an early public-private partnership for site presentation in this country. The house and portions of the original Royall lawn to the immediate east and west of the mansion are owned by the Royall House Association, which opened the property to the public in 1910. It is to this organization that we are indebted for the survival of the house and slave quarters, for the estate had been slated in 1908 for subdivision, sale, and development, and it was the RHA that had the foresight and organization to rescue what remained (Blake 1998:22–24; Finney 1974:31).

The Slave Quarters

There is some controversy surrounding the Royall House slave quarters. A long oral tradition has maintained that the slaves were housed there, as the modern name of the structure indicates. In fact no documentation from the Royalls' occupation survives to confirm this unequivocally, and the first identification of the structure as the slave quarters comes from the antiquarian literature.

The structure was referred to as an "Out Kitching" in the 1739 probate inventory of Isaac Royall, Sr. That does not, however, preclude that African Americans lived in the structure, and it even makes it likely (see, for example, Grady and Chappell n.d.; Tate 1965; Upton 1988; Vlach 1991; Delle 1999). It is a two-story, part-brick, part-wood frame. The original structure is most likely a product of Isaac Royall, Sr.'s construction endeavors or may even have stemmed from the Ushers' occupation, since the architecture suggests a pre-1740 construction, but the building also seems to have been built in three phases—a very small one-story brick kitchen, replaced with a two-story brick kitchen around 1739, and, several years later, a wood-frame addition (Grady n.d.; Grady and Chappell n.d.; fig. 20).

The lower room houses a large fireplace, 9.5 feet long, and a brick oven and is interpreted as the kitchen where slaves prepared food for themselves, the Royall family, and any additional hired or seasonal labor. Technical drawings from the Army Corps of Engineers also record partitions that were supposed to have created three "cabins" for slave families on the bottom floor. The architectural his-

FIG. 20. View of the northern elevation of the slave quarters, facing the courtyard it shares with the mansion house. (Photograph by author). The Historic American Buildings Survey of the slave quarter's floor plans states that the bottom floor of the clapboard section seems to have originally been divided into three rooms for slave families, each with its own door onto the courtyard (RHA files).

torians Anne Grady and Edward Chappelle (n.d.) believe that at least the large room above the kitchen, and possibly the entire upper floor, was intended for human occupation. Although probate inventories that record "Negro beds" in the kitchen, garrets, and hallways of the main house indicate that several slaves lived *with* the Royall family, Finney (1974:30) states, but without any indication of evidence to back it up, that at least a portion of the slaves "lived in the brick 'Out Kitchen' built at the same time as the mansion." In Isaac, Sr.'s probate inventory, however, there is a distinction made between two slave men named Peter and House Peter. Furthermore, although the inventory lists only 13 individuals, six more were added in a retroactive inventory in 1752, and 19 had already been bequeathed to other family members in the estate division (Middlesex County Probate 1739). What that means is that for the first two years the Royalls inhabited the house, they owned at least 38 slaves—far more than could be accommodated within the great house. This scenario suggests that the Royall estate, in many ways, is laid out like a typical southern or Caribbean 18th-century urban townhouse compound (see Tate 1965; Vlach 1991).

In urban settings most enslaved people were housed with their owners. Among larger, wealthier families, however, who had more slaves than could be comfortably accommodated in a single structure, some servants and their families would be housed in a separate building behind the main house, in close enough proximity to be at the master's beck and call (Vlach 1991). These structures would usually be two stories in height and house a kitchen, laundry, or workrooms on the first floor and slave quarters on the second (see also Tate 1965). Contemporary terminology would often reflect such a layout, as many such structures were called the kitchen quarters (Tate 1965:108); they would be built substantially and made to complement the great house architecturally (Vlach 1991).

Between the main house and the slave quarters and, of course, behind the slave quarters themselves, would be work areas where numerous domestic, work, and social activities would be carried out. Because of cramped living quarters, many tasks and activities were done outside. As Upton (1988) points out, the slaves' domain extended much further than the walls of their quarters, and this was recognized by both black and white. It enabled a degree of autonomy and a certain amount of clandestine behavior. Urban masters could often be lulled into a sense of security, feeling that they surveyed all from their commanding central posts. Slaves in such a setting could become seen but not seen, heard but not heard (Delle 1999; Upton 1988). Such known historical phenomena invite speculation about the cultural landscape of the estate and how statements of power were made and received from both white and black perspectives. Upton (1988), McKee (1992), and Hall (1992) provide good models for studying the intended meanings conveyed versus the actual meanings perceived of cultural landscapes in the past and show there was almost always a disjunction between the two, which is discussed later.

Mustering the Evidence

Historical archaeologists are fond of telling people that they spend as much time digging through archives as they do digging through dirt, and archaeological investigations at the Royall House have been combined with intensive documentary research to establish what happened at that site (socially, economically, and culturally) during the forty years that the Royalls lived there with their slaves. Historical research has provided an ethnographic, social, historical, and archaeological context for the study of slavery and race relations, first in the Caribbean and then in Massachusetts. It has allowed us to place the site in the wider context of New England slave society and economy and provides a context for the interpretation of archaeological remains recovered there.

One priority has been to reconstruct the demographic profile of different households and slave populations under the Royalls during the time they inhabited the house. Another has been to reconstruct the nature of the estate itself, how it operated as an economic system, its role in the regional or even global economy, and how these things compared to what was going on at the Antiguan estate. This provides a context against which to place interpretations of African American material culture in Medford. Royall family papers, letters, economic ledgers, vital records, and court records—both here and in Antigua—have been examined, as have Massachusetts tax valuations and African community organization membership lists in Boston.

Secondary sources have examined the population structure of the Boston area, the Massachusetts Bay Colony, and New England at large, and these studies were consulted to shed light on the social context in which the Royalls and their slaves found themselves and within which they each would have been forced to negotiate their ideas of spirituality, identity, self-expression, and cultural, social, or racial affiliation.

Summary

In introducing the research undertaken at the Royall House, it has been important not only to outline the history of the site but also to be explicit about the fact that "reconstructions" are also "constructions," and "knowledge" an inherently social enterprise. While things such as the succession of ownership, the life events of those who lived there, or the landscape and architectural improvements the site experienced through time can certainly be listed in chronological sequence, what we make of these facts, how we interpret them, is often governed in part by our own conscious and subconscious agendas. Being as explicit as possible about our biases and preconceptions, however, as well as about our theoretical point of view, can go far toward "constructing" history critically.

At this site, we use the metaphor of discourse to understand the material world of the Royalls and their many slaves. Using material symbols such as personal effects, architecture, and landscape, the Royalls were able to make powerful statements about who they were and how they expected to be seen, by social peers and inferiors alike. It is also arguable that these "statements" in the material were an organic part of perceived differences between "black" and "white," as they were then emerging.

By the same token, such statements of power and dominance were only effective insofar as they were heard or heeded by their intended audience(s), and there is evidence at the Royall House, again in the material, that the Royalls' side of the discourse did not go uncontested by the people they held as slaves.

Chapter 2
Introducing the Royalls: The Royall Family and the Royall House Property

He delights to display his riches, and 'tis said will bleed
freely when honor calls.
                —Contemporary of Isaac Royall, Jr.,
                        Quoted in Hoover, 1974

When you make men slaves you deprive them of half their
virtue, you set them in your own conduct an example of
fraud, rapine, and cruelty, and compel them to live with
you in a state of war.
                —Olaudah Equiano, former slave, 1789

The Royalls in Antigua

Before they were the "the elegant Royalls of New England" (Hoover 1974), they were the Royalls of Popeshead, Antigua, and the family's wealth stemmed from their participation in all three of the principal elements of the Triangular Trade. They had a sugar plantation and refinery, a rum distillery, and one foot in the slave trade.

Isaac Royall, Sr. (1677–1739) was born of modest means to a carpenter and his wife in the wilds of North Yarmouth, Maine. Fear of Indian attack brought his parents, William and Mary Royall, to Dorchester, Massachusetts, when Isaac was three years old (Hoover 1974). Isaac must have been imbued with great ambition and a sense of adventure, for records show him many thousands of miles from his birthplace and many fortunes richer than he or his parents had probably ever dreamed, and that by the time he was 23 years old. He became a merchant mariner as an adolescent and at the age of 20 married Elizabeth Eliott Oliver, a teenaged widow, in Boston (NEHGS 1907). Within two years, however, the young groom was himself a widower, having lost Elizabeth and an infant son, Aseph, named for Elizabeth's father (NEHGS 1907). Isaac struck out on his own and decided to seek his fortune in the slave trade. Just how, when, or why he arrived at this decision, history does not say. We do know, however, that he landed in St. Johns, Antigua, in 1700 and by 1703 was recorded as merchant and co-owner with his uncle Joseph of the sloop *Mayflower,* built in Scituate, Massachusetts (MHC *Archives* 7:304).

Antigua was an exciting new world, but it was also a foreign and dangerous one of which Isaac probably had little direct knowledge or understanding. Within a year of his arrival, Major Samuel Martin was murdered by his own slaves on Christmas Day, 1701, sending a panic through the island (Oliver 1894:lxxiii). In 1702 provisions were granted for the erection of a cage, pillory, stocks, whipping post, and ducking stool in each town to try to force compliance through visual intimidation. An act soon followed to punish enslaved and free blacks (of whom there were a total of 17) for striking and wounding a white person with slitting of the nose, cutting of a member, or death, at the judge's discretion (Oliver 1894:lxxiii).

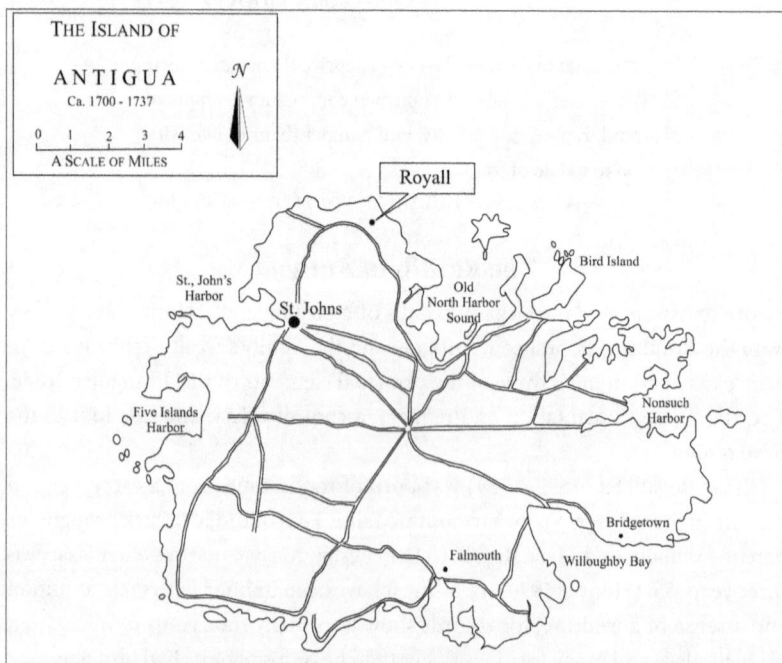

FIG. 21. Map of Antigua, ca. 1700–37, showing key townships, the road system, and the location of Isaac Royall's sugar plantation approximately four miles outside the capital of St. Johns. (After Oliver [1896: title page].) Original by Herman Moll, date unknown.

Whether Isaac Royall's resolve ever faltered in the early years or whether the social unrest he encountered there merely strengthened his steadfastness of purpose, we will never know. He stayed in Antigua, though, and by 1707 had settled himself sufficiently to marry Elizabeth Browne, a widow with a young daughter named Anne. In 1712 they were granted six acres in Popeshead by Governor Walter Hamilton, about four miles outside the island's capital of St. Johns (Oliver 1899:58; fig. 21). It was a small town that in the 1712–13 census recorded 22 white families, 28 women, 73 children, 27 men fit to bear arms, and 364 "negroes" (Oliver 1894:lxxxvi).

For the next 33 years, Royall remained a relatively small but successful sugar planter, rum distiller, and slave trader on the island (see table 1 below). His son referred to it much later as "my little Estate there," for it had only one windmill while others had two, three, or even six (Royall Correspondence: May 29, 1779; Oliver 1896:title page map).

Isaac procured slaves for such illustrious personages as the Governor of Massachusetts, Jonathan Belcher, who signed all of his letters to Royall and requests for more "boys" affectionately "JB" (see Royall Correspondence: Sept. 4, 1731; Jan. 18, 1732). Precisely how many slaves the Royalls owned at this time, or how much sugar and rum their operation was producing, Antigua's island records do not say (AHS: Miscellaneous Records, 1720–29), while their own accounts are seemingly incomplete. The accounts receivable section of the Royalls' account book (1724–49), for example, where most sales can be expected to be listed, is much more fragmentary than the accounts payable section, having some missing pages, years with suspiciously little activity, and whole years where nothing is recorded at all (table 1). Additionally there are several unspecified entries in £50, £60, £85, and £100 amounts that may represent the sale of human cargo, such as "By Cash recd of Collo Coddington £85" (Account Book:Sept. 1, 1729). The year 1737 is especially frustrating because it has several pages missing in the accounts receivable section, which amount to £14,860 in transactions.

Isaac's brother, Jacob, was his middleman and received a 5 percent commission on all transactions he completed on Isaac's behalf (Account Book:1724–49). Jacob Royall was a merchant in Boston and frequently advertised slaves recently imported from the West Indies (see *Boston Gazette:* May 19–26, 1729; June 2–9, 1729). Isaac, Elizabeth, and Anne must have led comfortable lives as Caribbean sugar planters and island elite, and Isaac had become a major, a colonel, and a judge, politically high-ranking offices. The family was not, however, without personal sorrows. Isaac and Elizabeth had numerous children over the years, but only two—Isaac, Jr. (b. 1719) and Penelope (b. 1724)—survived childhood (Maine Historical Society n.d.: n.p.). Unfortunately for them, just as joy in their personal lives was finally granted, ominous clouds were gathering on the horizon.

TABLE 1.

The Royalls' sales in slaves, sugar, molasses, and rum, based on figures given in the accounts payable and accounts receivable portions of the account book, 1724–49

	Slaves No.	Value in £	Sugar No. Hhds	Value in £	Molasses & Rum
1726	33	£396[a]	—	—	—
1728	—	—	—	£687	—
1729	46	≥ £3063[b]	—	—	—
1731	2	£138	—	—	—
1732	58	£1309[c]	—	—	—
1733	3	£265	—	—	—
1734	121	£7141	≥ 20	£788	—
1735	1	£90	≥ 60	£3190	—
1736	2	—	—	—	—
1737	3	£278	—	—	—
1738	—	—	—	—	—
1739	4	£475	—	—	—
1740	—	—	—	—	£872[d]
1741	—	—	—	—	—
1743	1	£130	—	—	—
Total	**274**	**£13, 285**	**80**	**£5537**	**£872**

Notes: [a]Half of the proceeds of a joint venture with Christopher Stoodley and brother-in-law Jonathan Cheney.
[b]Some amounts illegible.
[c]Seven-twelfths of the proceeds of a joint venture, partners unknown.
[d]Sugar, molasses, and rum combined for 1740.

In the 1710s and 1720s, drought and failed crops had ushered in an era of economic stress in Antigua that compounded an already seething social atmosphere. The growing crisis was extensively covered in the ubiquitous "excerpts from letters from [such-and-such a place]" that were published in newspapers throughout the colonies at the time as sensational firsthand accounts of important current events (see *South Carolina Gazette* 1736:no. 4). Water shortages and the island's flagging ability to pay for imported foodstuffs resulted in the declaration of public rationing and fasts, as well as in the rise of social unrest, as relief ships from Guadeloupe and Montserrat distributed water to the wealthy, who could afford to buy water, even at the staggering cost of 15 shillings per hogshead, rather than to the poor, who could not (Oliver 1894:xcvi).

In 1725 drought had lasted eight months and destroyed two years' crops, and the price of imported water had gone so high that it had "occasioned the loss of many of the Cattle *and Negroes*" (Oliver 1894:xcvi, emphasis added). Trade ships sent for rum and sugar were forced to leave the harbor half full and "some just in their ballast alone" (Royall Correspondence: Aug. 15, 1736). By August 1736 things had come to such a head that Royall wrote to his friend Edmund Quincy that he feared he should "be obliged to distill salt water for my people [slaves] to drink if it shall not please God to send us rain within eight or ten days" (Royall Correspondence: Aug. 15, 1736). During that crisis it was reported in the mainland colonies that "We are burnt up, have had little Rain since January last . . . good Water is scarce to make a Bowl; most of the Taverns pay from £1–6 to 2£ per Pail. It is very hard with the Poor, who are daily begging for a Drink of Water" (*South Carolina Gazette*, 1736:no. 4).

A massive hurricane hit the island in 1733, and a series of severe earthquakes struck in 1735 (Gaspar 1985:226). So many years of hardship—indeed, a veritable "conjunction of adversity" (Gaspar 1985:226)—may have contributed to Royall's decision to buy John Usher's Massachusetts farm in 1732, a 504-acre estate on the banks of the Mystic River, for £10,500. Isaac thought it to be a good situation, although Governor Belcher remained skeptical (Royall Correspondence: Aug. 15, 1732). Town records indicate that Isaac made many trips back to New England during the Antigua years, usually in the spring, picking up where he left off in public life there, attending the Stoughton town meetings (where he had an additional home), performing marriages, and almost certainly overseeing the construction of his new seat in Charlestown (Church of Jesus Christ of Latter Day Saints: Records of Stoughton, MA 1717–1860). He also wrote instructions to his brother, Jacob, when he could not be there in person, on what was to be done to the property.

I have desired my Brother to dam in forty or fifty acres of my salt meadow at my Charlestown farm, to cut all the Wood down, but a shade for the cattle and to break up all that ground as soon as conveniency will permit and after it has been manured for two or three years, to lay it down with grass seeds. (Royall Correspondence: Aug. 15, 1736)

Isaac, Sr., appears to have begun sending slaves north in the late 1720s as well, possibly in anticipation of the family's eventual arrival there. The account book shows Isaac paying £3 a head for the passage of "2 Negroes" on July 23, 1726 (probably Isaac, Jr.'s young enslaved companions), and that of "Beven [an indentured servant], Ruth, & Nan" on September 12. He paid £4 a head importation tax on Cuff and Peter (probably the two boys sent in July) November 8, 1726, and on Ruth and Nan May 4, 1727. In 1731 he shipped the family's chariot north

(Account Book: Dec. 10), and in 1733 he paid the freight of nine more "Negroes" (Account Book: June 4). They were most certainly getting ready to leave.

In 1727 Isaac had bought 220 acres in Stoughton (now Walpole, Massachusetts) and, a year and a half later, an additional 140 acres (Account Book: May 4, 1727; Oct. 19, 1728). By 1735 he had also purchased a 122-acre farm in Freetown (now Bristol, Rhode Island; Account Book: Feb. 12). And in 1736 he added 400 more acres there (Account Book:April 12). Thus, before they had even arrived in Massachusetts, the Royalls had three farms and at least 13 slaves in the Boston area. Initially thought to be provisioning estates for the Royalls' principal residence in Charlestown (the estate was later annexed to Medford), the account book suggests that in fact Isaac Royall, Sr., used Ten Hills Farm to provision the Stoughton and Freetown farms, although not in any apparently systematic way. The account book lists the movement of cattle, sheep, goats, rum, sundries, and at least one slave from Ten Hills Farm to Stoughton and Freetown (see, for example, June 25 and Dec. 5, 1737; Jan. 19, 1738). At least for one year, Isaac, Sr., rented the Freetown farm to Jonathan Farrow for £100 (Account Book: May 21, 1737), but we cannot find that he did so again.

The farms may have been part of Isaac's self-imposed familial duties, since his brother, Samuel, was a poor relation and was allowed to live modestly as a house carpenter in Freetown, apparently with no lands or slaves of his own (Middlesex County Probate 1739; RHS 1743:326). Samuel received cash allowances from time to time from Isaac (see Account Book: Oct. 21 & Dec. 6, 1737), and he once allowed Isaac (but not Jacob) to pay the balance at a shop where he owed over £51 (Account Book: Sept. 14, 1731). When Samuel recorded his last will and testament in 1739, he wrote simply, "My Will is that my Grandson Royall Paine Shall have my Chistt after my dec's" (RHS 1743:326). Who was living at Stoughton is not now known, although Isaac's son-in-law, Robert Oliver, did rent a house and barn from him in 1736 and was still living there in 1737, location unspecified (Account Book: Dec. 7, 1736; Mar. 7 and Sept. 12, 1737). An advertisement for its lease in 1743 describes it as "a Good Farm," containing 600 acres, "200 of which is cleared, with a good House and Barn" (*Boston Evening Post:* March 14, 1743).

Isaac was also at least partially responsible for the financial well-being of three other of his siblings—Sarah Dunton, Martha Cheny, and Mary Bird—as well as their children (Account Book 1724–49). A 1752 retroactive probate inventory of Isaac, Sr.'s holdings after his death records the buildings, lands, and slaves held on both of these farms (Middlesex County Probate 1739). They are much smaller than Ten Hills Farm, with one yoke of oxen, four cows, 17 sheep, and four slaves at Stoughton and one yoke of oxen, six cows, and two slaves at Freetown. The only other items listed were farm equipment such as carts, plows, hoes, spades, chains, shovels, or axes (Middlesex County Probate 1739). These farms do not appear to have been economically vital to Isaac Royall, Sr.'s wealth, and so his provisioning of them seems more likely to have stemmed from personal motivations or family obligations. Otherwise the farms were used for rental income.

Thus the account book records several years of preparations before the Royalls returned to Massachusetts, but not everyone seemed to be ready to go. Isaac's wife, Elizabeth, feared the northern winters and had to be reassured by Governor Belcher that "we have plenty of good wood and can keep our house warm enough in the coldest winter" (Royall Correspondence: Jan 29, 1732/33). He went on, perhaps with a twinkle in his eye, that she would not want to give so good a husband grounds for divorce "for want of paying him due honour and respect" by staying behind.

Antigua had also become an inhospitable place in its own right, and not just for want of rain. For decades it had been plagued too by war with the French (who owned the neighboring islands of Nevis and St. Kitts), political corruption, and intrigue, and the "Negro problem" of course remained a constant. By 1723, when blacks outnumbered adult white men four to one, it had become "customary to declare martial law" on Christmas Day and the two days following, which were slave holidays (Oliver 1894:xcv). Because great numbers of slaves had fled to the mountains and begun to descend on surrounding plantations in armed bands, a bounty of £3 for killing any runaway and £6 for live capture was posted the same year. How the situation had advanced to such a state is easier to understand when one considers how the Atlantic slave trade exploded in the 18th century. Island records (AHS: Miscellaneous Records, 1720–29) reveal that in 1720 the island had imported 251 slaves from Africa. By 1728–29, 2,846 Africans arrived on Antigua's shores—an 11-fold increase, with little corresponding increase in the white population.

On an island with a total free population of about 4,000 and only 1,337 adult men fit to bear arms, Africans vastly outnumbered their oppressors by the end of the decade. This could not have been lost on the black population, for the 1720s were rent by frequent "savage and bloody" slave rebellions, followed by regular executions of their leaders (Hoover 1974:7). In 1727 6.5 percent of the island's total public expenditures—which included things like cleaning of the island's ponds, upkeep of the forts, and compensation for military widows—was spent on the "Executing of Negroes for runing away and for fellony" (AHS: Miscellaneous Records 1720–29). Nor could the island's inhabitants look to their political leaders for help, for the government was foul with corruption. Daniel Parke, governor when Royall first arrived in Antigua, was assassinated in 1710 in a *white* insurrection that accused him of illegal acts, such as threatening to have the army open fire on the assembly and put the speaker in irons (Gaspar 1985; Oliver 1894:

lxxxi ff.). Isaac Royall was part of an extreme, incendiary—and perhaps naively misguided (for Royall's concern with honor plays itself out again and again in the documentary record)—minority that argued in Parke's favor. The assembly accused him in 1712 of "fomenting disturbances" for trying to obtain depositions in the dead governor's favor (Oliver 1899:58). Parke's successor, Governor Douglas, was little better. He regularly adjourned assembly meetings to prevent bills contrary to his own interests from being passed and received hush money from various people accused in the Parke rebellion. He made Royall a political prisoner in the fort in August of 1712 for reporting that he "heard Your Excellency say certain words reflecting on your honour" (Oliver 1899:58). Governor Douglas himself was eventually imprisoned five years for such acts (Oliver 1894:lxxxix).

The defining moment at this time for the troubled island, however, occurred in 1736, but four miles from the Royalls' home in Popeshead and less than a year before they left forever. Although the Royalls had been preparing to leave Antigua for some time, it seems clear that this incident provided the final impetus for them to do so. According to a "Letter from Antigua," a vast slave conspiracy in St. Johns, in which two of the Royalls' own were implicated, was discovered quite by chance and at the last possible minute before its execution.

> Here has been a general Stop to all Business, occasioned by the Happy Discovery of an accursed Negro Plot. . . . The Plot was thus, viz. One Court, a Negro Man, belonging to Thomas Kirby Esqr. was the chief Person in this affair; Tomboy, a Negro Man belonging to Mr. Thomas Hanston; and Hercules, a Negro Man belonging to Mr. John Christophers were to have been this King Court's Generals, and while the Gentlemen and Ladies were diverting themselves at the [King's Coronation Day] Ball . . . they were to convey a great Quantity of Gun-Powder into the Cellar and blow the House up. (Oliver 1894:c)

The plan from there was for each of the "Generals" to lead a party of 400 men armed with cutlasses from three directions into town and to fall on all white men, women, and children. Seven "Strong Guards" would be set up at the city's perimeter to block white reinforcements. The rebels had purportedly established an elaborate system of fire signals from all of the island's peaks to communicate with other slave enclaves across the island and to signal their own insurrections, seizing arsenals, distributing arms, and committing general murder and mayhem until every white soul on the island was dead. A new African or Creole government would then be installed, to make Antigua the first African nation in the New World. An execution list shows that Isaac Royall's slave driver, Hector, was burned at the stake for his alleged involvement in the conspiracy (Gaspar 1985:30ff.). One of his other slaves, Quaco, occupation unknown, was banished to Hispaniola (Gaspar 1985:30ff.). Isaac's son-in-law, Richard Oliver, also lost a driver, who was also named Quaco, to the executions (Gaspar 1985:30ff.). Terrified, outraged, and vengeful, island administrators compiled what they claimed to be a complete report of the conspiracy in *A Genuine Narrative of the Intended Conspiracy of the Negroes of Antigua* (1737 [1972]), which was extracted from the court's official report to the Crown. By this account the slaves' intended crimes were grim indeed, but so too was the punishment meted out by whites in retaliation.

From a modern perspective, it seems that the economic strife and drought of the previous years that had led to starvation and thirst, as well as generally less tolerable conditions for enslaved people, should have left no one surprised that things had erupted in such a way. Nor was it without specific forewarning. In *A Genuine Narrative* (1737:6–7), the court reported that whites on the island first learned from the testimony of other slaves that "King" Court had in fact formally and publicly declared war on his enemies, by performing the *Ikem* dance in broad daylight. This dance was an Akan royal ritual meant to seal the support of one's countrymen, while also giving public and fair warning to those one intended to attack. Gaspar (1985) explores in convincing detail the Akan underpinnings of the ceremonies leading up to and including Court's *Ikem* dance that preceded the intended revolt. White spectators had no idea of the actual meaning behind the spectacle, however, thinking it an entertainment put on by and for slaves. But in fact, by this ceremony, "King" Court was ensuring his generals' and soldiers' support and allegiance and demonstrating to the enslaved population of the island who had been let in on the secret that the revolt was no longer an abstraction but now to be put in motion. Those who understood the ceremony's meaning had been recruited at slave feasts and entertainments where they had been convinced to take an oath of secrecy and fidelity. The oath was administered by giving a concoction of rum or some other liquor infused with grave dirt and sometimes cock's blood, frequently in the presence of an Obeah man, an Akan shaman-type figure, who lent the ceremony spiritual gravity. The neophytes would then have to swear to be true to each other and the cause, to kill all whites indiscriminately, and to suffer death rather than expose the plot (*Narrative* 1737:13). "Evidence" for having taken this oath (usually just a verbal accusation by a fellow slave who might enjoy banishment over execution if he or she "complied") was one of the principal criteria used by the British colonial court to convict the slaves of conspiracy. All those sentenced to death or banishment were reported to have taken the oath and thus shown unequivocally their intention to do harm to their masters. Testimony in the ensuing months also revealed that enslaved people had met regularly in the forest for years; that one night, many years before the revolt, more than 2,000 of them had reportedly gathered and crowned Court their king and leader; and that he had since that time assumed that role among the island's blacks.

For their daring, "King" Court, Tomboy, Hercules, and two other principals named Tony and Harry were broken on the wheel (Gaspar 1985:30–36). Seventy-seven more (including Hector) were burned at the stake, six were gibbeted alive, and 37 were banished from the island. As if all this were not enough to send planters running for cover, disease was also rampant. "Black leprosy" (the tuberculoid form of leprosy) and "joint evil" (a severe septicemia in newborns, entering through the umbilical cord and causing joint inflammation, arthritis, and commonly death) were so bad among the island's enslaved population in 1734–35 that Bird Island—a small island off the northeast coast of Antigua—was set up as a Negro quarantine (Oliver 1894:xcix). Then in 1736 smallpox broke out.

Thus Royall arrived in Boston Harbor with his family and an unknown number of slaves on the ship *Unity* on Wednesday July 27, 1737, having escaped economic hardship and physical peril (*Boston Gazette* 1737: July 25–Aug. 1). In December of 1737, he paid £60 for the importation of 15 more of his slaves, presumably brought from Antigua (Account Book: Dec. 6). The slave conspiracy had hit close to home, and the family must have felt the full weight of its serendipitous escape from certain death. If two of their own "people" had known about and participated in the conspiracy, were there others? Could they ever feel safe in their own beds again? How would this affect the Royalls' treatment of their slaves in the future? How did the enslaved perceive the move? There was likely no love lost between Hector, the driver and Master's minion, and the other laborers, but the memory of his gruesome end less than six months before must have been still fresh and terrifying. And who was Quaco, banished to Hispaniola? A son? A brother? Another driver? How did the participation of two of their own in the most overt and dangerous form of retaliation against their masters affect the psyches of those who remained?

Whether African-born or West Indian–born, none of the people the Royalls brought with them was accustomed to the austere northern winters or the different natural environment. Most likely separated from friends and even family, they were also arriving in a place where they would no longer have strength in numbers, for Massachusetts was but 2–3 percent black (Greene 1942; Piersen 1988). There would be no maroon societies in the hills, capable of swooping down in a vengeful and terrifying horde against their oppressors, no secret forest meetings where 2,000 or more of their own could gather to crown a king—although New England's Black Election Day was a public and socially acceptable version of the same ceremony (Gaspar 1985). On the other hand the cycle of mutual terror and retribution that characterized the Caribbean slave experience was broken in New England. Whites perhaps felt safer with but few blacks in their midst. There was one whipping post in Medford Square, but if it was used often in the punishment of blacks and whites, documents do not survive to tell of it. In fact, from 1700 to

1800, there was just one discussion at the Medford town meetings regarding the control of black behavior, and that was to set up a nine o'clock curfew in 1745, on pain of public flogging in the square or fine to the master (MHS: Medford Town Records through 1830).

"A Fine Estate for a Gentleman to Live On"

It is thought that only a simple saltbox structure from the 17th century remained on Lieutenant Governor John Usher's farm at the time of its purchase by the Royalls, although the architectural antecedents of the present house are uncertain. At least five years of renovation and construction had transformed the humbler dwelling into a luxurious Georgian mansion with slave quarters, farm outbuildings, apple orchards, landscaped gardens and walks, and a summer gazebo some distance from the house with a statue of winged Mercury adorning its roof (fig. 22). Architectural grandeur was one way a gentleman could legitimate his role as a leader in society (Yentsch 1994). Isaac, Sr., must have recognized the fine situation of the house and its reasonable price, but there was never a question of moving into the structure as it was. It would not befit his station to do so. Governor Belcher wrote to Royall in August of 1732 to inform him of how the purchase was progressing but added that he would surely have to include an additional £3,500 into his calculations, "as the Buildings and Fences are all in aruinous [*sic*] Condition and the Lands desperately worn" (Royall Correspondence: Aug. 15, 1732). A man of Royall's taste kept good company and had impeccable manners, but also had an appropriate environment in which to display them (Pendery 1987:5). Governor Belcher reassured Royall four years later, however, by saying that "When you have done what you intend at Medford, it will be a fine Estate for a Gentleman to live on" (Royall Correspondence: Nov. 16, 1736).

Architectural and archaeological evidence at the site indicate that what Royall "intended" was elaborate, indeed. Changes to the house included

- Raising the structure to its current three-story height.
- Encasing the old brick structure in wooden clapboards, which were more economically elaborated upon than wood or stone.
- A center door and passageway that would open onto the courtyard, gardens, and summer house.
- And of course, all of the interior renovations required such as new floors, new doors, carved and painted woodwork (like the faux marble in the master bedroom), new wall paper, etc.

Nothing but expert carpenters and woodcarvers were hired from Medford, and the "tradition of gracious living and lavish entertainment of the Antigua

Fig. 22. Photograph of the Royalls' summer gazebo before it was demolished sometime in the 19th century. (Photograph courtesy of the Medford Public Library.) The Royalls would have entertained guests and suitors here, and the view from the hill would have afforded a fine prospect of the gardens, orchards, and Royall lands that stretched to the horizon. The slightly larger-than-life wooden statue of Mercury remains in storage at the Royall House.

days . . . was continued in Medford" (Hoover 1974:22). Indeed, when the estate was appraised in 1739, its worth had increased four-fold to almost £40,000, making Royall one of the richest men in the colonies, inflation notwithstanding (Middlesex County Probate 1739). The landscape design was purportedly borrowed from John Bartram of Philadelphia, and the house is said to have been inspired by that of a wealthy planter in Antigua whom Isaac Royall, Sr., had admired (Morrison 1952). Fragmented and damaged island records have left no information on the physical appearance and layout of Royall's own Antiguan estate, making it unclear whether he transplanted any components of it to Medford, but again archival, architectural, and archaeological evidence converge to indicate that alterations to the landscape included

- Expansion of a small, one-story, brick outkitchen into a much larger, two-story structure meant to serve as summer kitchen and quarters for slaves.
- Construction of a "French drain" (or dry well, a new technology in the 18th century) to keep the structure, built with a basement, from flooding.

- Construction of an expertly laid cobbled surface in the courtyard shared by the mansion and the kitchen quarters.
- Stripping of topsoil from behind the new kitchen quarters, possibly for various landscaping activities on the estate.
- Installation of plantings and formal walkways in the East Lawn of the mansion, fronting on the main highway to Medford Square (now buried beneath Royall House Park, but revealed again through remote sensing techniques and test excavations).
- Construction of numerous support outbuildings to do with the running of the farm, including barns, a corn house, a dove cote, and an unidentified outbuilding recovered archaeologically in the slave quarters' west yard.
- And although no archaeological remains have been recovered for it, archival evidence of the Tax Valuation of 1771, maps, photographs, and eye-witness accounts indicate planting of an apple orchard; construction of formal gardens, a hillock, and a summer gazebo in the West Lawn of the mansion, beyond the cobbled courtyard; and the planting of magnificent elms along the long carriage drive leading to the courtyard.

Unfortunately Isaac Royall, Sr., lived only two years to enjoy his new country seat; he died in 1739 at the age of 67, commemorated on his tombstone in Dorchester as "a faithful Husband, a tender Father, a kind Master, and a True Friend." It was at this time too, however, that his slaveholdings, along with the rest of his estate, were divided among his heirs, and people who had had less than two years to rebuild their lives and forge a home were forced to move on yet again, some with and some without the comfort of bringing loved ones with them. Frederick Douglass once wrote that he had not the words to describe the "deep anxiety" among the enslaved that accompanied the death of a master or mistress, for what it might mean to even one's deepest ties (Douglass 1845:312). In fact, over the course of the next 40 years, the people the Royalls enslaved would repeatedly face such challenges to the forging of home, family, and community, as the Royalls made their ascendancy to social preeminence.

Isaac's eldest surviving son and namesake inherited the estate at the age of 20. The family continued to be a prominent slave-trading family in Massachusetts and of considerable standing in the community. A two- to three-gallon silver punch bowl mentioned in Isaac, Jr.'s will (Harvard Law Library Special Collections 1778) would probably have been kept full of rum in the receiving hall for guests, a material symbol of the family's connection to exotic ports and the trade in human cargo. Hoover (1974) states that both Royalls, father and son, could also frequently be seen around town with their prominent guests in a four-horse carriage driven by a fine-liveried coachman, presumably enslaved. Thus, although many of the ways in which the Royalls have been historically portrayed tend to obscure the family's involvement in the Triangular Trade that involvement was an organic part of their projection of self and claims to legitimacy in the world they inhabited.

Isaac Royall, Jr., was born in Antigua in 1719, a child of his parents' middle age and the only son to survive. Although in his later years he was noted for his timidity and inability to make decisions, in his youth he was handsome, headstrong, and rash, and he seems certainly to have inherited some of his father's sense of adventure and daring. In July of 1726, at the age of seven, Isaac, Jr., had been sent to be schooled by his uncle Jacob, a successful merchant in Boston. Two young black companions, probably Cuff and Peter mentioned in November of the same year, accompanied him, and were entered into Isaac, Sr.'s account book for expenses paid on their behalf for room and board, clothes, mending of clothes, and medical care (see Account Book: April 1, June 1730). Isaac stayed in Boston for nine years until, chafing under the "unhandsome treatment of his Tutor," he ran away and showed up unexpectedly at his father's doorstep back in Antigua (Royall Correspondence: Aug. 15, 1736). The agitation in his son's mind over returning to the very place he had just fled was "one great reason" for Isaac, Sr.'s decision to put off the move north for another year, despite the social and economic upheaval there—a fateful decision for all involved (Royall Correspondence: Aug. 15, 1736). The years away from home and reaching adolescence in the absence of old friends and family had, in Isaac, Sr.'s opinion, given Isaac, Jr., too much "his own way." He had in fact come back from New England "wild" (Royall Correspondence: Aug. 15, 1736). But endeavoring to do all that he possibly could and what was incumbent on him as a father to do and to leave the rest to "Infinite Providence," Isaac, Sr., did not despair of his son "finally answering [his] expectations, and proving a blessing to his parents" (Royall Correspondence: Aug. 15, 1736).

In the end his hopes were realized. Once back in New England, Isaac, Jr., quickly became one of the colonial elite in Boston. He married the 15-year-old Elizabeth McIntosh in 1738. Their fathers had been friends, and it is possible that they met at one of the Royalls' lavish parties. The day the young couple registered their intention to marry, Isaac, Sr.'s account book indicates that he hired a black musician belonging to the barber, Winship, and bought spruce and oysters to celebrate (Account Book: Mar. 16, 1738). Isaac, Jr., and Elizabeth had a daughter, Elizabeth, in 1740, and another daughter, Mary (whom everybody called Polly), in 1744. In 1747 Isaac lost his mother and his daughter Elizabeth, had another daughter whom he and his wife also named Elizabeth, and became the justice of the peace for Suffolk County, beginning a long life of social, philanthropic, and political engagements in the community. He served on the Governor's Council for 23 years, was the chair of the selectmen in Charlestown and Medford for nine years running, and the deputy to the General Court of Boston from 1743 to 1752, the salary for which he donated to the poor of Charlestown (Hoover 1974). He was a proponent of public education, giving £80 to the school in Charlestown in 1745 (Hoover 1974). In his will he also left 100 acres of land to Medford "for the use and better support" of the schools of that town (Harvard Law Library Special Collections 1778). Isaac, Jr., seemed to delight in his role as the "benevolent aristocrat, kindly tolerant and protective of his people [slaves]" (Hoover 1974:49). Indeed Isaac, Jr., spent the first few years after his father's death enlarging and beautifying the mansion. He frequented all the import houses in Boston for furniture and china, and he commissioned silver from Paul Revere. He greatly exceeded his father in elegance and entertainment with his frequent parties, balls, and "musicales" (Hoover 1974:51). He also renamed Ten Hills Farm "Royallville" (Harvard Law Library Special Collections 1778).

In 1739, the month after his father had passed away, town records show that Isaac, Jr. took his father's place at the town meetings, symbolically demonstrating his new role as head of the family and the family's continued presence in political affairs. In 1754 he became the town meeting moderator, a position often held by his father (MHS: Medford Town Records Through 1830). A member of the Provincial Militia, he was made the first brigadier general in the colonies in

FIG. 23. John Singleton Copley's 1769 portrait of Isaac Royall, Jr., in his later years as a public figure and philanthropist before he was forced to flee in 1775 (photograph © 2007 Museum of Fine Arts, Boston) and Copley's portrait of his wife, Elizabeth McIntosh Royall, shown here probably about age 35–40 (Virginia Museum of Fine Arts, Richmond, gift of Mrs. A. D. Williams, photograph by Katherine Wetzel, © Virginia Museum of Fine Arts).

1761 (Hoover 1974). When the Harvard University library burned to the ground on November 12, 1767, Royall made a major contribution to rebuild it. Politically he had long had ties to "patriot causes" in the tumultuous years before the Revolution, but he remained a loyalist in the eyes of many because he combined a "natural affection and attachment" to his own country with a "high regard and esteem for the Mother Country" and sought compromise and peace between them (Royall Correspondence: Jan. 1774; fig. 23).

In fact it seems he did not so ardently desire compromise as he did to remain on the winning side. In an effort to reconstruct Royall's opinions and conduct prior to the Revolution, the Committee of Safety in Medford took depositions from his professional colleagues in 1778. In them it is clear that Royall oscillated between patriotic bravado, where he showed off his "arms and accoutrements" to his guests claiming his determination to stand for his country, and gloomily predicting dire defeat and retribution by 10,000 Russian mercenaries he felt sure would be sent over to deal with the colonists (quoted in Brooks and Usher 1886:148). At the time of the Battle of Lexington (April 15, 1775), Isaac Royall, Jr., was in Boston dining with his daughter and son-in-law, Mary and George Erving, and decided to flee directly to Halifax, Nova Scotia, intending to catch the first ship to Antigua (Royall Correspondence: May 29, 1779). In 1776, however, the British evacuated Boston, and the family urged him to join them in England instead. There he died of smallpox in 1781 at the age of 62, fairly wallowing in self-pity and still claiming he had never done anything wrong but to hope for peace between his native land and the Crown. His last years were spent writing what can only be characterized as sniveling and obsequious letters to friends and various officials in London and the new United States. He complained incessantly of his failing health and newfound poverty that allowed "but few diversions and little gaiety," although he thanked God he had not the inclination for it anyway, as he had had in his younger days (Royall Correspondence: May 29, 1779). He wrote appeal after appeal to the Crown for financial aid in his medical expenses and help in regaining his lost New England estate, but to little avail (Royall Correspondence: May 31, Aug. 6, 1777). His popularity in the town and the generally good testimony given by his friends and colleagues had spared his estate from being confiscated and his possessions auctioned for some years. His two sons-in-law were not so lucky—George Erving and Sir William Pepperell were both named in the Conspirators' Act, their homes were sold, and the proceeds were put into the Treasury of the State. Nevertheless Isaac's failure to return to Medford, mostly because of his failing health, was eventually taken as "going voluntarily to our enemies," and the Medford, Freetown, and Stoughton estates were finally confiscated as well. Even while perceiving himself to have suffered ill treatment from his mother country, Isaac Royall continued to be emotionally attached to his erstwhile home. He left other property in his will to Medford for use for the schools there, and 2,000 acres to Harvard that were to be sold and the proceeds put toward funding a professorship of medicine or law—today's Royall Professorship of Law (Harvard Law Library Special Collections 1778).

Summary

While this chapter has introduced the Royall family and their property, in Antigua and Medford, using a variety of documentary sources, including personal letters, contemporary newspapers, miscellaneous records, and secondary sources, what it has not really done is tackle "questions that count" (Deagan 1988). It does not capture what might be considered to be the essence of the Royall family. It does not situate them at the center of a moral and social dilemma that had seized New England society by the viscera in the decades leading to the War for Independence. A key challenge for the family was how to maintain slavery and the principles of inequality on which it stood in a society being challenged from within to reinvent itself as a republic. Also worth addressing is the materialization of aspirations, fears, hostilities, or uneasy compromises in the realm of objects, architecture, or landscape. Questions remain: What did they mean by doing or saying or building that? To whom were they addressing themselves? What was the reply? These are questions that can and should be asked, with the understanding that "an archaeology that does not work within the integrative framework of discourse runs the risk of merely being an illustrator's practice" (Hall 2000:43)—a mere handmaiden to history. As I have suggested, the best discursive framework for understanding the Royalls is under the rubric of colonial discourses of power. The task at hand then is to attempt to come to an understanding of how specific events in the lives of specific people—some of which have been outlined here—fit within, and thus derived meaning from, a global discourse of colonialism. We must situate the individual, particular, and fleeting within "an economic and cultural system that girded the world" (Hall 2000:43).

The background context is not yet complete, though. The economic importance, and social and cultural experiences, of the Royalls' many slaves and their African and African American contemporaries in New England society, culture, and economy must be examined.

Chapter 3

"FIT FOR TOWN OR COUNTRY": AFRICAN AMERICANS IN NEW ENGLAND CULTURE, SOCIETY, AND ECONOMY

> To be sold [by Isaac Royall, Esq.], a likely Negro GIRL, fit for Town or Country.
>
> —ADVERTISEMENT,
> *BOSTON GAZETTE OR WEEKLY JOURNAL, 1756*

> My feelings are always outraged when I hear them speak of "kind masters"—"Christian masters"— the "mildest form of slavery"—"well fed and clothed slaves," as extenuations of slavery; I am satisfied they either mean to pervert the truth, or they do not know what they say.
>
> —JAMES W. C. PENNINGTON,
> FUGITIVE SLAVE FROM MARYLAND, 1849

Self-Reflection in Interpretation

In 1721 Cotton Mather addressed African American bondsmen in a publication called *Tremanda,* telling them that if they were free, "many of you would not *Live* near so well as you do. . . . Your *Servitude is Gentle*" (Twombly 1973:11; emphasis in original).

Mather's statement raises the question: what was the nature of life for the enslaved in colonial New England? How might it have compared with the lives of the enslaved in plantation contexts? The people the Royalls held as slaves did lead quite different lives in New England from the ones they had held in larger plantation contexts. This fact was largely a function of economic and demographic differences between the two regions. And, yet, let there be no mistake. The depth of degradation and despair imposed on one human being by another in slavery defined the institution everywhere that slavery existed. We know from surviving documents that people enslaved in northern contexts felt this keenly and expressed it eloquently, as had those in other areas, and whatever differences that can be identified in New England as opposed to other regions are best thought of as alternative permutations of the same devastating system.

It is not that enslaved people were unable to influence or shape their experience under slavery or to engage in positive social action to improve the circumstances of their bondage. But the fact that New England slaves may sometimes have been well clothed, well fed, and well housed; were sometimes literate; and had certain legal rights that southern and Caribbean slaves did not have (see, for example, Greene 1942, 1944; McManus 1973; Twombly and Moore 1982; Piersen 1988; Berlin 1998, for discussions of some of the physical conditions found under northern slavery) does not alter the basic reality that these people were still enslaved. The social fact of their enslavement cannot be separated from the analysis, for it was only within the larger framework of slavery that all other aspects of slave life were structured in the first place (see Howson 1990). Kolchin (1993:148–49) states that in an effort to

> rebut images of slave passivity and docility, [many historians of slavery] . . . have also come dangerously close to replacing a mythical world in which slaves were objects of total control with an equally mythical world in which slaves were hardly slaves at all.

Keeping that in mind, however, Eugene Genovese (1974:xvi) also writes that studies that focus too tightly on the mechanisms of slave control and oppression miss an important opportunity. The trick is to find the balance. McKee (1994:6) concurs and reminds us that

> the simple part of slavery is that it was a vile and violent system whereby one group stole the lives and labor of individuals in another group. The complex part is studying the variety of ways this oppression was implemented and the variety of ways it was resisted.

There is little point in debating with Cotton Mather the "quality of life" of slaves in colonial New England; it is a phrase that implicitly suggests a scale from low to high, and thus is an inappropriate unit of analysis to accompany the study of slavery. What is of more consequence is to establish the importance of the slave trade to the New England economy and to describe what we know about slave life in New England. This will provide the necessary historical framework (for example, the social, political, and economic contexts) within which to interpret the documentary and archaeological evidence particular to the individuals enslaved by the Royalls at Ten Hills Farm.

The Massachusetts Slave Trade in the 17th Century

In February of 1638, Governor John Winthrop wrote in his journal that Captain Pierce of the Salem ship *Desire* had returned to Boston from a seven-month voyage to the West Indies, bringing with him "some cotton, and tobacco, and negroes, etc. from thence, and salt from Tertugos" (Donnan 1932:4). This, as far as anyone knows, was the beginning of the New England slave trade. Massachusetts was the leading slave trafficker in New England in the 17th century, and Boston the largest, if not the only, slave port (Thomas 1997:260). Its dominance was eclipsed only by Rhode Island in the 18th century (Coughtry 1981:11–16; Greene 1942:27; Thomas 1997:260–61). Africans and Creoles increasingly became the sole source of cheap labor, as Native Americans and white servants were gradually phased out as eligible slaves by law, economics, and custom, and they entered all sectors of the complex northern economy. As early as 1645, Emmanuel Downing, the brother-in-law of Massachusetts governor John Winthrop, doubted the colony would survive without "a stock of slaves sufficient to doe all our business. . . . And I suppose you know verie well how wee shall maynetayne 20 Moores cheaper than one English servant" (Donnan 1932:8). Those who did not own slaves, such as many artisans and small businessmen, were still eager participants in their exploitation through the hire-out system.

Massachusetts was the first British colony in North America legally to sanction the institution of slavery and the transatlantic trade with Africa in human cargo. In fact it incorporated the trade into its first code of written laws, the Body of Liberties, in 1641. This code did not specifically define slavery by race, allowing for all "lawful Captives taken in just Wars, [and such strangers] as willingly sell themselves or are sold to us," which would have included black, Indian, and European alike (Donnan 1932:4). It is a curious document, however, because it captures the contradictions and ambiguities of early New England attitudes toward slavery. It expresses abhorrence of "Bond-slavery, Villenage or Captivity" but sanctions it in the context of just wars or as the result of a legal purchase. It mandates that such slaves shall be given the "Liberties and Christian usage which the Law of God established in Israel . . . doth morally require," but it condemns the exemption from servitude for those "who shall be judged there by Authority" (Donnan 1932:4). In 1645 a Captain Smith and his mate, Keyser, were imprisoned for "kiling, stealing, and wronging of . . . negers, etc." (Donnan 1932:8). The slaves were returned to Africa because they had been obtained fraudulently and forcefully.

Massachusetts legislation began to tighten within the first few decades of initial settlement, however, and the plight of Africans in the colony quickly deteriorated, as the terms "African" and "slave" became more and more interchangeable and mutually defined. A 1649 law against the illegal enslavement of Native Americans, combined with further refinements of indentured servitude laws, saw to it that, in practice, only blacks would be enslaved. By 1670 the Body of Liberties had been amended to make slavery a permanent and heritable condition (Greene 1942:65).

In fact the chronic labor shortages that followed initial colonization and expansion ensured that "*every* colony became a slave colony," because only slave labor was stable and reliable enough to transform wild outposts of empire into "a viable society" (McManus 1973:2). In New England, as in many places, the first bondsmen were Native Americans. Prisoners taken during the Pequot War of 1637 were enslaved by the English or traded in the West Indies for blacks, who were considered to be more docile and better physically suited to the kinds of labor they were to be put to. In 1646 the New England Confederation codified this practice when it declared that all Indian captives should immediately "be shipped out and exchanged for Negroes" (Donnan 1932:6). Thus slave labor had quickly become the norm in New England and was considered to be key to the region's prosperity, the trade further playing an important role in all manner of secondary industry and shipbuilding. An economic interdependence among New England, the West Indies, and Africa—known as the Triangular Trade—developed overnight, as sugar and molasses were imported from the Caribbean in return for slaves and farm equipment and refined in New England to make rum to be traded in Africa for more slaves. Most slavers were also built in New England shipyards (Thomas 1997:678). Thus New England was heavily implicated in the slave trade, in direct as well as indirect ways.

Relatively few African-born bondspeople were brought to New England in the 17th century. The West Indies was by far the largest market for African-born individuals. Still, the New England market was not ignored, and there was plenty of internal trade. Despite the general preference in New England for West Indian slaves who had been "seasoned" in the islands and were more accustomed to colonial culture, work habits, and language—and thus deemed more suitable for the close working contact typical of the northern slaveholding system—there was always some direct trading between New England and Africa. In 1680 Governor Bradstreet wrote that "one small vessel about two years since, after twenty months' voyage to Madagascar, brought hither betwixt forty and fifty Negroes, most women and children sold here for £15 and £20 apiece" (Thomas 1997:207). Other references abound for ships leaving Boston and other New England ports for "Guinea." By the first quarter of the 18th century, such trade seems to have been relatively commonplace, with ships setting sail for Africa from Boston, Salem, Newport, and New York. Even after the institution of slavery had been abolished in the North, the trade continued on a highly intensified scale, with perhaps as many as forty ships setting sail each year for the African coast from ports such as Salem, Boston, Providence, and Philadelphia (Thomas 1997:284).

The Massachusetts Slave Trade in the 18th Century

The English had lagged behind the Portuguese, Dutch, and Spanish in the slave trade by nearly two centuries, but, by the early years of the 18th century, they "dominated the enterprise," and slavery and the slave trade were fast becoming the foundation for British colonial industry and commerce (Horton and Horton 1997:4). By the 1730s insatiable labor demands in the South and the sugar islands created a surge in the trade of Africans, and the shippers in British North America who met this demand were overwhelmingly New Englanders (Thomas 1997:260). New York, Boston, Philadelphia, and Newport, Rhode Island, were the principle suppliers for their regions throughout the century, and all manner of secondary industry boomed in response. Profits in shipping, northern business investments, insurance companies, rum distilleries, and manufactured goods companies skyrocketed. In the northern colonies, it was not so much slaveholding that amassed great wealth and supported the economy, as the direct and indirect effects of slave trading, which led to a very different socioeconomic structure from the cash-crop plantation economies of the South and Caribbean (Horton and Horton 1997:5).

A statute passed in Britain in 1750 made it "lawful for all His Majesty's subjects to trade and traffick to and from any port in Africa" (Thomas 1997:265). So ensued the age of the independent trader, who paid the English Crown a duty for the permission to enter the trade but then had free reign of the seas and could transport as many slaves as could possibly be sold. The importation of Africans to the New World exploded in this century, and the controversial questions pertaining to the trade were restricted still to "method" rather than "humanity" (Donnan 1931 [1969]:liii). From 1720 to 1730 the number of slaves imported to Antigua, for example, increased more than 11-fold (AHS Miscellaneous Records 1720–29). Nor did the strong Puritan ideals of the northern colonies pose a hindrance to slave ownership. Indeed the highly patriarchal tendencies of Puritanism and the explicit biblical definition of the master–servant/slave relationship seemed a justification for such an institution, as long as it was carried out, from their own perspective, in a properly Puritan and conscientious manner. With few notable exceptions, even the Quakers did not object to the institution of slavery at first but sought only to mitigate the cruelest treatment (Soderlund 1985). The Yearly Meeting did not forbid slaveholding among its members, for example, until 1776, and up until that point the different stances and degree of antislavery sentiment among the Friends were widely divergent and long debated (Soderlund 1985:3–4, 12).

The numbers of enslaved blacks in New England never reached the proportions they did in the South and the Caribbean. The nature of the New England soils prohibited the extravagant and sprawling plantations with opulent wealth and huge slaveholdings found in these areas. Nevertheless the black presence in New England was significant from early on, and the concentration of slaves in economic, political, and social centers exaggerated the effect of their apparently small numbers (Greene 1942:320). Evidence that contemporary white society also perceived this to be true lies in the fact that during the late 17th and early 18th centuries numerous laws were passed in the region to tighten white control over a restless and subjugated population. In March of 1693–94 an act was passed in Massachusetts

> forbidding taverns, common victualers, and inn holders to allow apprentices, servants, or Negroes to sit around tippling for more than an hour, or to allow them to have drinks of any manner without orders from their respective masters. (MHC *Archives* 47:142, 144)

In 1695, "harboring or entertaining Indians, Apprentices, and Negroes" became a punishable offense (MHC *Archives* 47:162). In 1698 it became forbidden to conduct business with any Indian, black, or mulatto servants (MHC *Archives* 47:178). There were strict curfew ordinances, and Massachusetts was the only New England colony to enact a stringent antimiscegenation law, in 1705–6, for the "better preventing of a spurious and mix't issue" (Greene 1942:208). In March of 1745–46, Medford voted in the affirmative to institute a nine o'clock curfew for its slaves, on pain of whipping in the market place "not exceeding ten strypes" (MHS: Medford Town Records Through 1830). It was not until the eve of the Revolution, when the "inconsistency of maintaining slavery with one hand while pleading or striking for freedom with the other, compelled a reluctant and gradual change in public opinion on this subject" (Donnan 1931 [1969]:71).

During the second quarter of the 18th century, just when the Royalls immigrated back to the area, the nature of northern slavery was beginning to change as well. Although New England never experienced anything like the plantation revolution of the South that yielded full-blown slave societies with a planter class and staple commodities, the significance of northern slavery in the overall economy grew. Meanwhile it also moved toward the center of the northern economy itself (Berlin 1998:178). Increasing African importation had serious implications for the structuring of the African American community. The growing number of blacks allowed more interaction and resulted in the emergence of many African American institutions in the North that went beyond the clandestine forest and burial-ground meetings of lore. The black population increased step by step with the white population, while in Rhode Island it far outstripped the white expansion (Berlin 1998:178). In Massachusetts too, between 1690 and 1750, the white population increased 150 percent, while the black population—enslaved and free—grew at twice that rate, although never exceeding more than 2 percent of the total population (Piersen 1988:tables 6 and 7, 168–71). Particularly as the economy and job market in Europe improved and when the Atlantic trade routes were especially lucrative or during periods of war (for example, the Seven Years' War, 1756–63) when white wage labor was scarce, slave importation and the dependence on slave labor increased. In many of the middle colonies, such as Pennsylvania and New York, the black population hovered steadily around 12–15 percent of the total population (Berlin 1998:178), but in Massachusetts it remained steadily around 2 percent (Piersen 1988:table 6, 168–169).

New England continued to be family- and wage-labor-oriented, but as urban life began to spread, so too did the disproportionate dependency on slave labor in urban centers of production. Among the urban elite of New York, Newport, and Boston, the very way of life was "fully invested in slavery," while even among artisans and the middling small business sorts, slaveholding or the use of slave labor was "commonplace" (Berlin 1998:179). As early as 1687, a French refugee recounted that "there is not a house in Boston, however small may be its means, that has not one or two [slaves]. There are those that have five or six" (quoted in Thomas 1997:207). Thus, in the 18th century, there was a shift in slave labor from domestics and farmhands on country estates that characterized the 17th and early 18th centuries, to workers in urban artisan shops and industry in the latter half of the century. This move from the outskirts of urban production to a more centralized role was an important turning point in northern slavery. Slave labor, in workshops and factories, became in a practical, if not ideological, sense equivalent to white (wage) labor, and this greatly affected the black experience in New England. For one, whites simply could not compete with skilled slave labor, and there were loud complaints throughout the northern colonies from at least the 1720s about the loss of jobs to slave labor. Meanwhile shop owners and industrialists came to depend on skilled slave labor that was not easily replaced. The power structure in the North, then, was different than in the South, and would define the contours of the slave experience in a very different way. Importation into New England increased from the 1720s to 1740s, with many slaves coming directly from Africa. The New England slave trade was no longer an incidental side arm of the general exchange system, but rather was "an enterprise in and of itself" (Berlin 1998:182).

Slavery as Business—the West Indian Connection

The slave trade was so economically vital that no stigma was attached to participating in it. Dealing in human beings was a proper gentlemanly pursuit, as much so as the growing of crops or the selling of manufactured goods. Slave traders were often the very pillars of society and occupied the most revered public offices, for religion and the law supported their position (McManus 1973). Judges, publishers, postmasters, philanthropists—all could trade in slaves on the side with impunity. Jonathan Belcher was a slave merchant and owner as well as the governor of Massachusetts. Isaac Royall, Sr., was a colonel and procured several of Belcher's slaves for him. Isaac, Jr., became a brigadier general and a justice of the peace in Suffolk County, was the chairman of the board of selectmen for 16 years, and was often voted town representative of Medford. The best and brightest of society engaged in the trade, and their actions had powerful legitimizing effects. Slave trading and slaveholding were part and parcel of colonial life. Hugh Hall sold slaves at his warehouse along with rum, sugar, and other "sundry European goods" (McManus 1973:25). Josiah Franklin and William Nichols did the same at their taverns (McManus 1973:25). Enslaved people were treated just as the other merchandise with which they were sold. One could pay cash on the barrel or set up an installment plan. Some came with land or a business, in the latter case being specially trained in whatever trade it was being sold. And in the end the enslaved too could be disposed of to settle debts or liquidate assets; they could be bestowed as a personal gift or inherited; or they might be sold simply as a profit-producing endeavor for their owners. All were equally valid, and examples of each can be found in the account book and probate records of the Royall family in Medford (RHA: Account Book 1724–49; Middlesex County Probate 1739, 1778; Harvard Law Library Special Collections 1778).

British North American shippers involved in the Triangular Trade were overwhelmingly from New England, and though the clientele was generally from the South or the islands, there were slave markets in northern ports all along (Thomas 1997). Because of limitations posed by the soils and topography of the region, however, New England's real wealth continued to lie in the *trade* in slaves and the indirectly affected industries of shipbuilding and rum distilling. New England's economy simply could not absorb the sheer numbers of Africans and African Americans that the South and the Caribbean could.

Thomas compares the "barren colony" of Rhode Island, for example, to Hong Kong of the late 20th century, with Rhode Island's gargantuan economy centered on the bustling port and slave-trading center of Newport (Thomas 1997:260). By the 1760s there were distilleries in Massachusetts and Rhode Island specifically meant to outfit slave ships with rum, which had become the preferred medium of exchange with the West Indies and Africa—New England rum above all others (Bailey 1998:12; Coughtry 1981:106–18; Thomas 1997:260), and Medford was one of the centers of production. Rum in fact represented 84 percent of the region's total exports to Africa during this time (Bailey 1998:10). This boosted rum production and made it one of New England's most important industries, for trade with Africa was one of the only sources of *surplus* revenue in the colonies. This

fact made it particularly critical to the New England economy, which was perpetually in debt to Britain during the colonial era. Thus, while the slave trade by itself
amounted to only a small part of the overall colonial exchange system, when one
takes into account all of the other commodities produced in response to and specifically for that trade, as well as trade done with other slave-based economies in
the West Indies and Africa, an astounding 75 percent of all New England exports
were tied in some way to the slave trade in 1770 (Bailey 1998:11).

This state of affairs was largely a result of the fact that the West Indies placed
such an extreme emphasis on sugar production that the colonists there became
heavily dependent on the mainland colonies and countries abroad for necessities
and foodstuffs. Antigua's principal imports in the 1720s, for example, were beef,
pork, butter, herrings, Madeira wine, white sugar, cotton, wool, ginger, molasses, and coconuts—largely foodstuffs and textiles (AHS: Miscellaneous Records
1720–29). Its exports for the same period were white and brown sugar, ginger,
indigo, lignum vitae (whose bark could be used for medicinal purposes), rum,
molasses, and lime juice (AHS: Miscellaneous Records 1720–29). New England's
side of the exchange, in 1770, shows that by this time 100 percent of New England's horses and livestock exports went to the Caribbean; 98.5 percent of the
beef and pork; 84 percent of the pine, oak, and cedar boards; 54 percent of the
barrel staves and headings; 51 percent of the bread and flour; 35 percent of the
fish; 31 percent of the wheat, oaks, and maize; and 27 percent of the rice (Bailey
1998:11). Thus the Triangle Trade was unabashedly the mainstay for the New
England shipping industry as well as the industries involved in the production
of all of these goods. New England was therefore linked inextricably to the slave
trade, even after slavery itself had been abolished there. Although there are those
who would argue that New England was never ostensibly a slave society (but
rather a society with slaves), it is undeniable that New England's profits, if not
always derived directly from trading in human cargo, came from trade with slave-
based economies or the use of slave products. The West Indies, and through that,
slavery and the slave trade, were the cornerstone for the economic prosperity of
the North throughout the 18th and even 19th centuries.

Black Labor in New England—the Specialists

Population statistics of 18th-century New England, although fraught with ambiguity because of fragmentary and/or inconsistent records and reporting, indicate
that the region was at least 95 percent white and the per-family ownership was very
low compared with other colonies—those who owned slaves often had between
only one and five. But the New England economy was diverse, and slave labor
was incorporated into every aspect of economic life, where the influence of the

enslaved could be felt much more strongly than their actual numbers would lead one to believe. Slaves worked as "carpenters, shipwrights, sail makers, printers, tailors, shoemakers, coopers, blacksmiths, bakers, weavers, and goldsmiths"—in short, the "whole range of free labor" (McManus 1973:ix). Having a skill or craft usually gave enslaved people a competitive edge over their unskilled counterparts and even over free white labor, equipping these slaves with the wherewithal to actively negotiate and gain control over certain aspects of their life and labor. Many earned wages, enabling them to provide small extras for their families to ease their hardship, and even occasionally to buy their own or their family's freedom. Skilled workers were often favored by their owners as profit-producing investments, and favored slaves could influence a master's decisions about their or their family's fate—such as to whom they would be hired out, sold, or bequeathed; whether they could keep their family members with them; whether their masters would take care to find a "good" situation for them if forced to sell. Isaac Royall, Sr., kept Black Betty, her five children, and five grandchildren together as a family unit at the division of his estate on his death in 1739 (Middlesex County Probate 1739). In 1776 Isaac, Jr., wrote to his agent, Simon Tufts, about the liquidation of his assets, including several slaves: "As to Betsey, and her daughter Nancy, the former may tarry, or take her freedom, as she may choose; and Nancy you may put out to some good family by the year" (quoted in Hoover 1974:83). Other, less valued slaves did not receive such consideration. Of Stephen and George, Isaac, Jr., had only this to say: "they each cost £60 sterling; and I would take £50, or even £15, apiece for them" (quoted in Hoover 1974:83).

New England was certainly not the only place to use skilled slave labor; both the South and Caribbean had well-developed hire-out systems that made use of slave artisans and craftsmen and specialists of all other sorts. What was unique about New England, however, was that the majority of slave labor there was skilled (Kolchin 1993:16). Slaves were indispensable, even in small numbers, to the running of the household, business, and economy at large, for even those who did not own slaves frequently hired their services. The hire-out system gave owners lucrative returns on their investment, for it relieved them of the considerable costs of caring for their slaves year-round and brought them added weekly or monthly income. Small businessmen, farmers, and households of moderate means got the labor they needed for much less money than buying slaves for themselves or paying wages for white labor, and there was not a task to be done that could not be performed by a specially trained slave. Slaves, of course, could also be hired for the purposes of general labor. It is not clear, however, what the economic, physical, or psychological effects of the hire-out system were on the enslaved themselves, and Kolchin (1993:53) points out that there was a difference between having "more privileges" and receiving "better treatment," because specialists also faced obstacles that others did not. It may on occasion have given them a measure of economic independence, allowing them to save a small portion of their cash wages for their own use or gratification. It perhaps allowed them to ply a trade that was stimulating and challenging to them. It might have provided a welcome respite from a cruel or tiresome master, or if one was lucky, put one in closer proximity to family members for a spell. Frederick Douglass (1845:349) stated that when he became a skilled caulker at the shipyard, "my pathway became much more smooth than before; my condition was much more comfortable," because he now was of "some importance" to his master. But he qualifies that statement by adding that

> I have observed this in my experience of slavery,—that whenever my condition was improved, instead of its increasing my contentment, it only increased my desire to be free. (1845:349)

The weekly handing over of wages to his master was an especially galling experience for Douglass (1845:349–350). Thus enslaved trades- and craftsmen, artisans, and musicians might have felt their condition improved by having a skill and being allowed the privilege of hiring themselves out, but it does not follow that it lessened the burden of their bondage. Chances were equally good too, if not better, that they would receive harsh treatment in their new situations because they were merely rented property (cf. Stevenson 1996:184–85 on the variability of treatment in the hire-out system). When Douglass was an adolescent, he was rented out to Edward Covey, who owned no slaves of his own, but got much work done on his farm for a good price every year because of his valuable reputation in the white community as a "nigger-breaker" (Douglass 1845:320). And being hired out by the year, as many were, including the Royalls' enslaved woman, Nancy (Hoover 1974:83), would have been no less destructive to slave families than being sold or bequeathed to another (see Cody 1982). Harriet Jacobs (1987:16), in the narrative of her own life as a slave, says that January 1 was the traditional hiring day in the South and that

> to the slave mother New Year's day comes laden with peculiar sorrows. She sits on her cold cabin floor, watching the children who may all be torn from her the next morning; and often does she wish that she and they might die before the day dawns.

What a bitter cup for Betsey, who had been granted her freedom by Isaac Royall, Jr., only to see her daughter consigned to perpetual servitude, having been let out to "some good family" rather than be allowed to live with her own.

Black Labor in New England—the Generalists

New England's inland landscape was dotted with small family farms. The coast enjoyed one of the richest marine environments in the world, and the fishing and whaling industries became extremely important in those areas. In the cities and port towns, shipbuilding, iron making, rum distilling, tanning, and, of course, the slave trade formed the basis of the economy. Enslaved people who did not have a particular craft were of necessity jacks-of-all-trades and often worked side by side with their owners, shared their living quarters, even at times joined them at table—facts of their material existence that did not necessarily mitigate the worst physical or psychological conditions of slavery. They had to have the flexibility to harvest crops, chop wood, press cider, tend livestock, do carpentry repair, "shoe a horse, print a newspaper, . . . even . . . manage his master's business" (Moore 1866:101). The Massachusetts Tax Valuation of 1771 (MHC Collections 1771) shows that Ten Hills Farm—now known as Royallville—was engaged in wool and cider production, the raising of livestock, and the growing of English and upland hay. With the exception of cider production, which required specialized—usually slave—labor (Garman 1998:148), these commodities would have been produced through generalized slave labor, and shipped on the Royalls' boat down the Mystick River to Boston markets by a specialized—and probably enslaved—boatman and loaders.

The more complex the New England economy became, the more unfree labor was worth. Young, healthy males were preferred because of the physically strenuous nature of many of the jobs to be filled. Enslaved people past the age of 40 might be relegated to the less physically demanding role of domestic and quickly lose their monetary value, as Royall's instructions to Tufts to take even £15 for Stephen and George indicates. At his peak form George, if indeed it is the same George, was estimated in a 1752 inventory of Isaac, Sr.'s estate, to be worth £100 (Middlesex County Probate 1739). And contrary to the slaveholding system in the South, where pregnancy was seen as a means to increase one's assets free of charge, sterility in women was prized in the North (McManus 1973:98). Pregnancy was a costly nuisance for urban or industrial owners, and frequently women were sold for no other reason than for having become pregnant, or their unwanted children were disposed of after birth. In 1739 a "Negro Child, a few days old, to be given away" was advertised in the *Boston Evening Post* (June 11). All of these factors led to a disproportionately male workforce in the North that would have posed a challenge to initial attempts to build community and family life. In the Massachusetts slave census of 1754, for example, which listed the number of slaves over 16 years of age by county and town, males outnumbered females colonywide nearly two to one, a demographic model that closely approximates the West Indian one. In Medford men outnumbered women by a factor of nearly four to one (MHC Collections 1754).

Large landowners, of course, held more enslaved people than the average New England farmer or artisan and used them as a sign of their high social and economic standing. Leading families, more than having a few hands for the sheer practicality of helping with agricultural chores, also had many individuals as domestic servants. In New England a small slaveholding gentry emerged that fancied itself the northern equivalent of the elegant southern planter. They had great estates and accumulated a relatively large number of slaves, often 20 or more, and sometimes up to 50 (Berlin 1998:55–56; Coughtry 1982). The Royalls belonged to this group, but the Royalls and their peers were not the majority in New England, and the region never developed a slave regime per se. Most of New England continued to be characterized by small agriculture, a far cry from the cash crop agriculture and gang field labor in the Caribbean, which was the occupation of most slaves there (Gaspar 1985). It was true for most enslaved people in New England, by contrast, that they might be in the field in the morning, driving the wagon to market in the afternoon, shining the master's buckles in the evening, manning the shop the next day, and mending fences on the following. Some shuttled back and forth from the farm to town for hire or to work independently on the weekends. The Royalls seem to have rented at least two of their slaves in town, perhaps more, and transported others between their farms in Medford and Stoughton wherever work was needed (Account Book: June 25, 1737; Hoover 1974:83). There was no way to keep tabs on all hands at all times. As there is no mention of overseers or drivers at the Royalls' New England estates, we must assume that at some point the Royalls would have had to trust that the individual or individuals assigned to a certain task were in fact carrying it out. At any given time, there might have been some in town, others in the hay fields, some in the orchards, others on the boat, some in the kitchen, and others simply unaccounted for. New England slaves therefore fit very much into the larger system of exchange in the North, frequently interacting directly and personally with the region's economy in a way that only a minority of southern and Caribbean slaves were able to do. This would have been doubly true of city slaves.

Race, Status, and the Law

The status of New England slaves before the law was a muddled one. They were, of course, by definition never allowed to become full-fledged citizens (though at this time neither were women, Catholics, Jews, or nonlandholding whites), but they were also not wholly relegated to "another realm of existence" (Twombly and Moore 1982:155). Puritan law idealized the status of slaves as being a part of the master's family in a "vigorous, stable, and godly society" (Twombly and Moore 1982:147). The Body of Liberties expressed this sentiment by stating that the slaves be given "all the Liberties and Christian usages which the Law of God . . . doth morally require" (Donnan 1932:4). They therefore hovered legally between person and property, and indeed they were both. Puritans of the 17th century were certainly not any more enlightened on the subject of race than other British colonists, but they did firmly believe in the universality of justice. Thus basic legal rights were extended to black people of all statuses in Massachusetts, a fact that nevertheless does not truly comment on how they were treated in daily practice. Black people in New England, enslaved and free, had the right to life and property, police protection, legal counsel, and trial by jury; they could be heir and inheritance in a master's will, and they could and did sue and testify in court (Twombly and Moore 1982; Greene 1942:177; McManus 1973:63). They could also be seized, foreclosed on, or sold at whim, however, to relieve debt or to increase an owner's income. And by the 1680s increasingly stringent social and legal measures arose to restrict black behavior. Twombly and Moore (1982:157) state that these restrictive laws were "not a premeditated program to debase the Negro," but rather a response to what the Puritans thought of as "manifestations of social disorder." As such, the explanation is seen to lie in the inherent characteristics of the Puritan religion, rather than in racial attitudes and discrimination. Here, though, it is perhaps relevant to enter a caveat on the topic of religion. Greene (1942:219) says that "religion . . . played an important role" in making New England slavery more tolerable:

> The fact that New Englanders regarded the slaves as persons divinely committed to their stewardship developed a patriarchal conception of slavery, which along with other factors, went far to mitigate the unhappy condition of their bondmen.

But religion has been indicted repeatedly by escaped and emancipated slaves in their narratives as one of the greatest frauds of the slave regime, used as a sanction for slavery and the cruel treatment of slaves rather than a benevolent force that eased their suffering (see Douglass 1845:363; Bibb 1849; Equiano 1789; Jacobs 1987; Truth 1850). Piety and religious fervor then is poor evidence of tolerable, tolerant, or just masters. To wit, Frederick Douglass (1845:319) cited one of his former masters as quoting a passage from the Bible whenever he delivered his brutal punishments: "He that knoweth his master's will, and doeth it not, shall be beaten with many stripes." Indeed, of all the transgressions of slaveholders, the one that seemed most to have offended Douglass was the "corrupt and wicked" misuse of Christianity to suit their own purposes:

> I am filled with unutterable loathing when I contemplate the religious pomp and show, together with the horrible inconsistencies, which everywhere surround

me. We have men-stealers for ministers, women-whippers for missionaries, and cradle-plunderers for church members. (Douglass 1845:363)

Other enslaved people in Massachusetts felt similarly, as evidenced when "An African" sent a letter to the editor of the *Massachusetts Spy* in Boston, saying

> So, Sir, christianity is made a cloak to fill their coffers and to screen their villainy. View these poor creatures in this miserable situation, a father fighting for his bosom friend, a mother for a beloved son, a brother for a sister, a friend for a kind companion—I say, to view them in this situation, I should think would make a Heathen blush, and a Christian shudder. (10 Feb. 1774)

Compounded with the fact that New England cannot really be said to have been a Puritan society anymore by the mid 18th century, there can be little argument that mitigating ideological nuances in New England lessened the harshness of servitude there. Hunter (2001:9–11) claims that Puritan asceticism was dead in Boston and Salem by 1740. An increasingly secular and commercial society where wealth was respected as much as, if not more than, moral or religious scruples did not concern itself extraordinarily with the finer distinctions of racial hierarchies, the injustice of slavery, or the human rights of slaves, as if its pious, Puritan forbears ever had.

All of the colonies had extensive legislative measures to control and regulate the activities, handling, and punishment of blacks. And a perusal of the documentary evidence defies any conclusion to the effect that slaves there found their condition tolerable. Advertisements for runaways, attempts by slaves to buy or sue for their own freedom, acts of violence or sabotage, suicide, and eloquently written letters and legal petitions reveal that slavery was detested by its victims in New England as much as in any other place, regardless of legal rights and definitions. Their increased legal rights simply allowed enslaved people in New England additional avenues for expressing themselves nonviolently and made possible attempts to use the system to address their oppressors in their own terms. Phyllis Wheatley, an African-born girl enslaved in Boston, who at the age of 20 had become an international sensation with her poetry, called on moral and religious principles in another letter to the *Massachusetts Spy* in Boston:

> ... in every human Breast, God has implanted a Principle, which we call Love of Freedom; it is impatient of Oppression, and pants for Deliverance; and [...] I will assert, that the same Principle lives in us.—God Grant Deliverance. (24 March 1774)

During the Revolutionary years, slaves also drew comparisons between themselves and their oppressors' fight for independence from Britain.

[We] can not but express [our] astonishment, that it has never been considered, that every principle from which America has acted in the course of her unhappy difficulties with Great-Britain, pleas stronger than a thousand arguments in favor of your Petitioners. (13 Jan. 1777; MHC *Archives* 212:132)

Throughout New England, including Massachusetts, there were curfews, restricted meeting laws, prohibitions on the carrying of any stick or cane that might be used as a weapon, and strict antimiscegenation legislation. The worse the infraction was, the harsher the punishment. An enslaved person out after hours in Medford could be whipped up to ten lashes, but one could also see enslaved people hanged or burned at the stake in Massachusetts for everything from poisoning to barn burning (McManus 1973; Twombly 1973). In 1755 two slaves were convicted of poisoning Captain John Codman of Charlestown; Mark was hanged, and Phillis was burned at the stake in front of a massive crowd of spectators (Twombly 1973:15). The people held at the Royalls' estate would surely have known, or at least known of, Mark and Phillis, and the brutality of their punishment would have reminded them that New England was not so very different from Antigua, whatever rhetoric their masters employed in public arenas. Social mores combined with the legal codes in Massachusetts led one group of petitioners to characterize their condition as being "in violation of the Laws of Nature & of Nations," so that

Your Honors need not to be informed that a Life of Slavery, like that of your petitioners, deprived of every social privelege [*sic*], of every thing requisite to render Life even tolerable, is far worse than Non-Existence. (13 Jan. 1777; MHC *Archives* 212:132)

It is undeniable then that even in New England the law and social codes were concerned with maintaining white hegemony and power and succeeded in rendering the lives of enslaved people, by all accounts, "intolerable." On the other hand, the strict laws meant to regulate black behavior do betray the precarious nature and claim of white supremacy there and white society's acute awareness of it. New England slaves as a group, as skilled labor with certain legal rights, were also living in a system that was more obviously and consistently beyond one-way power relationships than anywhere else in the colonies. While the reining in of black autonomy in law, ideology, and practice was formidable, New England blacks did succeed in building strong community ties, founding numerous social institutions such as churches, lodges, and fraternities—including the first Masonic Lodge for blacks in America, the Prince Hall Grand Lodge in Boston on March 6, 1775 (Kaplan and Kaplan 1989:203, 90ff.)—and using their expanded legal rights to become astute and vocal lobbyists for their own cause (see Horton and Horton 1979; 1997).

Assimilation

The degree of assimilation of colonial northern blacks has not really been the primary focus of any of the previous literature, but it has been implied that northern blacks might have been more quickly and completely assimilated into European cultural forms, value systems, and attitudes than in the predominantly black regions of the South and Caribbean (Twombly and Moore 1982; Berlin 1998; Piersen 1988). It is an argument that draws principally on demographic factors such as population statistics that show the low population density of the region and on anecdotal evidence of the supposedly close and often affectionate bonds between masters and slaves in a diverse and largely urban industrial economy. For example, Twombly and Moore (1982:155) say that New England slaves were allowed to "hover on the fringes of full participation in social and economic life." Piersen claims that "most bondsmen grew up with the family of a single master and were considered part of the household" (1988:31), and that

> the demographic evidence clearly suggests that since Afro-Americans were only a small percentage of New England's population, the cultural contact between African and Euro-American heritage was strongly weighted toward a rapid assimilation of the black immigrants. (1988:22)

Conclusive evidence of such claims, however, is hard to find. They may be hasty too, particularly for the colonial period, when the influx of native Africans and West Indians into New England was demonstrably at its highest, and the demographics of the region saw Africans and Creoles clustered in industrial and maritime counties along the coast (Greene 1942; Piersen 1988). Such population statistics suggest that Africans in these areas would have been a visible minority and that while there might have been some significant challenges to the process, the Africans ultimately would have been capable of forming community ties and relationships that were peripheral to European mainstream society. And in truth, why should slaves have been incorporated into larger colonial life in the North or more rapidly assimilated to Euro-American cultural forms, simply because there were fewer of them? Gomez (1998:25–26) writes that raw numbers can be misleading and generally "disclose very little" about actual black-white relations or the level of intimacy between the two groups.

In fact the lives of most early African slaves and their Creole descendants are too obscure to be reconstructed with any surety by historians (Lee 1986). At most one can try to reconstruct demographic factors such as black population density or the ratio of white to black in the region; try to trace demographic change such as the rate of natural increase over foreign importation and the presumed emergence of a Creole generation; or try to reconstruct adult sex ratios and draw conclusions about opportunities for establishing stable family life and a means of cultural transmission (Lee 1986; Kulikoff 1974, 1978, 1986). But these attempts are often futile and the relationship between numbers and behavior is unclear. Raw numbers, for example, are often given in colonial records without any reference to actual geographic dispersal. The 1754 Massachusetts Slave Census lists slaves only by number and sex per town, and sometimes only by number. It records 34 enslaved individuals in Medford over the age of 16, with 27 men and seven women—but not where they lived or to whom they belonged. Brooks and Usher (1886:355) provide some of that information, shown in table 2, but do not cite their sources, and their data contradict the slave census, showing 22 men and 12 women. The data also do not reveal how those men and women might have been interrelated through kin networks—how many families they represented, how many were married, how many might have been offspring of those unions—or how many were native born and how many were recent immi-

TABLE 2.

Slave ownership in Medford, 1754

Owners	Slaves	Owners	Slaves
Rev. E. Turell	Worcester	Mr. Brown	Caesar
Dr. Simon Tufts	Pompey	Mr. Pool	Scipio
Capt. Thomas Brooks	Rose, Pomp	Squire Hall	Peter, Nice
Capt. Francis Whitmore	Peter	Stephen Greenleaf	Cuffee
Simon Bradshaw	London	Joseph Tufts	Isaac
Deacon Benjamin Willis	Selby	Henry Gardner	Aaron
Benjamin Hall	Prince	———	Chloe
Widow Brooks	Punch	Mr. Boylston	Negro girl
Stephen Hall	Flora	Dr. Brooks	Negro woman
Hugh Floyd	Richard	Isaac Royall	Joseph, Plato, Phebe, Peter, Abraham, Cooper, Stephy, George, Hagar, Mira, Nancy, Betsey
Capt. Kent	Dinah		

Source: Brooks and Usher (1886:355)

grants. What the census does show is that 73 bondsmen in Middlesex County (20 percent of the county's enslaved population) lived in townships that had ten or fewer adult slaves; 17 (4.7 percent) lived in towns with fewer than five (MHC Collections 1754). In Suffolk County these numbers were reduced to 1.8 percent and 1.2 percent, respectively (MHC Collections 1754; tables 3 and 4). The adult sex ratios of males to females in the two counties were more similar—100:71 in Middlesex County and 100:88 in Suffolk County. These are rather startling numbers, but at most they suggest that except within city limits in places such as Boston, Salem, Providence, or Newport, it was often difficult for New England blacks to interact with each other in large groups on a continual or regular basis or to create broad community and family ties that crossed town or regional boundaries. They do not allow for a substantive assessment of the "degree of assimilation"

TABLE 3.

Slave census by town for Middlesex County, 1754

Town	Males	Females	Total	Town	Males	Females	Total
Charlestown	–	–	–	Dracut	–	–	–
Watertown	7	5	12	Weston	8	2	10
Medford	27	7	34	Lexington	13	11	24
Cambridge	33	23	56	Littleton	3	5	8
Concord	10	5	15	Hopkinton	–	–	15
Sudbury	9	5	14	Holliston	–	–	–
Woburn	9	8	17	Stoneham	6	2	8
Reading	14	6	20	Wastford	–	–	5
Malden	16	5	21	Bedford	2	4	6
Groton	7	7	14	Wilmington	4	3	7
Billerica	3	5	8	Townsend	2	1	3
Chelmsford	–	–	8	Acton	1	0	1
Marlborough	3	3	6	Waltham	2	2	4
Dunstable	–	–	–	Shirley	1	0	1
Sherburne	3	0	3	Pepperell	–	–	–
Stowe	–	–	–	Natick	0	3	3
Newtown	10	3	13	Lincoln	16	7	23
Framingham	–	–	–				

Sources: MHC Collections 1754; Greene 1942:339–40.

TABLE 4.
Slave census by town for Suffolk County, 1754

Town	Males	Females	Total	Town	Males	Females	Total
Boston	647	342	989	Milton	15	4	19
Dorchester	18	13	31	Wrentham	13	3	16
Roxbury	38	15	53	Brookline	10	7	17
Weymouth	12	11	23	Needham	1	0	1
Hingham	–	–	–	Medway	4	3	7
Dedham	–	–	17	Bellingham	1	1	2
Braintree	20	16	36	Walpole	0	1	1
Hull	7	4	11	Stoughton	6	2	8
Medfield	3	1	4	Chelsea	–	–	35

Sources: MHC Collections 1754; Greene 1942:339.

experienced by New England slaves in such an environment. It would certainly have been true that the poor souls who were the sole adult slaves in Shirley or Acton, Massachusetts, would have been forced to lead a culturally truncated and socially isolated existence. They may even have adopted some of the material and behavioral manifestations of white New England culture, deprived as they were of much or any opportunity to interact socially or otherwise with others of their kind, but more than that we cannot say.

Assimilation is a cultural process that has no real diagnostic symptoms. Its rate or degree cannot be mapped by the presence or absence of cultural traits. The concept of assimilation implies a kind of internalization that goes beyond mere physical manifestations or their suppression.

We cannot assume that because they were the only adult slaves in Shirley and Acton, the two men from the slave census automatically internalized European attitudes, values, or belief systems more quickly than slaves anywhere else, from Boston to St. Johns. And even if they were restricted by their particular situations in the mode of their material cultural self-expression, focusing on physical manifestations of assimilation (which, it should be remembered, census data do not allow in the first place) fails to recognize that there can be a real and significant difference between traits and culture, norms and ideals (Howson 1990; Gutman 1976). Recall the Chinese merchants from I Street, whose mixed use of Euroamerican and traditional Chinese material culture may well have facilitated the projection of a carefully constructed persona to their white associates and sponsors, but whose true "ethnicity" may forever elude us (Praetzellis, Praetzellis, and Brown 1987).

Most enslaved people in New England in the mid 18th century were either West Indian or African born. Many of the Royalls' slaves appear to have been African born too, as the names listed in Isaac Royall, Sr.'s probate inventories suggests (table 5). More specifically, many were likely from the Gold Coast, which encompassed portions of modern-day Ghana, Nigeria, and Ivory Coast. Belinda, for example, who does not appear on the Royalls' slave lists until the baptism of her children, Joseph and Prine, in 1768 (NEHGS 1907), stated in her petition to the General Court of 1783 that she lived on the Volta River as a child and was paying homage to Orisa when she and her parents had been kidnapped and sold into slavery. Orisa refers to the roughly 400 minor deities of the Yoruba people of southwestern Nigeria and parts of Benin. In addition Quamino, Quaco, Cuffee, and Abba are all day-names of the Akan-speaking peoples of the Gold Coast. As New England's preference for slaves who had been seasoned in the islands became more pronounced, the West Indian and African (direct and indirect) influences on an emerging African American subculture in New England would have increased (Bower 1991).

TABLE 5.
Slaves listed by name in Isaac Royall, Sr.'s probate inventories, 1739 and 1752

Men	Women	Children/ Adolescents
Fortune	Trace	Six year old girl[a][b]
Barron	Ruth	Quacoe
Ned	Sue	Diana
Peter	Jonto	John
House Peter	Black Betty	Nancy
Cuffe	Abba	Betty
Smith	Abba	George
Phillip	Old Cook[a][b]	Sarah
Quamino		Jacob
Robin		Jemmy
Captain[a][b]		Robin
George, about 45[a][c]		Coba
Santo, Lame 50 years old[a][b]		Walker
Old Negro Man, about 70[a][c]		Nuba
		Trace
		Tobey
		Present

Notes: [a]Individiuals added in a retroactive inventory of 1752.
[b]Individuals held at Stoughton, Massachusetts, farm (now Walpole).
[c]Individuals held at Mount Hope Farm (Freetown, Massachusetts—now Fall River]).

Even to qualify assumptions about assimilation by saying that these slaves were "less overtly African" than Caribbean slaves becomes problematic without any primary documentary evidence to address the point explicitly. Implicit evidence suggests, however, that white New Englanders at least did not perceive African and Creole slaves to be an assimilated or organic component of their own society, but rather an alien presence that could be alternately amusing, irritating, or menacing.

At about the time that Isaac, Sr., brought his family to Medford, his wife's grown daughter, Ann (half sister to Isaac, Jr., and Penelope), and her husband, Robert Oliver, also came to Massachusetts and settled in Dorchester, bringing many of *their* slaves with them as well. Robert Oliver is said to have looked with "scornful pity" on his slaves who refused to see the merits of the "proper use of a Yankee wheelbarrow" and persisted despite his efforts to carry all of their burdens on their heads (Jackson 1907:4). It appears not to have been an unusual phenomenon. Piersen (1988:97) provides a quote from the southern slaveholder Edward Kimble:

> you show [an African] how to hoe, or drive a wheel-barrow, he'll still take the one by the bottom, and the other by the wheel; and they often die before they can be conquered.

The fact that many of the Royall slave children, who would have been island or Massachusetts born, also had Akan names, such as Abba, Quaco, Coba, Jemmy, and Nuba, further suggests that the people belonging to the Royalls and their immediate family were still actively cultivating their African heritage in New England. Nor was it just their names that would have sounded strange on European tongues. Their skin color, hair, and facial features were frequently commented upon by white observers in mocking or disgusted tones, as were methods of self-adornment that were seen at times as unappealing or frightening, at others as strange and fanciful (see White and White 1998:37–62).

One place to find documentary accounts of these people's physical appearance is in contemporary newspapers, particularly in advertisements for fugitive slaves. Lorenzo Greene (1944:126) claims that "nearly every issue" of a New England newspaper between 1704 and 1784 carried such advertisements (see also Twombly 1973:21), and indeed even a brief perusal of contemporary newspapers, at least of the Boston area, reveals this to be true. Greene (1944:127) surveyed 62 of these advertisements from 11 different newspapers in various New England colonies and reported on names, age, sex, stature, complexion, physical traits, personal traits, and personal accomplishments of individual slaves, trying to reconstruct "the slave personality" in New England, admittedly a rather suspect agenda and of limited use here. Some of the data he presents, however, are revealing if interpreted for our own purposes, which is to assess the evidence, such as it is, of increased black assimilation in New England. For instance, 40 of the 62 fugitives (65 percent) had either classical or African names, probably reflecting the relatively high proportion of African-born individuals in the region, as well as suggesting that Africans, who had been born free, were more likely to run away. It also supports the idea that their presence in New England towns lent an exotic, and perhaps disagreeably foreign, air to their surroundings. Mastery of the English language was by no means a given in the 18th century. Many were said to speak "good English," "pretty good English," or "tolerable good English" (quoted in Greene 1944:138). When Joseph Gould of Lynn advertised for the return of his "Negro Man named George, formerly belonging to Isaac Royall, Esq. of Medford," the runaway was said to speak only "broken English" (*Boston Gazette and Country Journal* 1759:Sept. 24).

Fugitive slaves were most often described in traditional European attire, but that was true of most enslaved people in the Americas, and there is oblique documentary evidence that some enslaved people in the New England might have continued to cultivate an African aesthetic in their self-adornment and self-presentation. A young runaway in 1767, for instance, was described as having a shaved forehead, which was probably an African or African-derived hairstyle, possibly "Coromantee" or Mandingo (*Boston Gazette and Country Journal* 1767:23 Nov.; White and White 1998:48). White and White (1998:39) look at the social dimensions of 18th-century African American hairstyles and conclude that the styling of hair was one area in which blacks were left a "relatively unhindered scope for cultural expression." They seem to have exploited that niche to maximum effect in the 18th century (though not as much in the 19th), flaunting their distinctiveness, coming up with syncretistic styles influenced by traditional African forms, Native American forms, and even European wig fashions of the day. White and White (1998:47, 54–55) say that the "striking arrangements" 18th-century African Americans came up with were both jarring and confusing to white observers but could have served as an "affirmation of difference and even of defiance" for the enslaved. They also might have communicated sex, age, status, tribal association, or occupation to those who could read such signs (White and White 1998:41).

Other styles of self-adornment American colonials might have encountered on occasion are suggested in Pontoppidan's (1760:11) description of Africans encountered while still on the Gold Coast—the birthplace or ancestral homeland of many of New England's slaves in general and the Royalls' slaves in particular. He says that they "wear now one, now another, absurd object, especially in their hair on their heads, which always must have something or other hanging from it." Webber (1978:121) also states that even in the mid to late 19th century, generations after the last African had landed on America's shores, enslaved children in the South continued to wear "different kinds of greegrees and charms" on the body to ward off disease, while older individuals frequently wore voodoo bags around their necks to protect themselves against witches. Such things were probably commonplace throughout the colonies. A possible *nkisi* charm and a hand-drilled stone bead, for example, were recovered from the Royall House slave quarters excavations—scant but evocative archaeological evidence of a non-European aesthetic and possible belief system being cultivated among the enslaved population at Ten Hills Farm. They seem to support the contention that the enslaved people of New England, in the 18th century at least, were not necessarily more assimilated into Anglo-American culture than enslaved people anywhere else were, although their scarcity in numbers might have reduced the effective cultural expression of their otherness to more private and individual episodes and venues.

That is not to say, of course, that assimilation in New England did not occur; a certain amount of creolization was inevitable, especially given the preference of many New England masters for young or American-born slaves. Clearly whites and blacks in New England influenced and shaped each other's experience in the New World in mutually profound ways. What is not so clear, however, is how, if it is possible, to determine the rate at which the process happened, the degree and kind of the mutual influence, how economic and demographic factors affected white and black cultural behavior, or how much these processes differed from similar ones taking place in more predominantly black areas such as the American South or the Caribbean.

Literacy and Christianity, where present, do seem to have been potentially enculturating factors in New England that were not as readily available elsewhere; many enslaved people were made, or succeeded in becoming, moderately literate to read the Bible, and nearly all of the slave narratives I have encountered, from North and South, spend extensive time talking about the importance of literacy in turning brutes into men and heathens into Christians. There were no laws expressly prohibiting the education of enslaved people in New England; Phyllis Wheatley, who was raised from infancy in a white family and educated as one of their own, became famous as a poet and was hailed as a paragon of moral and religious virtue. She represented perhaps the best possible scenario, from the white perspective, for the integration of blacks into white New England society. The general consensus in the colonies, both North and South, however, was that "it made Negroes saucy to know how to read" (A Lady of Boston 1832:26).

Chloe Spear's Boston master threatened, when she was a child, to have her hung by her two thumbs and severely whipped when he happened on her with a spelling book (A Lady of Boston 1832:26). And in truth few enslaved people in the colonial era ever converted to Christianity either—let alone the harsh and unforgiving form of it commonly found in New England. Chloe Spear informed her biographer that she and her fellow bondspeople in 1760s Boston were seated separately from the rest of the congregation at Sunday meetings, and she admitted that they "did not understand the preaching, they took no interest in it, and spent the time in playing, eating nuts, &c. and derived no benefit whatever" from it (A Lady of Boston 1832:21). Cato Pearce (1842:1), who was born and raised in slavery in North Kingston, Rhode Island, and eventually did find what he called "ligion," had this to say about his early days when he would sometimes attend revival meetings, sometimes with friends, sometimes alone, apparently for their entertainment value:

> Many came forward and some of them, before they got up off of their knees would be converted [sic]—be praising the Lord. But all that didn't have no effect upon me. I cared nothing' about it—no otherwise than I used to set and laugh at them. (Pearce 1842:8)

Court and legal documents do show some New England blacks adopting the political and religious rhetoric of the day, and slave narratives, too, are almost universally written in romantic, moralistic, and preachy tones that were very characteristic of writing of the time. These documents can be viewed as evidence of an adoption, through the influence of literacy, of Christianity and Anglo-American cultural values. But they may also have been an attempt to make a case against human bondage in language and rhetoric that white oppressors and lawmakers would understand. Yellin (1987:xiv), for example, attributes Harriet Jacobs's tone and mode of address in her narrative very much to a desire to win female abolitionist favor and support and to depict herself not just as a slave, but as a fellow woman in a sisterhood of suffering at the hands of men. Such documents then too must stand as only equivocal evidence of greater black assimilation in New England or at least as evidence of assimilation among only selected elements of New England black society.

Resistance

Regardless of individual cases 18th-century records betray a general white frustration and chagrin at the stubborn tenacity of many non-European ways in speech, religion, and other modes of behavior and self-expression among the black population in their midst. And the expense and dangers of keeping human chattels were, of course, largely a result of enslaved people's lack of assimilation and resistance to the system, expressed in all manner of ways, from lethargy to murder. Resistance, for lack of a better word, is seen here as a form of everyday resilience or self-help, and not necessarily as a calculated strategy. As McManus

(1973:125) has eloquently pointed out, it was not "that every theft was a blow for freedom, but rather [...] a [...] logical response to slavery."

Insurrection and conspiracy were the most dreaded acts, and reports of entire families being murdered in their beds fueled the flames of terror that underlay every colony's strict social and legal codes, but such incidents were relatively rare and almost never successful. Twombly (1973:14) does call the frequency with which enslaved blacks perpetrated violence on an individual level against whites, though, "astonishing" and "very much a part of life in colonial Massachusetts," from arson to rape, poisoning, and murder. He turns to the public press for information on slaves' resistance to their servitude in that colony and finds that blacks were so much a part of life in eastern Massachusetts that "after 1704, when the first American newspaper began publication in Boston, hardly an issue failed to mention them" (Twombly 1973:13). In 1763 the *Boston News-Letter* (9 June) reported "a most shocking Murder" by a slave belonging to Dr. McKinstry, in Taunton, Massachusetts:

> a Sister of the Doctor's getting up early in the Morning to iron Cloaths, the Negro (after making a Fire) got his Master's Horse, and left him at the Door, and finding an Opportunity took up a hot Flat Iron, with which he struck the Woman on the Back of her Head, and stunned her, he repeated the Blow, then dragged her down in the Cellar, and rubb'd over her Face, flicking the Point of it into her Eyes, whereby she was scorche'd considerably; after he had done this, he took the Horse and rode off—The Family soon got up and found the Woman in the above Condition: she continued till the Evening of the next Day, and then died: The Negro was pursued, and taken up at Newport, and confess'd the Fact.—What induced the Fellow to perpetuate this Crime is not known, as he was always treated well, and there had been no Difference with him in the family.

Twombly (1973:37) notes that the *Boston Evening-Post* of the following week provided some additional commentary on the occurrence.

> The Boy was an exceedingly good Servant, & remarkable for his obsequious Behaviour, nor was there the least surmise of his bearing Hatred to the deceased, or of the least Occasion for it; tho' since this Affair some Things have come to light which shew the maliciousness of his Mind, and the bad Effects of Negroes too freely consorting together. (13 June 1763)

The reports of this incident demonstrate the profound lack of understanding among New England masters of the burdens of slavery and the desperate acts they could drive an individual to commit. For the Taunton man, it was not the fact of his involuntary servitude that was blamed for the murder—indeed he had always been "treated well"—but rather a character defect of blacks in general.

The shocked bewilderment of whites contemplating the reasons for perpetrating such an act shows that white New England society had no appreciation whatever for black resistance and violence being "a logical response to slavery." The incident also calls into question the possibility of ever characterizing slaveholders' treatment of their human chattel as kind.

Such occurrences were certainly sensational, but they were also relatively rare. Many more New England blacks found escape in drinking, gambling, or flight and chose less violent means of retaliation such as sabotage, feigned illness, or feigned stupidity. These too were individual means of rejecting the role that white masters had imposed upon them. They were also a sign of cultural resilience, accommodation, and adaptation. To recognize that slaves in New England were neither content nor complacent and often actively resisted their bondage is not to say that they rejected Anglo-American culture wholesale. The basic human desire to establish human contacts and have normal social interaction with others, particularly after the horrors of the Middle Passage, when many slaves assumed they were to be cannibalized, might have predisposed some to assimilate as much as possible once they discovered that they were merely to be put to work (Twombly 1973:45; Equiano 1789:73–79). For those who had come directly from Africa, Anglo-American culture also provided the common matrix for their interactions with others from diverse backgrounds. The emergence of a distinct subculture then, informed and influenced but not dictated by Anglo-American culture, was both inevitable and desirable, for it would eventually provide a "reservoir of stability" on which to draw (Piersen 1988:146). This community subculture was at the core of an everyday resistance that gave enslaved people's lives meaning, direction, and definition that the cruelties, inconsistencies, and tyranny of slavery could never fully eradicate.

Sundays and holidays were often spent feasting, storytelling, singing, and dancing, and most festivities in urban milieus cross-cut race and class, creating a general unease among the elite about the seemingly unlikely fraternization among the baser folk in its midst. Racial divisions were not forgotten, but they were overcome in certain circumstances by the common conditions of daily life among the disenfranchised. The strict "vertical focus of American society" that reigned until the end of the 18th century made for strange bedfellows (Horton and Horton 1997:51). Vibrant subcultures emerged. Strange alliances were struck, especially at the docks and wharves where social codes were relaxed anyway. There they communed and caroused with each other and with working-class whites and others who were unfree in one or another respect (Berlin 1998). "Alley society," writes Twombly (1973:27), "although illegal and dangerous . . . seems to have been an organic component of urban slavery, especially in Boston." The slightest errand might turn into a social gathering in the streets, and taverns and brothels always had a hefty black patronage. The *Boston Evening-Post* reported in 1740 that

> last Friday Night a Gentleman of this Town went over to *Roxbury* to look for his Negro Woman, who had been gone from him a few Days; and hearing a Noise in the Tavern, he went in, (past Nine o'Clock) and found about a Dozen black Gentry, He's and She's, in a Room, in a very merry Humour, singing and dancing, having a Violin, and Store of Wine and Punch before them. They all belonged to Gentlemen in this Town: and 'tis much to be wondered at, how they can be absent from their respective Families without their Masters Knowledge: And 'tis yet more to be wondered at, if they obtain their Masters leave to attend these Nocturnal Frolicks, which must needs be very expensive, and 'tis well known that their own Revenues are very small. (14 Jan. 1740)

Sixteen years later whites in Boston still found black social life vexing and no more under their control than it had ever been. In 1756 the Massachusetts General Court passed "An act for preventing all riotous, tumultuous and disorderly assemblies or companies of persons, and for preventing bonfires in any of the streets or lanes within any of the towns of this province" (*Massachusetts Acts and Resolves* III Province Laws 1756–57, 4th session, ch. 14:997). The act was in response to the observation that

> many and great disorders have of late years been committed by tumultuous companies of men, children and Negroes, carrying about with them pageants or other shews through the streets and lanes of the town of Boston, and other towns within this province, abusing and insulting the inhabitants, and demanding and exacting money by menaces and abusive language [. . .] horrid profaneness and gross immoralities. (*Massachusetts Acts and Resolves* III Province Laws 1756–57, 4th session, ch. 14:997)

What whites failed to realize is that blacks probably got together in alley society because they found comfort and pleasure in each other's company. They meant less to "cause disorder" than "to satisfy the more mundane needs of body and soul" for resistance to slavery in Massachusetts never did produce "a mass movement or even a good-sized conspiracy" (Twombly 1973:26, 31).

Ironically it was in the very categories that were ignored by white owners as a threat that blacks probably gained the greatest degree of autonomy, such as it was, in their lives. Much black resistance to slavery took place in personal acts and private episodes whose cohesive force whites did not understand or recognize. Magic was one early keystone in the formation of black community. Charms against evil or to promote health and happiness were ubiquitous, while sent sickness, poisoning, and witchcraft were common complaints among enslaved people wherever they lived. These categories of belief and knowledge were too close to the white notion of superstition to have instilled much fear in slave owners, but they became important and unchecked factors in the creation of black identities, and they gave the enslaved a sense of control and agency in a time and place when there was little opportunity for either. Henry Bibb once resorted to sprinkling a powder of cow manure, red pepper, and white people's hair all around his master and mistress' bed and in their bed linens to prevent their whipping him by turning their anger into love. All he succeeded in doing was to cause a violent coughing and sneezing fit in them both, at which point he became "convinced that running away was the most effectual way by which a slave could escape cruel punishment" (Bibb 1849:449). His "great faith in conjuration and witchcraft" during his youth, though, was widespread among slaves, sometimes out of a real faith in the practice and sometimes as a last-ditch effort to improve circumstances that had taken a dangerous or undesirable turn (Bibb 1849:448).

Modes of personal adornment, such as the use of beads, bright colors, and bold styles considered vulgar by white onlookers (see White and White 1998:5–6), and the "joy in physical attractiveness" that disregarded the modesty that would be required of a bondsman, might have been borrowing from African notions of beauty and were another form of everyday resistance (Piersen 1988:101). Keziah Brevard, a plantation mistress from South Carolina, once complained that her maid, Dolly, "would never go to church unless as fine and fashionable as possible" (quoted in Fox-Genovese 1988:216). Fanny Kemble (1984:93–94) concurred, saying

> You cannot conceive anything more grotesque than the Sunday trim of the poor people. . . . Their Sabbath toilet really presents the most ludicrous combination of incongruities that you can conceive—frills, flounces, ribbons; combs stuck in their woolly heads, as if they held up any portion of the stiff and ungovernable hair; filthy finery, every color in the rainbow, and the deepest possible shades blended in fierce companionship round one dusky visage; head handkerchiefs, that put one's very eyes out from a mile off. . . . Beads, bugles, flaring sashes, and, above all, little fanciful aprons, which finish these incongruous toilets with a sort of airy grace, which I assure you is perfectly indescribable.

Runaway slave advertisements frequently emphasized the fineness of dress of slaves in New England (Greene 1944), and Cato Pearce, after falling into the role of preacher for fellow slaves in Rhode Island, spent the money he earned on a new outfit.

I got into the wagon with my ruffle shirt on, and breast-pin and white gloves and stockings. I thought every body would know I was a minister, and never hardly any body felt as big as I did. (Pearce 1842:18)

White and White (1998:6, 13) suggest that such pride in physical appearance, which slaveholders often claimed made their slaves forget their "lowly station," perhaps signified a "worrisome loss of control" to masters. A well-dressed slave could arouse suspicion that that individual was up to no good and ire that he or she was not suitably modest. And yet whites were largely powerless to control slave dress. White and White (1998:10) call white attempts at sumptuary legislation in 18th-century South Carolina, for example, nothing more than "idle dreams." The great variety and flamboyance in slave apparel, as evidenced in historical documents reveals some of the ways that enslaved people were able to find a degree of "social and cultural space" through personal adornment and appearance (White and White 1998:10).

Satire and mockery of the system that enslaved them through oral traditions, trickster stories of Buh Rabbit, and practical jokes provided another outlet for aggression that was safer than open rebellion (see Webber 1978). And then there were festivities, frolics, Sunday markets, traditional music, religion, and the black 'Lection Day to give New England blacks a sense of self and common purpose (Piersen 1988; Berlin 1998).

Summary

In terms of raw population statistics, New England in general and Massachusetts in particular may be considered to have been a society with slaves rather than a slave society. Nevertheless one can hardly overestimate the importance that the slave trade had in New England industry and commerce at large. The benefits of the Triangular Trade were both direct and indirect—and manifold—with Africa and the Caribbean constituting the largest markets for everything from rum to livestock, cedar boards, and foodstuffs. Slavery and the slave trade were at the very foundation of the New England economy for more than 200 years.

Slavery itself and the status of blacks, however, was rather different there from in the Caribbean and the South. Although there was a small elite of slaveholders, such as the Royalls, who might have owned several dozen slaves and styled themselves a sort of northern plantation gentry, New England's wealth did not lie in large-scale agriculture, but in small family farms and urban industry.

As a result not nearly as many of the enslaved could be absorbed into New England as elsewhere in the Americas. Nevertheless the nature of an economy that centered on urban and industrial areas saw to it that even the relatively small numbers of Africans in New England's midst were clustered in a few places to make a visible minority that, except in a few extreme cases, would probably have been able to confer with each other and form community ties better than mere numbers would suggest. In urban areas most everyone with any means owned at least a few enslaved domestics, while small business owners and farmers who did not own their own slaves could still make use of their labor during busy seasons through the hire-out system. A diverse economy required a diverse and flexible labor force, and enslaved people in New England tended to be skilled and versatile, which could arguably have provided them with a negotiating power in securing certain freedoms that only a minority of their southern and Caribbean counterparts might have had. Under Puritan law, too, New England blacks were granted many more rights than enslaved people under other regimes, which provided them with an avenue for resistance that was wholly legal and worked within the system.

Laws governing and controlling their behavior, however, were many and strict. One's status as a black individual in New England was thus complex and often contradictory, and it seems that where certain freedoms were gained, others were sacrificed in the differences between the two slave systems. One could argue, as has been done in the past, that close working and living conditions resulted in increased familial affections and mutual understanding in the North. However, there is little direct evidence of this and much evidence to the contrary. Mutual misunderstanding and distrust seem to have lain deep wherever slavery occurred. Enslaved people in New England might not have been so easily replaced as the typical field hand in the cane fields; the diversity of their tasks also would have carried them frequently beyond the eye of the master or an overseer and given them an opportunity to meet with others or run personal errands (see Garman 1998). On the other hand, while at home, intimate living conditions would have granted little escape from such surveillance, and enslaved people there were perhaps not as independent as at first thought (see Jones 1990; Fitts 1996; chapter 5, this volume). They were probably less free to carry out old cultural traditions openly, and the low density of others of their kind would have prohibited their roaming the countryside "invisibly" as they often could in the islands or the South. Sparse populations in the countryside and the highly skewed sex ratios that characterized the 17th and 18th centuries would also have posed real, though perhaps not insurmountable, challenges to forging community ties and networks (Kulikoff 1974, 1978; Lee 1986). Despite these setbacks, however, there arose in the 18th century in New England various African and African American institutions and a growing subculture that drew from West Indian, African, Native American, and American colonial influences.

Chapter 4
THE "BENEVOLENT" ROYALLS
IN THE AGE OF REASON

Goods are neutral, their uses are social; they can be used
as fences or bridges.
      —MARY DOUGLAS AND BARON ISHERWOOD,
                                    1979

The whole blue world sings with meaning.
                        —HENRY GLASSIE, 1995

The Order of Things

Isaac Royall, Sr., was a self-made man, but he came from respectable stock. His
letters reveal that he was well educated, modest, affable, and articulate, and it was
not just his money that allowed him intimate access to the highest levels of society. He was a gentleman through and through, despite his low birth. In the 18th
century being a gentleman referred not just to chivalrous manners, but to a whole
mode of being that had its roots in the Italian Renaissance and was epitomized in
Baldasar Castiglione's 1528 publication, *The Book of the Courtier* (Aresty 1970).
A gentleman was married to the daughter of a gentleman. He was well traveled,
well read, and an accomplished conversationalist—casually witty, graceful, and
unaffected. He knew his history and had opinions about current events; studied
chemistry, philosophy, medicine, and architecture; took an interest in agriculture and horticulture; and dabbled in the arts. He was a good Christian and an
honorable businessman, but he was also a dancer and a sportsman—a horseman
and a hunter. A gentleman took his role as head and protector of his household
seriously and endeavored to be an indulgent husband, good father, kind master,
true friend, and gracious host in all of his dealings. Such characteristics were
described in detail in Issac's epitaph on the family tomb in Dorchester:

Here lyes the body
Of the Honble ISAAC ROYALL Esqr
who departed this Life at his Seat in Charlestown
June ye 7th Anno Domni 1739 Ætatis 67
He was a Gentn of Superior natural powers & great
acquired knowledge
Civil affable courteous & Just to all men
Remarkably Dutiful to his Parents,
Kind to his Relations & Charitable to ye Poor
He was a faithful Husband a tender Father a Kind Master
& a True Friend
Delighted in doing good.
He was highly esteemed & respected during his residence at Antigua
which was near 40 Years
and advanced to ye most Honourable & important Publick
employments Civil & Military
which he discharged with ye heighest reputation and fidelity.
He Returned with His Family to New England His Native Country
July 27 1737
Where His death which soon followed was greatly Lamented
By all who Knew Him
But as He Lived a Virtuous Life
So He was removed by peaceful Death
Leaving a SON & DAUGHTER
To inherit a plentifull Fortune which He was Blessed with
And an exemplary Pattern for Their imitation
At His desire His Remains were here
Interred with His Parents For whom He Erected this
MONUMENT*

This definition of a gentleman, however, was recent and relatively broad, and it represented "a new model of gentry culture" in the 17th and 18th centuries (Beaudry 1999:ix). Land and title were replaced with simple polite deportment and genteel dress as the hallmarks and defining characteristics of a gentleman (Beaudry 1999:ix). In the secularizing and socially volatile world of Isaac Royall, high rank could be acquired, not just conferred by birth.

*The text of Isaac's epitaph (reproduced in Hoover 1974; also Oliver 1899:59) is also typical of the Georgian secularization of death in which the emphasis is shifted away from death itself entirely to memorializing the individual and his or her life (Deetz 1996:89–124).

Isaac was living in a very different world from his parents, born at the cusp of a cultural transition that has been the subject of a pantheon of studies in archaeology, sociology, history, and American culture and termed the "Georgianization" of the American colonies (see Deetz 1996; Isaac 1982). This transition represented an entirely different Western worldview and a reinvention of the role of humanity in the universe and its relationship to nature. This was the difference between being medieval and modern. It was the Enlightenment, the Age of Reason.

The Age of Reason, as its name suggests, placed new emphasis on and belief in *order* and *control.* The "rediscovery" of the classical scholars, artists, and architects resulted in the rise of scientific thought. Essentially the Renaissance had come 150 years late to America and broken down the old cosmology and religiously based society. The new society was secular, and with it came a preoccupation with the mechanical, symmetrical, and individual. The Reverend Devereux Jarratt, for example, writing in late-18th-century Virginia, bemoaned the fact that hardly anybody went to church anymore except on Sundays, and many not even then, preferring "cards, racing, [and] dancing" instead (Jarratt 1806:23). This new society manifested itself materially in a variety of ways, from the rigorous bilateral symmetry of newly built houses, to a new organization of the living space within, to a new importance of the individual in everything from food consumption to burial practices (Isaac 1982; Deetz 1996). It also cut across regional lines and served to homogenize a patchwork of folk cultures that had characterized the early colonial period, making them into something new and more profoundly European than ever before.

In the Chesapeake the economic strife of falling tobacco prices in the 18th century has been blamed for a social hierarchy that became more and more rigid and exclusive as the century wore on (Isaac 1982). Constant erosion of the planter gentry's economic position led to its members receding and trying to isolate themselves at the top of this unstable social pyramid (Isaac 1982). The greater the social and economic chaos in their society, the more they reacted by trying to exert control over that society and make it appear rational and inevitable. This was expressed in the Georgian Order, a behavioral as well as material cultural phenomenon that segmented, ordered, and created hierarchy in all things, as well as implicitly linked them to the mysterious workings of nature, which were beyond question. Everything from architecture to interior decor, landscape, dance, dress, and manners was rallied to provide the isolation needed to hinder an attack on the crumbling social order (Aresty 1970; Deetz 1996; Isaac 1982; Leone and Shackel 1987; Pendery 1987; Shackel 1992).

The Georgian Order presided in New England too by the early years of the 18th century, although the region had its own sources of social instability. The Crown's restrictions and regulations on all manner of provincial trade and production were heightened during the 18th century, and this limited the gentry's prosperity in all of the colonies. In a letter to his lawyer, Edmund Quincy, Isaac Royall, Sr., stated that he feared "one half of the men must turn hunters and cloath themselves with bearskins" if the newest proposals of the Crown to "cramp" them in "everything" were not blocked in Parliament (Royall Correspondence: Aug. 15, 1736). Oppressive taxation was imposed on colonists to finance the Crown's imperial objectives of "manifest destiny" into the interior and wars with the French and the Indians. Frequent wars and inflation also made the new trade-based economy susceptible to instability. In the 1730s the Massachusetts Bay currency had fallen in value in excess of 7 percent per year for six or seven years straight (Royall Correspondence: Aug. 15, 1736). Isaac, Sr., equated success in mercantile trade in these tumultuous years with "throwing the die." He maintained that it was all well and good for a man with nothing to engage in trade and shipping, because one in ten might strike it rich, as he had. But, from his own experience, for a man with a "good estate to run such risks, I think it is a madness" (Royall Correspondence: Aug. 15, 1736).

An originally agrarian society had been transformed by the 18th century into a mercantile one in which social interaction was no longer governed by kinship, community, and religion, but by common occupation (or gentlemanly lack thereof) and uncertain profit (Pendery 1987). The further stress of having an economy that hinged on the slave trade and a society whose functioning depended on maintaining a strict class system by keeping blacks and poor whites peacefully subjugated left even New England's gentry on shaky ground. Thus it is apparent that in the decades leading up to the Revolution, there was reason from Boston to St. Johns for a growing nervous unrest among the upper classes that their position was untenable. In embracing science and a Galileo-Newtonian universe that could be distilled down to mechanical tenets subject to inalienable, constant, predictable, and universal laws, perhaps they sought to rationalize their own apparently chaotic society. If physics could bring the very planets and stars under the control of human understanding, then one could believe in good faith in the infallibility and inevitable triumph of human reason to bring order to all things.

If the Age of Reason was nothing else, it was at its most basic level an attempt to demystify and rationalize the universe and everything in it. Nothing was too big or too small—from the stars of the firmament to the slave in the field—to have its place in the order of things (Isaac 1992). A gentleman farmer would make experiments and observations in agriculture, horticulture, and labor to achieve maximum efficiency scientifically. This was based on a new natural philosophy of cause and effect, of balances based on numbers, weights, and measures. No longer was the will of God to be humbly accepted, as had been done in the organic, medieval world. There was a distinct (and unprecedented) sense that we could make our own destiny, that through reason, we could improve our God-given lot in life, for in the secularizing optimism of the Enlightenment, God helped those who helped themselves. When this segmentation and mechanization of the material world was applied to "natural" elements of the environment, such as house form, use of space, gardens, vistas, the heavens, native peoples, or slaves, it became easy to confuse the imposed order with a natural one. Afloat in such self-conscious reveries (Isaac 1992:419), the 18th-century gentleman could be lulled into believing that however shaky one's position might seem now, this was how it had always been, though it was not, and how it must be, though it need not.*

The Age of Reason at Ten Hills Farm

By 1775 New England was full of "mansion people" (Sweeney 1984:231). Profound social, political, and economic changes in the Western world had created, perhaps for the first time, a fluid social structure. This was particularly true in the colonies, in whose wilderness people of all backgrounds were frequently reduced to practical equality. Sumptuary laws were adopted in the 17th century to prohibit the lower echelons of society from trying to pass for something they were not. By the 18th century, however, New England was participating in a new Atlantic economy that was based almost exclusively on trade—with Great Britain, Spain, Portugal, France, the Netherlands, and the West Indies (Pendery 1987)—and social and cultural life was reshaped around this "consumer revolution" (Hunter 2001:5). Boston was one of the nodes of this new trade-based economy, as was Charlestown (Ten Hills Farm was identified as being in Charlestown until it was annexed to Medford in 1754). In a description by a gentleman traveler in 1744, Boston Harbor was said to have always "above 100 ships . . . besides a great number of small craft" even in slower times of trade (quoted in Hunter 2001:2). In these international seaports a distinct middle class of merchants, sea captains, mariners, shipwrights, sail makers, craftsmen, and artisans emerged—something that had never existed before—and it was full of aspirations. It was a culture that "emphasized the

---

*In short, as a means of naturalizing and thus masking the arbitrariness of the social order, the Georgian Order can be conceptualized as a kind of ideology (Leone 1984:26, 29), but not one inevitably rooted in a deeper human psyche or manifested among all social groups. Although material manifestations of a Georgian mindset were widespread—found in colonial contexts from Boston to London to Cape Town—there can be no doubt that they were messages in social discourses that were historically and contextually specific. Hodder (1982:13) states that culture is not an "extrasomatic means of adaptation" but "meaningfully constituted." Statements of power and resistance through material objects are viewed here then as at least on some level intentional, individually motivated, and historically derived from specific societal conflict and contradiction. These stories may be "subjective, local, and fleeting," but they are not irrelevant for it was only through the accumulation of thousands of stories like theirs that there was a Georgian Order to speak of at all (Barrett 1994: 2).

value of material objects"—from timber to rum to tea to porcelain—"in defining self and creating community"; it was the "age of the public man" (Hunter 2001:4, 74). It was distinctly irritating to the self-styled "upper class" because it was apparent that this middle class no longer "knew their place" (Aresty 1970:129). Even the Reverend Devereux Jarratt, himself a lowly carpenter's son turned respected clergyman in 18th-century Virginia, observed in the latter part of the century that

> In our high *republican times* there is more *levelling* than ought to be, consistent with good government. I have as little notion of oppression and tyranny as any man, but a due subordination is essentially requisite in every government. (Jarratt 1806:15)

As a result of such "insubordination," the upper class adopted a rigorous code of manners, modeled after the European courts but "composed also of numerous private ceremonials observed in certain cliques and sets" whose rules one could not learn but had to know (Aresty 1970:129). In the colonies, especially, because the colonial gentry were themselves rarely more than a generation removed from humble beginnings (provincial parvenus in Europe), manners became important in the struggle for cultural legitimacy, civic influence and power, and forging alliances (Goodwin 1999:2ff.). With plenty of disposable income and freedom from material toil, this expanding commercial class "turned its attention to niceties and refinement" (Hunter 2001:75). Shared behavior (from dress to manners) within occupational groups was used to symbolize group solidarity, and a long-term commitment to investing in material goods—or abstaining from them—served to communicate such information to others of one's own kind (Pendery 1987). "Gentry cliques" with strong ties to county courts and to each other began to transcend local community and form an exclusive class of gentlemen and their families and political and social luminaries, all of whom were largely interrelated by blood or marriage and collectively ruled the province (Sweeney 1984:231).

When we examine public and genealogical records, it is clear that the Royalls were tied through blood or marriage or both to many of the elite families in the Boston area. The Royalls, Vassals, Olivers, Tailers, Ruggles, Borlands, Lechmeres, Lees, and Phipses were all intertwined, and nearly monopolized posh Brattle Street—"Tory Row"—in Cambridge (Jackson 1907). Among these families were colonels, majors, judges, lawyers, merchants, and Lieutenant Governors William Tailer and Spencer Phips. Close personal friendships existed between the Royalls and the Quincys, Tufts, and Governor Jonathan Belcher himself. Material statements of this distinctiveness—visual evidence of their authority—were an important part of the legitimization process and were meant to garner unquestioned respect from outsiders and to constantly reaffirm their rightful membership to insiders (see Hall 1992). The gentry of the 18th century took their bearings from material things—from houses and fields [to] the folks who lived in and tended them—[that] were read as tangible evidence of success and failure, or ties to friends and the community, and of membership in the local social network or a wider social net, or both or neither. (Hudgins 1990:59)

How did people in the past understand or imagine their environment? What meanings and desires were invested in the artifacts we recover? Questions concerning the use of the physical world to make cultural statements have been many in recent scholarship. How material things took on meaning and shaped social and political relationships as well as gave meaning and context to daily life through social action has been one of the primary preoccupations of postprocessual research (see Beaudry, Cook, and Mrozowski 1991; Hall 1992; Hodder 1982; Howson 1990; Isaac 1992; Stewart-Abernathy 1992). The material world can be read as "texts without words" that can be all the more powerful because such texts are ambiguous and hence have ever-changing significance (Hall 1992:373). The Georgian mindset then is perhaps a misnomer, for historical and archaeological evidence suggests that it was but one of several coexisting and competing mindsets—a part of an active social discourse whose participants were continually reinventing themselves in opposition to an Other. When we examine the Royalls' side of the discourse, we see an attempt to legitimate their claim to power to not only their social inferiors, but also, and perhaps most important, themselves and their own inner circle (Cook, Yamin, and McCarthy 1991; Hall 1992; Shackel 1992).

Historical texts and artifacts recovered archaeologically from the Royall House have helped to reconstruct how the Royalls lived and how they might have manipulated the material world to define themselves and negotiate their own place in the order of things. It is perhaps useful to look first at the use of probate records—wills, inventories, and accounts of administration—in historical and archaeological research. Probate inventories in particular are one of the most widely used and informative sets of historical documents in terms of reconstructing lifestyle. They are often used to address functional uses of space within a house (Cummings 1986; St. George 1986), to identify various household furnishings, or to identify material goods that may indicate changing lifestyles. Some have also tried to apply ideological analyses by addressing the "symbolic and active meanings" of the objects listed, such as their manipulation to create and magnify social inequalities (Shackel 1992:205). For the Royall household, inventories were filed at the deaths of Isaac, Sr. (Middlesex County Probate 1739), and his son-in-law, Henry Vassal (Middlesex County Probate 1769), and while Isaac, Jr., was in exile in England (Middlesex County Probate 1778). All reveal to what extent the Royalls and their various in-laws were integral members of the New England elite. The inventories also reveal a well-established concern with functional division of space that is characteristic of a "modern organizational framework" (Yentsch 1994:84), and one of the defining characteristics of the Georgian Order.

The classic Georgian style of architecture, exhibited at the Royall House, has its roots in the Renaissance of Europe, supposedly introduced to England by Inigo Jones in the early 17th century (Deetz 1996:156). It is an essentially academic design, constructed from books on the topic that flooded the market beginning in the late 17th century (Deetz 1996) and borrowing classical design elements that falsely linked an independent European tradition with classical antiquity. It constitutes a bilaterally symmetrical facade and floor plan, with a central hall or passage that served to isolate or protect the family and visitors from outside (fig. 24). No inner room was directly accessible from the formal entrances of the house, and the owner was thus able "directly and individually" to control circulation through, and access to, such space (Upton 1986:321). This was a marked departure from the early colonial period "organic" house forms, whose living spaces were small, multifunctional, and corporately used, with little or no distinction made between public and private space. In the earlier, two-

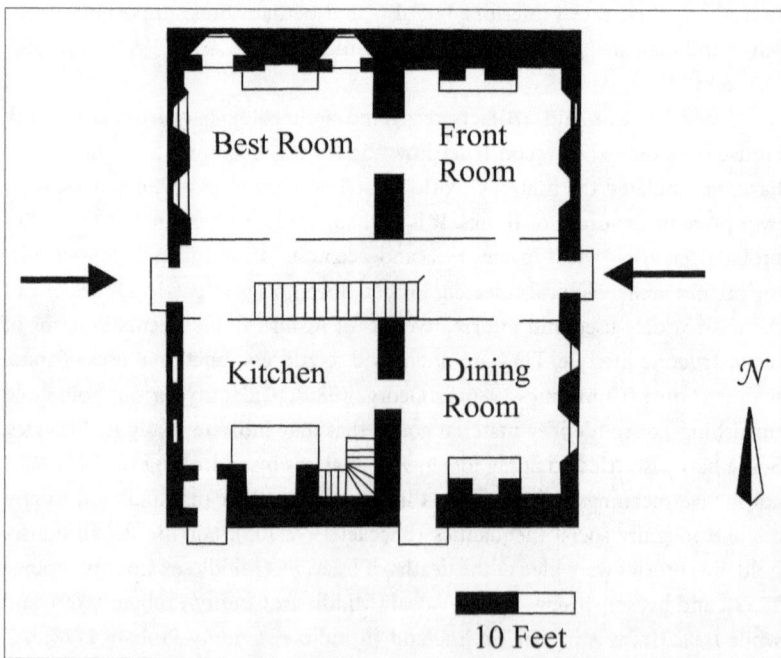

FIG. 24. Floor plan of the Royall House. (After *Colonial Homes* 1989 15 [5]: 101.)

room house plan of hall and parlor, one might cook, eat, sleep, and entertain in the same room, and the entrance to the house usually opened directly into the heart of the action. Inventories of this early period often reflect this organization in the hodgepodge of goods listed, written down apparently as they came into view or into mind. With the advent of a Georgian floor plan, privacy took on a new and much more central meaning. A central hall with several doors leading off from it served to separate the visitor or servants from family activities. On the second floor, bedrooms were sealed off from the central stairwell in the same fashion, representing a sharp division between public and private space. Behind closed doors, too, there was a growing degree of spatial specialization and categorization that separated work from social space or servant from served. Each social function had its own room—a place for everything and everything in its place. Cooking took place in the kitchen or out kitchen, spinning in the spinning garret. Guests were received in the best room. People took their meals in the dining room. Each family member likely had his or her own bedroom.

A house might also have many auxiliary structures to accommodate all of the new special-function spaces needed, so that "when you come to the house of a person of some means, you think you are entering a fairly large village" (Dauphine, quoted in Hudgins 1990:67). Isaac, Sr.'s 1739 probate inventory reveals that the Royalls had ten special-function outbuildings in the immediate vicinity of the house, and as many as 15 all told (Middlesex County Probate 1739). Inside the house this social division of space is reflected not only in the room names, but also in the artifacts that are listed in the probate inventory (Middlesex County Probate 1739). The house is divided by room name, and the artifacts that belong in each are then listed accordingly. There are matching sets of chairs, a set for each room that had use for them; bedsteads for each individual; several full sets of dishes; and other special-function objects or pieces of furniture that both reflected and helped to define the purpose of each space. The Royalls had 11 special-function rooms or spaces in their house. The Vassals (Isaac Sr.'s daughter Penelope and son-in-law Henry), who lived on fashionable Brattle Street in Cambridge, had 21 (Middlesex County Probate 1769). Within these spaces were all of the social trappings of wealth, power, and influence that reassured them of their own position and helped to project their self-image out to the world.

Table 6 shows an amenity index for Boston-area households of varying wealth levels between 1740 and 1750. Individuals were subjectively chosen for the spectrum of class, occupation, and degree of wealth they represented. The presence of almost every amenity listed, and in relatively large amounts, shows to what extent the Royalls incorporated nonessentials and luxury items into their daily lives, in relation to members of other socio-economic classes and occupations. It may seem obvious to say that a man worth £27 could not afford the amenities

TABLE 6.

Amenities index for Boston-area households, ca. 1740–50

Amenities	Isaac Royall, Sr.	Capt. Samuel Wade	John Inglesby	John Whitmore	Josiah Franklin	Grace Knight	Andrew Hall
Linens (bed and table)	£334	£13	£1	£1	£6	£119	£108
Earthenware	£1	£13	—	—	£0:3	—	—
Knives	—	—	—	—	—	<£1	—
Forks	—	—	—	£0:2	£0:1	<£1	—
Spices	a	—	—	—	—	£0:5	£29
Fine tablewares (including pewter)	£88	£6	£1:8	£4	—	£9	£20
Tea and tea services	£16	—	—	—	—	£18	£12[b]
Wigs	a	—	—	—	—	—	—
Watches and clocks	£60	—	—	—	£2	—	£85
Turkey carpets	£40	—	—	—	—	—	—
Books	£136	—	—	£1	£3	£12	£10
Paintings	a	—	—	—	—	£3	£2
Silver and gold	a	—	—	—	£3	£49	£307
Value of amenities	£635+	£32	£2:8	£6:2	£14:4	£212	£551
Inventory total	£36992	£1236	£27	£46	£313	£1887	£40942
Place of residence	Charlestown	Charlestown	Boston	Medford	Boston	Boston	Medford
Occupation	Merchant/Slave Trader/Esquire	Potter	Shipwright	Housewright	Tavern Keeper	Widow	Distiller/Shop owner/Shipper

Notes: ªPresumed present because indicated in the estate ledger of accounts payable, 1724-1745.
ᵇ£11 silver belongs in both "tea" and "silver" categories, hence the £466 total amenities sum
Source: adapted from Yentsch 1994: 44

of a man worth £40,000, but the difference is not just indicative of purchasing power (Stone 1968). It also reflects a difference in the way of life, as well as a difference in what were likely considered to be essentials and nonessentials based on one's occupation and social group.

Andrew Hall (Middlesex County Probate 1750), who was worth about £41,000, was nonetheless a tradesman. He was not a great reader—investing mostly in a large Bible—and although he did have luxury items, he seems not to have engaged in the social display of elegant entertaining to the extent that the Royalls, who were worth less than he, did. Much of his wealth can be accounted for by the goods he sold in his shop. Although the table indicates that he had £12 of tea equipage in his home, more than £11 worth of that is represented by six silver teaspoons. Nor did he invest in many fine tablewares. The large value of silver listed refers only to a silver-hilted sword, two porringers, one tankard, 15 spoons, and a cream pot. To him, then, perhaps portraying himself as an educated gentleman and procuring items to do with establishing his home as a center of hospitality were nonessential. Perhaps the Halls thought themselves too pragmatic for such ostentation. Indeed, what fine tea and tablewares they did have were all found in the kitchen, not the best room, which indicates that they were not an important part of the visual backdrop of the home. Here we have an example of one of the richest men in the colony living relatively simply. How to explain this, in light of all the rhetoric about a Georgian mindset? It is an exemplary illustration of the Georgian mindset being tied to individual tastes and desires that might have been not only historically specific, but actually individually so.

Henry (1991) looks at the internal and external influences on people's consumer behavior in the past and concludes that social class and subculture are powerful reference points for an individual's worldview, life values, personality, and ultimately consumption patterns. Wall (1991) examines the use of fine teawares among 19th-century women of different social classes, for example, and concludes that lower-middle-class women had less fancy wares not because they had less money, but because they entertained only family and close friends, for whom social display was not necessary. To return to our present example, Andrew Hall happened to be very successful at his trade, but the values of his social class and early upbringing might have proved more influential with him than the possibilities presented by his upwardly mobile finances.

Henry also concedes that the internal influences (that is, those that come from the individual's own mind) would also have been important in shaping that person's consumer behavior, but she seems content to dismiss it as an unknowable "Black Box" and hence irrelevant to archaeologists (Henry 1991:9). While it is true that the precise inner workings of another's mind will forever remain something of a mystery for others, I do not believe it impossible to reconstruct plausible scenarios based on sound historical evidence. Andrew Hall may have been a very rich man, but he likely did not habitually move in gentlemen's circles. His probate inventory shows that he did not have the proper possessions to do so. We may speculate that, given his occupation, in his mind he was still just a plain man with a plain man's tastes. He also appears to have liked it that way, for he did not change things even after he had ample means to do so. He might have found the aristocratic obsession with things, pomp, and ceremony affected and unattractive, and he may thus have concentrated his efforts instead on the acquisition of land and the development of his businesses.

On the other hand, the widow Grace Knight (Suffolk County Probate 1749), who was only moderately well-to-do, had invested a sizable portion of her total amenities in fine tablewares and tea services—all used for entertaining and social display, something that a widow of moderate means might engage in quite frequently. Is it impossible to know why she, who had so much less money than Hall, invested so much more heavily in items of elegant hospitality? In her particular case, we might imagine that as a widow with no husband to support her, such means of forging and maintaining reciprocal social relationships would have been critical. They would have ensured her continued place in society and a wider social support network in her vulnerable husbandless state. As the widow of a moderately well-to-do man, she must also have been the daughter of one, and thus she had grown up accustomed to some of the niceties, if not opulent splendors, of a comfortable life. She would have entertained as a wife, and when she continued to entertain into widowhood, she was simply doing what she had always done—constantly reaffirm her position in society and her group, a belonging that would ensure her future survival.

Isaac Royall, Sr., presents an interesting contrast to the previous two (Middlesex County Probate 1739). The social class he was born into seems not have been the primary reference point that would shape his consumer behavior as an adult. He was of humble beginnings—his father had built houses for a living—and, according to his epitaph, he remained "Remarkably Dutiful to his Parents." But the simple life of an honest tradesman obviously did not hold the same allure for him that it did for Andrew Hall. Although the Royalls had been in New England for some 80 years, mostly working as coopers and carpenters, Isaac had itchy feet by the time he was a teenager, when he became a merchant mariner, which was one common way for members of the nonelite to get a start as merchants.

By his early twenties he was in the West Indies pursuing a lucrative and exciting career in sugar and the transatlantic slave trade. St. Johns would have been cosmopolitan—seething with life, excitement, danger, and Continental influences—in a way that Dorchester, Massachusetts, simply was not. These clues from his past, we find, foretell and account for what we discover many years later evidenced in his probate inventory: that Isaac had been restless with his lot in life and had striven to change it, in his mind, for the better.

He seems to have used a higher social class than his own as a reference point for his own behavior and adopted all of the material accoutrements to go along with the lifestyle, in some ways probably outstripping those he strove to imitate. His travels must have made him worldly, but he must at first have also felt keenly his ignorance of so many of the things that gentlemen discussed glibly as evidence of their rightful belonging to a group apart. As a young man with great aspirations, he must have studied gentlemen he met, picking up their mannerisms and comportment. He studied law, consulted books, and when he made a fortune, devoted himself wholly to the reinvention of self, which the secular optimism of the Enlightenment would have allowed as an entirely possible endeavor. Morrison (1952) has said that Isaac borrowed the architecture of his Medford home from that of an Antiguan planter whom he admired, and the landscaping from John Bartram of Philadelphia. He had an extensive library that comprises a menu of how to make a perfect gentleman (Middlesex County Probate 1739) and was commemorated on his tombstone as a man of "great *acquired* knowledge" (emphasis added). In letters from his later life, there is no hint that he was not born and bred a gentleman. He was certainly more eloquent than his own son, who had been. Thus Isaac Royall, Sr., epitomized everything that the Georgian Order was all about, and yet we need not believe that this was beyond his control. Rather he was conscious of his own actions, and a contextualized look at his own personal history suggests the specific reasons for acting the way he did. The Georgian Order was simply a backdrop from which he could draw his ideas of what would be logical and effective means of engaging in that particular discourse.

Isaac Royall spent over £40 in December of 1730 on "Makg a Tomb at Dorchester" for his deceased parents in the Dorchester Burying Ground (Account Book:Dec. 1730; Maine Historical Society n.d.). It was the fanciest thing William Royall, carpenter, and his wife, Mary, had ever had, and the large sum spent on its construction was probably more of a tribute to their son's own accomplishments and newfound status than a memorial to them. Meanwhile there was hardly an amenity to be had that their son did not own and have perfect mastery over. Isaac Royall, Sr., died a celebrated social figure both in Antigua and Medford, a self-made gentleman. Thus the terms "essential" and "nonessential" should perhaps be considered relative terms. Particularly among the merchant elite of the 18th century, where business and pleasure (or society) were inextricably intertwined, polite behavior and entertaining assumed all the more importance because this was where all social and economic life was created and reproduced (Goodwin 1999:119–31). A tea service was certainly nonessential to the Royalls' or Mrs. Knight's physical survival, but it would have been absolutely essential to their social survival among their desired peers. What is more, in the high presence of these essential nonessentials, and in the details of their fleeting individual histories, we also gain insight into the personal desires and motivations that influenced their purchase.

The Secular Rituals of Elegant Living

Documentary and archaeological evidence combine to reveal the Royalls not just as "rich," but well equipped to lead an aristocratic lifestyle that revolved around conspicuous consumption, social display, and numerous "secular rituals" of sociable dining and drinking that defined and perpetuated their place at the center of the social order (Yentsch 1994:133).

The ceramic and glass vessel assemblages from the Royall House grounds belong to three principal categories: tablewares, for the serving and consumption of food and drink; tea wares and other vessels for the consumption of exotic beverages such as coffee, chocolate, and punch; and utilitarian vessels for the care and running of an enormous household, such as cooking and storage vessels; commercial containers for food, condiments, or extracts; and pharmaceutical bottles. A total of 303 ceramic vessels and 203 glass vessels were recovered archaeologically from this site, and each is examined in greater detail below.

The Royall House Ceramics

The first step in a ceramics analysis is to determine the minimum number of vessels (MNV) present. A single plate may be broken into 100 pieces or five pieces, but the number of sherds is not as important as the number of vessels they actually represent because it is the vessel that contains the cultural information about the people who acquired and used it. MNVs are, of necessity, conservative and, as their name indicates, represent only the *minimum* number of a certain kind of vessel represented. While it is usually best to err on the side of caution in our interpretations, there are inherent biases that must be kept in mind as a result. For example, in 3,274 sherds of creamware recovered, we can count only 28 separate vessels for certain, while 62 sherds of Westerwald stoneware can be said to represent at least 11 different vessels. Particularly when we are dealing with plain, undecorated wares that have little to distinguish them between them and their neighbor (as is often the case with creamware, redware, or coarse, undecorated stonewares), there is an inherent risk of underrepresentation of those wares in our MNV counts.

Sherds are assigned to a single vessel based on a variety of characteristics: glaze, decoration, vessel form and size (where identifiable), and diagnostic features, such as rims, footrings, spouts, and handles. A teacup can have only one footring, for example, while a 5-inch rim cannot mend with a 4-inch rim.

Based on the methods outlined above, we determined that the nonutilitarian ceramic assemblage at the Royall House consisted of a minimum of 129 vessels, or 42.57 percent of the total ceramic vessel count. The fact that the utilitarian assemblage represented well over half of the total MNV (n = 174, or 57.43 percent) is probably a measure of the effort required to keep a household of up to 50 people fed and cared for.

Among the table- and teaware assemblages, a variety of different ware types and vessel forms bespeak the Royalls' standing in the community and place them at the vanguard of Colonial-period consumption (tables 7 and 8). Porcelain vessels, for example, outnumber those of any other material, representing over a third of the nonutilitarian vessel count. Nearly a third of those consisted of the prestigious "burnt" china, or overglaze enameled porcelain (fig. 25). Porcelain is followed by a number of different refined stonewares (nearly 20 percent of the total), including white salt-glazed stoneware; Nottingham; English scratch-blue; and red dry-bodied stoneware. Creamware too seems to have been one of the preferred tablewares, making up over 18 percent of the total number of nonutilitarian vessels.

Other wares were recovered in smaller amounts and include painted tin-glazed earthenware, Westerwald and English Brown stoneware, and Jackfield, Buckley, English Mottled, and Whieldon Clouded refined earthenwares. Thus the Royalls set a colorful and refined table with vessels from the latest shipments from abroad. Of equal import is the variety of vessel forms these wares represent, showing in this case a concern with display and elegant hospitality (fig. 26). Tea sets, coffee or chocolate cups, custard cups, punch bowls, plates, platters, bowls, mugs, and a salt cellar are all represented.

The documentary record helps put these finds in wider context, demonstrating how these independent lines of evidence—document and artifact—complement each other. It is not surprising, for example, that the numbers listed in Isaac, Sr.'s probate inventory of 1739 differ somewhat from the patterns observed in the ground (tables 9 and 10). Pewter made up 24 percent of the total value of inventoried plate in the documentary record, but it was totally absent from the archaeological record. As a material of value and of relative indestructibility, it is unsurprising that the Royalls' pewter did not end up in the trash heap. On the other hand, utilitarian earthenware is shown in the inventory to make up only 13 percent of the number of vessels listed, while archaeology has shown it to account for well over half of the vessels in the ground. In this case the difference may reflect more the earthenware's economic insignificance in determining the total worth of the estate than its actual absence from the household. Inventory takers may not even have troubled themselves to itemize many of the pieces because they were so cheap and easy to come by. Archaeology has also shown just what an array of things might have fallen under the somewhat opaque, vernacular umbrella of "cheney," or china.

At least one of the trends in the probate inventory documents, however, supports the archaeological pattern: a preponderance of porcelain and an emphasis on vessel forms for entertaining and elegant hospitality. Of Isaac, Sr.'s total 1739

FIG. 25. "Burnt china" porcelain saucer, recovered from the foundation hole of the small outbuilding in the slave quarters' west yard.

FIG. 26. Porcelain coffee/chocolate cup recovered from the foundation hole of the small outbuilding in the slave quarters' west yard.

TABLE 7.

Nonutilitarian ware types in descending order of frequency

Ware Type	MNV	% of Nonutil. MNV
Porcelain	44	34.11
"Burnt" china or overglaze enamel	14	10.85
Stoneware (refined)	25	19.38
White salt-glazed	18	13.95
Dry-bodied	2	1.55
Unid., rouletted	2	1.55
Scratch blue	1	0.78
Nottingham	1	0.78
Creamware	24	18.60
Redware	16	12.40
Tin-glazed earthenware	9	6.98
Stoneware (coarse)	5	3.88
Westerwald	2	1.55
English brown	2	1.55
Unid. gray-bodied	1	0.78
Jackfield	2	1.55
Buckley ware	1	0.78
English mottled	1	0.78
Whieldon clouded	1	0.78
Total	129	100.00

inventory of plate, 71 percent of it was Chinese porcelain—26 percent the prestigious "burnt china" described above and 31 percent for the consumption of exotic beverages such as tea, coffee, and chocolate. The abundance of vessels for exotic beverage consumption (as well as porcelain and glass trays for their presentation) establishes not only the adoption of the full-blown English tea ceremony, but also the Royalls' home as a center of hospitality by the early years of their residence in Medford.

Tea was a luxury and a novelty before midcentury, implying the wealth needed to own the equipage, the knowledge of the appropriate rituals to use it, and the leisure to indulge (Goodwin 1999:123). The Royalls would have used such exclusive ceremonies and polite rituals to wield tangible influence over and promote solidarity with their social peers. This "polite sociability," which also included things such as dancing, concerts, and card playing, was at the heart of the Georgian gentleman's world (Hunter 2001:109). And in the absence of a "native aristocracy" (Goodwin 1999:29), since most of these rituals were dependent on merchants' commercial activities and transatlantic connections, merchants quickly rose to the top of the American colonial hierarchy.

But it was not just *what* one did, but also *where* one did it that signified. Isaac Royall's probate inventory is especially useful in this regard, for the spatial information it contains about the family's table- and teawares when they were still in use. How these vessels were dispersed around the house and where they were set up as props in life is not retrievable from the ground, but it is vital to the interpretation of their meaning. Remember Andrew Hall's probate inventory, which showed all of his most expensive wares being kept in the kitchen, away from public view. Isaac Royall, Sr.'s probate inventory, by contrast, shows that all of the porcelain could be found in the best room, the front room, and the dining

TABLE 8.
The Royalls' ceramic tableware and exotic beverage forms in descending order of frequency

Vessel form	MNV	% of Tableware/Exotic Bev. MNV
Unid	39	30.23
Plate	22	17.05
Mug	21	16.28
Saucer	16	12.40
Teacup	8	6.20
Bowl	7	5.43
Teapot	3	2.33
Punch bowl	3	2.33
Dish	3	2.33
Coffee/chocolate cup	2	1.55
Custard cup	2	1.55
Platter	2	1.55
Salt	1	0.78
Total	**129**	**100.00**

room, meaning that the Royalls were self-conscious consumers of the fine goods they accumulated. They bought them to show them off. Thus the probate inventory suggests that the ceramics found in the ground, which at the very least confirm the Royalls to have been rich, were also an important part of the visual symbolism with which the Royalls cloaked themselves as wielders of power and occupants of the inner circle of the colonial governing elite.

TABLE 9.

Inventory of tablewares belonging to Isaac Royall, Sr.[a]

Item	Value in £
A Sett of Cheney [china] for [a Japanned tea table]*	13:0
A parcell of Cheney for [a mahogany tea table]*	3:0
1 doz. burnt Cheney plates	7:0
1 doz. of blew and white Do	6:0
3 Cheney Dishes @ 60/	9:0
2 Small Cheney Bowls	2:15
1 Glass Decanter	0:10
1 doz. burnt Cheaney plates	7:0
8 Cheney Dishes @ 30/	12:0
1 fruit plate	0:10
6 wine Glasses and nine tumblers	3:0
5 Custard Cups	0:15
2 blew and white Cheney Dishes	3:0
6 Cheney Salvers [serving trays]	3:0
1 Glass Salver	1:10
1 doz. of burnt Cheney plats	7:0
1 Glass Decanter	0:2:6
2 Glass Salts	0:8
1 Tubler [tumbler]	0:4
18 milkpans	0:18
115 lbs. pewter @ 4/6	25:17:6
Total No. of Vessels: 138	**106:16:0**

Note: [a]A tea set would likely contain a minimum of 12 vessels: the pot, the sugarer, the creamer, the slop bowl, and at least four teacups and saucers.

TABLE 10.

Breakdown of Isaac Royall's inventory of tablewares by type and/or function

Type	MNV	% Total Inventory of Plate (n = 106)
Exotic beverages (tea, coffee, chocolate, punch/wine/port)	43	31.16
Burnt china	36	26.09
Chinese porcelain (not tea, etc.)	33	23.91
Earthenware	18	13.04
Pewter[a]	115 lbs.	*

Note: [a]Pewter makes up 23.58% of the total value of the plate but was not itemized for a percentage of the total number of vessels to be possible.

Fortunes made by trade, argues Goodwin (1999:64), were still not entirely respectable until the family was at least one generation removed from the source of wealth. She uses the concepts of luxury, novelty, and patina in polite rituals to understand the uses of material goods by New England's merchant elite in their struggle to gain and maintain genteel legitimacy (Goodwin 1999). In a mercantile capitalist society where luxuries were increasingly easy to come by, it was the quest for novelty that helped to distinguish between those who owned luxuries and those who understood their social implications and proper use. In colonial American society, luxury and novelty were the saving grace for an elite that was newly rich and newly possessed of land and social rank (figs. 27 and 28). Although members of America's merchant elite often sought to imitate it, they could not by definition have the "true hallmark" of gentility—patina—that seemed to confirm not only present status but the longevity and historical derivation of that status (Goodwin 1999:144).

FIG. 27. Robert Feke portrait, oil on canvas (56 3/16' x 77 3/4'), of Isaac Royall, Jr., and his family, 1741. (Courtesy of Art & Visual Materials, Special Collections Department, Harvard Law School Library.) From right to left are depicted Isaac, Jr.; his wife, Elizabeth; first daughter, Elizabeth; sister-in-law Mary McIntosh; and sister Penelope. Isaac was 22 years old at the time and had recently assumed the role of master at Ten Hills Farm. The Turkey carpet on the table and the book in Isaac's hand establish the Royalls as a wealthy, leisured, and educated family with access to exotic, imported goods. Penelope seems to share the limelight, suggesting that the painting had been commissioned to convey the Royalls' greatness, not that of their in-laws.

Fig. 28. John Singleton Copley portrait of Mary (Polly) and the second Elizabeth Royall, ca. 1758. (Photograph © 2007 Museum of Fine Arts, Boston.) In addition to their obvious finery of watered silks and a generous amount of lace, Mary, on the left, holds a trained hummingbird, imported from the Caribbean or Latin America. The King Charles spaniel in Elizabeth's lap wears a flower necklace and would have been imported from England, where the ownership of spaniels was restricted by law to the aristocracy (Staiti 1995:64). It is not known whether the Royalls actually owned the animals depicted here, but Isaac, Jr.'s probate inventory of several decades later does list a birdcage among the items left behind in Medford.

New England's merchants were in a unique position to exploit luxury and the quest for novelty to their own advantage. International trade and shipping exposed them to a wide world and what was au courant in the fashionable centers of Europe. As merchants and "leaders of civic and social activities," they were the gatekeepers of commodities flowing into the colonies, and at the vanguard of their novel uses, incorporating "products of foreign commerce" effortlessly into their everyday lives (Goodwin 1999:44–45; Hunter 2001:107). In effect, then, those who were part of this elite were able to style themselves as the makers of the very manners required to become and remain elite. Goodwin further argues that entertaining became increasingly popular in the 18th century because it provided an arena for putting manners and one's familiarity with novelties on display, helping in the self-definition and perpetuation of a New England merchant class.

In 1737, Isaac, Sr., bought one-quarter pound of cocoa for £12 sterling—that is, at a cost of £48 per pound (Account Book: Oct. 28). It was roughly half of what he paid for his son's mahogany desk the same year—this in an era when an average man might receive 6–12 shillings (there are 20 shillings in a pound) for a day's menial labor (Account Book: Oct. 28, 1737). It was not only expensive but also exotic. Most colonial people had probably never drunk chocolate and might not have known the difference between a teacup and a chocolate or coffee cup. We return to Reverend Devereux Jarratt, himself the son of a carpenter, writing of his boyhood in 1730s and 1740s Virginia, who said

> We made no use of *tea* or *coffee* for breakfast, or at any other time; nor did I know a single family that made any use of them. . . . I suppose the richer sort might make use of *those* and other luxuries, but to such people I had no access. (Jarratt 1806:14, emphasis in original)

The Royall House Glass Assemblage

The methods for determining a minimum number of glass vessels were very much the same as those employed in the ceramic count. More than 4,300 glass sherds were assigned to individual vessels based on type, size, and form; and diagnostic characteristics such as rims, bases, design elements, or manufacturing technique. A wine bottle can have only one neck and one base, for example, while two opaque-twisted port glasses might have slightly different twists. Because of the undifferentiated nature of most forms of glass, however, the MNV for the Royall House glass is probably more conservative than for the ceramics.

A minimum of 203 glass vessels were identified from the Royall time period and fall into the categories of alcohol; commercial containers (for pickles, preserves, spices, condiments, mineral water, extracts, or snuff); pharmaceuticals; and table glass (table 11). As is the case with ceramic vessel types, the glass vessel form is often the most useful unit of analysis for understanding past cultural behaviors. Archaeology at the Royall House has revealed an array of drinking vessels, ceramic and glass—many for the serving and consumption of exotic beverages—that shows how the Royalls made "novelty" and "hospitable drinking" part of the "social scene" at Ten Hills Farm, most particularly when Isaac, Jr., came of age (Goodwin 1999; Yentsch 1994:134, 136–37). Where the average colonial New Englander drank beer, ale, or cider from rough earthenware or stoneware mugs, the Royalls were drinking tea, coffee, and chocolate and toasting each other with punch, gin, rum, and Madeira and Vidona wine—all from vessels made specifically for each (fig. 29). Nearly three-quarters of the identified glass vessels were precisely for such purposes.

TABLE 11.

Royall house glass vessel types in descending order of frequency

Vessel Types and Forms	MNV	% of Total MNV
Alcohol	116	50.43
Wine	93	45.81
Port/liqueur	9	4.43
Case gin	5	2.46
Unid.	5	2.46
Decanter	3	1.48
English beer	1	0.49
Commercial containers	42	20.69
Table glass	35	17.24
Stemware	17	8.37
Unid.	7	3.45
Salt	6	2.96
Tumbler	4	1.97
Butter dish	1	0.49
Pharmaceuticals	33	16.26
Unid.	2	0.99
Total	**203**	**100.00**

DISCUSSION

Archaeology, which concerns itself perhaps most often with the study of material culture, is a useful research tool for addressing various aspects of historic period consumer behavior patterns (see Henry 1991; LeeDecker 1991; Klein 1991; Klein and LeeDecker 1991). Newspapers, merchant daybooks, commercial documents, and the like can provide data on consumerism at a broad community level, but archaeology provides the kind of household-specific information that is by and large unobtainable from the documentary record (Hardesty and Little 2000:120). What people are said to have bought and what they actually bought or what the consumer use of those goods was may not be one and the same.

But while the presence or absence of particular ware types and decorative styles can be used as temporal indicators of site occupation or general markers of the somewhat elusive idea of "socioeconomic status," this part of the analysis should be a means to an end, not an end in itself. Scientists of course want to characterize the nature of collections as accurately as possible, but as humanists it is imperative to include a discussion of the symbolic meaning behind the patterns we discern. The most critical informational value that artifacts have lies not just in what they can tell us about dates and purchasing power, but in what they might have meant to the people who made and used them and how they would have been mobilized in social action to make statements about who those people thought they were; who they wanted to be; how they saw themselves; and how they strived to be seen.

FIG. 29. An array of specialized drinking vessels recovered archaeologically from the Royall House grounds. Tea, port, coffee or chocolate, and punch are all represented. The porcelain teacup at the far left stems from the Yung Cheng Dynasty (1727–33) and indicates the Royalls' adoption of the tea ceremony long before it was very accessible. Goodwin (1999:131) attributes the new custom of punch drinking and toasting—represented here by the tin-glazed earthenware punch bowl to the right and the air-twisted port glasses and wheel-engraved tumbler—to an Asian influence. In the colonies it was incorporated into public and semipublic alcohol consumption. (Goodwin 1999:131; photograph by author.)

The principal shortcoming or pitfall of consumer behavior studies that focus only on the temporal and economic information of artifacts is that they suffer from what might be called a drastic underconceptualization of the individual (Cowgill 1993:551). That is, they overlook material culture as a medium of communication. With notable exceptions (for example, Beaudry et al. 1991; Cook et al. 1996; Orser 1996; Wall 1992), commodities are typically treated as objects acquired for use and then disposed of. Meanwhile the consumers themselves are cast as "faceless blobs"—if they are cast at all (Tringham, quoted in Cowgill 1993:560). Colonial period consumption, for example, is often explained as a function of accessibility or market availability, or sometimes of the rather abstract and amorphous concept of "socioeconomic status" (Cook et al. 1996:51), where facile equations between social and economic status are made, though the two are really not the same. We saw this with the example of Andrew Hall, who was rich, to be sure, but was not equipped to move in a rich man's circles. It is also often assumed that both social status and economic status will have specific archaeological correlates that can be "read" from the material record or that ethnicity too can be given an index value, provided enough samples. Archaeologists have for some time now, however, been grappling with the reality that things such as culture, identity, social relations, or status cannot be mapped in any one-to-one fashion in the ground.

And indeed material culture should be conceptualized as the medium, not just the outcome, of social action. It structures and perpetuates social relations as much as reflects them. If we accept Hodder's contention (1986:1) that culture is "meaningfully constituted," strictly economic, rational-actor models for why people bought what they bought are profoundly unsatisfactory. The question of real interest for us here, then, is not just whether the widow Grace Knight, the Halls, or the Royalls entertained guests over a cup of tea but what it meant to them if they did—and what it meant to them if they did not.

Isaac, Sr.'s account book shows preparations for his New Year's Eve party in 1737 (Account Book:Dec. 29). On December 29 he hired two extra coaches, posted a parcel of letters, bought lemons, oysters, and gallons of Madeira and Vidona wine. I imagine that a slave had polished the brass sconces and gilt-framed mirrors to a high shine in the best and front rooms, whose pocket doors had been opened to connect the two. That evening the mirrors and brass must have captured the candlelight and reflected it in a warm glow, catching the guests' eyes and flushed cheeks as they arrived from the midwinter cold. The wine and punch glasses would have sparkled. The lemons heaped in a bowl on the table ("Citrus in winter!," perhaps the guests remarked), the trays of oysters, the dozens of colorfully enameled porcelain dishes, and the black faces of the slaves who stood silently along the walls, waiting to jump at the master's call, would have shown dully in the candlelight. Isaac, Sr., might have raised his hand in a toast— to King George, to family, to absent friends and new acquaintances—perhaps uttered a witticism that sent rippling laughter through the room, assuring all that they were indeed in the presence of as fine a man as any in the province. He then might have signaled his musicians (sometimes slaves from other estates would be hired for this sort of affair) and called for the dancing to commence.

The costly imported wine was probably brought out with a studiously unaffected flair, that everyone might casually notice how it was bottled with the family crest and motto stamped on the front: "Pectore Puro" (Pure of Heart; see figs. 30 and 31). Three sheaves of wheat stand on a shield, perhaps an allusion to British landed aristocracy, or perhaps even to the family's broadly agrarian background, modestly implying that Isaac was a simple man, a farmer—salt of the earth, unconcerned by the fortune with which he was blessed. Isaac, Jr., could not claim such humble beginnings himself, but in the absence of an American aristocracy, there was an aesthetic of the self-made man unique to the colonies. The elaborate tomb erected for his carpenter grandfather was evidence that his

FIG. 30. Remains of several chamfer-cornered liquor bottles with the Royall seal.

FIG. 31. A close-up of the seal stamped on a similar bottle and a drawing of the same seal to show detail. Five such seals and countless similar bottles were recovered from the outbuilding foundations. Isaac, Sr., also used a printed version of the seal on the inner cover of his books, some of which survive from his original library at the Royall House today.

father, and probably he as well, was proud of where they had come from and what their family had been able to accomplish. While Isaac, Jr., himself would never have sullied a lace sleeve with physical labor, he might have liked thinking he came from men who had. His father had started with six acres of land, and now here they were with more than 1,000 (Middlesex County Probate 1778).

The Royall seal seems to allude to modest parentage, but only insofar as it contrasted sharply with the Royalls' acquired station. In claiming a simple past, they were loudly illustrating how grand they had become. At the same time, on the seal a lion rears on its hind legs above the shield—a symbol since medieval times of purity, bravery, strength, and royalty—and it seems to claim the fortune with unabashed self-assurance. Such symbols were not lightly used. The allusions were purposeful and significant. They would have been understood and accepted as self-evident among the Royalls' colleagues and peers, who were finely tuned and trained to read such subtleties and nuances as they would any written text.

To ignore or dismiss the "esteem value" of an artifact in favor of its "use value" or "exchange value" (Orser 1996:192) because it is thought to be irretrievable or, worse, irrelevant, not only misses half of the story, but the true essence of commodities in the first place. The fact of the matter is that commodities—even industrially manufactured and globally distributed ones—have multiply inscribed meanings that archaeologists must work hard to tweeze out. They may mean one thing on the factory floor that lends itself well to price indexing and comprehensive TPQ lists today (see Glossary; Miller et al. 2000), but they would have acquired other meanings entirely through the context of their acquisition and use by the individual consumers who once used them. These meanings would have been fluid, not fixed, and the alternative transformations in meaning undergone by commodities as they were consumed would have allowed them to become active components in an individual's creation and presentation of self (Cook et al. 1996:55). Consumption itself—the very act of shopping—*is* agency, influenced by a combination of self-identity and -perception, intention, and the object's own utilitarian function (Cook et al. 1996). In the remains that historical consumers such as Grace Knight, Andrew Hall, or Isaac Royall leave behind, then, they communicate with us not just about their status or when they lived there, but about their ideas and ideals and their daily taken-for-granteds.

The Rules of Polite Behavior

The rise in the number of different kinds of material culture, as retrieved from the Royall House grounds and supported by Royall family documents, indicates the need for an escalating knowledge of the proper rules of polite use associated with each form. The proliferation in the rules of civility from medieval times to the Enlightenment was marked and indicative of deep social changes at work. One can easily imagine the age-old scenario of a commoner, posing as something he or she is not in society, being embarrassingly exposed when faced with not one but three forks at dinner, playing out perfectly at an 18th-century table. Forks, of course, however, were a relatively new item at that time, and a commoner would have been bewildered by their use at all (fig. 32). It is also unlikely that a commoner would ever have made it to a rich man's table in the first place, for the rules of 18th-century politesse were both intricate and rigid.

The Royalls might have spent over £240 (9 percent of their total expenditures, not counting what they paid for slaves and poor relations) on clothes and accessories in their first year in Medford alone, but clothes alone did not make the man. Meals were segmented into individual servings with special-purpose tools and vessels. For instance, in 1729 LaSalle prescribed no fewer than three utensils at each place setting (each with its function explicitly defined), a plate instead of a trencher, and napkins for a "polite" table (quoted in Shackel 1992:209).

All of the Royalls' plate and table linens were in matching sets of 8 or 12, allowing each individual of a rather large group to have his or her own table setting. In addition there were teapots, coffeepots, fish dishes, fruit plates, custard cups, soup tureens, and butter boats—none of which could have served the purpose of another. The use in the 18th century of an increasingly broad spectrum of objects—from a proliferation of drinking and dining equipment, to scientific, mechanical, and/or manufactured items such as musical instruments, clocks, globes, barometers, surveying equipment, spyglasses, or sundials—served to standardize, segment, and rationalize daily routines and behavior (Leone and Shackel 1987:51).

When Isaac Royall, Jr., swallowed the last of his morning chocolate, dabbed the corners of his mouth, set his red damask napkin down, and looked at the clock on his way out the door to survey his prodigious grounds and check on the progress of the day's work thus far, he was implicitly reinforcing his own notion of the order of things. He was the central figure in his own mental play, in which the proliferation of material things around him served as only so many props. In this way, even as the girls went off to their needlepoint or spinet playing and his wife went to the kitchen to dictate the day's menu and House Peter (perhaps the same Peter who was sent with him to Boston as a child in 1726) helped him into his great coat, and even as he finally set out on horseback alone—down the long avenue of elms leading to the road—he was still being conspicuous, if only to himself. From his elevated seat on horseback, he might have contemplated the vista he encountered—his land, nearly to the horizon—and the obsequious bowings and scrapings of his slaves as he came upon them at work, and he might have reflected that this was what he had been born to. In every direction he turned was evidence of his rightful ownership of land and men, even as its days were numbered.

Fig. 32. Iron and bone-handled flatware from the Royall House, conserved.

Summary

The 18th century in America was a time of growing reliance on the visual symbols of material things to navigate the rapidly changing social and economic environments. The rise of an artisan and merchant middle class made American colonial society upwardly mobile for the first time and resulted in efforts by some of the upper class to make class distinctions more intricate and rigid. The adoption of a vast array of new and luxury objects, as well as a bewildering growth in the rules of etiquette that dictated their use, assured the elite of its unassailable social position, even as its economic one was continuously undermined by the violently fluctuating colonial economy, and astute observers such as Isaac Royall, Sr., could learn the rules and enter the elite on the sly. The manipulation of the material world has always been a powerful way to make social statements about position and group belonging, but this was used in the 18th century more rigorously than ever before. Such statements could be used to forge one relationship and hinder another.

The rules were not, however, universal. Within this larger explanatory context, it was the personal agendas, fears, and desires of actual people with "subjective, local, and fleeting" histories that were most important in influencing these people's actions (Barrett 1994:2). How one chose to manipulate the material things around one, and what statements one chose to make in a social discourse, often reflected the values and attitudes one got from one's social class and/or occupational subculture, as well as the particular social discourse in which one was engaging. Isaac Royall, Sr., provides an example of how the material world could be manipulated not just to reflect the self (presumed fixed and inevitable), but to actually redefine it, making identity a fluid phenomenon, ever-changing in the face of an equally dynamic Other.

The Royalls were part of a specific social discourse that was historically derived and individually motivated but also informed by the larger forces and processes that governed their society. Isaac, Sr., used material culture to make a new identity for himself. Every china set, every book in his library, probably served as a reminder to him of just how far he had come. Isaac, Jr., on the other hand, used these things to enhance his already-high position, perhaps taking them for granted. He took pleasure, by his own contemporaries' accounts, in showing himself wealthier and more fashionable and more at the heart of things—and thus even more deserving of his riches—than his respected father had been. Both chose to define themselves in opposition to their humble family beginnings.

In order to achieve this, they would have found within the confines of Ten Hills Farm a microcosmic mirror of the universe at large. They would have seen the order of things right in front of them; they would have incorporated it into their daily lives and interpreted it as their individual needs, desires, and histories dictated. But this perception and projection of self would also have been a never-ending work in progress, constantly adjusting to contradictions and new challenges from various "Others." They represented the highest end of the spectrum only insofar as their many slaves represented the lowest. With every material statement they made about who they were, there was an equal but opposite statement, unspoken but understood all the same, about who they were not.

Historical and archaeological research at the Royall House has revealed many of the material statements of power the Royalls chose to use on their own behalf, and it has hinted at some of the idiosyncratic influences that might have affected their decision-making processes in that. It is also more than just an interesting parochial tale, however; for in the isolated particulars of the Royalls' story, we gain potential insight into the ascendancy of an entire class.

Chapter 5

BLACK BETTY AND HER CHILDREN AND THE TRAGEDY OF GEORGE: BLACK FAMILY AND MASTER-SLAVE RELATIONS AT TEN HILLS FARM

They were noble souls; they not only possessed loving hearts, but brave ones. . . . I never loved any or confided in any people more than my fellow-slaves. . . . I believe we would have died for each other. We never undertook to do any thing, of any importance, without a mutual consultation. We never moved separately. We were one; and as much so by our tempers and dispositions, as by the mutual hardships to which we were necessarily subjected by our condition as slaves.

—FREDERICK DOUGLASS
ON SLAVE COMMUNITY, 1845

I have no language to express the high excitement and deep anxiety which were felt among us. . . . A single word from the white men was enough—against all our wishes, prayers, and entreaties—to sunder forever the dearest friends, dearest kindred, and strongest ties.

—FREDERICK DOUGLASS ON THE PSYCHOLOGICAL
EFFECTS OF ESTATE DIVISION, 1845

Creating Identities—Private Personae in the Quarter

In my various interactions with Medford locals and community members during the course of excavations or at public presentations, I frequently encountered a sentiment likely quite common among the general public. It takes no significant amount of imagination to see that archaeology might be an important tool for finding out about the daily lives of slaves. But when it comes to the Royalls, it is perhaps not readily apparent what archaeology really has to offer. What could it reveal to us about these historically very "visible" people that we did not already know? As one prominent historical archaeologist and writer, Carmel Schrire, wrote, in *Digging through Darkness* (1995:111), "This frames the question wrongly. The issue is not what new facts were revealed but what new emphases were stressed."

It was this vein—finding new emphases—that led in the last chapter to casting the physical world in a new light: not as lifeless, or even silent, but as actively engaged in social life, another actor or player, if you will, in daily human drama. Discussions there presented artifacts, architecture, and landscape as communicators of self and social relations, inscribed with the attitudes, values, and ideals of the people who inhabited that world.

The Royalls arguably provide an example of how material things were manipulated not just to reflect identities but to recast them according to personal fears, desires, and aspirations. It was this cultural fluency that made it possible for an ambitious carpenter's son to use material statements of legitimacy—porcelain tea sets, a commanding house, or symmetrical pleasure gardens—to achieve access to the highest levels of society.

Ironically, though, the material world does not discriminate. Anybody can communicate with objects, and indeed everybody does, on conscious as well as unconscious levels. The obvious question that remains for us here, then, is this: as the Royalls were building mansions and formal gardens; toasting each other with rum, punch, and wine; and importing coffee, tea, and chocolate, what symbolic world were slaves creating (Ferguson 1991 [1996]:262)? For we can be sure that the Royalls' slaves were also communicating with material symbols, negotiating their own identities in a liminal space somewhere between how they defined themselves and how they were defined by others.

Identity, says Wilkie (2000:4), is the way that individuals "define and present" themselves, but also how they are defined and perceived by others. Because identity has multiple components—such as race, gender, kinship relations, age, occupation, or socioeconomic status (Wilkie 2000:6)—that depend to some extent on the different circumstances, settings, and players involved in each encounter, identity is constantly being negotiated. It is continually constructed from within and imposed from without. We have seen some of the ways that enslaved people's identities as slaves were imposed from the outside by white society, but historical archaeology offers a more intimate portrait of how these people might have constructed identities as individuals in the privacy of their families and the quarter community. While public personae are often partially externally imposed, private personae are usually created by and for oneself (Wilkie 2000:225) and based or centered in the private interactions and encounters of the household and family. Daily routines, practices, and experiences in the home shaped the way private personae were created. Wilkie (2000:164) says that "Meanings become embedded in the mundane tasks of everyday existence: cooking, work, childcare, eating, dressing. People become who they are through the ways that they engage in those activities."

The yards surrounding the Royall House slave quarters had not only the most prolific number of artifacts and features at the site, but many of the deposits there could also be linked to the Royall period of occupation, and several artifacts recovered from these areas seem to open a window onto the more intimate personal, family, and spiritual lives of the people enslaved there. In particular, small trash pits and the stone-lined foundation hole of a small outbuilding in the west yard, as well as sheet refuse from the east and south yards, have yielded artifacts reflective not only of work, but also of leisure time activities, childhood, craftsmanship, personal adornment and self-presentation, folk religion, and possibly healthcare. Such artifacts contribute to an archaeological portrait of these components of African American identity, and in many ways they seem to indicate some of the ways that the Royalls' slaves attempted to live decently as human beings despite the realities imposed by their legal status as slaves. Some of these components of their identity might have assumed particular importance because of their status as slaves, as a means of coping with the challenges and dangers of being human property, whose fate was ultimately subject to the whims, uncertainties, and foibles of another. As such they are less indicative of African ethnic traditions than they are material markers of just what constituted the color line in 18th-century Massachusetts.

Indian Summer

Jemmy was first awake in the kitchen chamber. He, his two brothers, and one of his sisters were crammed cross-wise on one of the beds. He looked across the room and saw his mama, Abba, and oldest sister, Betty, sharing the other. They had both been up late again, knitting eleven pairs of warm stockings for the family. These mild September days, everyone knew from last year, were deceptive. Abba and Betty worked on them whenever they had a spare moment during the day, but nighttime was always spent taking care of family, and many were the mornings when Jemmy awoke to see his mama still slumped in a chair over her sewing or some such other task, buttons scattered at her feet. He knew how late they had been up this time because he had hardly been able to sleep himself.

He grinned in anticipation and snuck down the servant stairs to the kitchen below where he saw his four aunts and uncles still breathing heavily on beds fitted haphazardly into corners and behind tables, so that there was hardly space to step. Uncle John seemed to be getting a little too big for his bed, thought Jemmy, mirthfully noting the way his uncle seemed to overpower the little structure and the way his big feet just didn't seem to fit, no matter which way he tried. Jemmy scanned the possibilities in his mind of startling him right off his precarious perch but thought better of it in the end. Uncle John had grown long arms and a short temper since he and some of the other boys from the kitchen quarters had started work last year.

Instead Jemmy simply knelt by the hearth and shoved his hands into the ash—soft, and still warm from last night's fire. At last his wriggling finger-tips located the smooth surfaces of several hard little spheres, and he let out a muffled sound of glee. He raked them out and blew the ash away. A handful of red marbles, all different sizes, sat in his palm. He inspected his handiwork and then, because he couldn't help himself, he placed the shooter between thumb and forefinger and flicked it across the wooden floor, where it rattled its way (in a straight line, he noted with satisfaction) across the room and clicked against the leg of a chair. Uncle John let out an angry grumble, swatting at the air as if he could bat the sound right out of it. Time was, Jemmy thought, when Uncle John would have wanted to play marbles with him. Jemmy had rolled them himself the night before from a lump of clay he and his brother, Jacob, and friend, Tobey, from the quarters, had gathered on one of their adventures down by the riverbanks. Usually they were supposed to be doing something like finding starter sticks for the fire or taking lunch and water out to the men in the orchards, or even buffing Master Royall's buttons and buckles to a high shine. Last week, Jemmy had helped shoe the horses. Uncle Smith said nobody could pick out just exactly the right nail every time like he could! But in between such chores, there was always time to explore. . . .

Looking out the window, Jemmy saw Gran in the courtyard, the stub of her old red tobacco pipe clenched between her teeth, as she hauled the water up from the well with her sinewy, still-powerful arms. She had been the one to show them how fire magically transformed clay. He could hardly think of a time when she did not have that thing either stuffed in the corner of her mouth or slipped in the waistband of her dress. Even in later years, the rich, dark, and musty-sweet scent of tobacco would still smell to Jemmy of bright teeth and dark, sensible eyes.

Lightly steaming pans of milk already standing on the table told him that Gran had been up for some time. He dipped a small finger in the cream that was accumulating on the top. He should have known she would be up already. Today was bath day, and the whole household was getting scrubbed, whether they liked it or not. She would be hauling water for hours. Jemmy *knew where he was going to be: out of reach. He retrieved the marble by the chair, stuffed the whole collection into his pocket, and peered out the kitchen door, one foot over the threshold. While Gran was settling the weight of two large buckets over her shoulders, Jemmy raced silently on unshod feet around to the back of the kitchen quarter, where there sat Tobey, lining up each of his new marbles in a row, smallest to largest, in the dirt-swept yard. Jemmy grabbed a stick and flopped to his knees in front of his friend, his own marbles held out in the palm of his hand, ready for inspection. He raked the stick around in an arc, inscribing a large circle in the yellow dirt. Tobey dumped the marbles in the circle, and both boys stood up, held their newly made shooters to the tip of their noses, looked at each other and giggled, and let them drop. Tobey's landed closest to the edge of the circle without going outside the ring. Once again they fell to their knees. "Okay," said Jemmy. "You go first. . . ."*

It Begins

Isaac Royall, Sr., passed peacefully from the world June 7, 1739, at the age of 67 (Maine Historical Society n.d.; *Boston Gazette* 1739:4–11 June). He had tried to live a virtuous life, and in his tombstone's epitaph his death was said to have been lamented by all who knew him (see page 98). There was great grief in the garrets above the master bedroom where he had died, as well, in the kitchen chamber across the hall, in the kitchen downstairs, and in the out kitchen out back, where anxious whisperings and murmurings were likely made among the slaves when they thought nobody was by. They might have met at night or gotten together in the kitchen, work yards, or the orchards, when they had an opportunity, to talk in strained voices about what all knew was coming. They might have speculated out loud about which of Master Royall's children would be their new master or mistress. Who would go with Master Royall's stepdaughter, Anne, to Dorchester? Who would be left to his daughter, Mistress Penelope, fifteen years old and soon of marriageable age, thereafter to go who knows where? Who would stay here at Ten Hills Farm with young Master Royall? Would any of them be sold? They might have discussed too what each person's chances were of being separated from family. Would they be able to keep their children with them? Would husbands be allowed to go with wives? The former slave John Brown remembered the great sorrow in the slave quarters that accompanied the death of a master or mistress; he said, "The women who had young children cried very much. My mother did, and took to kissing us a good deal oftener" (quoted in Webber 1978:114). And as the legalities of will execution and estate division dragged on, the anxiety probably grew palpable; rumors might have flown, imaginations run wild; tempers flared, and many tears been shed. Those in the slave quarters might have turned hopeful eyes to the house servants, who were often important sources of information for the enslaved community, for any word on the goings-on and conversations in the great house that might put an end to the insufferable not knowing (Webber 1978:227–28). And when the Royalls' "people" were finally called together, perhaps in the cobbled courtyard between the great house and the quarters and perhaps by Master Royall's son and heir, Isaac, Jr., to be informed of their fate, the dread, fear, and grief must have been great.

Reconstructing Family and Community

When Ulrich Phillips (1929:199) first wrote about the early black community in the old South, he portrayed an inferior culture gradually becoming civilized through contact with whites. Once in the New World, he hypothesized, blacks eventually forgot Africa and adapted to white ways. The sociologist E. Franklin Frazier (1939) also saw a slow assimilation of blacks into white culture—led by house servants, artisans, and people of mixed heritage—but attributed it not so much to the inferiority of the originating African cultures per se as to the brutality of enslavement in the New World. The influences of slavery in North America, he argued, "completely stripped" blacks of their social heritage there and tended to make them "take over the attitudes and sentiments of his master toward religion, sex, and marriage, and the other relations of life" (Frazier 1939:21, 35). Thirty years later Daniel P. Moynihan (1965:4—5) identified a purported "deterioration of the Negro family" as the "single most important social fact of the United States today"—which he also supposed to be rooted in the peculiar brutality of North American slavery. He documented a veritable "tangle of pathology" in 1960s lower-class black America that he argued was a disaster of epic proportions and the direct result of three centuries of oppression and exploitation (Moynihan 1965:29).

Though they were writing in different decades, within different social and political milieus—from Jim Crow to the civil rights movement—and had differing agendas for their research, these authors had in common a reactive model for African American family and community formation. In these portrayals enslaved and free black society was a tepid reflection or outright perversion of white society, caused either by blacks' own intellectual and cultural inferiority or by their victim status in their systematic exclusion from the mainstream. More recent scholarship has suggested, however, that the African American family under slavery, while perhaps individually unstable, was never crippled as an institution, and these early scholars had drastically "underestimated the adaptive capacities of the enslaved" (Gutman 1976: xxi). Family continued to serve as a mechanism for the education and socialization of children into the realities of slavery and as such was the crucible for a developing African American folk culture that was not disorganized and reactive, but rather "cohesive" and "indigenous" (Kulikoff 1986:335, 357; Gutman 1976:36). For anthropologists this is significant, for it means that in family lies the key to culture.

Unfortunately the process of family formation among the charter generations of Africans and Creoles is, of necessity, largely conjectural. Many scholars agree, however, that the slave system set the outward bounds of slave family activities, and the possibilities and opportunities open to them, but that it was Africans and their descendants who gave actual meaning to the relationships between parents and children, among siblings, or in a more extended kin network (see Gutman 1976; Kulikoff 1974, 1978, 1986; Lee 1986). "As they interacted daily among themselves," writes Kulikoff (1978:227), "slaves learned to cope with ordinary problems of working, eating, marrying, and childrearing under the conditions of slavery."

What is unclear, however, is how accurately the lives of most 17th- and 18th-century slaves, obscured through time and tradition, can be reconstructed in the first place (Lee 1986:337). A broad range of variables further complicates the situation. How and why did specific institutions emerge in particular areas? How might the demographic and economic structures of a place have affected, limited, or encouraged the specific social and cultural forms that slaves were able to create there? What was the timescale for such a process, and did it proceed at different rates in different environments? These are questions we find are often impossible to answer, but this should not stop our asking.

Alan Kulikoff's studies of the Chesapeake contain several key points of relevance to the issues at stake in New England and deserve mention. Kulikoff (1974:173ff.; 1978:228; 1986:317–319) isolates four key factors influencing early Africans' ability to establish viable families and communities in the colonial Chesapeake: the size of the working units; the density of the black population; the pattern of African immigration and natural increase; and the proportion of blacks to whites in the area. Other factors, such as the master's economic strategy and particular rules and attitudes or the male to female sex ratio in the area would have made for slower or faster community development, more or less stable family lives, or varying degrees of African influences in the resulting regional black culture (Kulikoff 1986).

Kulikoff (1974) also argues that enslaved black family structure on the eve of the Revolution was different from both African and European American family systems and had, of necessity, derived in part from adaptations to the slave order; that the Africans who made up New World slave populations were far too diverse for a recreation of West African kinship systems in the New World to be possible; but that 18th-century slaves did at least continue to conceive of kinship as the principal way of structuring their social relations with others in their community (Kulikoff 1974:173; see also Mintz and Price 1976:35). The ability of Africans to create stable family lives, though, he sees principally as a function of the economic and demographic variables of the region (Kulikoff 1974:172; Kulikoff 1978, 1986). For example he finds that the first two out of three demographic stages he identifies in Tidewater Maryland and Virginia made the 17th and early 18th centuries in that area "hostile to most forms of family life" (Kulikoff 1974:173–74).

In the period 1650–90, blacks made up roughly 3 percent of the population in the Chesapeake, usually lived on small plantations with fewer than 11 slaves, and were almost all immigrants from the West Indies, all of which Kulikoff claimed led to less black autonomy and greater assimilation into European-American culture (Kulikoff 1978:229). In addition he cited the sex ratios that showed men outnumbered women two to one during this period to suggest that these early Africans would have had difficulty establishing a regular family life (Kulikoff 1978:231; see also Morgan 1998:4). The importance of kinship as a concept was probably never forgotten or diminished in the minds of the enslaved, but Mintz and Price (1976:37) argue that in certain situations, such as the one described above, there might have been "practical limits" to an individual's ability to establish a kin network where the relative stability and continuity necessary for family and community formation were "the exception rather than the rule."

The conditions identified for the Chesapeake were markedly different from those in the lowcountry at the same time (see Gomez 1998; Morgan 1998; Wood 1974), where blacks were the majority in every sense of the word (total numbers, pace of immigration, and rate of natural increase) by the 1720s (Wood 1974:145). The land and labor exigencies of rice cultivation saw to it that enslaved Africans were held in large units with little white interference or interaction, although Stevenson (1996:159–60) cautions that even though large slaveholdings are often thought to have afforded domestic stability and promoted nuclear family formation and monogamous marriage, they are "hardly indicative" of such. Meanwhile opportunities for family life in the early-18th-century Chesapeake were tenuous and even dismal (Morgan 1998:503).

Things worsened for Africans in the Chesapeake in the period 1690–1740, as heavy black immigration led to greater white oppression and frequent conflict among the slaves themselves. Infusions of new Africans were supposed to have disrupted fledgling black social institutions (Kulikoff 1978:243–44). But in the period 1740–90 important demographic changes took place that would have made the region more conducive to family life, the establishment of widespread kin networks, and the emergence of a settled African American community life (Kulikoff 1974:175ff.; 1978:245ff.). Among these were a sharp decline in immigration and corresponding increase in the native-born population that resulted in a more natural demographic curve and the presumed beginnings of a Creole generation; increasing plantation size with many more people living in groups of 20 or more; increasing overall black population density; better road systems that allowed more frequent and easier travel between communities; and the sale, transfer, or migration of slaves over time that disrupted the composition of particular households but could scatter family members and friends over an entire county or region and help to develop widespread kin and community networks (Kulikoff 1974:175ff.). By the 1770s, he claims, most adult slaves in the Chesapeake would have been able to marry and would often have had grandparents and great-grandparents who were native born (Kulikoff 1978:249).

Kulikoff's description of the 17th- and early-18th-century Chesapeake closely resembles the economic and demographic characteristics of 18th-century New England, while the ameliorating circumstances he then contrasts it with in the period between 1740 and 1790 were only partially present in New England. For example the 18th century saw the construction of more and better roads in Medford in response to its growing importance as a hub for trade and travel (Seaburg and Seaburg 1980:14); Royall family papers do document the dispersal of families through sale and transfer across several farms and townships; and Piersen (1988:170–73) shows an increasing black population density in New England, particularly in urban and coastal areas. On the other hand, the overall proportion of blacks in the population was still very low (Piersen 1988:166–69), while African imports, in Boston at least, were demonstrably at their highest in the 1740s (Bower 1991:60), so that in 1750 fully half the slave population was still foreign born (Piersen 1988:18).

Meanwhile the sex ratios in Massachusetts did not even approximate a natural demographic curve (MHC Collections 1754); and there were almost no New England masters outside of Rhode Island who owned more than ten people. It may also be that Kulikoff has exaggerated blacks' ability to build stable community life even in the latter period. The rates of demographic change that Kulikoff bases his three-stage argument on have not been established, while population statistics often leave historians with little notion of how raw numbers were dispersed geographically, let alone what the specific family connections were among individuals (Lee 1986:337). Indeed the argument may be moot, for in comparison with, say, Jamaica, or even 19th-century Russian serfdom, all North American slaveholdings were relatively small and thus restricted the possibility for enslaved people to lead "autonomous lives" in any real sense of the word (Kolchin 1983:584). On small farms of 5–10 slaves, or even 20–30 slaves, people often had to marry abroad or not marry at all; in either case family stability was compromised (Kolchin 1983:588). Given all of the above considerations in the

Chesapeake, the question presents itself, could colonial Massachusetts also be said to have been "hostile to most forms of family life?" What were the "practical limits" of family and community formation in the 18th-century Boston area?

Regardless of population statistics that indicate that New England in the colonial period was never more than about 2–3 percent black (Piersen 1988:166ff.), slavery in New England was neither insignificant nor inconsequential, and there really might not have been quite the isolation that those numbers imply. From 1700 to 1750 the black population increased by 50 percent each decade, compared with only a 30 percent corresponding population increase among whites (Piersen 1988:18). Half of Massachusetts' entire enslaved population of roughly 2,700 adults lived in Boston and surrounding Suffolk County in 1754, while Boston itself was at least 10 percent black from the 1740s on (Piersen 1988:15). Africans and their American descendants then were arguably becoming an increasingly sizable and visible component of daily life, at least in Massachusetts. The clustering in maritime and urbanized counties and townships was important because it enabled blacks to interact with other blacks, both American and foreign born, and allowed them against all white efforts to the contrary to create a subculture of community feeling to draw upon. In truth there was no other way for such a subculture to emerge in a region that was so statistically white. An enslaved person in Boston, for example, would probably have had little difficulty congregating with others of his or her station even if he or she was the only unfree person in her master's particular household. Evidence that this was so can be seen in the annual election of black "kings" and "governors" in New England by fellow bondsmen, which took the form of public celebrations, parades, and general public tumult. Piersen (1988:123–24) particularly describes the "bustle of the holiday" in Boston and the "rowdy army of revelers attracted to the black activities on the common" every May. He quotes a poem composed circa 1760 about the polyglot crowds and the level of revelry that accompanied Boston's black election days:

> The city swarms with every sort
> Of black and white, and every sort
> Of high, low, rich and poor;
> Squaws, negroes, deputies in scores
> And ministers and Counsellors
> Are seen at every door.
>
> Long before Phoebus looks upon
> The outskirts of the horizon,
> The blacks their forces summon.
> Tables & Benches, chairs, & stools

Rum-bottles, Gingerbread & bowls
Are lug'd into the common.

Thither resorts a motley crew,
Of whites & Blacks & Indians too
And trulls of every sort.
There all day long they sit & drink,
Swear, sing, play paupaw, dance and stink
There Baccus holds his court.

Thus, urban and maritime centers were probably a good setting for the emergence of vibrant African American subcultures. The many and various acts and resolves previously reviewed that were enacted by white legislators in the 18th century to control the most troubling manifestations of these alley societies, as well as contemporary newspaper reports describing their doings, bear witness to the fact. The documents also suggest, though, that full participation in such subcultures would not have been possible for people held in servitude outside these clustered populations and that even in areas with relatively large black populations, the demographic profile was such that even alley society did not function as a normal community in the 18th century. The 1754 Massachusetts slave census indicates, for example, that even in areas such as Middlesex and Suffolk counties, which did have sizeable black populations, men still outnumbered women almost two to one, while in smaller towns such as Medford, they outnumbered them by three or four to one, and in Shirley, Acton, or Walpole, a single adult might represent the entire enslaved population of the town, male or female (MHC Collections 1754; tables 3 and 4). What that means in practical terms is that only half of Massachusetts' enslaved men had any hope of finding wives and establishing stable family lives, such as they could be, under slavery, even without the added isolation of rural living.

The per-family ownership rate among New England masters was also very low, rarely exceeding five people, which, as suggested above, might not have posed much of a problem in Boston, given the "sprawling comradeship, if not kinship" of even small slaveholdings (Stevenson 1996:173), but would have been a considerable obstacle in the country, where the majority of one's daily social interactions would have been with members of one's own household. Kulikoff (1978:240) in fact, in looking at plantation contexts, claims that settled black social life would have been difficult or impossible on plantations whose quarters housed fewer than ten slaves, while Fox-Genovese (1988:295) states that only households of 20 or more enslaved individuals could provide a solid basis for slave community life.

In truth, though, the number of people was really not as important as having all of what Lee calls the five gender and age categories on the plantation;

only with a wide demographic spectrum could the "full range of daily contacts occur" (Lee 1986:352). Where that spectrum did not exist, enslaved people were forced to lead a "truncated existence of one kind or another" (Lee 1986:352): children without regular parental supervision or any black adult role models at all; adults without children or spouses; older people without younger ones to educate, instruct, and advise; and younger people without elders from whom to seek guidance, comfort, or support.

Reconstructing Family at Ten Hills Farm

The Royalls were not slaveholders of the sort that might have been found in various parts of the South and the Caribbean, where slaveholdings could number in the hundreds and in fact a single plantation could contain the entire population of Medford in 1736. But nor did anyone in Massachusetts ever own more slaves than they. Throughout their tenure in that colony and by any standard of measurement, the Royalls were quite important with much property. The names and appraised values of many of the people the Royalls owned were recorded in Isaac Royall, Sr.'s probate inventory in 1739. Others were listed in the 1754 Massachusetts slave census as taxable property. In that document the Royalls were reported as having 12 slaves over the age of 16 in Medford, listing seven men and five women; Captain Thomas Brooks and Squire Hall each were reported to have two; and all of the other 18 slaveholders in town were listed with only one (Brooks and Usher 1886:355; refer to table 2). Even having reduced their holdings from an all-time high in 1738 of 38 people, the Royalls were still without equal in the county.

Only the Royalls' enslaved population would have had anything approaching a normal social life at home in Medford. The 1754 slave census shows that only 1.9 percent (n = 23) of the slaves in Suffolk County (which includes Boston) lived in townships with ten or fewer adult slaves in the whole town (MHC Collections 1754; refer to table 4). By contrast fully one out four of the slaves (n = 90) in Middlesex County (which includes Medford) lived under such conditions (MHC Collections 1754; refer to table 3). Outside the city limits of Boston and some of the surrounding townships such as Cambridge, Dorchester, Roxbury, Braintree, or Chelsea—which were the only other towns besides Medford with more than 30 enslaved people—Massachusetts slaves in general were probably not leading full social lives, as defined by Lee (1986), on a regular or continual basis.

There is good reason to believe that the Royalls employed more than just field hands, though, and the nature of some individuals' work might have given them occasion to visit or even spend considerable time in and around Boston or other towns with large black populations. As mentioned, one individual seems to have been "let out" to the Boston baker, Henry Neal, in 1737 (Account Book: June 25), and Nancy was put out "to some good family by the year" in 1776 (quoted in Hoover 1974:83). Another "likely Negro Girl" was advertised for sale in 1756 as being "fit for Town or Country," which probably reflects her role on the Royalls' estate up until that time (*Boston Gazette or Weekly Journal* 1756: March 15).

In addition there was likely one or more boatmen to carry the hay, cider, and wool that were the principal produce of Ten Hills Farm down the Mystic River to Boston, and their trips would probably have kept them in town for two or three days at a time. But while many New England slaves were relatively mobile, such contact with larger black communities would have been temporary and even fleeting. There were many people too who had no reason to leave their masters' estates at all. And even in towns such as Medford that were reasonably important to the regional economy and had many comings and goings from the surrounding area, extended contact with larger, more established black communities, such as the one found in Boston, must have been intermittent at best (Lee 1986:344).

The 34 enslaved people in Medford no doubt knew each other rather well, and several among them at least were probably interrelated through marriage or consanguinity. They likely socialized when the opportunity arose. For their New Year's Eve party in 1737, the Royalls hired "Prince Holm's the Cook" for three days; a year and a half later, they again "pd Prince for dressing victuals at ye farm" (Account Book:Dec. 29, 1737; July 16, 1739). It is entirely possible that Prince the cook was the Prince listed years later as the sole adult slave belonging to Benjamin Hall in 1754 (Brooks and Usher 1886:355). Borrowing, lending, or hiring each other's "people" among the white townspeople would have brought those who were enslaved into more frequent contact. But the fact that more than half of them, such as Prince, were the only adult slaves in their masters' households would also have meant that time at home was isolating. And Medford had one of the largest slave populations in all of Massachusetts.

Regardless of the challenges involved, reconstructing family relationships and the opportunities for, as well as challenges to, creating them, remains one of the crucial first steps in trying to understand the experiences of the enslaved in Massachusetts. Their ability or inability to create family would have structured their experience under, and adaptation to, slavery. On the other hand, even among the Royalls' own holdings, the opportunities for family and community life would not have been uniform.

The Royalls, as mentioned, kept people at their Stoughton and Freetown estates as well, where the home social life would have been decidedly more restricted than that of the people kept in Medford. The farm at Freetown had only George, a 45 year old worth £100, and an old man about 70 years of age, who apparently had no monetary value (Middlesex County Probate 1739). The

Stoughton household had Captain, who was infirm; Santo, who was lame; "one Negro named old Cook," gender unspecified; and a six-year-old girl (Middlesex County Probate 1739). The people held as slaves in these households might have loved or hated each other, been related by blood, felt family-like ties, or both or neither; they were of course social beings and would have had complex social relationships with all of the individuals, white and black, around them, but they were not leading full social lives at home. Their slave "families" and "community" would have been a more or less functional substitute for the real thing.

In the summer of 1999, archaeologists recovered a small, rounded pebble of un-identified light-colored stone, possibly quartz, from the west yard of the Royall

FIG. 33. A hand-drilled stone bead, recovered from the outbuilding foundation in the west yard of the slave quarters. It might have been worn in the hair or have been one of several similar beads worn as part of a necklace or in a string around the waist. It may be indirect evidence of the transmission of African and Creole ideals of womanhood, from one generation to the next, and might have strengthened symbolic ties of kinship through their physical embodiment in something tangible.

House slave quarters in Medford. Among the jagged-edged brown, gray, and orangey-red pebbles that typified the stone and gravel inclusions on the site, this stone stood out and appeared symmetrical and water worn in contrast. Brushing the dirt away for a closer look revealed that a hole had been hand drilled right through the center. This pebble, perhaps for its unusual characteristics, had been turned into a bead, and might originally have been but one of several (fig. 33).

Clearly reflecting a non-European aesthetic, the stone bead was the first specific artifact at the site to invite a consideration of material expressions of black identity (including family) at the Royall House, and it is a good point of departure here. Many of the ways that Africans and their American descendants expressed themselves are, of course, lost to us. Certain hairstyles, modes of dress, or manners of speaking and working are fleeting and do not preserve in the archaeological record but would have been as integral a part of a person's social environment as any tangible object left to be found by archaeologists. One contemporary observer noted, for example, that it was common among Ibos to talk to their tools while using them—earnestly, as if talking to an old friend (Yentsch 1994:189). More than just a whimsical tale, such observations remind us that some of the most significant ties between people and the objects they used are beyond our reach. Nevertheless the physical characteristics of an artifact can often point toward social meanings the object might once have had.

This particular bead has none of the gay, vibrant colors typically associated with beads from other slave quarters, which were part of an African American woman's "garments of gladness" (John Davis 1803, quoted in Yentsch 1995:52). Beads have long been found at, and associated with, slave sites, and Yentsch (1994, 1995) has situated the role of beads within an African American cultural framework of maintaining ideas of African womanhood. She argues that African American girls wore beads because their mothers and grandmothers had. Dismissed by whites as decorative baubles of the weaker sex, beads became an often unchecked means among African American women of expressing themselves and of forging transgenerational kinship ties in the physical (Yentsch 1995:48–49).

On the other hand, it should not be overlooked that men in many parts of West Africa also wore beads for various cultural, political, and aesthetic reasons at this time (Ogundiran 2002). Indeed beads as prestige goods had played a role in establishing and maintaining social hierarchies and relationships in West Africa since the 11th century and could be mobilized in public arenas as a kind of social and/or political capital—to reaffirm status or consolidate and legitimate power (Ogundiran 2002:433). In this sense beads were very much more than mere personal adornment and were often restricted to persons of authority. Of course, the very act of transporting millions of Africans to the New World would have torn the cultural fabric within which such symbols had originally been used and had significance. Nevertheless, while the Middle Passage and the new cultural context of enslavement would have altered the precise meanings and social valuations of beads, the idea of "beads as peculiarly social objects" may well have continued to signify for Africans and their descendants in the New World. Within an American context of forced servitude, beads could still have generally been understood among the enslaved to distinguish among persons of different status, authority, respectability, or desirability—both for women and for men.

The stone bead recovered from the Royall House is plain, handmade, and somewhat crude in comparison with the various glass, ivory, semiprecious stone, or coral beads found at other American sites. It may be argued, however, that the task of drilling it by hand reveals something of its symbolic importance to the person who made and wore it. As an item of handcraftsmanship and personal adornment, we must assume that this bead—and the labor required to make it—*meant* something. On the one hand it shows pride in personal appearance and would have reaffirmed the basic humanity of the person who wore it. On the other, it might even have served to strengthen ideas about identity or ties of kinship through their embodiment in something tangible. But what were these ideas? Can we talk realistically about enslaved people's ideas about family and identity at this site, 230 years after the last of these people faded from view?

The 1754 Massachusetts slave census (MHC Collections 1754), Royall family probate records (Middlesex County Probate 1739, 1778; Harvard Law Library Special Collections 1778), and town vital records (NEHGS 1907) have helped to reconstruct black family and household composition through time at the Royalls' estate. Family relationships among these people are rarely stated in the documents, and what information there is provides only a static picture, with little notion of the fluid processes involved in the evolution of households and families through time because of marriages, births, deaths, sales, relocations, or gift-transfers. However, table 12 lists all of the enslaved individuals mentioned by name in the Royall family papers and other documents between 1726 and 1778. It does not necessarily contain a full list of all the people the Royalls ever owned, and indeed this is almost assuredly not the case. For example, in 1762 Isaac, Jr., advertised the sale of a family (not necessarily to be sold together) who is seemingly unaccounted for in other documentary sources. He wrote:

A Likely Negro Wench to dispose of, who understands Houshold Business, and something of Cookery: Also Four of said Wench's Children, viz. three Girls and one Boy. (*Boston Evening Post* 1762: March 22)

Such advertisements were made regularly in the local newspapers and suggest a substantially larger number of people who passed through the Royalls' doors than has been reconstructed here. As there can be ambiguity even among individuals identified by name, however (again, see table 12), such anonymous sales were not considered in constructing the table. Meanwhile individuals mentioned only once were counted as having been in the Royalls' service only the year of their mention, though many of them probably stayed longer. It is likely, for example, that Black Betty and all of her family, who were mentioned only in Isaac, Sr.'s 1738 will, had been with the family since their Antigua days and that the family had grown to 11 people while under Royall ownership. The table also gives the minimal duration of each person's service for the Royalls and tells us something of the degree of stability and continuity they experienced and through this some of the challenges they would have faced in establishing long-term family and community ties. Thus documents have provided us with some "raw data"—something of the who, the when, the how long—but it is up to us

TABLE 12.

Slave tenure under the Royalls

Name	First and Last Dates Mentioned (Inclusive)	Min. Tenure in Years	Ultimate Fate
Hector, slave driver	1737	1	Burned alive for conspiracy to revolt
Quaco	1737	1	Banished to Hispaniola for conspiracy to revolt
Ruth	1726–39	14	Unknown
Nan	1726–27	2	Unknown
Cuff	1726–39	14	Unknown
Peter June	1732	1	Sale
Cuffee	1735	1	Unknown
Peter	1726–69	44	Death
Fortune	1725–39	15	Unknown
Captain	1737–39	3	Unknown
Black Betty[a]	1738	1	Gift-transfer
Abba[a]	1738	1	Gift-transfer
Quacoe[a]	1738	1	Gift-transfer
Diana[a]	1738	1	Gift-transfer
John[a]	1738	1	Gift-transfer
Nancy[a]	1738	1	Gift-transfer
Betty[a]	1738	1	Gift-transfer
George[a]	1738	1	Gift-transfer
Sarah[a]	1738	1	Gift-transfer
Jacob[a]	1738	1	Gift-transfer
Jemmy[a]	1738	1	Gift-transfer
Abba[b]	1738	1	Gift-transfer
Robin[b]	1738	1	Gift-transfer
Coba[b]	1738	1	Gift-transfer
Walker[b]	1738	1	Gift-transfer
Nuba[b]	1738	1	Gift-transfer
Trace[b]	1738	1	Gift-transfer
Tobey[b]	1738	1	Gift-transfer
Present	1738	1	Gift-transfer
Cato	1739	1	Unknown
Barron	1739	1	Unknown
Ned	1739	1	Unknown
House Peter	1739	1	Unknown
Robin	1739	1	Unknown
Quamino	1739	1	Unknown
Smith	1739	1	Unknown
Phillip	1739	1	Unknown
Trace	1739	1	Unknown
Sue (Susannah)	1739–58	20	Death
Jonto	1739	1	Unknown
Old Negro Man	1739	1	Unknown
Santo	1739	1	Unknown
Girl, 6 Years of Age	1739	1	Unknown
Old Cook	1739	1	Unknown
George	1739–76	38	Suicide
Abraham	1754–68	15	Death

TABLE 12 (cont.)

Name	First and Last Dates Mentioned (Inclusive)	Min. Tenure in Years	Ultimate Fate
Betsey[c]	1754–76	23	Manumission
Nancy[c]	1754–76	23	Let out
Cooper	1754–75	22	Death
Hagar	1754–76	23	Sale
Joseph	1754–61	8	Death
Mira	1754–76	23	Sale
Phebe	1754–65	12	Death
Plato	1754–68	15	Death by drowning
Stephy	1754–76	23	Sale
George	1759	1	Sale
Diana[d]	1761	1	Unknown
Joseph[d]	1761	1	Unknown
Belinda[e]	1768–78	11	Manumission
Joseph[e]	1768–78	11	Gift-transfer
Prine[e]	1768	1	Unknown
Priscilla	1778	1	Gift-transfer
Bathsheba[f]	1778	1	Gift-transfer
Nanny[f]	1778	1	Gift-transfer

Note: [a]Individuals shown with the same superscript belong to the same family group. Isaac Royall, Jr. stated in his will, "I hereby confirm my Gift unto my beloved son in law Sir William Pepperell Baronett and his heirs of my Negro Boy Joseph and my Negro Girl Priscilla" (Harvard Law Library Special Collections 1778). Joseph was likely the son of either Diana or Belinda (listed above in the "d" and "e" family groups), but there is no way to know which. I have treated him here as Belinda's son because Belinda was still in Royall's employ in 1778, and Diana had not been mentioned since 1761. This is an assumption based on the fact that the Royalls had kept mothers and children together in the past, but there is no evidence whatever of that here. It is equally possible that Diana was sold, but her son Joseph kept, or conversely, that Belinda was kept while her son, also named Joseph, was sold. In her petition of 1783, she mentions only a daughter, presumably Prine, baptized with her brother in 1768 (NEHGS 1907). Of course, the "Boy Joseph" of 1778 could also have been a different Joseph entirely. These are some of the challenges to reconstructing slave family at the Royall estate.

to make these "facts" speak to us more ethnographically about "different dimensions of black life" (Yentsch 1994:172). But how does one do this? And where do the artifacts fit in? One could start by observing that the Royalls owned at least 33 men and women without recorded spouses or families during their tenure in Medford; four single-parent families, consisting of a mother and her children; one single-parent extended family, consisting of a mother and her children, and one of her children's children; and two sisters, Bathsheba and Nanny. Having done that, one might go on to notice that men, by contrast, are without exception listed as single units, with no family relationships given. These observations lead us to the first question: what exactly constituted a "family" among the enslaved in Massachusetts at that time?

One possibility that must be considered is that fathers were considered by those who recorded the documents as separable—nonessential to the family unit. Another possibility is that "single adults" are evidence of "broad" marriages, where couples were spread across two estates and/or owners (Cody 1982:329). Both are likely to have been true at different times. Morgan (1998:499) points out that a woman listed with her children could also reflect "serial polyandry," and Stevenson (1996:160) says that, at least in the Chesapeake, there is little evidence that the "nuclear family," as constructed today, was an ideal among the enslaved anyway and that most Virginia slave families were not nuclear and not derived from long-term, monogamous marriages. A "malleable extended family" seems instead to have been the "most consistent norm" and the "most identifiable ideal," if indeed there was one (Stevenson 1996:161).

When Isaac Royall, Sr., died, Black Betty and her five children—Abba, Quacoe, Diana, John, and Nancy—and Abba's five children—Betty, George, Sarah, Jacob, and Jemmy—were bequeathed to Anne and Robert Oliver in Dorchester. Another woman named Abba and her six children—Robin, Coba, Walker, Nuba, Trace, and Tobey—and the "Girl Present" were given to the fifteen-year-old Penelope. Peter and Trace were given to Isaac, Sr.'s wife, Elizabeth, and the "remainder"— being 18 individuals—went to Isaac Royall, Jr. (table 14). Neither of the family groups mentioned includes a father, and no extended family relationships were mentioned at all outside those of mother and child. It seems then that the "slave family," as defined by the Royalls, consisted of a mother and her children and, in one instance, two female siblings.

Naturally, to those who were enslaved, "family" would have had meaning that went far beyond the obvious biological link between mother and child. Family would have been based on their own beliefs, experiences, ideals, and codes of conduct—rooted in part in their respective African traditions, but also a partial reflection of the "cumulative slave experience" (Gutman 1976:261, 308). We instinctively understand this to be true, and an ethnographic knowledge of some of the roles that beads played in West African societies hints at something deeper

TABLE 13.

Breakdown of the Royalls' slaves by duration of service

Minimum Tenure in Years	No. of Slaves	% Population
1-10	47	73.4
11-20	9	14.1
20-30	6	9.4
30-40	1	1.6
Over 40[a]	1	1.6
Total	64	100.00

Note: [a]Belinda stated in her petition to the General Court in 1783 that she had served the Royall family for 50 years, but her name does not appear in any of the records until 1768, when her children, Joseph and Prine, were baptized. She was therefore counted in the 11–20 year category.

TABLE 14.

Estate division of Royall's slave holdings in 1739

Anne and Robert Oliver	Penelope Royall	Elizabeth Royall	Isaac Royall, Jr.	
Black Betty	Abba	Peter	Fortune	Ruth
Abba	Robin	Trace	Barron	Sue
Quacoe	Coba		Ned	Jonto
Diana	Walker		House Peter	One old Negro man about 70 years of age
John	Nuba		Cuffe	George, about 45 years old
Nancy	Trace		Smith	Captain, Infirm
Betty	Tobey		Phillip	Santo, Lame and 50 years old
George	Girl Present		Robin	Old cook
Sarah			Quamino	Girl, 6 years of age
Jacob				
Jemmy				

Source: Middlesex County Probate 1739.

going on at the Royalls' farm than the documents would superficially seem to indicate. But, again, how are we to retrieve something as ephemeral as ideas about family or kin obligation beyond a basic, intuitive acknowledgment that they must have existed?

Names present one fascinating means of speculation. Several scholars have been able to use known historical family relationships, for instance, to reconstruct general trends in slave-naming practices in the 18th and 19th centuries and have found that names were not idly given (see Gutman 1976; Cody 1982; Kulikoff 1986). Gutman (1976:197) concludes, for example, that the naming practices of enslaved people in the 18th- and 19th-centuries show first and foremost the "sheer importance of kinship" in structuring interpersonal relations and defining one's place in society. Fox-Genovese (1988:325) says that a slave's name was often a symbolic "delineation of kin." "To the Negro," wrote William C. Gannett (quoted in Gutman 1976:185), "the plantation is his country and the 'family' his state," meaning that naming practices among slaves reflected enslaved people's conceptions of the ties between immediate family and the enlarged kin group.

Gutman (1976:185) found that children were frequently named for members of their immediate family, and sons often had their fathers' names.* An enslaved child was even more likely to be named for a member of the larger kin group—particularly in the absence of a father, when a woman's own parents and siblings would play a significant role in the lives of her children. Of the slaves on three of the plantations from the 18th and early 19th centuries that Gutman surveyed, 75 percent had grandchildren named after them (Gutman 1976:198). That aunts and uncles were also important in naming practices suggested that the new "nuclear" family was still tied to the family of origin and other immediate kin (Gutman 1976:200). Naming newborns after recently deceased immediate family members was also very common (Gutman 1976:192). Thus enslaved people did not adapt to slavery by simply adopting the "conventional 'nuclear' families" of their masters (Gutman 1976:97). Rather naming practices preserved in masters' slaves lists and estate ledgers suggest that African American families meshed through time, creating far-reaching kin networks that cut within and across generations and provided a family solidarity that carried through to the postemancipation era.

Another thing of note in the list in table 12 is that nearly three-quarters of the Royalls' 64 known slaves spent fewer than ten years with the Royalls (table 13). This is a startling statistic that suggests that making lasting ties of friendship, and possibly family as well, was difficult to do on the Royalls' estate. Documents reveal that by 1754 only three of the 38 people belonging to the Royalls mentioned in 1738–39 were still at Ten Hills Farm, the rest being scattered throughout Charlestown/Medford, Cambridge, Dorchester, Stoughton, and Freetown through sale or gift-transfer or otherwise simply disappearing from the rolls. The process of kin network and community development had begun.

This fact sheds significant light on the naming practices of the people on the Royalls' estates. Fig. 34 shows two possible family groups in Medford at the time of Isaac, Sr.'s death. The mother-child-grandchild relationships were explicitly given in Isaac, Sr.'s will, but it is noteworthy that some of the children also share names with other adult slaves belonging to the Royalls at the time. Given the degree of family instability under the Royalls, these children may have been named for close kin. And where actual family relationships are known, names seem to reveal what relationships were especially important to the Royalls' slaves.

On the one hand, Black Betty might have been named by the Royalls in honor of the many Elizabeths in their own family. The comical nature of her own name

---

*Daughters, by contrast, almost never had their mothers' names, which was a marked point of departure from white tradition. Isaac Royall, Jr.'s mother, wife, two of his daughters, one of his granddaughters, and a niece for example were all named Elizabeth. His sister-in-law, other daughter, and another of his granddaughters were named Mary (Maine Historical Society, n.d.).

and the fact that two of her children—Abba and Quacoe—actually had African names suggests that "Black Betty" was indeed an imposed appellation. On the other hand, Black Betty's granddaughter was also named Betty, and the fact that they shared a name could show a concern among the Royall slaves with making symbolic ties to older kin, regardless of the ultimate origin of the name. Even if the younger Betty had also been named by the Royalls, for instance, the symbolism of grandmother and granddaughter having the same name would have been recognized within their own family, as the name entered the tradition of both families (Sobel 1987:160). Not only did the younger Betty and her siblings know at least one of their grandparents then, but Black Betty seems also to have had a significant role in the family and in the socialization and enculturation of the children.

The importance of elders in the slave community is a recurrent theme in the literature. Frederick Douglass (1855:69–70) wrote:

> Strange and even ridiculous as it may seem, among a people so uncultivated and with so many stern trials to look in the face, there is not to be found among any people a more rigid enforcement of the law of respect to elders than [slaves] maintain. I set this down as partly constitutional with my race, and partly conventional. . . . A young slave must approach the company of the older with hat in

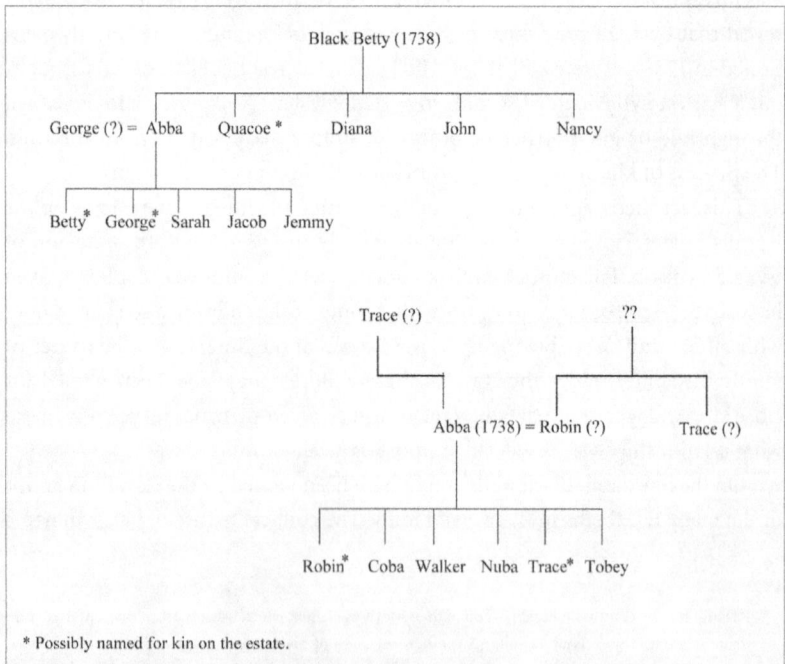

* Possibly named for kin on the estate.

Fig. 34. Family relationships, known and conjectured (marked with a "?"), among the Royall slaves under Isaac Royall, Sr., in 1738–39.

hand, and woe betide him, if he fails to acknowledge a favor, or any sort, with the accustomed "tank'ee" &c. So uniformly are good manners enforced among slaves, that I can easily detect a "bogus" fugitive by his manners.

Meyer Fortes, writing about the Ashanti of West Africa, said that "the grandparents are felt to be living links with the past" (quoted in Gutman 1976:218), while Frazier (1939:146, 148) characterized grandmothers in the American slave family similarly as the "guardian of generations," a repository of family history, folklore, proverbs, and wisdom, present at most births on the plantation, black and white, and generally a figure of great regard and importance both among slaves and their masters. Harriet Jacobs (1987) often spoke of her grandmother as caregiver, disciplinarian, nurturer, and a dominant influence in her family's relations. Even as Harriet's own immediate family crumbled, her grandmother remained the rock of her childhood: "My grandmother was all in all to me, I feared her as well as loved her. I had been accustomed to look up to her with a respect that bordered upon awe" (Jacobs 1987:28–29).

Two females named Trace, an adult and a child, might also have had a grandparent-grandchild relationship. Isaac, Sr., left the elder Trace to his wife, Elizabeth, and a young girl by the same name, with her mother and five siblings to his daughter, Penelope. The elder Trace might also have been an aunt to the younger or sister to Abba or to the father of Abba's children. Gutman (1976:200) found that adult siblings were important sources of names for one's children. He suggests that relationships of "mother's brother" and "father's sister" might have assumed particular importance and derived from similar West African beliefs about reciprocal kin obligations (Gutman 1976:200). Fig. 34 allows for each of these possibilities, the elder Trace as maternal grandmother or paternal aunt to the younger.

The boys Robin, George, and Quacoe also had the names of adult men owned by the Royalls at the same time. Their names might reflect father-son or "mother's brother" relationships with the older men of the same name. The rareness of recording fathers' relationship to their families in the documents arguably reflects the conceptual unimportance of "father," or indeed any adult male, in the minds of most slaveholders. This was largely a function of the fact that an enslaved child's legal status followed that of its mother (Gutman 1976:190). Slaveholders therefore defined slave families, if at all, mostly through their maternal line of descent. But Gutman (1976:190) argues that the frequency with which boys in his study were named for their fathers might have assured affinity and continuity within the family when fathers were more likely to be separated from the family than mothers were (see also Morgan 1998:546, 549–51).

The practice of naming sons for their fathers also partly contradicts the once-popular idea that black men were emasculated by slavery and stripped of their ability to have a significant role in the family because of it. Frazier (1939:164), for example, argued that the "Negro man acquired a permanent interest in his family and assumed a position of authority" in it only after emancipation. Meanwhile Moynihan (1965:30) stated that slavery had destroyed the black family, giving modern "Negro husbands . . . unusually low power" and that it was in this "weakness of the family structure" that one could find the source of "most of the of aberrant, inadequate, or antisocial behavior" that kept lower-class blacks in a vicious downward spiral.

But enslaved parents who named their sons after their fathers for over a century before emancipation were clearly reasserting to themselves the cultural importance of "father" to the family unit (Gutman 1976:190). Escott (1979:49) and Webber (1978:169) surveyed former slave narratives from the Federal Writers' Project to support the claim that fathers, uncles, grandfathers, and adult males in general did have symbolically important roles in the quarter community, usually taking their obligations seriously as fathers, providers, and protectors. These historians found that enslaved men often provided extra food, clothing, and small necessities to their families that made daily life more comfortable; they hunted, fished, gardened, and earned extra wages by hiring themselves out on weekends; they sometimes taught their particular skills to the next generation, often their own sons; and they were, as were most adults in the community, male or female, often ready to step in and fill the roles left suddenly empty by the sale, death, or migration of other people's biological kin (Webber 1978:170).

If Robin, George, and Quacoe were all named for their fathers, then the concern for delineating kin and maintaining familial continuity can be justified. The adult Quaco was banished to Hispaniola for conspiracy to revolt in 1737; Robin was separated from his conjectural family at the division of Isaac, Sr.'s estate; and George never would have lived with his in the first place, being principally held at the farm in Freetown. As young Robin, George, and Quaco grew up, however, their names would have reminded them of who they were and where they had come from, even if they suddenly found themselves alone and "without family."

One other possible father-son relationship can be identified between the man, Joseph, who died in April of 1761 after eight years of servitude for the Royalls, and Diana's son, Joseph, who was born the very next month, in May of 1761 (NEHGS 1907). Gutman has spoken of the frequency with which newborns were named for recently deceased family members (1976:192). Chloe Spear, a woman in Boston who had been stolen from West Africa ca. 1760, provides some insight into the possible reasoning behind such a practice. She said that she frequently wished for death in the early years of her enslavement because it was believed among her people that the first-born infant after the death of a family member was that very person reincarnate, so that by dying she was assured of a return to her village in Africa (A Lady of Boston 1832:17). Thus, while we cannot know whether Diana thought her son was actually Joseph come back from the dead, or even who the elder Joseph had been to her—husband, father, brother, or nobody—it is entirely plausible that there was a family relationship between the elder and the younger Josephs, whose respective death and birth were separated by only a matter of weeks.

Names are important because they can represent unmistakable evidence of the role of one's own beliefs, experiences, and ideals in the structuring of family and community. Such evidence has suggested repeatedly that the slave family was not just an "owner-sponsored" mechanism of "social control" (Gutman 1976:261), but actually a meaningfully constructed unit that shaped the lives and experiences of the enslaved in significant ways.

Names can also reflect intergenerational links that, where allowed to develop, would become the passageways for the traditions, values, and mores of an emerging slave culture (Gutman 1976:261). Kulikoff (1986:325–26) says that it was rare for masters who allowed slaves to keep their own names to also allow them to name their children for African kinsmen. In the names of the Royalls' slaves, however, we gain insight into these individuals' own ideals of proper family roles and kin obligations that contradicted white, matrifocal definitions. Naming their children for grandparents, fathers, aunts, uncles, or other older blood relatives showed an "effort to honor tradition and family ties" (Morgan 1998:454), to be sure, but also undermined white concepts of authority associated with ownership.

Far from slavery's having destroyed the black family, the instability caused by the ever-present threat of separation or violence perpetrated against loved ones might have given the slave family even greater depth of meaning, intensity of feeling, and strength of unity. Slavery doubtless destroyed many slave families and cut deeply the souls of countless individuals, but in naming practices we see small evidence of the creation of new cultural norms that kept the ideal of family and the importance of certain family relationships intact even when harsh realities worked to obliterate them. This cultural adaptation was part of the "built-in internal dynamism" and "adaptive flexibility" that Mintz and Price (1976:32) have argued were important in the formative period of African American family and community life. It also furthers our understanding of the processes of racialization.

For instance the kin-structured social relations suggested by naming practices at the Royalls' estate were perhaps of Old World derivation, but they would arguably have been imbued with peculiar import within the American context of slavery. The documentary history particular to this site reveals a host of circumstances that would have made this so. In the face of practical instability, a family's emphasis on the ideological importance of extended and honorary kin, through the use of names as well as familiar terms of address ("Auntie," "Uncle," "Gran,"

"Bro," and so on), would have assumed greater significance. This would not have been an ethnic difference in family and community structure, per se, though it might well have had African antecedents. Within the context of American slavery, such practices turned the entire slave community into an extended family with mutually reciprocal obligations. As partially a response to racism, then, they would also have been structurally connected to emerging notions of the differences between black and white, as these colors were perceived on both sides of the line. The stone bead too, as a *material* expression of identity, would have been structurally tied to the definition and maintenance of the color line—not so much for its different aesthetic (which was ethnically derived), but because of the potential transgenerational symbolism behind it (whose peculiar significance was racial).

Family and Community in Crisis

Family is one of the key elements for understanding life under slavery because it is slavery's disruption and destruction of family and community that most saliently emerges from the documentary record as rendering life most intolerable for the enslaved. A slave, as Patterson (1982:5) points out, was, by definition,

> denied all claims on, and obligations to, his parents and living blood relations [and] by extension, all such claims and obligations on his more remote ancestors and on his descendants. He was truly a genealogical isolate.

The systematic conceptual, as well as physical, separation of the enslaved from their kin is a process he calls "natal alienation" (Patterson 1982:6–7). Although enslaved people certainly experienced real social relationships with their families, these were not regarded as legitimate or legally binding in white society.

The slave system's disregard for the sanctity of marriage and the relationship between parents and their children was repeatedly indicted by African and African American witnesses as one of the greatest burdens under bondage and was a harsh reality of slavery regardless of the material conditions under which slaves might have lived.

In a petition to Governor Thomas Gage in 1774, "a Grate Number of Blackes of this Province [Massachusetts] who by divine permission are held in a state of Slavery within the bowels of a free and christian Country" described how slavery damaged families:

> Thus we are deprived of every thing that hath a tendency to make life even tolerable, the endearing ties of husband and wife we are strangers to for we are no longer man and wife than our masters or mistresses thinkes proper marred or onmarred. Our children are also taken from us by force and sent maney miles

from us wear we seldom or ever see them again there to be made slaves of for Life which sumtimes is vere short by Reson of Being dragged from their mothers Breest Thus our Lives are imbittered to us on these accounts. . . . How can a slave perform the duties of a husband to a wife or parent to his child. How can a husband leave master to work and cleave to his wife. How can the wife submit themselves to there [sic] husbands in all things. How can the child obey thear parents in all things. (MHS 1877:432–433)

The anxieties of slave parenthood, for mothers and fathers alike, are especially prominent in slave narratives and documents. Henry Bibb (1849:458–59), for example, writes, "Who could imagine what could be the feelings of a father and mother, when looking upon their infant child whipped and tortured with impunity, and they placed in a situation where they could afford it no protection" (Bibb 1849:459). He goes on to say

If ever there was any one act of my life while a slave, that I have to lament over, it is that of being a father and a husband of slaves. I have the satisfaction of knowing that I am only the father of one slave. She is bone of my bone, and flesh of my flesh; poor unfortunate child. She was the first and shall be the last slave that ever I will father, for chains and slavery on this earth. (Bibb 1849:459)

For Harriet Jacobs the awareness of the inevitable suffering of her children drove her to near despair:

The little vine . . . excited a mixture of love and pain. When I was most sorely oppressed I found a solace in his smiles. I loved to watch his infant slumbers, but always there was a dark cloud over my enjoyment. I could never forget that he was a slave. Sometimes I wished that he might die in infancy. (Jacobs 1987:62)

Sojourner Truth (1850:577), enslaved in Ulster County, New York, had two older siblings who had been sold as children, remembers how, even years afterwards, her parents, Mau-Mau Bett and Bomefree, would spend many of their waking hours

recalling and recounting every endearing, as well as harrowing circumstance that taxed memory could supply, from the histories of those dear departed ones, of whom they had been robbed, and for whom their hearts still bled.

The forcible break-up of marriages was, of course, also devastating, and it was terrible for husbands and wives to be forced to watch each other's humiliation or physical abuse. Fanny Kemble wrote in her journal about a narrowly averted breakup of a marriage among her husband's slaves at Butler Plantation in Georgia that evokes some of the desperation that such instances caused, as well as the nonchalance of many white owners in bringing them to pass:

Early the next morning, while I was still dressing, I was suddenly startled by hearing voices in loud tones in Mr. [Butler]'s dressing room, which adjoins my bedroom, and the noise increasing until there was an absolute cry of despair uttered by some man. I could restrain myself no longer, but opened the door of communication and saw Joe, the young man, poor Psyche's husband, raving almost in a state of frenzy, and in a voice broken with sobs and almost inarticulate with passion, reiterating his determination never to leave this plantation, never to go to Alabama, never to leave his old father and mother, his poor wife and children, and, dashing his hat, which he was wringing like a cloth in his hands, upon the ground, he declared he would kill himself if he was compelled to follow Mr. K[ing]. I glanced from the poor wretch to Mr. [Butler], who was standing, leaning against a table with his arms folded, occasionally uttering a few words of counsel to his slave to be quiet and not fret, and not make a fuss about what there was no help for. (Kemble 1984:136)

Physical cruelty and the separation of family members by sale, however, were not the only things destructive of slave families. Estate division, relocation to other estates, and leasing of slaves to other owners were also psychologically damaging and compromised family stability (see Cody 1982; Escott 1979:46–48), while the conflicting obligations of slaves to master and kin could cause great friction within intact slave families. Harriet Jacobs tells of a time when her younger brother was called by their father and their mistress at the same time:

He hesitated between the two; being perplexed to know which had the strongest claim upon his obedience. He finally concluded to go to his mistress. When my father reproved him for it, he said, "You both called me, and I didn't know which I ought to go to first." (Jacobs 1987:9)

Indeed Stevenson (1996:187–88) has pointed out that while many enslaved people had fond memories of certain aspects of their early childhood, childhood was also a time for children to become socialized into the work routine and system of reward and punishment under slavery. Being forced to watch parents and elders subjected to brutality and humiliation was not only traumatic, but also undermined the efficacy of their authority in the home, while children were often subjected to perverse punishments themselves. One Virginia boy remembered his mistress repeatedly forcing him to sit in the corner and eat dry bread "till [he] almost choked" (quoted in Stevenson 1996:187).

Documentary evidence reveals that the Royalls, regardless of their self-professed status as kind and benevolent masters, were throwing their slaves into crisis on a regular basis. While there is no surviving evidence of physical cruelty, sales seem to have been commonplace, some individuals were leased, and since even kind masters must die, estate division was inevitable. These were some of the crises that slave families and the slave community on Ten Hills Farm would have to have weathered.

It was within this documentary history and context that the discovery in 2000 of something made to look very like a Native American stone tool dramatically seized the imagination. The discovery some time later of an apparently genuine Native American tool only deepened the fascination and suggested that we might have stumbled onto something of real significance and been granted a rare insight into the lives and relationships of the enslaved at this estate.

Master-Slave Relations at Ten Hills Farm

The curation of Native American lithics, or stone tools, by enslaved and free Africans is a known phenomenon in the South, ethnohistorically as well as archaeologically (Orser 1985; Wilkie 1995, 2000). More than just the remains of old "arrowhead collections," however, such finds on slave sites are generally interpreted as falling within the realm of spirituality and are therefore linked to some of the most intimate levels of identity formation. This is because at its base, writes Wilkie (2000:166), spirituality defines one's understanding of the supernatural and the natural worlds; the nature of the body, health, illness, and appropriate treatments; and the principal explanatory model of one's place in the universe. To find evidence of small-scale "personal acts" of spirituality (Wilkie 2000:166) at Ten Hills Farm, then, is exciting indeed, and although it may not be immediately apparent why, they are a perfect place to begin the reconstruction of master-slave relations on the Royalls' estate.

While there may have been a puritanical religious zeal that set New England society apart from the other colonies, and the Puritan patriarch may have been a specific regional phenomenon or ideal, paternalism in general was not unique to New England. All over the Americas, from Boston to St. Johns, paternalism was proffered as the best method to ensure obedience and loyalty in one's servants. Samuel Martin wrote in his *Essay Upon Plantership:*

> Let us consider what is the right or rational method of treating Negroes; for rational beings they are, and ought to be treated accordingly; that is, with humanity and benevolence. . . . It is evident from experience, that he who feeds his Negroes well, proportioneth their labor to their age, sex, and strength, and treats them with kindness and good nature will reap a much larger product, and with infinitely more ease and self-satisfaction, than the most cruel Egyptian task-master. . . . Thus then ought every planter to treat his Negroes with tenderness and generosity, that they may be induced to love, and obey him out of mere gratitude; and

become real good beings by the imitation of his benevolence, justice, temperance, and chastity. (Martin 1745 [1765]:3)

Whether Martin practiced what he preached we may never know. His father was murdered by slaves on Christmas Day in 1701, and it was widely supposed to have been brought on by his own cruelty (Oliver 1894: lxxiii). Perhaps this was the "experience" of which his son would write, 45 years later. Most planters, when expounding on the subject, also implied, directly or indirectly, the existence of a mutual obligation between master and slave—physical, spiritual, and moral guidance and protection from the master was rightfully returned with gratitude, loyalty, and dutiful labor from the slaves (see Genovese 1974:91–93). Mrozowski and Beaudry (1990) have shown that even as late as the 19th century, among free industrial laborers at the Lowell Boot Mills in Lowell, Massachusetts, the concept of paternalism was a powerful means for management to disguise mechanisms of control as a benevolent concern for workers' welfare.

In 17th- and early-18th-century New England, paternalism took on a distinctly religious undertone. The biblical allusion to the patriarchs of ancient Israel was purposeful and at once reflected and defined the behavioral ideal. Here the head of household, God, and King George himself all became metaphorically tied to the concept of father and through this to each other (Isaac 1982:21; Piersen 1988:26). It served to raise everyday experience to the "highest levels of cosmology," sanctioning (and sanctifying) patriarchal authority (Isaac 1982:21).

Isaac, Sr.. and Jr. almost certainly did not think of themselves as patriarchs in the biblical, puritanical sense, but they were concerned with being paternalistic. No documents survive to directly attest their personal views on slavery or their rightful relationship with their slaves, but Isaac Royall, Sr., does refer to his slaves at one point as "my people" (Royall Correspondence: Aug. 15, 1736), which indicates the relationship he felt he ought to have had with his slaves and the image he strove to project to the outside world. Referring to slaves as "my people" or "my family" was a paternalistic way of naturalizing the master-slave relationship, casting the master's authority over the enslaved as a natural extension of the patriarch's obligations to his own family (Epperson 1990). It styled a demeaning relationship of domination and power that emphasized the treatment of adults as children as a more innocuous- and just-sounding "social contract" (Garman 1998:137, 154).

The danger of treating the relationship as a mutually obligatory "contract" between members of an extended family lay in the possibility that transgressions against the contract might be considered especially grievous because they came from within the family, and retribution in such cases might be swift and violent (Genovese 1974:91). It may not have been the cruelty alone that caused Major

Samuel Martin to be brutally slain by his slaves in Antigua in 1701, but the fact that he was their master and hence was perceived to have certain obligations to them that others did not have.

And so we return to the stone tools mentioned above. While the Royalls paternalistically spoke of their slaves as "their people" and thus have implicitly revealed to us their own perceptions of "master-slave relations" at this estate, what do the artifacts tell us about how "their people" perceived those same relations? The first artifact, in particular, was long something of a mystery at the site, found in the deposits filling the outbuilding foundation in the slave quarters' west yard. It consisted of a stone flake, crudely shaped into the semblance of an arrowhead. I say "semblance" because it is clear to anyone familiar with stone-tool making that the material is unsuitable for knapping—rough-grained and cleaving along jagged planes, not easily stream-lined, and difficult to sharpen. Except for the two side-notches chipped at the base, it is also only unifacially worked, with no attempt to create a cutting edge (fig. 35). What this means is that, whatever it resembled, this was no arrowhead. In flint-knapping terms it was a reworked, or utilized, flake. A small groove etched between the side notches may have been made to better secure the object from a piece of yarn or leather thong, and this to be hung around the neck or some other part of the body.

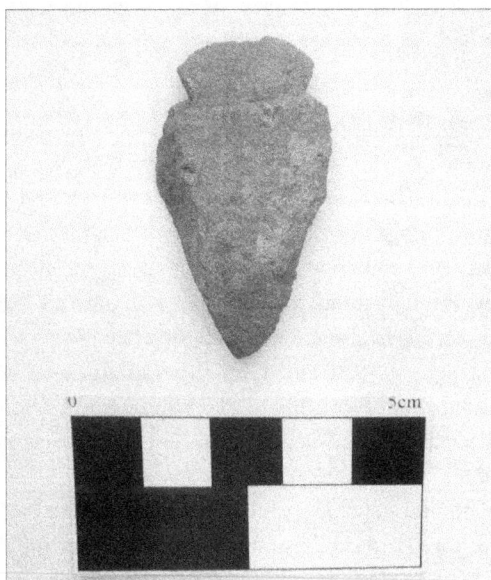

FIG. 35. An "arrowhead amulet," possibly of Akan derivation, recovered from the west yard of the slave quarters. A groove scratched between the side notches likely facilitated suspension, possibly from around the neck, by a length of yarn or leather thong.

The object languished in the archaeology lab at Boston University for nearly two years before I knew what to make of it: a troubling curiosity in the back of my mind, an object whose secrets were all the more scintillating for their being so well kept. And in fact it was not until I began to do background research for the discussions about naming practices that the pieces began to fall into place.

Several of the Royalls' slaves, as we have seen, had Akan day-names, and it was first in an ethnography of the Akan-speaking peoples of the Gold Coast that I found reference to a belief system in which prehistoric stone projectile points were believed to have magical powers. *Nyame akuma,* they were called, or God's axes: thunderbolts that resulted when lightning struck the earth (Ward 1958:32). It is a belief demonstrably carried over to parts of the Americas as well. Ed Murphy, one of Newbell Niles Puckett's conjure-doctor informants from 20th-century Mississippi, for example, informed him that Indian arrowheads were "not made by man at all, but were fashioned by God out of thunder and lightning" (Puckett 1926:315). Wilkie (1995:143) adds that "arrowheads" continue to be sold in New Orleans today as good luck charms. Often the piece itself was not the charm but was used to produce it:

> To use one for good luck, strike a spark from it with your knife (if the sparks fly readily you will know that you have a good knife) and let the spark fall upon a piece of powdered punk. Let the punk smoulder into ashes, which are to be wrapped in a piece of newspaper and carried with you always for good luck. (Puckett 1926:315)

The object at the Royall House was not a real arrowhead but seems rather to have been made by someone who was no doubt familiar with Native American lithics. Such items might have turned up periodically in fields and streambeds, but it may be that such things were hard to come by when they were most needed, and thus it was easier to make one or have one made for the purpose. Objects did not have to be accidentally found to be imbued with power. Chireau (1997:228) says "created objects" were also employed as a matter of course in housing the supernatural throughout West and Central Africa. Incantations or libations could invoke the ancestors over it and turn any object into a charm (Dr. Rosalind Shaw, Tufts University History Department, June 2001: personal communication; Puckett 1926:171; Wilkie 2000:188).

Of course, if an unusual object could be found, so much the better. Another discovery at the Royall House illustrates the point. From the deposits within the outbuilding foundation in the slave quarters' west yard came a stone pestle, pecked and abraded into a cylinder (fig. 36). What was startling about the object, however, was not only its cultural affiliation, which was most likely Native American, but also its very great age, appearing to stem from the Archaic Period, which lasted from about 8,000 to 2,000 years ago. Although it is conceivable that this artifact was used for simple secular and utilitarian purposes of grinding and mashing, within the historically and archaeologically established phenomenon of African curation of Native American lithics for religious or ritual purposes, it seems likely that there was more to the story. For example, as an unusual object with a powerful indwelling spirit, the pestle might have been used to grind and mash the ingredients of magic, ritual, or medicinal concoctions, thereby lending its own potency to the end product. As such it is potential further evidence of the "secret and sacred landscapes" that enslaved people created for themselves at Ten Hills Farm (Wilkie 1997:81).

These finds beg the question: what use was magic at Ten Hills Farm? And what would Isaac Royall have made of "his people" making incantations over strange objects and wearing charms on their bodies or beads in their hair? Frederick

FIG. 36. Pecked and abraded pestle recovered from deposits in the outbuilding foundation in the slave quarters' west yard, resembling those found on Native American sites from the Late Archaic Period. This artifact might have been found by slaves and either used for practical or magical purposes of grinding and mashing or simply kept for its peculiarity, as a ritual object or residence for protective spirits. Wilkie (1995:143; 2000:188), Orser (1985), and Puckett (1926:315) have all provided historical and archaeological documentation of African Americans' having curated Native American lithics for ritual purposes.

Douglass (1845:293) wrote that there was a maxim among enslaved people that "a still tongue makes a wise head." This adage referred to the fact that enslaved people's private beliefs and family lives were often kept secret from their masters. Charles Jones, a 19th-century slaveholder, seemed to recognize the veracity of the saying implicitly when he said, "[Whites] live and die in the midst of Negroes and know comparatively little of their real character" (quoted in Gutman 1976:93). Robert Smalls, a former slave speaking in 1863, told his interviewer, "No, sir, one life they show their masters and another they don't show" (quoted in Gutman 1976:93).

So if Isaac Royall knew about "his people's" private doings at all, he might have been more amused or contemptuous than angry. Particularly in the North American colonies, the forms of magic and religion that came to characterize black American "occultism" were "largely private, noncollective, and noninstitutionalized," which is one of the ways that the spiritual lives of slaves in North America most differed from those in the Caribbean (Chireau 1997:229). It may have been lucky for them that this made their particular brand of spirituality seem peculiarly nonthreatening to masters. Whites often dismissed African American spirituality in North America as harmless superstition (Piersen 1988:85; Wilkie 2000:165). Since both Isaac, Sr., and Isaac, Jr., styled themselves benevolent aristocrats and cast themselves in a protective, paternalistic role with regard to their families and their slaves, it seems likely that neither would have seen, understood, or appreciated the true nature of such "superstitious," small-scale, personal acts—neither their purpose nor their potential.

And why should they have? Their own private persona of being kind masters and good men was so deeply engrained that they cloaked themselves with it even unto death. Isaac, Sr., was commemorated on his tombstone as a "kind master and a true friend" when he died. This was a judgment coming from his family, of course, but they might have pointed out, if asked, that they routinely paid for the making and mending of clothes for their slaves that often went beyond the minimum, giving extra niceties to certain individuals. Between 1726 and 1739, Fortune, Peter, Nan, Ruth, Cuff, and Cato all received extra gifts of clothing (Account Book 1724–49; table 15). These were probably favored slaves or domestic servants who needed to look neat and presentable as part of the Royalls' own social display. Indeed "Kersey" and "Bays" (or baize) were textiles imported from England, while the "tayloring" of clothes in 1738 suggests more formal attire, probably for men, and may represent domestic uniforms or livery. On the other hand, "Ozanbrigg" (or osnabrig, osnaburg, and so on) was a cheap, durable, and sturdy cotton cloth that was also rough, and so it may not have been received especially gratefully by Peter and Cuff. Said one Virginia woman, "Dat ole nigger-cloth was jus' like needles when it was new. Never did have to scratch our back. Jus' wriggle yo' shoulders an' yo' back was scratched" (quoted in Genovese 1974:551).

TABLE 15.

Clothing purchases for slaves, 1724–49

	Fortune	Peter	Nan	Ruth	Cuff	Cato	Misc.
1726	Leather breeches	Clothing	Clothing	Clothing			Cloth, Kersey, Bays, etc. for 2 Negroes
	Shoes	Lined breeches	Shoes				
1727	2 shirts						
1729	Sundries						
1730		Ozan-briggs			Ozan-briggs		
1736		Felt hat					
1737	Hose						Making Negroes' cloath
	Mittens						4 pair sealskin jackets for Negroes
							Mend-ing for Negroes
1738	Felt hat						Shoes for Isaac's boy
							Taylor-ing for the Negroes
1739						Worsted cap	

Note: "Isaac's "boy" might have been either Peter or Cuff, who were sent with him to Boston as his companions in 1726 (Account Book: Nov. 8); they were referred to as "his Negro's" in 1730 (Account Book: April).

Source: Derived from the Account Book (1724-1749).

The distribution of clothing, on some level, was meant to underscore the Royalls' "own benevolence and to evoke gratitude for the supposed gift"; as such it was also part and parcel of the Royalls' perceived obligations (Genovese 1974:555). It also suggests a division in the slave hierarchy on the estate, however, which might have been the source of conflict, jealousy, or hostility among the enslaved. Documentary evidence that also suggests that the Royalls not only occasionally bestowed their favored slaves with gifts, but gave them special consideration in both work and family matters, provides a context that is a potentially important one for interpreting artifacts of conjuration at the Royall estate.

By and large it seems that the biggest challenge for the Royalls' "people" was to create and maintain lasting family ties in the face of sale, estate division, and gift-transfer. Artifacts of conjuration may represent enslaved people's own endeavors to harness higher powers to protect themselves from, or prevent the worst effects of, family and community instability. Indeed Wilkie (1995:138) has argued that, as "family was the most important social relationship in the African American community," the continuation of African-based spiritual traditions in New World contexts of slavery served principally to give enslaved people some sense of control in the preservation of those families and communities.

Both primary and secondary literature support the idea that there was an almost "implicit belief" among slaves in conjuration, witches, ghosts, and spirits, that there not only was a spirit world, but that it also regularly interacted with the earthly one—indeed that they were "equally convincing realities"—and could at least partially be affected and controlled by human agency via a set of practices called hoodoo (Webber 1978:118). Puckett (1926:168) wrote that "any inexplicable or unexpected calamity" could be blamed on witchcraft or hoodoo practices, from constipation to insanity, while hoodoo practitioners could prescribe a course of action for individuals to lift these hexes and/or inflict them on others.

Beliefs in magic and magical practices, says Wilkie (1997:84), persisted on the one hand because they were "intrinsic to the ways in which enslaved Africans defined themselves, their families, and their relationship to life, death, and the world around them." But they were not necessarily indicative of an inherent cultural or religious conservatism. That is, they were not just "African holdovers." Puckett points out that enslaved people, "lacking overt and natural means of obtaining justice," often turned in a last-ditch effort to supernatural forces (Puckett 1926:167), but Wilkie (1997:84) concedes that "the secret maintenance of magical practices" was also partially "a means of exerting control over circumstances of life or of resisting planter authority."

What is more, Conjure continued to play a significant role in the daily lives of 19th-century African Americans, even after an ostensible conversion to Christianity, because each practice—Conjure and Christianity—had its own place in addressing a diversity of "needs and interests" (Chireau 1997:227). In this way folk beliefs to do with religion and ethnomedicine have taken on a renewed significance for scholars, not just as cultural retentions intrinsic to an African-based way of life, but also as a culturally dynamic and socially active response to the challenges of slavery and oppression. Through various aspects of their folk religion, which may or may not have been derived from Old World traditions, enslaved people were able to "counter the negative view of their spiritual and physical nature" that existed among their masters (Earl 2003:7). Hoodoo was implemented not just for lofty religious purposes, but in all of the "practical affairs of life," from finding lost or stolen objects to getting luck in gambling or love to exacting revenge or evading corporal punishment (Puckett 1926:283, 300). Henry Bibb (1849:447) wrote, for example, "There is much superstition among the slaves. Many of them believe in what they call 'conjuration,' tricking, and witchcraft; and some of them pretend to understand the art, and say that by it they can prevent their masters from flogging them."

In particular many enslaved people seemed to believe in the power of talismans and amulets to protect against evil spirits and hexes and to bring good luck (Piersen 1988:86; Laguerre 1987:83); by wearing them on the body it was supposed that one could produce "desirable results of all kinds," physical and supernatural (Puckett 1926:313). This was true throughout the black Atlantic world. One New England slaveholder was quoted as saying that "In one form or another fetish worship . . . was almost inherent" (Piersen 1988:80; see also Thompson 1983:117). Actually fetish worship is not, strictly speaking, the accurate term. Both Puckett (1926:170) and Thompson (1983:117) point out that it was not the object itself that was being worshipped but the indwelling spirit within it. The world of spirits and ghosts, as stated, was real and near, and able to meddle endlessly in the affairs of the living. With the proper rites and ceremonies, these spirits could be harnessed and centered in almost any object to effect good for oneself or harm to another (Puckett 1926:169).

On the Gold Coast of Africa, such charms and amulets (called *minkisi*, the plural form of *nkisi* [Thompson 1983:117]), which were really just a temporary habitation for an invoked spirit, were regarded as "spiritual, intelligent beings who make the remarkable objects of nature their residence" (Puckett 1926:171). In short they were alive (Thompson 1983:117). Unusual or peculiar objects were especially sought because, in a circular kind of logic, the object's peculiarity was thought to stem from having an indwelling spirit within it (Puckett 1926:173). Only a priest or conjurer could invoke a spirit to reside in an object, though, and such specialists or experts achieved particular standing in the community for their ability to control the supernatural; interpret dreams, visions, and signs; and provide health, protection, and prosperity (Chireau 1997:228; Wilkie 2000:194).

The "arrowhead amulet" and the stone pestle, as potential artifacts of conjuration at the Royall House, are evidence of enslaved people's active attempts to gain control over the rigors and dangers of a life under slavery. Their use was ethnically derived but racially "required" and reinforced and thus was no passive indicator of African ethnicity. These artifacts became part and parcel of what it meant to be black and enslaved in 18th-century Massachusetts. As many spiritual dangers were perceived to come from fellow bondsmen, rather than from white owners, these artifacts may also be the only clue we have to a divide among the enslaved population on the estate arising from the Royalls' preferential treatment of certain individuals. In either case they are strong evidence that the Royalls' perception of having a paternalistic and protective relationship to their slaves was a one-sided one.

In 1748 Peter Kahn, observing the conjuration practices of slaves in New York, noted that "the negroes commonly employ [them] on such of their brethren as behave well toward whites, are beloved by their masters, and separate, as it were, from their countrymen . . . " (quoted in Piersen 1988:83). A man named Fortune seems to have been most "separate from his countrymen" at the Royall House, receiving leather breeches, shoes, two shirts, sundries, mittens, a pair of hose, and a felt hat. He was also occasionally entrusted with large sums of money to carry out errands for the household, such as buying meat or wool cards (Account Book: May 10, 1738). Four others were given sealskin jackets, likely to protect them from the wet in their work as boat- and rivermen (Account Book: May 22, 1737).

Morgan (1998:442) reminds us that "romantic interpretations of black life often overlook evidence of divisiveness and too easily speak of a cooperative ethos and communal solidarity magically present in the slave quarters." Such an interpretation underestimates the kind of social and psychological pressures of slavery and the social tensions that often exist among people who are simply thrown together. That is not to say that slaves were incapable of cooperating, working together, and establishing mutually agreed on standards of behavior, but Morgan (1998:443) states that explorations of "community formation among slaves must . . . encompass conflict and cohesion." It was a dangerous thing to be black and enslaved in the 18th century. One had to protect oneself as best one could. A survey of former slave narratives suggests that, from an enslaved person's perspective,

> a good master, "as masters go," was one who fed bountifully, set a fair task, whipped only when absolutely necessary, allowed quarter slaves to do as they wished with their leisure time, stayed out of their internal affairs, and refused to sell slaves in even the direst circumstances. (Webber 1978:75)

The Royalls would probably have been counted as either conflicted or fickle by this definition. Provisioning records are sporadic in the accounts payable portion of the account book, suggesting that Ten Hills Farm was largely self-sustaining, requiring only periodic replenishment of supplies. The faunal analysis further supports this conclusion, as the body part distribution indicates that the majority of animals recovered from the site would have been raised, butchered, and consumed there. There is little evidence of getting meat from markets or of the Royalls butchering their own meat for resale (Newman and Landon 2002:8). In the account book the purchased food supplies are not labeled specifically as slave provisions, although the sheer quantity of some of the entries suggest that slaves would have been receiving rations from those stores. Nevertheless the vagueness and infrequency of the entries leave us with very little notion of what the size, frequency, and variation of the slave rations might have been. Consider the following excerpt from June of 1726 in the account book:

To 4 Bbles Alwives	£ 5..12..0
4 Bbles Mackreles	7..0..0
Truckg Coopa & Primage	..6..0
1 bble Rye meal	1..6..6

Or this excerpt from June of 1728:

To 5 hhds Indian Corn	£ 29..2..9
27 1/2 bushls Do @ 6/6	28..8..9
5 Hogs & Truckg	3..3..9
2 bbles Bass & Trucking	3..5..0

What survives of the Royalls' papers records no whippings or punishments of any sort, aside from the execution of the slave driver, Hector, and the banishment of Quaco, for conspiracy to revolt in Antigua, but those were punishments administered by the island of Antigua, not the Royalls. On the other hand, the threat of corporal punishment, whether resorted to or not, was essential in any slave regime, because what was most important to a slaveholder was teaching or training his slaves to be competent and effective in all of the jobs and tasks needed to keep the plantation running smoothly and making them do it willingly (Patterson 1982:4; Webber 1978:41–42):

> On a well-run plantation the whip did not crack often or excessively; the threat of
> its use, in combination with other incentives and threats, preserved order. . . . From
> colonial times to the end of the regime intelligent masters tried to reduce their
> dependency on the whip but admitted they could not do without it. (Genovese
> 1974:65)

Sale must also be considered a potential form of punishment, meted out by slaveholders to intractable slaves. The Royalls are known to have sold people in specific instances, and they did not have to be in the "direst circumstances" to do it (Webber 1978:75). Many people whose names simply disappear from the slave lists over time are likely to have been sold as well (see slaves whose "ultimate fate" was "unknown" in table 12).

Isaac, Sr.'s account book (1724–49) occasionally records the sale or advertising of a "Negro," but, except in the case of Peter June, who was sold in 1732 (Account Book: March 15), never provides names or indicates the reason for selling, so that it is impossible to know in any particular instance from this document whether the person sold was an individual from Royall's own estate holdings or a recent import purchased for the purpose of selling at a profit. Nor can we know then whether these individuals were being
punished or simply liquidated into cash assets.

Newspapers suggest that it was often the latter. Isaac, Jr., routinely assured potential buyers that his "Negroes" were being sold for no particular shortcoming. Of one of his properties in Medford, he advertised:

> Also to be sold three likely Negro Men, one of which is not more than 20 Years old, all used to farming Business, and can be recommended, one of which is also qualified for Household Affairs, and suitable to wait on a Gentleman; also a Negro Woman. Said Negroes are not to be disposed of on any other Account, than that said Royall has determined to let his Farm. (*Boston Evening Post* 1752: February 24)

Four years later, he wrote:

> Also to be SOLD, Two likely Negro MEN, fit for the Country Business, and a likely Negro GIRL, fit for Town or Country, neither of which are sold for any Fault (*Boston Gazette or Weekly Journal* 1756: March 15)

Likewise, the "Negro Wench" and her four children, mentioned earlier, were being sold for "no other Reason but Want of Employ" (*Boston Evening Post* 1762: March 22).

It seems then that the Royalls sold slaves—even members of their own household—almost as a matter of course and with no real intent to punish. But punishment is what it must often have been for the people involved. There was also the possibility that no matter how bad one's condition was with the present master, things with the next one might be worse. In 1759 one Joseph Gould, of Lynn, Massachusetts, advertised a reward for the capture of a runaway once belonging to the Royalls:

> RUN away the 12th Instant from his Master [. . .] a Negro Man named George, formerly belonging to Isaac Royall, Esq; of Medford, who had on when he went away a stript worsted Cap, a coarse Linnen fly Coat, red Waistcoat, a Fustian Pair of Breeches, Yarn Stockings, and a Pair of Shoes. His Stature is short and

small, speaks broken English, his Age between thirty and forty Years. Whoever will apprehend and take up said Negro, or bring him to me his said Master, shall have TWO DOLLARS, and all necessary charges paid. (*Boston Gazette and Country Journal* 1759: September 24)

This George would have been about the same age as Abba's son of the same name, who was mentioned in 1738, but the fact that he spoke only broken English suggests that he was an African by birth and therefore a different individual. In either case, having been sold by the Royalls, he was clearly unhappy with his new master.

Jones (1990:39) points out that sales not only severed family ties but also separated people from all that was familiar, where they had "toiled, loved, borne children, and buried their dead." When Gould specified that George had once belonged to Isaac Royall, in Medford, he was implicitly acknowledging the strong ties to "home" and the possibility that George had returned to the Royalls' estate or might be seen thereabouts.

The Royalls might have justified their actions by pointing out that even "kind" masters were forced to sell slaves from time to time and divide them among their heirs at their deaths. Both father and son tried to preserve certain family relationships when they broke up their slaveholdings, and they occasionally took care to find good situations for the ones they rented out. These would seem to be the actions of kind masters. On the other hand, consideration for family at this estate was inconsistently given. Isaac, Sr., recognized a mother's relationship to her children, but not a father's, and Isaac, Jr. saw fit to favor some family units over others.

Isaac, Sr., might have congratulated himself on keeping together 11 members of Black Betty's family in his will, as well as seven members of Abba's family; but if the conjectural family relationships provided in fig. 34 are accurate, at least four husbands and wives were separated on his death; 11 children were separated from their fathers; and Trace might have been separated from her daughter and six grandchildren. Many years later, Isaac, Jr., also proved a fickle master with regard to family. His advertisement for a "Negro Wench" and her four children makes no stipulations for a group sale. He also eventually manumitted Betsey and Belinda in their old age, essentially to fend for themselves when they were past their productive years, but kept their children in bondage (Hoover 1974:83; Harvard Law Library Special Collections 1779). Betsey's daughter, Nancy, as stated, continued to be hired out by the year, while the Boy Joseph, whom I hypothesized above to have been Belinda's son, was given to Isaac's son-in-law, Sir William Pepperell, who had by this time resettled in England (Harvard Law Library Special Collections 1779). Meanwhile the sisters Bathsheba and Nanny he kept together and left to his daughter, Mary Erving (Harvard Law Library Special Collections 1779).

As with corporal punishment, the threat of sale or separation could be almost as traumatic as the deed itself, and the knowledge that the Royalls could sell them or their dearest loved ones at any time for any reason must have weighed heavily on the Royall slaves' minds. In fact it was precisely because family could be a mitigating institution for the enslaved that it could also be a pacifying one (Jones 1990:61). Masters used family as their trump card in exacting obedient behavior from their slaves and widely acknowledged the threat of sale as the "most effective long-term mechanism of control" (Jones 1990:37).

In 1746 the *Boston Evening-Post* (December 8) reported a double suicide of a couple threatened with the woman's imminent sale to the country. The man slit her throat with a razor and then shot himself in the head. When Isaac, Jr., was in exile in Halifax, Nova Scotia, he found himself in reduced financial straits and wrote to his agent, Simon Tufts, on March 12, 1775. He instructed Tufts to sell several of his slaves in Medford and to take as little as £15 for Stephen and George (Hoover 1974:83). Unbeknownst to Isaac, Jr., George, who may have served the Royalls for as many as 38 years and may have been by this time well into his eighties, had perhaps anticipated his master's course of action and slit his own throat the day before (NEHGS 1907). On March 16 his clothing was appraised, and his "Buckiles, Buttons, etc." were eventually sold for £1.7.6 (Middlesex County Probate 1778). They more than covered the expense of the funeral and burial, which had cost only 15 shillings (Middlesex County Probate 1778). Many masters would not have paid for a funeral at all, and though numerous individuals died on the Royalls' estate over the years (see table 12), George is the only one for whom there is documentary evidence of having been paid last respects by the family he served.

Another way in which the Royalls probably kept up appearances was to spare no expense in providing medical care, paying, among other things, over £8 to Dr. Ware for salivating Peter June in 1732, which refers to a grim procedure of force-feeding mercury to a patient in order to cause excessive salivation (Account Book: April 29). Later the same year they paid £15 for salivating "the Negro Boy" (Account Book: Sept. 1). Then on Christmas Eve in 1737, £17.13 went to Dr. Boylston for medicine and attending Captain, who was "infirm" (Account Book:- Dec. 24; Middlesex County Probate 1739). These were sizeable sums and probably represent the Royalls' good faith efforts to provide the best medical care, as it was then known, that money could buy.

Besides being morbidly ineffectual, though, such practices represented a European-based understanding of health and the body and completely ignored the fact that many early African Americans and their more modern descendants believed that illness had both a natural and a supernatural component (see Laguerre 1987; Puckett 1926:204; Thompson 1983:117; Wilkie 2000:166–70). Medical treatments such as the ones for which the Royalls paid so dearly were, from a black perspective, not only bad for the body, but bad for the soul.

A black-glazed, coarse earthenware teacup was recovered from the outbuilding in the slave quarters' west yard (fig. 37). It is an artifact that can possibly be interpreted within the framework of ethnomedicine, or folk medical knowledge and practice. Along with possible artifacts of conjuration, such finds implicitly evidence a broader "sympathy toward the metaphysical realm" of magic, ghosts, spirits, and witches, and would have belonged to a set of practices that served, among other things, as a kind of preventative medicine (Wilkie 2000:180).

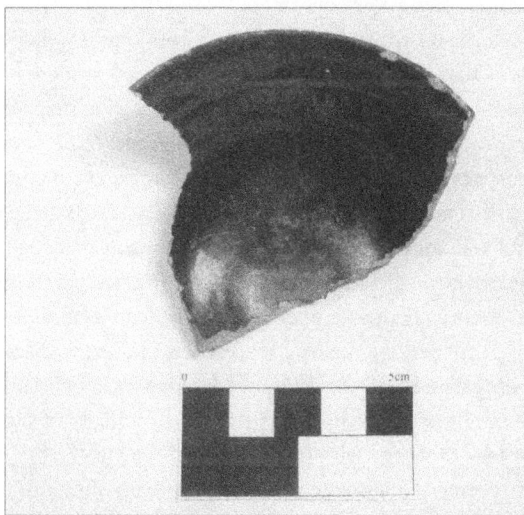

FIG. 37. Black-glazed earthenware teacup, recovered from the outbuilding foundation in the slave quarters' west yard and showing heavy-use wear on the bottom. It is one possible component of the Royall slaves' body of folk medical knowledge and practices at the site.

But while the talisman and pestle might have been best used in treating and preventing supernatural ills, the teacup more likely belonged to the folk medical knowledge concerning the treatment of the body—the natural component of an illness. Wilkie (2000:170; 1996:124) has argued for the incorporation of teacups into traditional African American ethnomedical practices at Oakley Plantation in Louisiana. Of course, there were times when a teacup was a teacup, used to drink tea or coffee or any other beverage, even water. But the evidence at Oakley Plantation seems to point to additional, and alternative, uses that might have included making and containing medicinal ointments or consuming medicinal teas or brews (Wilkie 2000:170; 1996:124). While there are other teacups at the Royall House (MNV = 10), this particular teacup is different because it is the only one of coarse earthenware recovered from the site and because it shows heavy use wear on the bottom, indicating frequent use, apparently of mashing and/or stirring. The heaviness of the wear suggests that it should at least be considered as a possible component of enslaved people's own tradition of medical or ritual self-help.

Laguerre (1987:26) states that most slaves had a repertoire of folk treatments and cures for minor illnesses and ailments, based on their own experiences, as well as individual and collective memories. These often diverged greatly from their owners' perceptions of illness, and so enslaved people were often forced to treat themselves in ways that seemed proper and effective to them. When an ailment exceeded their own knowledge or ability, they frequently sought the help of a root doctor, who may or may not have been a conjurer as well. Ethnohistorical evidence suggests that enslaved people often considered root doctors to be more effective than white physicians, and this because they were prepared to treat not just the natural component of the illness, but also the supernatural one. Said one 19th-century southern woman, "Chile, her sickness ain' nat'ul, and edicated doctor's medicine is pointedly ag'in it" (quoted in Puckett 1926:204).

So powerful was mind over matter that if a person truly believed him- or herself to be hexed, he or she might actually begin to show psychosomatic symptoms and even eventually die—a phenomenon called "voodoo death." Cannon (1979:372) has grounded the reality of voodoo death in the disastrous physiological effects of fear-induced shock. Likewise, if a person believed in the power of hoodoo, he might convince himself that he was actually recovering. Puckett (1926:211–13) tells the story with great mirth of how he, posing as a hoodoo-doctor himself, prescribed a hoodoo-doctor informant with a backache a mash made of, among other things, fried worms, lard, and hair from a strong man, and that not only did the man believe himself cured, but also became eager to talk shop with Puckett. This was true in historical times, as well. One former slave, William Newkirk, stated,

> Well, the root doctor was all we needed. They [were] better than the doctors nowadays. There wasn't all this cutting and when you [were] sick, the root doctor would make some tea and give you . . . something to rub with and that's all. Then before you [knew] it, you [were] all right. (quoted in Laguerre 1987:26)

This observation raises the point that root doctors may indeed have been more effective simply in the lack of physical harm they caused. White medicine in the 18th and much of the 19th centuries would be considered unscientific and barbaric by today's standards—part of what Savitt (1978:3) calls the "medically hostile atmosphere" of white society to black sensibilities. In plantation settings, the master and/or overseer were generally in charge of determining whether someone was sick and in need of treatment, as well as of taking the necessary steps to provide it (Savitt 1978:156).

Account book entries show that the Royalls relied principally on white physicians and apothecaries for all of their health-care needs, which might have fit very well in their own understanding of human anatomy and the "etiology of diseases," but probably not those of their slaves (Laguerre 1987:35; fig. 38).

The discovery in the Royalls' account book of the salivation procedure underscores the fact that white physicians could doctor their patients to further illness, pain, or even death with their "Herculean medicines" (Laguerre 1987:30) of bloodletting, purging, blistering, or puking or the forcefeeding of chemical

FIG. 38. Two pharmaceutical bottles recovered from the Royall House. Several account book entries record the purchase of "sundry Medicines" and "Druggs" from the apothecary's shop (Account Book: April 8, 1726; Feb. 27, 1739; Feb. 19, 1741). Whether used for themselves or for their slaves or both, these bottles are probably reflective of the Royalls' own conceptions of illness and appropriate treatment. They fit within the European medical tradition, which is based on the classification and treatment of "natural illness" (Wilkie 2000:171).

elements such as mercury, arsenic, or antimony (Laguerre 1987:30; Savitt 1978). Not only did such treatments ignore the spiritual side to illness, the latter three were also deadly poisons. Home remedies and folk medical knowledge would have been essential to every slave community's arsenal of psychological self-help, as well as physical survival (Savitt 1978:216). Enslaved people would have had their own folk conceptions of the medicinal properties, real or imagined, of various plants; their own classifications of natural and supernatural illnesses; and their own understanding of what constituted appropriate treatments. The amulet, stone pestle, and earthenware teacup at the Royall House may represent these enslaved people's attempts to take diagnosis and treatment of their illnesses and afflictions, both natural and supernatural, into their own hands whenever they could. Documents suggest that the alternative—to seek medical care from the Royalls' white physicians—would have been an unpleasant and even dangerous undertaking.

Sales, hire outs, family break-ups, illness and unsatisfactory medical treatment, deaths, and a suicide—these were the things that seem to have characterized the Royalls' relationship to their slaves, and they stand in stark contrast to the Royalls' own pretensions to benevolence. In addition there is the nagging question of what had induced Hector and Quaco to enter the conspiracy to revolt in Antigua in 1736, when their master, Isaac Royall, Sr. was widely considered to be "kind." Did he break the social contract in some way? Lapse into a fit of cruelty or show indifference at a key moment? Or did "kindness," such as it was, backfire and paradoxically make enslaved people feel the injustice and hopelessness of their position more keenly? Frederick Douglass wrote that whenever his condition was improved, it only increased his desire to be free (1845:349).

Records abound for violence perpetrated against masters whom their attackers themselves acknowledged as kind or gentle or at the very least not intolerably cruel. All of those individuals executed or banished for their involvement in the 1736 conspiracy in Antigua were skilled labor, house slaves, drivers, or people otherwise privileged above the rest in the hierarchy of slave labor and in the estimation of their masters. All of the ringleaders were characterized as "valuable Tradesmen and Sensible Fellows" (*New York Weekly Journal* 1737: April 25). Nat Turner, the infamous leader of a bloody 1831 rebellion in Southampton County, Virginia, stated in his confessions that his master, Joseph Travis, had been a kind master and Nat had never had any reason to complain of his behavior toward him (Gray 1832:11). And yet Travis and his wife died in their nightgowns, under the sword, the very first of the rebellion's 55 victims (Gray 1832:12). Hector was the Royalls' slave driver, a position that was third in command on a plantation, answering only to the overseer and the planter himself. The Royalls would have trusted him implicitly. Quaco's occupation was not given, although he was likely a high-ranking individual also. The conspiracy had been most flabbergasting to Antigua's white population because it had been perpetrated by the "very top Negroes" of the island, completely trusted by their masters, and "it was with great difficulty, any Crime was believed against them" (a concerned citizen, quoted in Gaspar 1985:4).

Thus, while the Royalls might have thought themselves benevolent masters and striven to project that image to their peers, it is questionable what the Royalls' "people" really thought of them, "as masters go" (Webber 1978:75). The Royalls might not have kept all family members together, but they kept some together. They might have allowed at least some of the people they held as slaves to keep their own names and name their children according to customs that they themselves deemed appropriate or important. Certain individuals seem also to have been especially favored, receiving gifts, and achieving a degree of autonomy to accomplish their tasks and move about the landscape. What the documents also indicate, however, is that in several circumstances other enslaved people have singled out in their narratives as the most traumatic or important in their lives, the Royalls were acting in a way that we, as modern observers, have no other choice than to interpret as reflecting insensitivity, indifference, or, at the very least, an imagined powerlessness to do otherwise. Recall the nonchalance with which Fanny Kemble's husband, "Mr. Butler," informed one of his male slaves that he was to be sold away from his family—leaning against a table with arms folded, "occasionally uttering a few words of counsel to his slave to be quiet and not fret, and not make a fuss about what there was no help for" (Kemble 1984:136).

Hector and Quaco were driven to a desperate act, and Hector paid the ultimate price, while Quaco probably never saw a single person of his acquaintance again. Belinda's own anger in her petitions of 1783 and 1787, though expressed through the words of another, comes through with chilling clarity over two centuries later. George's last wretched "act of hope and despair" was extreme (Piersen 1988:74–75), but slave suicide was not uncommon and speaks volumes about the pitfalls inherent in the search for evidence of kindness in masters. It is also possible, for example, that Plato, who drowned at Ten Hills Farm in 1768, was another suicide (NEHGS 1907). Piersen (1988:75) attributes the purposeful self-drowning of two Massachusetts men, Cato and Tom, to the "common Afro-American conviction that drowning could be a supernatural method for returning to Africa—as well as affording an escape from slavery."

The numerous "practical limits" the Royalls set for their slaves in establishing full, rewarding, and stable family lives and community ties have shed significant light on the nature of master-slave relations at that estate. That there is also abundant evidence of how these people sought, within practical limits, to structure their lives meaningfully and to create personal identities and relationships that belied their status as slaves, however, is also testament to the resilience of the enslaved. These private personae and relationships partly arose in response to, but also helped people adapt to the inescapable fact of, their enslavement and thus were organically incorporated into the process of racialization. The differences we see in the daily lives and modes of self-expression among the Royalls and the people they held as slaves were not so much the differences between African and European, as they might once have been interpreted, but rather the emerging and crystallizing differences between black and white.

Work and Play

Over 8,000 fragments of coarse earthenware, representing a minimum of 98 vessels associated with the kitchen duties of enslaved women in food preparation, serving, and consumption, were recovered from the Royall House grounds (tables 16 and 17). The fact that they represent 29 percent of the total ceramic vessel assemblage of the household reflects some of the formidable task of preparing food for the Royalls' larder (such as milk, cream, butter, preserves, and so on) that fed, at the maximum size in 1738, the 37 black and white members of the household. Then there was the additional task of preparing meals at least three times a day for dozens of people, including the Royalls, their many slaves, and any seasonal or day labor they had hired. There would also have been meat to cure, laundry to wash, candles and soap to make, wool carding, spinning, and weaving to do. The monumentality of the task of keeping such a large household running smoothly is hard to imagine and would have fallen heavily on the shoulders of the women. Fox-Genovese describes in detail the work of enslaved women:

> Slaves worked in the kitchens and smokehouses . . . to produce three meals a day.
> . . . Slaves waited on table. Slaves washed and ironed; took up and put down carpets; carried the huge steaming pots for the preservations of fruits; lifted the barrels in which cucumbers soaked in brine; pried open the barrels of flour; swept floors and dusted furniture; hoed and weeded gardens; collected eggs from the poultry. Slaves suckled, washed, and minded infants, freeing the mistress to shop, or visit, or read, or write. Slaves spun and wove and sewed household linens and "negro clothes." Slaves quilted. Slaves did whatever their mistresses needed or wanted done. . . . (Fox-Genovese 1988:137–38)

On the other hand, in the routine nature of such basic household production, enslaved women might have found an opportunity to work together with minimal supervision. There they might have forged a camaraderie through the drudgery of their work, traded gossip and idle chit-chat, and brought a new generation up into their "sisterhood" (Fox-Genovese 1988:186). These relationships

TABLE 16.

Coarse earthenware fragment and vessel counts

Vessel type	No. of sherds	MNV
Milkpan	931	53
Jar/crock	350	33
Mug/pitcher	13	3
Basin	1	1
Unidentified	6740	8
Total ceramic kitchenware assemblage	**8035**	**98**

TABLE 17.

Refined earthenware, stoneware, and porcelain fragment and vessel counts

Vessel type	No. of sherds	MNV
Plate	1108	38
Mug	166	22
Saucer	246	20
Chamber pot	113	19
Bowl	81	13
Teacup	57	10
Teapot	20	3
Salt	1	1
Unidentified	5320	106
Total domestic, tableware, teaware, and exotic beverage ceramic Assemblage	**7014**	**240**

would have carried over after working hours and been invaluable in creating a supportive social network.

Such relationships of work and play among enslaved women are also evoked among the plant remains collected from the site. The original research questions with regard to the floral analysis were ambitious and relatively few floral remains with which to address them were actually recovered. Ideally we might have been able to determine, for example, whether and to what extent the Royalls' slaves were foraging in the nearby marshes and forests for edible or medicinal wild plants and whether they were cultivating small garden plots of their own. Plants not native to the area, for instance, or clearly of a domesticated strain, might be considered to reflect cultivation on garden plots as a dietary supplement or source of economic surplus for the enslaved.

Nine soil samples from the site were floated and analyzed by Julie Hansen of Boston University in 2002 (Hansen 2002; appendix), yielding a small number of fruit fragments, seeds, and charred wood. The samples were taken primarily from the slave quarters' west yard, from the outbuilding foundation, and from an 18th-century debris layer in the south yard. These were the best closed contexts on site that dated to the Royall occupation (Chan 2003: chap. 5).

The charcoal samples were few in number and fragmentary in nature. Where identifiable, the wood came from oak, maple, plane, and locust trees, all of which grew abundantly in the region. More than the somewhat obvious fact that these species were being burned for warmth and cooking, it is difficult to say.

The seeds, however, were more evocative. A mixture of various unidentified species of *Rubus* (which includes Allegheny blackberry, cloudberry, northern dewberry, black raspberry, and red raspberry); elderberries; and grapes were found. Seeds were confined to the outbuilding foundation deposits and were found to be mineralized rather than carbonized. Mineralization occurs most frequently in deposits where there is a high concentration of organic waste. The few remains recovered here might therefore have come from a context where hearth or oven refuse was dumped with other organic, including human, wastes (Hansen 2002:1). Although the outbuilding was too shallow to have been an outhouse, the idea of the seeds' having come from hearth or oven refuse and kitchen waste disposal is consistent with the large amounts of ash and charcoal recovered from the feature, as well as the prodigious amount of other food remains in the form of bone and shell.

All but two of the seeds recovered were wild, showing no indication of garden cultivation. Only the size and shape of the grape seeds recovered seem to be of a domesticated variety (Hansen 2002:1). As there is no documentary evidence to support the cultivation of grapes at Ten Hills Farm, however, if they were being grown at all, it was probably on a small scale for the Royalls' own benefit. Otherwise it is most reasonable to assume that the grape seeds came from raisins, which would have been bought at market.

What the rest of the remains seem to be telling us, though, is principally that the enslaved people at Ten Hills Farm were collecting berries, no doubt partially consumed as fresh fruit—as any berry picker will tell you—but mostly for the purposes of making preserves, jams, jellies, juices, pies, or flavorings. These would have been an integral component of the women's work in the kitchen, and mothers and daughters or groups of women might have collected berries together over the summer to fill the Royalls' larder for the winter. The various *Rubus* species and elderberries are summer fruit, ripening in June and July, and yielding fruit for most of the summer. *Rubus* plants are found in thorny thickets that grow in hedgerows, along fence lines, or in forest clearings, while elderberries tend to grow on small shrubs found in meadows, clearings, and alluvial forests (Hansen 2002:1).

We might imagine then that berry-picking season was a highly anticipated one among the enslaved women on the estate. It would have provided an occasional, and legitimate, respite in the dog days of summer from standing over steaming cauldrons or in front of blazing fires. It might have relieved sore fingers from the endless task of spinning in the sweltering stillness of the third-floor garrets. The work their men did—sons, fathers, brothers, husbands—often took them far afield, and we may wonder how many women, young and old, listened with envy to tales of things done, seen, or heard by their men while they were away. A woman's work was close to home. Berry-picking excursions would have been one of the few opportunities to get away from the confines of the kitchen and the great house. It might have been that gossip was traded on such excursions and advice given, a sweaty face lifted to catch a breeze. The feeling of being away from Mistress Royall might have lightened one's step, made one a little quicker to laugh, less careful to do it quietly. Perhaps feeling a little reckless, grievances might have been aired too, with the knowledge that none could hear and none would tell. Tired and cramped legs might have been stretched in jubilant sprints across a meadow, and there would be time also to collapse breathless beneath a tree and sample the bounty of one's handiwork and—sticky, sweet, and tired— relish this time away.

As a scientist I must concede that none of this can be read directly from a few hundred berry seeds, but as a humanist I am not so concerned about that. I can say it no better than Anne E. Yentsch did over a decade ago, when she insisted that we

> use empathy as one means to achieve understanding and let emotion enter the discussion.... Laughter vanishes faster than sorrow marked on a grave and while the latter becomes part and parcel of the archaeological record, many things which delight the human mind do not. (Yenstch 1992:308)

The floral analysis did not yield the kind of data that would allow for a fine-grained interpretation of economic, subsistence, or medical activities of the enslaved people at this site. The presence of wild berry seeds on a historical domestic site is hardly surprising, nor might we suppose to have blazed a trail by depicting berry picking as a pleasurable experience or seek to claim that this was so only for slaves. And yet the seeds at this site are by no means uninformative, for within the context of a slave quarters deposit, even a few hundred seeds can evoke small pleasures that would have been especially gratifying, satisfying, and important in dealing successfully with an otherwise bleak and oppressive existence. The camaraderie of such group activities, says Yentsch (1992:308), would have been healing and so should not be overlooked or underestimated.

Piersen (1988:96) states that throughout the 18th century the black folk life in New England that arose around such camaraderie was "more Afro-American than Yankee." At the Royall House, the stone bead and possible artifacts of conjuration described above are the only artifacts recovered from the grounds that seem to reflect any peculiarly ethnic behaviors. And even of these we have argued throughout that they may best be interpreted, in an American context, as arising from the process of racialization. The rest of the artifacts of black folk life and leisure time activities are distinctive—and they are associated here with the enslaved population—because they are either handmade or are mainstream artifacts that have been reworked for alternate purposes. This fact probably stems principally from enslaved people's restricted access to goods and their creativity in making do with what they had. The result, however, might have been the development and accumulation of a whole range of material things that gave the color line wide tangible expression. Such material signals gave the makers and users of such artifacts a distinctive "Otherness" that both resulted from as well as informed the crystallization of race as it was then understood.

Nights in particular were times for "quiet family pleasures" such as folk songs, storytelling, play, talk, or additional work to meet the family's own needs (Webber 1978:17). Three marbles were recovered from the Royall House slave quarters—two commercially produced white clay ones from the courtyard and the slave quarters' west yard and a handmade red clay one from the slave quar-

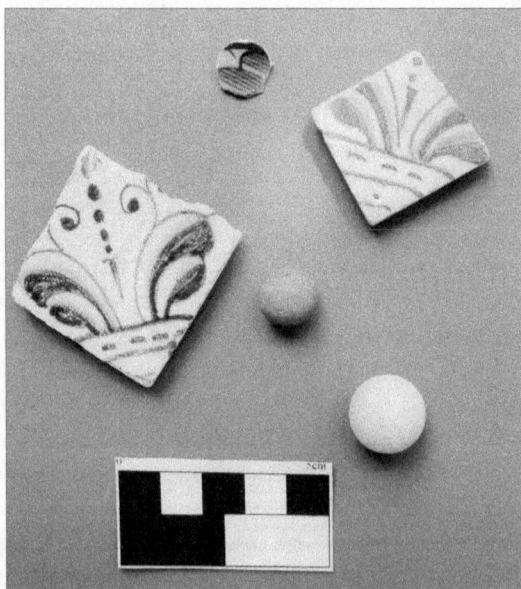

FIG. 39. A collection of leisure-time artifacts from the Royall House slave quarters, including the two marbles (handmade, left; commercially made, right; recovered from the slave quarters' south and west yards, respectively). Former slave narratives indicate that slave boys were especially fond of playing marbles and often made their own marbles out of local clay and fired them in the kitchen hearth (Webber 1978:180–82).

ters' south yard (fig. 39). Documentary evidence suggests that young slave boys were often passionate about playing marbles and made their own marbles of local clay, firing them in the kitchen hearth. Tom Hawkins, a former slave from South Carolina, recalled, "De best game us had was marbles and us played wid homemade clay marbles most of the time" (quoted in Webber 1978:180–81). Frank Gill concurred, saying that he and his friends "played ball, and marbles, 'specially marbles, hit was our big game" (quoted in Webber 1978:182).

The marbles are evocative because they are likely archaeological indicators of the presence of children. What is more, marbles in the 18th century was a boys' game, and although slave girls might have gotten away with playing it, white girls—particularly of the slaveholding class—were unlikely to do so. Isaac Royall, Jr. was already 18 years old before moving into the house in Charlestown, and he had only daughters. Thus the marbles likely represent the leisure-time activities of enslaved children, probably boys, at Ten Hills Farm.

In 1739 there were 15 children—eight boys and seven girls—at the Charlestown estate, all of whom were black (Middlesex County Probate 1739). In fact the only white children ever to live on the site during the Royalls' occupation were Elizabeth Royall (1740–47), who died in childhood, and her sisters, Polly (b. 1744) and Elizabeth (b. 1747). We can also probably assume that the Royalls owned several other children, but since censuses taken for tax purposes only counted slaves over the age of 16, they would have gone unrecorded.

Childhood was often recalled with pleasure by former slaves, as some of their only carefree days under slavery. They describe exploring the countryside, roaming through the woods, collecting small finds, playing games, wading, or fishing, either alone or with playmates, white and black, and seem generally not to have realized their station in life until they reached an age when they were forced to start work or were faced with forcible family breakups (Webber 1978:181). Harriet Jacobs (1987:5) starts her narrative with "I was born a slave; but I never knew it till six years of happy childhood had passed away." The friendships and ties forged in play, as well as work, during childhood were important in the socialization of children into the slave community, helping them to make the transition together from carefree childhood to the sorrows of being an adolescent or adult slave (see King 1995:44). The "roles, friendships, values, attitudes, and understandings formed within the peer group . . . continued, and served as an important foundation upon which slaves acted as adult members of the quarter community" (Webber 1978:190).

Evidence of adult rest and relaxation at the Royall House comes principally in the form of tobacco pipes and gaming pieces. A minimum of 37 clay tobacco pipes were recovered from the site, consisting of 388 stem and bowl fragments. Table 18 shows the frequency distribution of tobacco pipes at the Royall House.

These pipe fragments likely represent the smoking activities of both the Royalls and their slaves, but three specimens are of especial interest with regard to recreation among the enslaved. One is a pipe, possibly hand built, made of local red clay (fig. 40). Two other commercially produced white clay pipes have been altered by the incision of the letter "M" in several places, which may have been an initial meant to mark ownership (figs. 41, 42, and 43).

Only one person, black or white, lived at Ten Hills Farm whose name began with "M": a woman named Mira, listed in the 1754 Massachusetts slave census. Both men and women enjoyed smoking tobacco pipes in the slave community. Laurie Wilkie (2000:217) quotes one old informant from 1940s Louisiana as saying, "De gals now'days smokes cigarettes; dat's bad for deir health. I smokes a pipes [sic]. . . . A pipe's healthy. . . . A pipe's de best way for a woman to use tobacco." Howson (1990:85) also suggests that smoking was an important part of social life in the quarter and that it was often over a pipe that enslaved people were able to create and maintain "an alternative society to that envisioned by planters."

For this reason it is worth digressing for a moment to consider briefly the significance of finding artifacts of recreation on slave sites. When Charles Fairbanks started investigating the archaeological remains of the life of enslaved Africans in Florida in the 1960s, he was the first to do so, and one of the most startling things he found was the abundant evidence of recreation. Somehow time for leisure or play did not fit preconceived notions about what slave life must have been like.

TABLE 18.

Clay tobacco pipe frequency distribution

Location	NISP	% Total	MNV[a]	% MNV
Courtyard	98	25.26	10	27.03
SQWY	122	31.44	13	35.14
SQEY	52	13.40	8	21.62
SQSY	77	19.85	5	13.51
SQNY	1	0.26	–	–
Park	34	8.76	1	2.70
West garden	3	0.77	–	–
Mansion east yard	1	0.26	–	–
Total	**388**	**100.00**	**37**	**100.00**

Note: [a]MNVs were calculated based on diagnostic portions of the pipes: complete or nearly complete bowls, stamped makers' marks, heels, and mouthpieces. The clustering of most of the tobacco pipe fragments in the slave quarters' work yards may either reflect the fact that slaves were the principal smokers on the site or that the work yards, as discussed in chapters 5 and 8, were considered the most appropriate venues for waste disposal. The fact that only 37 individual pipes can actually be identified, however, makes generalizations about "who smoked more" at Ten Hills Farm relatively meaningless.

As the archaeology of early African America has burgeoned in the last decades, however, Fairbanks's unexpected anomaly has come to be seen as almost characteristic of slave sites. Why?

Recreation among the enslaved was important not just because it allowed them a physical and emotional release from the rigors of slavery, but also because leisure time "belonged to them, not to their masters" (Genovese 1974:556). Evidence of games or other forms of recreation in the archaeological record then is more than just quaint. In recreation we see an active reassertion of humanity

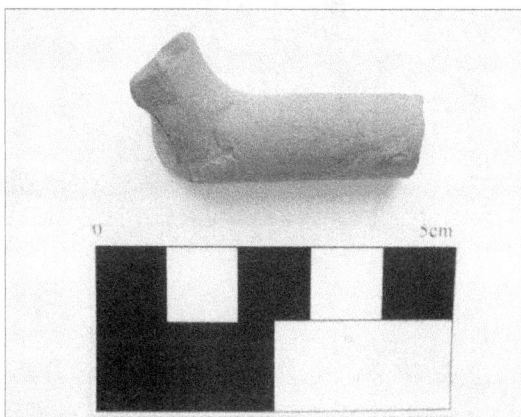

FIG. 40. A tobacco pipe made of local red clay, recovered from the slave quarters East Yard.

FIG. 41. A commercially produced tobacco pipe, incised with the initial "M" three times. Recovered from the slave quarters' west yard outbuilding.

FIG. 42. Reverse view of the same pipe bowl, showing a third "M" incised on the left side.

FIG. 43. What may be the fragment of another "M"-incised pipe bowl, although the discoloration caused by heavy use makes positive identification difficult. Recovered from slave quarters' west yard.

within the worst of dehumanizing conditions. The prevalence of such evidence on slave sites across the country attests to its importance, as do the often-creative ways these people seem to have had in ensuring that they would have such items.

We cannot know for certain that Mira owned these pipes or even that the "M" was meant to be an initial marking ownership, but the pipes' reworking suggests that they can be associated with the slave community and that they had been singled out among one's personal belongings as having peculiar social import, perhaps because they were imported and difficult to come by. Many other artifacts with incisions and inscriptions have been found on slave sites as well and interpreted as personal marks of ownership (see Klingelhofer 1987:114). The role of such artifacts in status differentiation within the slave community should also be considered, however, as inscriptions would have at least implied literacy, even if the individual was not actually fluent.

The third specimen of interest here is the local red-clay tobacco pipe recovered from the slave quarters' east yard. Made in the style of the commercially available European white-clay pipes of the time, it is possible that it was made in imitation of these imported pipes because imported goods were too expensive or too hard to come by for slaves. Henry (1979:14), for example, has linked the prevalence of terracotta pipes on 17th- and 18th-century English sites during certain time periods in Virginia and Maryland to major economic depressions in the region. She suggests that their presence on these sites indicates a "strong tendency toward greater self-sufficiency" when affordability and availability of English goods was low (Henry 1979:16). Wilkie (2000:216) has also pointed out, however, that, at least in the 19th century, stoneware and redware pipe bowls, made for use with disposable reed stems, sometimes came free with a pouch of tobacco. The context in which the red-clay pipe was found at the Royall House dates solidly to the mid 18th century, with no creamware and only three sherds of pearlware present, suggesting a TAQ (see Glossary) of no later than the 1770s. Nor was the pipe made commercially for use with detachable stems. If slaves were responsible for making this pipe, it can be seen as further evidence of the importance of smoking as a leisure-time activity in the slave community, as well as of the craftsmanship and resourcefulness required to make it when commercially produced ones might have been difficult to obtain.

Emerson (1999) has discussed at length the heavy concentration of locally made tobacco pipes in the late-17th-century Chesapeake Bay region in plantation deposits and has suggested that these pipes were produced by slaves who desired European pipes but had little access to imported goods. These pipes are hand- or mold-made and often incised with abstract designs, and sometimes initials, which Emerson (1999:57) interprets as having a "strong decorative affinity" with West African aesthetic traditions in ceramic and pipe production. There is both documentary and archaeological evidence that suggests that English colonists and Native Americans were also making clay tobacco pipes in the Chesapeake during that time, though, and Emerson's interpretations are not unchallenged (compare Mouer et al. 1999, who argue that the Native American role in the production of Chesapeake pipes for trade with plantation owners and their slaves has been severely underestimated). Whether enslaved people were making

FIG. 44. Pearlware gaming piece recovered from the slave quarters' west yard.

the pipes or not, though, they were certainly using them, and the presence of locally made pipes in plantation contexts supports the importance of smoking as part of the social life in the quarters.

Other hand-made objects include three ceramic sherds recovered from the slave quarters that have been reworked into geometrical shapes and are interpreted here as gaming pieces (figs. 44 and 46). In fact the two squares, made from Dutch fireplace tiles, while different in size, are made from the same place in the pattern, suggesting that they might have been made as part of a matching set (figs. 44 and 45).

A French faience plate gives further evidence of the Royall slaves' reusing discarded, lost, or stolen materials from the great house. Once likely of considerable value, the plate was broken into several large pieces and mended with a tarlike substance that left thick black seams across the surface of the plate (fig. 47). It is unlikely that the plate was mended in such a manner for use on the Royalls' table. Their items of social display were impeccable. Unlike the probate inventory of Isaac, Sr.'s son-in-law, Henry Vassal, which recorded several broken and mended items—from earthenware to fine china, jugs to candlesticks—neither Isaac, Sr.'s or Isaac, Jr.'s inventories reflect any such thing (Middlesex County Probate 1739, 1769, 1778). Schmidt and Mrozowski (1983) also point out that faience was a smuggled good so that it is possible that the Royalls, as Loyalists to the Crown, might have tried to divest themselves of such incriminating evidence once the political atmosphere began to get tense. And perhaps someone from the Kitchen Quarters retrieved the plate from the trash and mended it to brighten a dingy table, deriving a certain tingling pleasure from owning something that was once admired but seemingly forever out of reach.

Fig. 45. Portions of Dutch fireplace tiles recovered from the Royall House property.
Isaac Royall, Sr. likely obtained these decorative tiles from his brother's shop in Union Street.
Jacob Royall advertised in the *Boston Gazette* (1729: Sept. 8–15) some "Very good Fig. d Dutch
Tyle for Chimneys, to be Sold by the Dozen."

Fig. 46. Two possible gaming pieces made from Dutch fireplace tiles, which took advantage of the
same part of a fleur-de-lis pattern and may reflect an attempt to make matching pieces. Recovered
from the slave quarters' west yard (left) and East Yard (right).

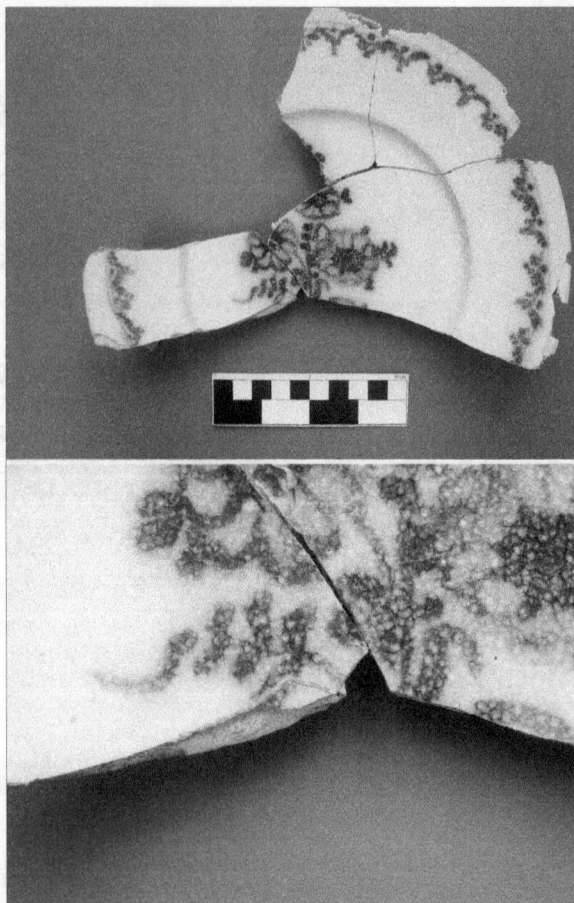

FIG. 47. French tin-glazed and, curiously, salt-glazed plate from the outbuilding foundation in the slave quarters' west yard. Broken into at least six pieces and mended with a tarlike substance that still clings to the body of the ceramic, the thick black seams are plainly visible across the surface of the plate (see enlargement and the seams in the white areas). Tar still adhering to the open edges of the plate shows that, when the plate was complete, the mending seams would have gone from one edge of the plate to the other.

Two thimbles, three straight pins, and a pair of scissors were also recovered from Royall-period contexts (fig. 48). Whether these particular artifacts were used by enslaved women or Elizabeth Royall and her daughters, the artifacts of sewing and clothing certainly reflect the fact that enslaved women often had to sew and mend their own clothes as well as those of their masters and that young slave girls were taught to perform minor sewing tasks as part of their generalized domestic training and frequently learned from their own mothers (Fox-Genovese 1988:153). Tending to the family's own sewing and mending needs took place after hours, and it was here too that plain clothes received from the master could be dressed up to reflect more of a personal aesthetic and sense of style.

Genovese (1974:557) says that one of the things enslaved people did to spruce up drab clothing was buy or make their own buttons to decorate the garment. What appears to be a very free form, but roughly square, button carved from bone was found in the outbuilding foundation in the slave quarters' west yard (fig. 49). It might have been made from scrap materials for utilitarian purposes, but its unusual character evokes a sense of unique self-expression. In New England, Piersen (1988:101) says, enslaved people combined their "owners' used clothing and their own purchases" to make bold statements in dress that underscored a great "joy in physical attractiveness" that was unseemly and unbefitting to white observers. On Sundays or for Saturday night parties and holidays, slaves often dressed themselves, as one slaveholder put it, "to death" (quoted in Genovese

FIG. 48. Artifacts of sewing and clothing from the Royall House slave quarters. The scissors, thimbles, one of the straight pins, and the possible button all came from the outbuilding foundations in the slave quarters' west yard The other straight pin was recovered from the slave quarters' east yard from the same context as the pearlware gaming piece.

FIG. 49. The presence of an eye at the back of this object makes it appear to be a bone button or something else meant to be sewn to cloth. It was recovered from the slave quarters' west yard outbuilding foundation and provides possible evidence of slaves' own endeavors in sprucing up drab clothing received from the Royalls and giving it a sense of personal style.

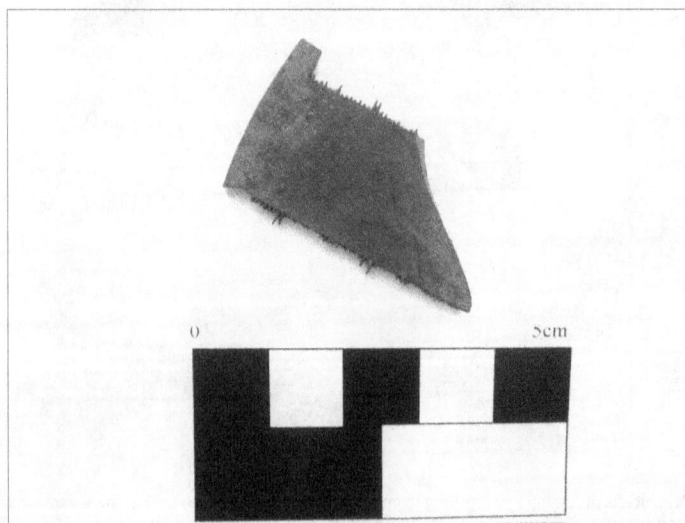

FIG. 50. Portion of a double-edged horn lice comb. The comb is typical of lice combs that can be found between 1600 and 1800, but its presence in the slave quarters' south yard among artifacts that date to the last half of the 18th century and the first quarter of the 19th century makes it possible, and even likely, that it was used by slaves. Genovese (1974:552) says that it was the responsibility of women to rid their husbands, children, and each other of lice in preparation for church services or other special occasions.

1974:556; fig. 50). Sundays were important, as were holidays, for games, contests, visits to and from friends and relatives (with parents and siblings dispersed over a wide area or among different owners), and going to Sunday markets and generally for interacting with a wider community of one's peers. During the first half of the 18th century, God-fearing Bostonians were dismayed at the swarms of black slaves who came to town every Sunday, "not with prayer books, but, as the selectmen complained, 'with corn, apples, and other fruit of the earth to the great disturbance of the public peace and scandal of our Christian profession'" (Piersen 1988:102). These markets did not just reflect slaves' own economic initiative, however, for they were also great "social attractions" for which people dressed in their finest, interacted with great hilarity with friends and family, and even snuck in a little "surreptitious drinking and gambling" as well in a carnival-like atmosphere (Piersen 1988:102–3).

Unfortunately the floral remains at this site, as discussed, give no evidence of the Royalls' slaves having been able to bring produce of their own to these Sunday markets, although that does not mean that they did not sometimes participate. Evidence of taking pride in personal appearance and hygiene as well as possibly exerting a personal sense of style indicates that there were opportunities for socialization and personal display.

Animal Remains

In addition to the archaeobotanical investigation, a faunal analysis was commissioned from Elizabeth Newman and David Landon, both of the University of Massachusetts at Boston (Newman and Landon 2002; appendix). The aim of the faunal investigation was similar to that of the floral one, to be able to trace foodways at the site from procurement to disposal and to determine what parts of what animals were being eaten, how they were prepared, and whether they were likely to have been rationed, scavenged (stolen), or foraged. In reconstructing such subsistence patterns, considerable light might be shed on the role that enslaved people played in the economy of the Royall household. Of particular interest too would be to find out what kind of, if any, private subsistence activities the enslaved were engaging in for themselves. Food, like family, can be a deeply personal, profoundly social phenomenon. The methods by which it is procured, the ways in which is prepared, and how and with whom it is consumed can provide invaluable insight into all kinds of social, economic, and cultural aspects of people's lives.

Numerous archaeological studies have been able to link species, body parts, and the spatial distribution of butchery techniques to the lower economic status and possible ethnic culinary preferences of slaves on plantation sites in the South (see McKee 1987, 1999; Reitz, Gibbs, and Rathbun 1985; Singleton 1991). Reitz, Gibbs, and Rathbun (1985:183), for example, state that on plantations located in coastal or estuarine environments, the evidence indicates that "planters, slaves, and freedmen all used wild resources extensively." Singleton (1991:172) also maintains that "at every slave site where food remains have been recovered and analyzed, there is evidence that African Americans consumed at least some wild foods." This would have stemmed in part from the fact that many masters expected their slaves to provision themselves to a certain extent, but also from the fact that hunting and providing extra food for one's own family was an empowering activity and therefore engaged in willingly (McKee 1999).

McKee (1987) has also found that of the domesticated barnyard species, such as cows, pigs, sheep, goats, chicken, and geese, which were presumably provisioned by the estate, enslaved people were getting a disproportionate amount of the lower utility cuts of meat (see head, tail, foot, or lower leg elements) and that these were being intensively processed to extract as much nutrition and other use out of them as possible. Differences in the butchery techniques may indicate ethnic preferences in food preparation and consumption. McKee (1987) argued, for example, that chopped bones in the slave quarters may have stemmed from an African American culinary preference for stews and pottages while sawn bones may have reflected the masters' European-derived preference for roasts and steaks.

More than 4,000 faunal specimens were recovered from the Royall House—86.5 percent of which were found in the yards surrounding the slave quarters—and mammals, birds, fish, shellfish, and amphibians were all represented. The Royall House faunal collection is interesting, however, in that it is totally divergent from expectations derived from other slave sites, and one is left to wonder whether this is the result of some systemic differences in the slave economy of New England or of some idiosyncratic circumstance of this particular site.

In terms of composition, the assemblage seems to represent standard New England fare, notable only for consisting of "exclusively domestic" or market species (Newman and Landon 2002:4). In fact the only wild animals recovered from the site were the remains of three rats, one toad, and one rabbit, the former two of which are almost certainly accidental inclusions and not part of the dietary repertoire of the Royalls or their slaves (Newman and Landon 2002:1, 3).

Among the mammals, cow, pig, cat, sheep/goat, dog, rabbit, and rat are represented. In terms of both sheer number of bones and total living biomass, the standard barnyard species (MNI = 19) show an "overwhelming predominance" (Newman and Landon 2002:6). Cows alone represent 52 percent of the total number of individual specimens (NISP). Add to that the sheep, goats, and pigs, and the number rises to 86.4 percent. The one rabbit recovered, which may or may not have been wild, represents only 0.01 percent of the total collection's biomass (Newman and Landon 2002:4).

Birds represent a distant second as a class of bones (2.2 percent of the assemblage, 1 percent of the biomass) and those represented include Canada goose, chicken, and turkey—which were identified to the species level—as well as several bones identified to the family level of swan/duck/goose, pigeon/rock dove, and chicken/turkey (Newman and Landon 2002:2). Documents record the presence of a pigeon house on the estate (Middlesex County Probate 1739; Account Book 1737:Sept. 12). The Royalls also apparently kept geese, paying 12 shillings in 1726 to build a coop to house them (Account Book 1726:Nov. 8). Doves and geese would likely have made their appearance on the Royalls' table on holidays and as part of their elegant hospitality in dining. In truth, though, these were not truly exotic, and the Royalls seem to have been decidedly unimaginative in their cuisine, contenting themselves with standard, homegrown New England fare. This finding was surprising given all of the documentary and artifact evidence presented thus far, which seems to point to a life of luxury, social display, and the Royalls' eye for detail in all things. Perhaps luxury was manifested instead through special modes of preparation, the use of exotic spices, and the presentation of rather ordinary foods in abundance on fancy tablewares in beautiful rooms of a commanding house.

There is no documentary mention of chickens or turkeys, but it is reasonable to assume that they roamed the grounds too, more or less at will. The recovery of gizzard stones (bits of ceramic that have been eaten and passed through the digestive tracts of birds, emerging with a smooth, water-worn appearance) further indicates that this was so. Even if some of the unidentified bones did belong to ducks or wild geese, though, as the ones identified only to the family level might, they do not necessarily reflect the hunting activities of slaves, for the shooting of game fowl was a proper gentlemanly pursuit.

The remains of six fish were recovered, representing haddocks, the cod/hake/haddock family, and two unidentified specimens (Newman and Landon 2002:2). Whereas others have done beautiful studies that link fishing to African American slave activities and culture (see Yentsch 1992), haddocks are deep-water species that would have been bought at market, and while they were perhaps consumed by the Royalls' slaves—as evidenced in the numerous purchases of barrels of fish in the account book—they were certainly not caught by them (Newman and Landon 2002:4). It is possible that they engaged in other fishing activities, though, either on their own or for the Royalls, but there is no documentary evidence of that, and, archaeologically, fish bones are more likely than other bones to be underrepresented because of their small size and tendency toward poor preservation. Only the preponderance of shellfish (8.72 percent of the total assemblage) might reflect subsistence activities of the enslaved. Eastern oysters, northern quahogs, soft-shell clams, and mussels are all represented—among which the oysters, at least, could have been collected from the nearby Mystic River (Brooks and Usher 1886). Oysters, of course, could just as easily represent the Royalls' own cuisine, and Isaac, Sr., did purchase oysters and lemons for his New Year's Eve party in 1737 (Account Book 1737:29 Dec.).

Of the total number of bones, only 394 (9.9 percent of the total assemblage) showed any signs of butchering: 314 cuts, 64 chops, 410 shears, and 33 saws were identified (Newman and Landon 2002:8). Contrary to expectations, chop marks were in the minority, although the low percentage of butchered bones of any kind makes the kind of fine-grained analysis that McKee (1987, 1999) did so elegantly somewhat inapplicable to the Royall House collection. There was evidence for high intensity butchering, but this was restricted primarily to low utility parts of the animal, so that it is not clear how much this reflects distinctive cultural or culinary behavior and how much the "basic mechanics of butchering the lower utility parts," which simply require more effort to process (Newman and Landon 2002:12). And as there was no dramatic spatial differentiation between high and low utility cuts of meat or of especially intensive butchering methods, the food remains alone do not seem to carry any indication of the economic, status, or racial differences between master and slave at Ten Hills Farm.

Thus, taken as a whole, the faunal remains seem at first glance to reflect nothing in particular about the enslaved at this estate, what they were eating, how they were getting it, or how it might have differed from the Royalls' fare. There is nothing particularly African American or reflective of slavery about the faunal assemblage, but remember that the assemblage is by its nature just a sample of the total recoverable collection. What all the negative evidence does imply, though, is that the Royall slaves were not engaging in many activities to supplement their diet, according to preference, taste, or necessity. Although they would have been in charge of raising, slaughtering, and preparing the livestock for the Royalls' and their own consumption, they do not seem to have provisioned the estate through independent activities. It is not likely that they hunted prestige game animals as elegant fare for the Royalls' hospitable dining. Nor do they seem to have exerted any Afro-Caribbean influence on what was eaten or how it was prepared.

Rather, if lack of any differentiation can be taken as a clue, they seem to have been eating more or less what the Royalls were eating, probably with the exception of the elegant preparation and presentation, and perhaps receiving more pork than beef and less meat overall than the Royalls. There is no evidence of a preference for stews or gumbos; no presence of small forest game, aside from a single rabbit; no evidence of fishing; only equivocal evidence of shellfish gathering; and few plant remains. This pattern differs a great deal from what has been observed of the subsistence activities of people enslaved in the South and Caribbean, who seem to have been intimately familiar with their natural surroundings and regularly engaged in clandestine hunting and foraging activities to supplement niggardly rations or simply to regain a sense of humanity and independence in their lives (Ascher and Fairbanks 1971; Ferguson 1992; McKee 1987). Given that many New England slaves were employed in diverse tasks that often dispersed them across the countryside and gave them a certain amount of unsupervised time, one might expect to find even more evidence of the exploitation of wild resources. But, as stated, there is next to none.

At present there are no directly comparative data to be had that might help establish the Royall House pattern either as a trend or an anomaly, but a couple of interpretations can be explored. On the one hand, it may be that the faunal remains at Ten Hills Farm reflect the Royalls' generosity in the distribution of rations; that their slaves were well fed, perceived themselves to be so, and were perhaps even thankful that food was one less thing they needed to worry about. After all they were relatively recent transplants to a new and unfamiliar environment and perhaps ill equipped to exploit the natural resources the way they might have done in the Caribbean.

On the other hand, I think it reasonable to wonder whether the Royalls' slaves did not miss trudging to the forest at night to check traps and snares; the challenge of outwitting nature's creatures; or the satisfying smell of a home-cooked meal, seasoned to sweet, juicy perfection with the feeling of achievement. Indeed it is possible, and even likely, that the nature of northern demographics and the northern slave system inherently restricted certain kinds of movement, outside normal waking, working hours. A black person out after nine o'clock in Medford—in violation of curfew there—would have been much more noticeable than one out in Popeshead or St. Johns and more quickly missed from the great house and nearby slave quarters than from a slave village a quarter-mile distant.

I had originally hoped—and even expected—that the floral and faunal analyses would fit well within a discussion of the creation and maintenance of "private personae" and black community life in the quarters. I had no reason to assume otherwise. All historical and archaeological evidence thus far had pointed to exactly this. But the plant and animal remains from this site are perhaps more informative in what they do not tell than in what they do.

Berry picking would have been one important way for enslaved women to escape the physical confines of slavery, much the way that enslaved men were able to do on a more regular basis because of the nature of their work. But freely roaming the countryside, while perhaps part of many enslaved people's workaday world, does not seem to have figured prominently, if at all, in independent subsistence or economic activities and thus does not seem to have been an active arena for the further development and support of private identities and family and community life.

The floral and faunal remains suggest that the Royalls' slaves were doing little or nothing to supplement the provisions they got from the Ten Hills Farm stores, either through the exploitation of wild resources or the cultivation of domesticated ones. What this means is that while the varied and dispersed nature of much of the labor engaged in by northern slaves would have provided opportunities to become autonomous in ways unknown among slaves in other parts of the Americas, the close living quarters and relatively low density of blacks in the region also gave northern slaves less freedom of movement in their natural and cultural environs. This must have been a great loss in autonomy. Indeed, since African American folk culture in other areas is known to have sprung up and flourished in physically marginal areas such as fields and forest clearings and depended largely on enslaved people's ability to get away from the plantation, the possibility that the Royalls' slaves were curtailed in that kind of movement has serious implications for their ability to create and maintain social, cultural, and economic ties outside the bounds of Ten Hills Farm. Once again we see how the practical limits of slavery, even in the North, were manifold and sometimes unimagined.

Summary

Reconstructing the outer constraints of a life under slavery in creating and maintaining stable family and community ties—both in Massachusetts in general and at Ten Hills Farm in particular—relies on the presentation of documentary and archaeological evidence. This includes considering some of the ways in which the enslaved worked within those limits to define themselves as individuals and social beings and to structure their roles and relationships with others in a meaningful way that belied their legal status as slave but might also paradoxically have helped them cope with that fact of their existence.

Theory on black family and community formation has progressed greatly in the last 80 years. Originally thought to have destroyed black social institutions and left a legacy of pathology in the modern black community (see Phillips 1929; Frazier 1939; Moynihan 1965), the reversals of fortune that were the inevitable and unhappy lot of most African Americans under slavery are now understood to have been a social reality, but not one that was necessarily internalized and absorbed into "slave culture" as "the norm." Gutman (1976), Mintz and Price (1976), Kulikoff (1974, 1978, 1986), Lee (1986), Cody (1982), and others have focused on the adaptive capacities of those who were enslaved and on the role of family and community as a source of strength and solidarity and an agent of cultural transmission.

Kulikoff (1974, 1978, 1986) also outlined some of the economic and demographic variables he saw as being either conducive or hostile to most forms of black family and community life in the Chesapeake. By these standards it seemed to me that in the 18th century New England, outside urban and maritime centers such as Boston, Newport, Salem, or Providence, would have tended toward hostility. The overall black population density in New England remained very low, and the sex ratios did not even approximate a normal distribution, with men outnumbering women by a factor of at least two, as in Boston, and sometimes of three or four, as in Medford. Furthermore most slaveholders had fewer than five adult slaves in their households, and many only one or two. Of the 34 slaves listed in Medford in 1754, 18 were recorded as the only adult slave in their master's household; four had one other adult, and only the Royalls had 12 (MHC Collections; Brooks and Usher 1886:355).

Even at Ten Hills Farm, though, there is much indirect evidence of family and community instability. More than half of the Royalls' slaves were recorded without spouses or families (33 out of 64, or 52 percent). Part of this might be an issue of representation—the result of white matrifocal definitions of the black family that sometimes recognized/recorded the relationship between a mother and her children but rarely any other family relationships. Part of it, though, surely also stemmed from the fact that nearly three-quarters of the Royalls' slaves stayed with the Royalls for fewer than ten years, making lasting ties of family and friendship difficult to maintain. Thus family disruption—or the threat of it—made family life under slavery inherently unstable, and this seems to have been no less true at the Royalls' estate. Nevertheless all indications at this site are that this did not make the concept of family less important to those who were enslaved. Naming practices at the Royall House show a concern for establishing symbolic ties to older kin and for forging wider intergenerational relationships that went far beyond the simple mother-child relationship recognized by the Royalls. Robin, George, Quacoe, Joseph, Betty, and Trace were all children on the estate who had possibly been named for grandmothers, aunts, or fathers, and this practice demonstrates a structuring of family and community that differed from the white mainstream. These differences were rooted in enslaved people's own beliefs, experiences, and social ideals and were surely derived in part from notions of kinship they brought with them from the Old World. Within the context of American slavery, however, these ideas about family helped to define the color line as it was then coming to be understood and became part and parcel of the racial transformation of "ethnic" Africans into "black" Americans.

In addition artifacts of leisure-time activities, childhood, craftsmanship, personal adornment and self-presentation, folk religion, and possibly healthcare have opened a window onto some of the processes involved in the creation of private personae within the quarter community, such as it was, at Ten Hills Farm. Some of these activities might have been a simple means of trying to live as decently as possible, despite the legal status of slave, while others, such as wearing charms or using home medicinal remedies might have been an active response to the perceived natural and supernatural dangers of a life under slavery. These also would have given the color line a unique tangibility and perpetuated perceptions of it as a result.

Originally expecting that floral and faunal analyses would fit well within a discussion of the creation and maintenance of "private personae" and community strength, we found the plant and animal remains from the site to be intriguing, but more for their silence than for anything else. As other contemporary sites from the region are excavated and published, they will provide an important wider context within which to interpret the finds at the Royall House.

We may imagine, however, that while berry picking would have been one important way for enslaved girls and women to escape the physical confines of slavery and while men were engaged in varied and sundry tasks across the landscape in the course of performing their tasks, freely roaming the countryside remained principally a part of enslaved people's workaday world. Evidence of independent subsistence or economic activities is virtually nonexistent. The floral and faunal remains at the Royall House give no evidence of either the exploitation of wild resources or the cultivation of domesticated ones, suggesting that the Royalls' slaves were doing little or nothing to supplement their rations from the Ten Hills Farm stores. This pattern may indicate the loss of one more area for the active development and support of private family and community personae.

Whether this apparently reduced exploitation of the environment was by force or by choice is not at present known, and as more northern slave sites are excavated, it will be of great interest to see if the same pattern plays out across the region, possibly hinting at some fundamental, systemic differences between northern and southern/Caribbean slave adaptations. For now, however, it remains one of the most fascinating aspects of the material culture at this site: that the one arena understood to have figured prominently elsewhere in the development of black identities under slavery seems singularly lacking at Ten Hills Farm.

In part the close living quarters and relatively low density of blacks in the region might have given enslaved people in the North less freedom of movement in their natural and cultural environs outside of normal working hours. But access on their own time to physically marginal areas such as fields and forest clearings enabled enslaved people in plantation life to develop an African American folk culture in other areas of the Americas; the possibility that the Royall slaves did not engage in such activities suggests what is likely to have been a great loss in autonomy.

In the next chapter, we turn to the use of landscape in master-slave discourses of power, resistance, and accommodation at Ten Hills Farm. We use the concepts of "multilocality" (Rodman 1992), "implication" (St. George 1998), and "processional landscape" (e.g., Barrett 1994; Upton 1988) to explore the Medford landscape as the manifestation of, and the means of constructing, ideology and meaning. Because the "experience" of landscape, however, is personal, and contingent on one's place in society and the circumstances of a particular situation, all landscapes have multiple levels of meaning. Ten Hills Farm was a patchwork of contested spaces and landscapes whose meanings differed vastly between the Royalls and their slaves, and the landscape of the Royall estate might have been "implicated" differently for each group.

Chapter 6
BRINGING THE OUT KITCHEN IN? THE EXPERIENTIAL LANDSCAPES OF WHITE AND BLACK NEW ENGLAND

Social life is lived out as a "seriality of encounters" between people.
—JOHN BARRETT, 1994

[The Royall estate] was a "fantasy of classical allegory and temporality of lost perfection regained."
—ROBERT BLAIR ST. GEORGE, 1998

An Introduction to the Study of Landscape

Almost everything archaeology does could be construed to fall under the rubric of landscape archaeology. Everything comes down to land use—advertent and inadvertent—in some way, on large and small scales. Rodman (1992:643) criticizes anthropologists for being slow to problematize the concept of place, stating that place "is more than locale, the setting for action, the stage on which things happen." Archaeologists, however, have long realized that people in the past as well as today lived in cultural and natural landscapes that varied widely and were experienced in multiple ways—what Rodman calls "multilocality," the "dynamic, socially constructed qualities of place" (1992:651). Broadly defined, landscape constitutes all the cultural and natural features "inside and outside human settlement: houses, bridges, waterways, trees, grass, mountains, [and] other settlements" (Orser 1996:368). Landscapes have not only reflected but also shaped human relations, controlled social interaction, and given meaning and context to everyday life. Yet if landscape studies have been able to do anything, they have demonstrated that at best we may treat the Georgian gentleman's preoccupation with landscape manipulation as his manipulation of artifacts—just one side of an ongoing discourse that might be more telling about his own fears and desires than about any universal 18th-century "social reality."

Who designed and ordered a particular landscape? Who built and maintained it and who altered his or her unobserved patch of it? Who displayed it, who visited it, and under what circumstances? And what do the answers to these questions imply about the way we should be interpreting that landscape's social meanings?

There are what might be called inadvertent landscapes too, and they can reveal the nuances of social life and relationships because they are often shaped by unconscious attitudes and values. Unlike purposeful landscapes the inadvertent landscape is not anyone's attempt to make a statement about anything, and yet it might come closest to the truth about many things. Ten Hills Farm would have been a patchwork of advertent and inadvertent landscapes that melded seamlessly one with the other. The Royalls and their slaves might have crossed the boundaries between them unknowingly, but they would always have been aware at some level of what the landscape was telling them about who they were, where they belonged, and where they were headed.

The Medford Landscape

When the Royalls arrived in Medford in 1737, there were fewer than 700 inhabitants (Seaburg and Seaburg 1980:100). By the time they fled to England in 1775, there were still fewer than 1,000 people in the town. Founded in 1630 as the personal plantation of Matthew Cradock, London Puritan, merchant, and governor of the Massachusetts Bay Colony before John Winthrop, Medford was never formally incorporated into a town but gradually acquired all of the offices of town government and functioned as a town by the last quarter of the 17th century (Seaburg and Seaburg 1980). Medford's location on the tidal Mystic River, whose steep banks and deep waters made it navigable by ships, rendered it an excellent situation for a trading venture. Early Medford inhabitants engaged in subsistence farming, fishing, and shipbuilding, and, from 1645 on, the Mystic was the main thoroughfare through the heavily wooded region that connected the hamlet directly to Boston markets (Brooks and Usher 1886:19).

The broad river ran in great undulating curves through vast, open marshes and wetlands that became saturated with Atlantic seawater twice daily. Here one could find geese, quails, partridges, and a variety of ducks in the spring. The river itself was home to bass, shad, frost-fish, and oyster beds (Brooks and Usher 1886). Annual runs of alewives and smelts choked the river and the many small freshwater streams and creeks that snaked their way into the salt marsh. The weirs that were set up there caught fish that would eventually find their way into the southern colonies and British West Indian markets.

Beyond the lowland salt marshes that immediately surrounded the river, there rose wooded uplands that had been smoothed into rolling hills by glaciers thousands of years before. "The Rocks" were a range of such wooded granite hills that defined the north-northwest boundaries of the town. By the time the Royalls arrived, most of the town had been cleared of forest and transformed into an agrarian landscape with signs of exclusive land ownership clearly demarcated through field boundaries, fences, bridges, and roads. The woods continued to hover at the outskirts, however, and not so far from human settlement. There the wolf, bear, wildcat, boar, and deer roamed at will. The woods were also a resource for food to supplement the meat of farm animals. Throughout the 18th century, there were annually elected town officers called deer reeves and hog reeves, whose job it was to preserve the wild populations of deer and boar in the forests (MHS n.d.).

Apart from the physical landscape, however, is the landscape that was perceived, interpreted, and experienced by its inhabitants. The fields, fences, bridges,

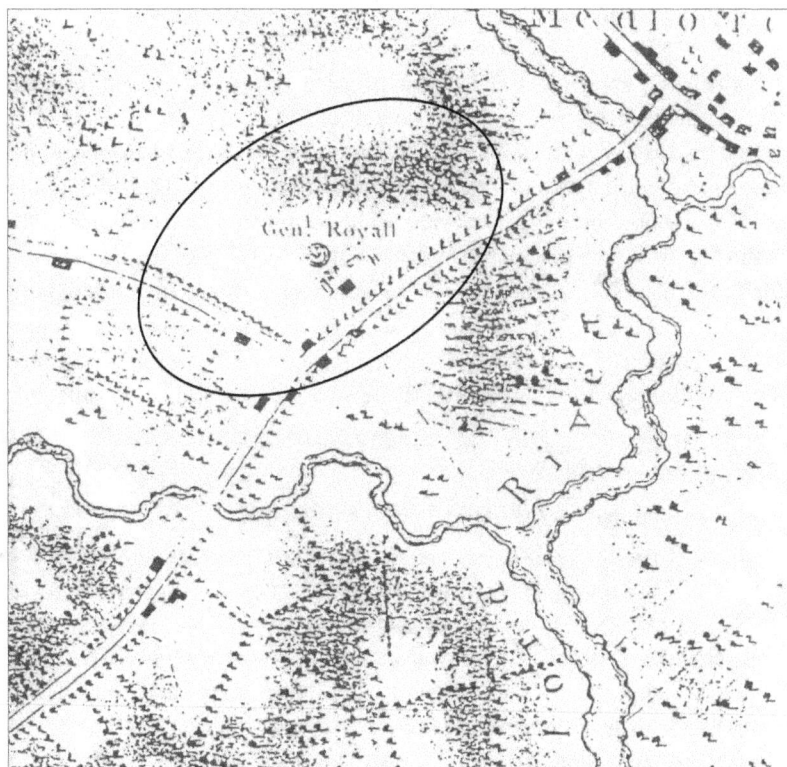

FIG. 51. Detail of the Pelham map of Medford, 1777, showing field boundaries dividing the town, which was by this time already largely cleared of forest. (Courtesy of the Royall House Association.)

roads, and boundary markers can be read as a map of relations between people and their environment as well as of the "distribution and control of access" to resources (Isaac 1982:19). As Medford carved its tiny niche of civilization out of the wilds of Massachusetts, it was purposefully shaped in accordance with social values about what was appropriate, desirable, or necessary. One of the great social values in the new colonies was that of private ownership of land. It was one of the primary attractions for colonists to come to the New World in the first place. The 1777 Pelham map of Medford shows to what extent the town had been divided and demarcated by that time into private property, with access to the resources in each plot exclusively controlled by whoever owned the place (fig. 51). Medford town records also show that these boundary lines would periodically be walked by town citizens, the boundary markers repaired or enhanced, as a kind of ritual to reaffirm that ownership and exclusivity of access. People passing these demarcations would think of the person who owned that land. The condition of the fields would reflect the owner's standing and respectability, the size of his labor force, and his ability to keep them in order (Isaac 1982).

Highways, roads, and lanes further divided the town. These grew in number in the 18th century as Medford became an important stopover for travelers going between Portsmouth and Boston or Salem, but they were still relatively few. By the mid 18th century there were three principal streets that went out from Medford Town Square like spokes on a wheel: the road to Woburn, the road to Malden, and Mystic Street (present-day Main Street), where the Royalls lived. In addition there were cart paths leading to places of business such as the Distill House or taverns, the brickyards, and the wharves (Seaburg and Seaburg 1980). There were likely other ways of moving about the landscape, however, that were not recorded in maps, for they were informal: footpaths that led from field to barn, highway to tenement, house to house, and field to forest. These would probably have been the domain of the lesser folk: common farmers, tenants, artisans, and slaves.

Figures in the Landscape

People were part of the landscape as well and informed one's perception and interpretation of it on a more intimate and detailed level. Of course age, gender, and occupation would all have shaped one's access, vision, and experience of that landscape, as well as contributed to others' experience of the same place.

The Royalls were conspicuous figures in the Medford landscape. They cloaked themselves with an authority that seemed to have been drawn from time immemorial. The "appropriate demeanor, dress, manners, and conversational style . . . accompanied by a familiarity with the sources of sacred, classical, or legal learning" led to a "presumption of gentility" (Isaac 1982:131). The Royalls met all of these requirements with apparently effortless ease. The estate ledger from 1724 to 1749 shows the degree to which both father and son concerned themselves with keeping au courant with the latest fashions. Expenditures on clothes and accessories were overwhelmingly the most frequent and expensive in the accounts payable portion of the account book, exceeding even food. Silk hose, wigs, hats, yards of lace, "puffs" (soft gathers of fabric, ribbon, or small feathers for accenting dress), gowns, greatcoats, breeches, gloves, pumps, gold buckles, silver buttons, and watch crystals were frequent entries in the ledger. Isaac, Sr.'s letters in particular reveal too that in addition to being well dressed, he was an educated, articulate, and genteel man. His erstwhile neighbor in Antigua, Samuel Martin, wrote that "A liberal education is undoubtedly the principal ingredient necessary to form a good planter; who ought at least to know the rudiments of all the sciences" (Martin 1745 [1765]:viii).

Both father and son studied law, and Isaac, Jr., became a Suffolk County judge during his tenure in Medford. They had numerous legal, scientific, and classical works on the shelves of their library, as a perusal of the catalog of books taken in 1739 will reveal, and almost certainly considered themselves to be among the heirs apparent of the ancient world's cultural legacy. Just six years later, Samuel Martin, Esq., once again expounding upon the genteel planter, drew comparisons between the modern and ancient worlds when he noted the similarities between the modern planter and the Roman husbandman in his *Essay Upon Plantership:*

> the best plowmen were the bravest generals, and the wisest politicians of the Roman commonwealth; as if the same qualifications were equally requisite to form those very different characters. This I confess seems a paradox at first view; but upon closer examination will appear not less true of a good planter. (Martin 1745 [1765]: viii)

Robert Blair St. George, referring specifically to Isaac Royall, Sr., suggests that

> Narrating his way through high republican theory to his summer house and back Royall could almost forget that the river across his fields was the Mystic and not the Thames. (1998:276)

A further method by which the gentry were able to justify their authority was to present themselves as purveyors of public good. They were deserving of their high station because they held it responsibly and kept the public's interest in trust as its representatives and caretakers. Goodwin (1999:96) suggests, for example, that Puritan ideology cast the emerging merchant elite in New England in a different mold from London merchants of the same class or even English nobility.

She argues that the American colonial elite were more conservative, concerned with virtue, morality, education, and self-improvement, and reviled the English aristocracy as decadent (Goodwin 1999:96). The merchant elite, embarrassed by the uncouth methods of amassing their fortunes and their own lack of gentlemanly patina, might have felt that "the 'stain' of trade that secures the family fortune is wiped away [only] when future generations were empowered to take on the more worthy business of public service" (Goodwin 1999:64).

This business of beneficence might have been manifested in the serving of public office without salary, as Isaac, Jr., did by donating his salary as court deputy to the poor or in the generous treatment of "humbler men," for which Isaac, Sr., was commemorated on his tombstone (Isaac 1982:132). This idea is perhaps best described in the words of one of Isaac, Jr.'s own contemporaries who spoke of him as a "benevolent aristocrat" (Hoover 1974:49). Ruling with grace and humility—or at least appearing to do so—was perhaps the gentry's most powerful weapon against their detractors, for if done properly, it gave them "local currency as conscientious benefactors" (Goodwin 1999:59).

Within the white world there were many shades of respectability. A person of the times would have been able to read the clues to another's station in life effortlessly from the style of clothes they wore, the materials they were made of, how clean or kempt the person was, and their manner of speech. Gentlemen of the caliber of Isaac, Sr., and Jr. would have been a small but highly conspicuous minority in the Medford landscape. Both Royalls are said to have paraded their illustrious guests regularly out on pleasure drives in their four-horse carriage driven by a fine-liveried coachman, who may or may not have been enslaved (Hoover 1974). The conveyance was impressive. In 1761 Isaac, Jr., advertised for a

> Pair of Coach Horses, to match the Pair he already has: —N.B. They must be black, with a white Spot on their Foreheads, fifteen Hands high, trot all, not above six, nor less than four Years old. —Said Royall also wants a Coachman, that can be well recommended, and understands driving a Coach and Four; and if he understands something of Gardening, he shall have the more Wages. (*Boston Gazette and Country Journal* 1761:June 8).

A common farmer, deeply tanned and gritty from the relentless demands of planting and harvesting crops, his simple unbleached linen sleeves rolled to the elbows and his hair a natural brown, might have paused to look up as the Royalls swept through the public landscape of Medford like elusive and exotic birds, in their colorful velvets and flowing silks. Such conspicuous, and at some level ritualized, performances served at once to underscore their authority by appropriating public spaces for personal pleasure but also, in so doing, re-created the Royalls as an elite anew every time.

The world of the less fortunate is much more fragmentary and elusive. Not much is known about the lives of common farmers, tradesmen, widows, migrants, the poor, the elderly, or servants and unskilled laborers. Court records are the primary source of information about their lives and often the only evidence of their existence at all. The fact that court records usually represent extraordinary circumstances rather than ordinary ones must be taken into consideration when trying to reconstruct the lives of townspeople of the 18th-century Boston area.

Women, for example, were members of the community rarely seen outside the context of court documents. After all, the best women of the 18th century were unremarkable (Goodwin 1999:160). Remarkable women, however, were frequently at the mercy of the General Court to settle their personal affairs and grievances.

Christain [Christine] Wainwright's plight must have been a common one at that time. A recent widow in 1742, she found when her husband died that some of his land that she had intended to sell to support herself had been entailed away from her to a distant male relative because she and her husband had had no sons. She petitioned the court to have the entail removed but was denied on the grounds that it was unlawful (*Massachusetts Acts and Resolves (MAR)* III Private Acts 1742–43, 1st session:67). At that time male inheritance rights reigned supreme, and women, though perhaps born and raised on a piece of land—be it subsistence farm or country estate—knew it not to be their own and themselves to be tenants of a sort in their own homes.

On the other hand, women were not always abandoned to their fate, as numerous successful suits for divorce from that century attest. Grace Parker, widow of the potter Isaac Parker of Charlestown, was another petitioner to the court, a successful one, and representative of a small minority of women who engaged in trade. She pleaded along with Thomas Symmes in 1742 for the continuation of the monopoly on stoneware production granted her husband before he had died, and she was granted it. She immediately went into business with her new partner (*MAR* III Votes and Orders:69). There were other husbandless women in the landscape, though, and these were less pitiable in the eyes of citizens and legislators. In 1758 the province passed an act citing the fact that "towns often have to take care, at considerable cost, of lewd women at their lying-in with bastard children, and for nursing and taking care of such bastard children" (*MAR* IV Province Laws 1758–59, ch.17:178). The new act made it lawful to bind such a woman to service for up to five years in order to repay the costs to the community of her and her children's care.

The frequent military campaigns of the 18th century made soldiers, mariners, and militiamen a common sight on the streets of Boston and the surrounding townships. Legislators concerned themselves with their accommodations and pay. War with the French and the Indians made numerous military widows who also had to be pensioned by the province.

Taverners, innkeepers, "common victuallers," and retailers were subject to special duties on all brandy, rum, spirits, wine, lemons, and limes sold at their establishments (*MAR* III Province Laws 1745–46, ch.2:236). Transient traders who moved from town to town, hawking their wares from wagons and carts, were also subject to special taxation—liable to the towns in which they conducted trade as well as to their town of origin (*MAR* IV Province Laws 1758–59, ch.2:17). Meanwhile other groups petitioned for tax exemption. The Quakers and Anabaptists, for example, were granted freedom from the church and ministerial taxes imposed on the rest of the townspeople. An Act for the Relief of the Poor Prisoners of Debt was also passed in 1736–37, whereby those people in debtors' prison who could swear and show that they had not the means to support themselves in prison should be released (*MAR* II Province Laws 1736–37, ch.13:831).

Then there were the Indians, now friends, now enemies, still a sizable presence in southern New England. Some were free, some were indentured to white families, some were pagan, and some were Christian (Bragdon 1988). Legislators alternately strove to encourage and regulate trade with local tribes and issued warrants for their scalps. The Royalls seem to have been involved with one Indian man, although the nature of their relationship is unclear. Isaac, Jr., was reimbursed in March of 1741 by the province for the cost of medical care and funeral expenses for a Zachariah Quock, Indian, of Stoughton (MHC *Archives* 31:310–11).

Occasionally there is also reference to petty crimes of theft or robbery. Victims were entitled to triple damages by an act passed in 1737–38, rather awkwardly titled "An Act in Addition to the Act Intitulated 'An Act for the Punishing Criminal Offenders'" (*MAR* II Province Laws 1737–38:59–60). Other threats to social order lay in the disorderly conduct of ne'er-do-wells, the undeserving poor, servants, and laborers. These threats could be dangerous because they were symptomatic of raw feelings of anger, hatred, resentment, and labor unrest that seethed below the surface of social relations in the 18th-century hierarchy. Among these disaffected were people who, even with some estate, "mispend their time and money . . . live idle, vagrant, and dissolute lives, as if they were poor, indigent and impotent persons . . . and neglect to take due care of themselves and their families" (*MAR* II Province Laws 1736–37, 1st session, ch.4:795). In 1756 it was also noted that

> Many and great disorders have of late years been committed by tumultuous companies of men, children, and Negroes, carrying about with them pageants or other shews through the streets and lanes of the town of Boston, and other towns within

this province, abusing and insulting the inhabitants, and demanding and exacting money by menaces and abusive language . . . horrid profanities and gross immoralities. (*MAR* III Province Laws 1756–57, 4th session, ch.14:997)

Robert Blair St. George (1998) documents the phenomenon of "house attacks" by an increasingly conscious and critical labor force. These plagued the coastal urban elite in the decades leading up to the Revolution. Angry mobs assaulted several Georgian mansions in 1760s Boston—gaudy and belligerent proclamations of class prerogative—burned their owners in effigy and paraded through the streets celebrating their "funerals." These were the faces in the world of 18th-century Boston and surrounding areas, and they appear to have been divided by vastly different planes of existence and spheres of interaction, with one group having rare occasion to experience or understand another group's existence or point of view. Isaac Royall and his colleagues and peers, who concerned themselves so much with "ruling with grace" and instilling love, obedience, and gratitude in their inferiors, might have been quite satisfied with the shows of obsequiousness they were met with in waking, working hours. They likely saw no connection between their own social position and such displays as the ones described above that had to be met with legislative action in 1756. They likely considered such behavior to be evidence of the inherent inferiority of such people—a character defect—of blacks and the poor. The elite could not fathom that such behavior was actually an act of aggression against a specific social system where it was not the content of one's character but the level of one's birth or the color of one's skin that determined the possibilities of one's life.

Court records indicate that the Royalls' lifestyle was not representative of the general colonial experience, but it would have been highly visible for its vast difference. Perhaps the second most conspicuous or visible portion of the population at that time would have been another minority—the numerous African and Creole (American-born) slaves that seemed to exist in a separate but parallel universe to the white world. As stated, Medford would have been about 4 percent black at the time of the 1754 colony-wide slave census, when 27 males and 7 females over the age of 16 were reported for the town, 12 of whom belonged to the Royalls (MHC Collections 1754; Brooks and Usher 1886:355). Thirty-four people, with some number of children and elderly, were certainly not many, but they would have been a visible and exotic minority—lending a distinctly foreign flavor to the town, and they probably knew each other well. Boston had about 1,000 enslaved Africans and Creoles at the time.

Owners' descriptions of their bondsmen in the advertisements for runaways surveyed by Greene (1944) reveal a contemptuous condescension that suggests that enslaved people, as figures in the Boston area landscape, were considered by whites to be unpleasant and irritating aliens in the environment. Some owners betray an outright revulsion at the physical appearance of their chattels, using disgusted and mocking tones. Cloe, for instance, could be recognized by her "flat face, blubber lips and large mouth" (quoted in Greene 1944:135); Sarah was a "short, thick wench" (quoted in Greene 1944:133). Quom, probably an Akan-speaker from the Gold Coast (whose name had been shortened from Quamina), who ran away from his Boston owner in 1754, was described as having a "wrinkled face, a mouth full of teeth and a large eye which he turns up when he is earnest in speaking" (*Boston Gazette and Weekly Advertiser:* May 14, 1754). A week later a different man was identified simply as having "a curled head of hair" (*Boston Gazette and Weekly Advertiser:* May 21, 1754). Still others were not described physically at all but rather were to be identified by their character defects, such as being "saucy," "surly," "cunning," "crafty and subtle," or "a great lyer" (quoted in Greene 1944:137–38). Decorative elements also provided some of the differences between the enslaved and the white population. We have seen some of the evidence of the Royalls' slaves' having cultivated a non-European aesthetic in the wearing of stone beads and possibly protective amulets. Various primary documents then have shown the Boston area landscape to be a bright and colorful place, with the Royalls and their slaves being two of the most visible elements of it, albeit on opposite ends of the spectrum.

Traveling through the Landscape

Upton points out that the 18th-century landscape was "neither uniform nor entirely dominated by the gentry" (Upton 1988:368). He further claims that the white world of the 18th century, contrary to the black, was designed to be experienced dynamically (1988:363). It is an interesting way of looking at landscape because it implies that social life, shaped by and played out in these very landscapes, is a kind of performance in motion, or *praxis* (Bourdieu 1977). The public landscape of roads, drives, public architecture, and the private landscape of a landed estate with mansion house, fields, and outbuildings are but a spatial context or a collection of visual referents to guide the intricate dance among participants in a discourse negotiating their positions and roles in reference to each other. Such performances create a kind of "cultural geography" from which people get their bearings and learn "how to act" (Barrett 1994:56, 19). In other words, it is only through the practice or performance of social life that the rules of social discourse are created, its meanings determined. The importance of place does not just derive from what occurs there, but equally from what has taken place there before and what is expected to take place there in the future (Barrett 1994). Robert St. George (1998:2) calls this phenomenon cultural "implication"—the poetic art of conveying thoughts, ideas, or things without specifically referencing them, bringing associations and evocations to mind as things, places, ideas, or words from another time and place and cultural milieu are appropriated into a new context. Place is a metaphor that gives what happens there meaning and power because it recalls other places, other events, other interactions. As a result each individual event or encounter takes on additional significance as one of an infinite number of referent points in an individual's mind for how to act in any particular instance.

The world of the 18th-century wealthy New England elite was a carefully contrived one, consisting largely of enclosures, barriers, and checkpoints, physical and social, that had to be passed in order to gain access to the inner circle of elite society. The ideas of enclosure and access are important ones, for implied therein is the distinction between those who have and those who do not have access—and among those with access, between those who lead and those who follow (Barrett 1994).

The Royalls' Georgian mansion was situated on raised ground that commanded a view of the hills and marshes that led down to the Mystic River itself. There the bustling ship traffic served as a visual reminder of the Royalls' personal connectedness to international markets, as their own boat took tons of hay, cider, and wool down that artery to Boston markets, where the goods then headed out to the world. The house was set back from Mystick Street, where most traffic coming in or going out of Medford would pass by and see its grandeur. In fact a long stretch of Mystick Street cut right through Ten Hills Farm, so that travelers would be surrounded for some time on all sides by the Royall grounds. Drake (1906:123) quotes one such traveler as saying

> On our journey past through Mistick, which is a small Town of abt a hundred Houses, Pleasantly Situated, near to which is a Fine Country Seat belonging to Mr. Isaac Royall being one of the Grandest in North America.

The links between the public landscape of roads, rivers, and wharves, however, and the private landscape of Ten Hills Farm, though seemingly part of a single articulated landscape, were carefully orchestrated with an eye to outside visuals and processional effect and to the establishment of a series of barriers to restrict access. From the public space of Mystick Street, one could see and admire the Royalls' house, grounds, and sprawling vistas, but one was also meant to be awed by the symbols of power that inhabited the landscape and to be intimidated by their inaccessibility.

The house itself could be approached on foot or horse through a gate on Mystick Street flanked by wooden posts and opening onto a "grand avenue . . . bordered with box" that led to the door (Drake 1906:120; see fig. 52). Farther to the north were massive stone gateposts that marked the entrance to the carriage drive that also turned off of Mystick Street and led, "under the shade of magnificent old elms," around to the cobbled courtyard in back (Drake 1906:121; see fig. 53). Here too was the separate entrance for the barn, stables, and coach house complex.

St. George (1998:273) claims that the Royall estate "represents the first documented impact of a new generation of English agricultural reform," which sought to keep animal yards "at a polite distance" from the house and to "segregate farm labor . . . from the fictive allegorical scene [Royall] was contriving."

The house was in a neoclassical architectural style that implicated the villas of ancient Rome and thus drew from their cool authority (St. George 1998). It was extremely fashionable, the more so for its relative rarity so long before the Revolution, and processing along the carriage drive allowed the privileged social visitor to admire the house from three sides before reaching the ornate front door. There they might enter the house and take tea in the best room, which overlooked the pleasure gardens and drew the eye to the distant and tantalizing focal point of the summer gazebo on a hill in the orchards. After tea one might be invited to take a turn in the gardens and catch the late afternoon breezes in the summerhouse, which, St. George (1998:273, 276) indicates was located perfectly according to John Mortimer's *Whole Art of Husbandry,* a book that Isaac, Sr., had in his library (Middlesex County Probate 1739).

The path to the summerhouse was aligned with the mansion's central axis, and led to the top of a hill that afforded fine prospects of the orchards, gardens, and lands. In fact, although the mansion house was of neoclassical design, the Royalls' estate might have more immediately implicated the English landed gentry and their country houses. Girouard (1980:3) states that the country house was the "image-maker" of the emerging English gentry in the 18th century and that the building of a country seat was the critical culmination of a gentryman's rise to influence and affluence. He goes on to say that people who lived in English country houses either already "possessed power, or . . . were making a bid to possess it" (Girouard 1980:2). Thus, while the classical references in the architecture of the house and summer gazebo would certainly have been recognized, the Royalls, who continued to be active and influential members of the Boston political and social scenes, might also, in retiring "to the country" in Medford, have been symbolically aligning themselves with the English ruling class. And, indeed, "walking round a garden or driving round a park, whether one's own or somebody else's, loomed large in the ample leisure time of people in polite society" (Girouard 1980:210). The Royalls, in coming to Medford, had really arrived.

The procession was truncated for people there to conduct business. The Royalls' office where they collected outstanding debts and loans is a single room annexed to the northern elevation of the house and has its own entrance. Debtors came and went without ever gaining access to the inside of the house or any of the hospitality and gentility that it seemed to promise. The placement of the office would have defined its visitors' relationship to the Royalls in no uncertain terms.

Then there were the people who had no business at the Royalls' estate at all—common farmers, tradesmen, servants, etc.—who passed the house day in and day out, driving their goods to market in open carts or running errands on foot. They could but imagine what lay beyond the massive stone gates that barred them from the Royalls' world.

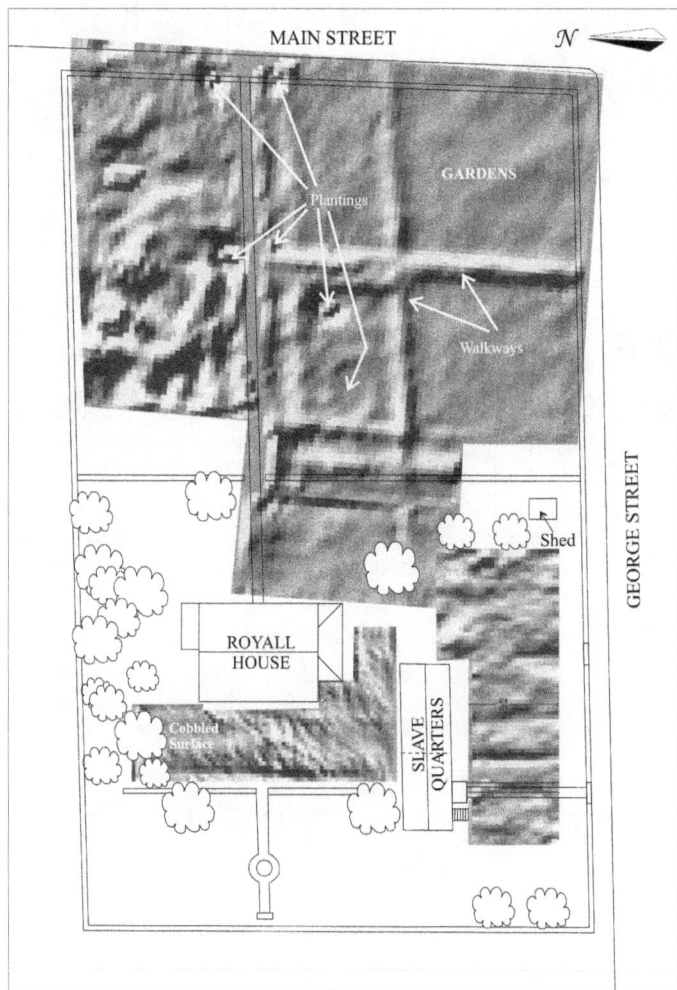

Fig. 52. Analytical hill shading of resistivity readings at the Royall House grounds superimposed on a site plan, showing buried formal walkways that were once part of the Royalls' carefully contrived landscape of power and elegance.

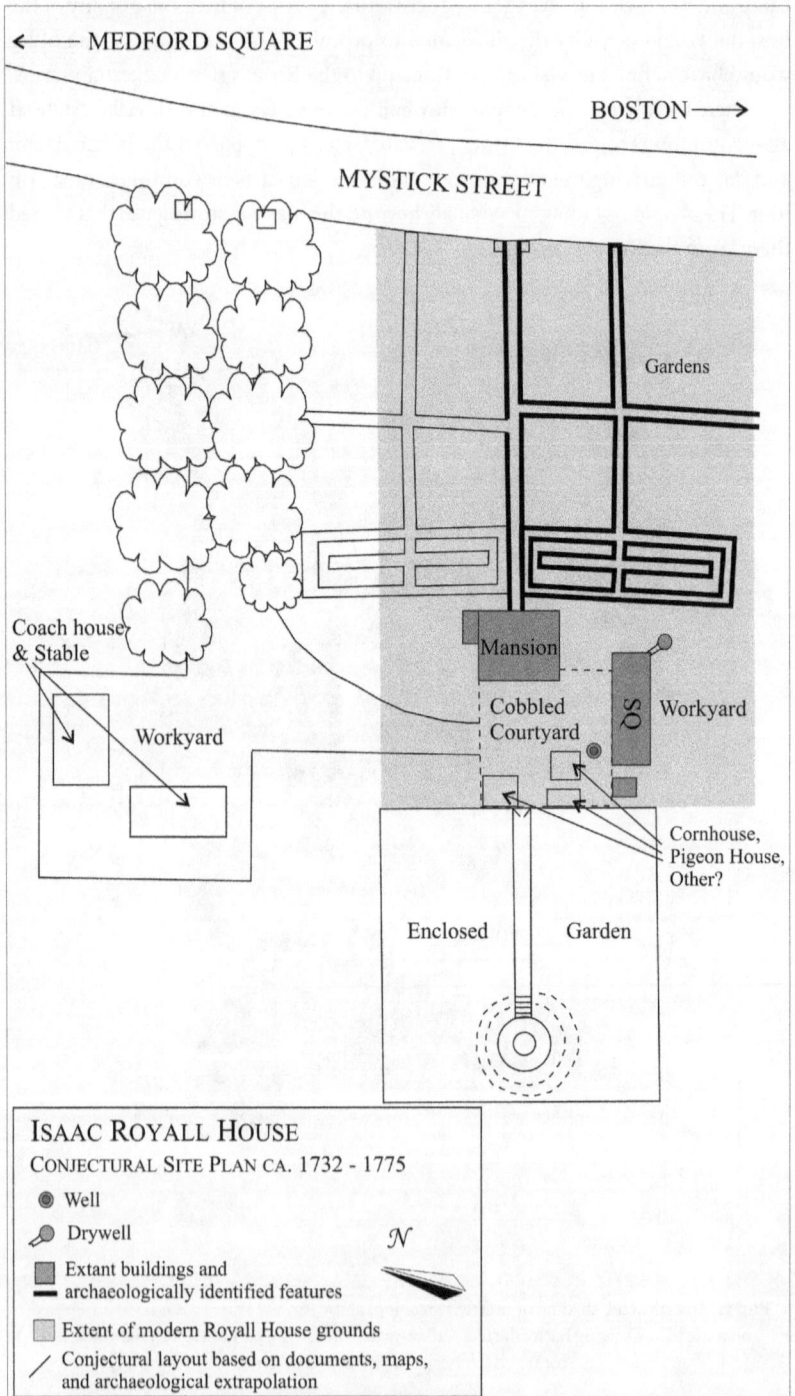

FIG. 53. Site plan with conjectural formal drive/entrances, ca. 1732–75. After Lamar (n.d.), the 1777 Pellham map of Medford, archaeological extrapolation, and Isaac Royall, Sr.'s probate inventory of 1739 (Middlesex County Probate 1739).

In the immediate vicinity of the house was, of course, the slave quarters, which—visible from the street—was one obvious, tangible symbol of their lordly stature in the landscape. There were other symbols, though, as well, in the built environment that seemed to justify the Royalls' authority and rightful domination in the town. The Royall House estate, as previously mentioned, is laid out much like an urban townhouse compound of the American South, such as one finds in Charleston, Savannah, or Richmond. In those cities large slaveholders kept some of their slaves in a building behind the main house, usually a two-story structure housing a kitchen, laundry, and other workrooms on the first floor and slave bedrooms on the second (Vlach 1991; Tate 1965). These buildings, as part of the social display of the whole estate because of its proximity to the main house, matched the main house in architectural design, detail, and integrity, and together they formed an L-shaped enclosure on a common courtyard. The whole design mirrored the social relationships of the people who inhabited the structures: the master's spatial control of the land and viewscapes that centered on the main house reflected the master and his place (Vlach 1991; Herman 1999). The Royalls' mansion house, with its neoclassical quoined corners and pedimented windows and doors would, according to Epperson (1990:31), have worked to "appropriate the ahistorical aura and authority of classical culture, making specific relations of domination appear timeless." By extending the same style to the slave quarters, the Royalls might have attempted to incorporate the quarters into the formal landscape of the estate and hence into the ideology of domination and control on which it rested (Epperson 1990:31).

But Isaac, Sr., was not just a master of black men. In addition to one white servant named William Beven whose indentures Isaac, Sr., held briefly in the 1720s, Isaac's account book shows that he collected rent from or held mortgages on the Skinners, Farrows, Fosters, and Clevelands of Medford and Charlestown (Account Book 1724–49). Isaac, Jr., held the same on the Tufts, Wises, Greys, Crofts, and Olivers. Some of these were tenants on the Royalls' property, paying rent to use houses, barns, and fields on Ten Hills Farm. Some, who were perhaps not directly on Royall property, were forced to relinquish partial ownership of their farms by taking out a mortgage with the Royalls for defaulting on payments for slaves or monetary loans that the Royalls put out at 6 percent (Royall Correspondence: Aug. 15, 1736).

Part of this money-lending scheme was Isaac, Sr.'s strategy to stabilize their fortune in a time of great inflation and uncertain colonial currency. Investing in land and putting money "out to interest," he thought, was the only way to make sure his fortune did not lose value over time, for he shrewdly guessed that land values in and around Boston would never fall (Royall Correspondence: Aug.15, 1736). Another part, however, was surely a means of establishing a kind of hegemony in the township. Girouard (1980:2) states that power in the 18th century was based on ownership of land, not for farming, but for the tenants who lived on it and the rental income it produced.

Isaac, Sr.'s account book (1724–49) shows that literally dozens of families were perpetually indebted to the Royalls, either for tenements, mortgages, monetary loans, or slaves. Tenant farms that dotted the landscape were another reminder to passersby, as well as to the tenants themselves, of the Royalls' stature and dominance in the town, akin to those of an English landed gentryman. Isaac, Sr., additionally paid for clothes, shoes, mending, and pocket money for his three sisters, one of his brothers, and all of his nieces and nephews. In so doing, he was establishing himself on the one hand as a benevolent patriarch, but on the other as a powerful man.

The Black Perspective

It may be that only white landscapes were designed with processional effect in mind—what we might call purposeful landscapes—but I do not agree with Upton (1988) that only white landscapes were dynamic. All landscapes are really processional or experiential, and all people moving through them processing, intentionally or not. Who one is will affect how one moves through a particular landscape and thus also how one experiences that landscape. Indeed Isaac (1982) has said that one's experience of a landscape is not just affected by, but actually contingent on, rank. So it is not that free and enslaved blacks, women, and common whites failed to process or that they were denied the opportunity to process; they processed differently, often through what I spoke of earlier as inadvertent landscapes, those that do not make a conscious social statement, but rather are shaped by and help to perpetuate unconscious values and attitudes.

By processing through the landscape in alternative ways, the Royalls' slaves would have made their own implicated places. Their different *praxis* would have resulted in a different *habitus* and ultimately a different *doxa* (Bourdieu 1977; See Glossary). The "social 'art' of living" (Bourdieu 1977:19) for a slave would have been very different from that of his master. His understanding of "reality" was shaped by personal experiences and interactions with the physical world and other actors in it that were themselves vastly different.

Most scholars of landscape agree that landscape as artifact works to reflect as well as shape social and class relations (Hudgins 1990; McKee 1996; Mrozowski and Beaudry 1990; Luccketti 1990; Orser 1988). Planters in particular designed their estate landscapes to be part of their "strategy of social control," meant to facilitate control over the lives and labor of their slaves and to maximize production and profits while convincing social inferiors to internalize their own inferiority (Delle 1999:151). Such statements of power were mitigated by the degree to which their intended audience saw or paid attention to them (see Hudgins 1990; compare also McKee 1992), but Garman (1998:133) claims that "conflict-driven models" of dominance and resistance are inadequate for understanding the complexities of master-slave relations in southern New England anyway. Piersen (1988:143) suggests a model of "resistant accommodation," which is more rigorously developed by Garman (1998), as more suitable to understanding the nature of the encounters between colonial New England masters and their slaves. Master-slave relations, under such a model, consisted of a series of mutually uneasy compromises and grudging concessions.

Blacks and whites in New England, because of their physical proximity in work and daily life, lived under a system in which white surveillance and monitoring of blacks (both formal and informal) were an inescapable part of daily life. Close living arrangements were coupled with curfews to curtail slaves' movements, legal acts to control their behavior, ability to engage in trade, attend houses of entertainment, or their right to assembly. At the same time, however, while segregation in everything from meals, work, and living spaces to processional access, church seating, or burial grounds cast enslaved people as inferior and as outsiders, it also ensured that they would have space and time to themselves (Jones 1990; Garman 1998).

The slave quarters at Ten Hills Farm were at the interface between two different landscapes—the white and the black—and they would have belonged in some ways to both (Upton 1988). On the one hand, there can be no question that they belonged to the white landscape the Royalls had explicitly created, centered on the mansion house, as part of the workscape and visual statement of the Royalls' dominance. On the other hand, they also belonged to the black landscape that included the quarters and surrounding yards but may in fact not have been centered on them, for the black domain could be far-reaching. These were "shared but contested" spaces (Garman 1998:134).

The three seasons of excavations at the Royall House have greatly helped to shed light on the way the Ten Hills Farm landscape might have been perceived by those who lived there, black and white. Although it may be argued that the estate was laid out in a way that seemed to proclaim the natural inferiority and dependency of blacks on whites and to draw the slave quarters physically into the center of the estate, the results of the excavation of the grounds suggest ways in which this centripetal force might have been counteracted.

Most notable is the evidence of a pronounced difference in the social and functional use of space surrounding the mansion house and the slave quarters, which relegated work, construction, and waste-disposal activities to the relatively out-of-sight side yard and backyard of the slave quarters. The north yard where the slave quarters fronted onto the courtyard that is shared with the main house seems to have been swept relatively clean. A certain amount of sheet refuse lay immediately atop the cobbled surface of the courtyard and in the matrix of the stones, but fully two-thirds of the artifacts in the courtyard came from a midden layer found beneath the cobbled surface and dating to the late 17th and early 18th centuries.

Thus the cobbles, believed to have been laid as part of the Royalls' beautification efforts of the estate when they first bought the property in 1732, mark a shift in the use of that space, from a work yard to a formal receiving area. No trash pits or significant refuse accumulations were located in the courtyard after the laying of the cobbles. The attention to cleanliness is not particularly strange. The Royalls entertained guests of the highest order, including the governor himself. To lead their visitors down the long avenue of elms only to greet them in a courtyard filled with stinking piles of rubbish would hardly have been appropriate.

TABLE 19.
Artifact distribution in work yards

Material	Slave quarters' west yard		Slave quarters' east yard		Slave quarters' south yard		Courtyard	
	No.	% Total from these areas	No.	% Total from these areas	No.	% Total from these areas	No.	% Total from these areas
Ceramic (n = 22,837)	13,492	59.08	2,090	9.15	4,662	20.41	2,593	11.35
Glass (n = 10,052	7,173	71.36	729	7.25	1,373	13.66	777	7.73
Organic (n = 8893)	4,411	49.60	546	6.14	2,539	28.55	1,397	15.71
Metal (n = 6534)	3,232	49.46	382	5.85	1,457	22.30	1,463	22.39
Other Mineral (n = 244)	111	45.49	40	16.39	93	38.11	–	–
Stone (n = 59)	32	54.24	6	10.17	18	30.51	3	5.08
Synthetic (n = 5)	–	–	2	40.00	1	20.00	2	40.00
Other (n = 593)	148	23.57	44	7.01	404	64.33	32	5.10
Unid. (n = 1)	–	–	–	–	–	–	1	100.00
Total (n = 49,253)	28,599	58.07	3,839	7.79	10,547	21.41	6,268	12.73

TABLE 20.
Average number of ecofacts/artifacts recovered per unit

Location	No.	No. of Units Sampled	Avg. Artifacts/ Unit
Slave quarters' west yard	28,591	13	2,199
Slave quarters' east yard	4,390	4	1,097
Slave quarters' south yard	10,457	10	1,046
Courtyard	6,274	15	418

Table 19 compares the artifact assemblages from the slave quarters' west, east, and south yards with those of the courtyard and indicates that the west and south yards of the slave quarters contained nearly 79 percent of the total artifact assemblage in these four areas. Because the yards were not equally sampled, table 20 was created to help correct for sampling error. The average number of finds per unit was determined in order partially to balance out the raw frequency distribution numbers, which do not take into consideration the fact that unequal numbers of excavation units were opened in each of the yards investigated.

Among the work yards, the west yard was more heavily used for these purposes than the south yard, and both were more heavily used than the east yard, probably because the latter two would have been visible from the street to passersby and the east yard would actually have been part of the house's main frontage on Main Street. In the west yard, small trash pits were dug to contain some of the larger deposits, while buckets of ash and the remains of the latest meal were thrown carelessly on the ground.

Rats and other small rodents rummaged for scraps, and pungent smells must have wafted across the grounds on hot days. Broken cooking and storage pots, discarded utensils, and rubble from old building activities were strewn across the ground, with little care given to appearances. It was in both of the side yards too that most of our artifacts suggestive of family life, leisure time activities, and craftsmanship of slaves were found, indicating that when the work day was done, these were the areas in which the slaves gathered to unwind, largely beyond the watchful eye of the master. Table 21 shows the wide range of activities represented in the artifact assemblage of the slave quarters' work yards. The west yard in particular has the whole range of artifact types listed and the artifacts there are numerically dominant in the assemblage as a whole.

The functional division in the use of space would have had various social implications as well. For one it would have made the slaves' domain an unpleasant one and reinforced slaves' inferior—and altogether separate—social position. It would also keep the most blatant and unpleasant evidence of human bondage out of sight and perhaps out of mind while the Royalls got down to the

TABLE 21.

Functional categories of artifacts from the Slave Quarters' West, East, and South Yards, and the Courtyard.

Functional Category	Slave quarters' west yard		Slave quarters' east yard		Slave quarters' south yard		Courtyard	
	No.	% Total from these areas	No.	% Total from these areas	No.	% Total from these areas	No.	% Total from these areas
Architectural (n = 16,549)	8,257	49.89	1,402	8.47	3,892	23.52	2,998	18.12
Beverages/ Condiments/ Containers (n = 4,379)	3,679	84.01	237	5.41	286	6.53	177	4.04
Currency (n = 12)	8	66.67	2	16.67	2	16.67	–	–
Domestic (n = 3,675)	2,184	59.43	416	11.32	725	19.73	350	9.52
Industrial (slag) (n = 508)	87	17.13	–	–	392	77.17	29	5.71
Kitchenware (n = 7789)	6,099	78.30	358	4.60	920	11.81	412	5.29
Leisure/Smoking (n = 363)	124	34.16	54	14.88	85	23.42	100	27.55
Magico/religious (n = 1)	1	100.00	–	–	–	–	–	–
Misc. (n = 4531)	2,106	46.48	146	3.22	1,324	29.22	955	21.08
Munitions (n = 4)	2	50.00	–	–	–	–	2	50.00
New beverages/ teaware (n = 262)	222	84.73	7	2.67	8	3.05	25	9.54
Pharmaceutical (n = 229)	155	67.69	14	6.11	60	26.20	–	–
Self-adornment (n = 15)	6	40.00	1	6.67	2	13.33	6	40.00
Sewing/Clothing (n = 59)	27	45.76	1	1.69	11	18.64	20	33.90
Tableware (n = 4,996)	2,579	51.62	741	14.83	1,318	26.38	358	7.17
Floral/Faunal (n = 4,734)	2,970	62.74	418	8.83	588	12.42	758	16.01
Unidentified (n = 433)	68	15.70	16	3.70	285	65.82	64	14.78
Total (n = 48,539)	**28,574**	**58.87**	**3,813**	**7.86**	**9,898**	**20.39**	**6,254**	**12.88**

Note: For this table certain functional categories that had been listed separately in the artifact catalog were combined for a simpler presentation of the data. Thus, the "architectural" category here includes nails/screws/spikes/rivets/tacks, window glass, brick, tiles, etc.; "domestic" includes things like chamberpots, flower pots, mugs, pitchers, vials, pen knives, ink wells, escutcheons, lighting devices, a house bell, etc.; "misc." includes undiagnostic glassware, unidentified glassware, iron hardware (sheet metal, wire, hinges, pintles, horse/ox shoes, etc.), pavement, and modern artifacts; "sewing/clothing" includes buttons, straight pins, shoe parts, clasps/snaps/hooks-and-eyes, scissors, thimbles, and a possible needle case; and "self-adornment" includes beads, buckles, cufflinks, paste jewels, a finger ring, a boot spur, and a military pendant.

serious business of entertaining and lavish living. Another possibility, although documents particular to the Royalls do not survive to support or contradict it, is that these areas were dirty in spite of the Royalls. McKee (1992) argues, for instance, that slave house yards were often untidy and unclean in spite of owners' best efforts to the contrary and that dirty house yards were in point of fact a form of workplace aggression on the part of slaves, in retaliation against the various controls placed upon their lives. He also argues that since few slaves were likely to feel any real emotional attachment to their quarters as a home and the "slave domain" extended far beyond the walls of the quarters in any case, there was even less reason to keep the yards neat (McKee 1992).

In light of the claim that northern bondage was more familial and incorporative in nature than southern or Caribbean slavery, the various interpretations presented above of the finds at the Royall House in this respect take on special significance. Although one can certainly argue that there is a difference between retaining and enforcing social distance, the observed spatial segregation between master and slave is, in either case, inconsistent with family-like relationships. The Royalls and their slaves were clearly not living together as a single social and economic unit. They were not using the land collectively as one might expect in a familial form of bondage. Rather our excavations present clear evidence of a social and spatial segregation of master and slave that is inconsistent with family-like relationships.

Taken together, the architectural layout of the farm seems to convey an ideal of incorporating slaves and their place into the center of the white-dominated landscape and its ideology, while archaeology seems to betray the inherent contradiction involved in giving such importance to social and physical segregation to make these attempts at spatial domination effective. Epperson (1999a, 1999b) points out, for example, that slaveholders were never able to reconcile fully the need to incorporate slaves, through landscape, into the ideology of their own inferiority, when their inferiority was defined in large part through their systematic exclusion from the white spatial domain.

Alternative Ways

The Royalls' slaves would not have experienced the formal approach to the house in the same way that Governor Belcher would, even if they were in a position to take it, because of who they were. What is more, taking footpaths and shortcuts and inhabiting marginal areas of the formal landscape—such as the side and back yards of the quarters—was not only likely a forced condition of their existence, but also one way for these people to make the formal landscape informal and familiar.

The Royalls' slaves did not see or experience the formal landscape in the same way as the Royalls themselves, their honored guests, or tenant debtors did, because they traveled through it differently. At the Royall House, in addition to the functional division in the use of space, there is evidence of alternative processional ways that would have allowed for multiple experiences of the landscape, depending on one's background, one's business there, and one's routes of access to various parts of the estate. An enslaved person's procession began not at the stone gates, but at the kitchen door at the back of the house. Excavations revealed a historical walkway that once connected the out kitchen to the main house kitchen door. From there a narrow servant stair made all three floors of the house accessible from the kitchen and this backdoor entry. On the one hand, it hid the inner workings of servicing the house from the Royalls and their guests. On the other hand, it also gave enslaved people a unique back-door view of all that happened there.

It is perhaps ironic that House Peter or Priscilla were probably more intimate with the house than any of the Royalls' visitors could be and more privy to the intimacies of the Royall family than even the Royalls themselves could imagine. They might have kept themselves abreast of the financial state of the family and the various events and happenings of the Royalls and their acquaintances; they might have listened for news from the outside world or rumors of imminent sale or other threats to slave family stability. This information they could then pass on to other of the enslaved on the estate (see Webber 1978:227–29), and they would have been invisible to the house and its occupants in a way that the house and its occupants were *not* invisible to them.

This idea has been illustrated in dramatic fashion by Bernard Herman (1999:88), who used court records from the defense of a slave named Billy Robinson in the 1822 Denmark Vessey insurrection trial to reveal the "cultural blindness in masters" in their perceptions of space. He argues that blacks were able to gain an invisibility "engendered by white custom, habit, and arrogance" that stemmed from the misguided belief that the spaces in an urban townhouse compound made the enslaved population "perpetually visible" (Herman 1999:100). Billy Robinson was able to take advantage of this false sense of security to help plan the insurrection under his master's very nose and then able to use the same presumptions of perpetual visibility to get himself acquitted of any wrongdoing. Urban townhouse compounds were tightly knit, incorporative landscapes that made the mansion house, kitchen, washhouses, quarters, privies, work yards, gardens, and other structures from sheds to warehouses appear to be part of a unitary whole.

As stated, the core of the Royall estate was set up much like the urban townhouse compound that Billy Robinson lived in. The Royalls, situated at the center, might have felt that they could survey all, while the architectural layout of the estate seemed to confirm "their people's" inferiority to and dependency on them.

Indeed the idea of perpetual visibility might have been especially seductive in New England, where most slaveholders housed many if not all of their bondsmen in their own homes—ferreted away in kitchens, garrets, closets, or hallways.

Isaac, Sr.'s 1739 probate inventory lists eight sets of "beds and beding" in the main house as specifically "Negro," although there may have been as many as twelve. Five were located in the kitchen; two in the kitchen chamber, across the hall from the master bedroom; three—a "Negro" cradle and two bedsteads (the latter not specified as "Negro")—in the spinning garret; and two more bedsteads in the front garret. The constraints and pressures of living in the main house in close proximity to the Royall family must have been formidable. Jones (1990) states that house servants paid a high price for the material improvements in living conditions they may or may not have had. They often worked long hours at the master's beck and call day and night and were under close surveillance that made slipping out for "nocturnal and illicit travels," crucial for forging and maintaining family ties, friendships, and community, more difficult (Jones 1990:116). Often their greater visibility also made them easy targets as "scapegoats for every fault and misadventure" of their masters, who subjected them to barbaric punishments for minor transgressions or merely for being in the wrong place at the wrong time (Jones 1990:122; see also Fitts 1996). Although Isaac, Sr., was called a "kind master" on his tombstone and Isaac, Jr., "kindly protective of his people" by his friends, no documents survive to elucidate the specific nature of their treatment of those they held in slavery—cruel, kind, or indifferent. Nevertheless there can be little doubt that the proximity of the slave quarters to the main house, and the housing of several individuals within the mansion itself, would have made absences or transgressions more immediately apparent. One can also see quite readily how masters might have been seduced into thinking in such a situation that they had a good idea of what their slaves were doing at all times.

Of course, the idea of perpetual visibility would not have been taken literally. There were several places in the immediate vicinity of the mansion house that would have been more or less out of sight from the Royalls' central living spaces. Indeed this fact partially explains the differences in the use of space around the mansion and slave quarters outlined above. And if Mistress Royall went to the kitchen daily to dictate the day's meals, she would have had little occasion to go to the kitchen chamber or the third-floor garrets. Thus these segregated areas and whatever was done or said in them, though easily monitored if desired, would have been mostly unsupervised. Likewise, in their servicing of the house and its inhabitants and visitors, perhaps standing discreetly by the wall or coming and going silently to serve and clear tea, lace up stays, or deliver wax-sealed letters, enslaved people became "backdrops" or "props" who found in their "transparency" a measure of autonomy (Herman 1999:97).

Not all of the people enslaved at the Royall estate lived in the great house, however, and in their varied and sundry tasks, they too might have been able to circumvent the formal landscape in unsuspected ways. Historical documents obliquely suggest that the Royalls, in addition to having a bevy of house slaves, also had in-house specialists for performing tasks from baking to boating to cider pressing. In 1737, for example, a black man, likely on the hire-out system, was "taken again of Henry Neal" (a baker in Boston) "and sent up to Stoughton, he not being able to pay for him" (Account Book: June 25, 1737). In June of 1768, Plato drowned (NEHGS 1907), leaving open the possibility of his having been the boatman responsible for taking hay, cider, and wool produced at Ten Hills Farm down the Mystick River to Boston markets. Garman (1998:148) has also demonstrated that cider production, which was engaged in at Ten Hills Farm, can be statistically linked to specialized and seasonal slave labor in New England.

These occupations likely afforded considerable unsupervised mobility. Fortune, whose occupation is unspecified, was sometimes entrusted with large amounts of cash and a degree of autonomous movement to buy things for the farm, as seen in account book entries such as "To Cash sent P Fortune . . . £25" and "To Cash to Fortain to buy beef 27/ 1 pr Wool Cards 10/ . . . £1.17" (Account Book: Nov. 21, 1737; May 10, 1738). He must have been a trusted servant and largely been able to go where he pleased on such errands. The baker's apprentice might also have been sent here and there regularly, and working in town would have allowed him access to the shadow lands and alternative landscapes of "alley society"—tavern, work yard, and waterfront life—among the city's 1,000 enslaved blacks and crowds of poor whites, free blacks, and Indians (Twombley 1973:26). He might have seen, or even participated in, the "gross immoralities" of "tumultuous companies of men, children, and Negroes" that plagued the streets and lanes of Boston at the time (*MAR* III Province Laws 1756–57, 4th session, ch.14:997). He might have heard news from abroad about slave conspiracies and revolts, smelled the ghastly odor in the air that signaled the recent arrival of a slave ship in Boston harbor, or seen the latest imports from Africa or the West Indies stumble ashore in all of their filthy misery, perhaps by now exotic and strange even to him. Perhaps he also attended festivals such as Black Election Day or met in private homes with Boston's free blacks to talk about life, the past, the future, and possibilities. We will never know. But we can reasonably expect that he brought news of what he had done and seen in town back to Ten Hills Farm. In so doing he would have been able to give his fellow bondsmen a feeling of belonging to a larger community of their brethren in suffering that went beyond the bounds of their immediate surroundings and existed in spite of the landscapes of inequality that seemed to deny their independence. Jones quotes a former slave named Benjamin Russell, born in 1849, as saying that many plantations were strict about [letting news get back to slaves], but the greater the precaution, the alerter became the slaves, the wider they opened their ears and the more eager they became for outside information. (Jones 1990:124)

Those enslaved people who, because of the nature of their work, had mobility and relative freedom of movement, became a ray of hope and the umbilical cord between those left at home and the wider black community. Jimmie was a coachman who drove his master's family around to church, weddings, parties, or meetings. "Frequently upon his return from one of these trips," said the Reverend I. E. Lowery, himself a former slave, "the slaves would gather around him—old and young—to hear him tell what he saw and heard. For days these things would be discussed by the body of slaves" (quoted in Jones 1990:125). Indeed it is telling that Fortune became one of the cofounders of the Prince Hall African Lodge in Boston after emancipation, and Prince Hall himself drafted Belinda's 1783 petition to the court because she could not read or write herself. These ties to the Boston black community were no doubt first forged under servitude, when the nature of several slaves' work for the Royalls took them far afield. In being hired out, the baker's apprentice escaped the confines of the Royalls' incorporative landscape of inequality and was exposed to alternative landscapes and ideologies, where the Royalls, if only temporarily, had no mastery over him (or her, as women could also be trained as bakers). Through his stories the people back home might have felt a vicarious thrill.

Back home, however, even the consummate generalists who were responsible for the daily ins and outs of running the estate were probably able to appropriate various landscapes of Ten Hills Farm as their own. These general farm hands and jacks-of-all-trades probably used the main Medford highways only to transport goods on their carts. They likely got their bearings from the backs and sides of houses and traveled along field boundaries, following the river, creeks, fence lines, or the edge of the forest rather than roads. There were orchards to be planted and maintained; herds of pastured livestock to care for, feed, and protect from predators; friends to visit at the next estate; and clandestine meetings to attend deep in the forest. Garman (1998:151) states that the necessary spatial dispersion of many New England slaves in the construction of "workscapes" undercut the "spatial proximity and surveillance" experienced by domestics and probably constituted a source of "constant interaction" and dialogue between master and slave. While masters probably had an idea of where each enslaved laborer was on a given day—which field, pasture, or orchard they were supposed to be working—they could never be sure until "the end of the day when individuals reported back" (Garman 1998:151). In the meantime, just what a master could expect from a day's work must have been at least partly negotiable:

For example, how many apple trees could be pruned in a day's work? Or how long would it take to transport a wagonload of salt pork to Newport? There were no established answers to these questions. Time expectations were likely set, contested, negotiated, and renegotiated. . . . Although they were not industrial factory workers, who could shut down a plant by walking off the shop floor, [Rhode Island slaves] must have found innumerable ways to slow down the pace of work when necessary. Conversely, with the threat of violence pervading any master-slave relationship looming in the background, they must have reached work levels that were at least tolerable to [their masters]. (Garman 1998:151)

The people enslaved at the Royall estate inhabited a patchwork of natural and cultural landscapes that they would have seen with two different sets of eyes, for they led a dual existence. On the one hand, they were members of a discounted and despised class of people who were bound for life to labor for another. From this perspective all the natural world seemed to be cut up and divided among the ruling class; the fields, the forests, the land, and the waterways belonged to Master Royall or his neighbors and were physical manifestations of the system and ideology that allowed him to own people as well (see Isaac 1982:53). Everywhere around them was evidence of their role as unfree laborers: the fields they planted and harvested, the orchards they tended, the pastures they grazed the livestock on, the fences and boundary walls they maintained and that seemed to enclose them too in a statement of all-encompassing power. Where Isaac Royall, Jr., might have looked at the land around his house and been reassured through its beauty and symmetry of the legitimacy of his position, the people he held as slaves must have looked at the same landscape and seen only the rigidity of their imprisonment.

On the other hand, slaves led an alternative existence as individuals. Through those eyes the landscape held countless personal and secret implications that had nothing to do with the cool authority of ancient Rome or the English countryside and were likely invisible to outsiders. In 1735 Sampson, an enslaved man of the town, was "sorely frightened" by a bear and her cub in the woods near Governor Cradock's house, which lay directly across the river from Ten Hills Farm (Brooks and Usher 1886:495). At first glance little more than an anecdote, the story of Sampson suggests that enslaved people in rural or suburban settings might have had a more intimate, organic relationship with their environment than their masters, and certainly that they had access to and perhaps sought solace in the forests.

While the Royalls tried to structure movement through the landscape, their human chattels roamed freely across paths and boundaries. Enslaved people were surrounded too by their own implicated places. Perhaps for Sampson the distant line of trees at the edge of the forest called to mind the smell of damp earth and the cool silence where confusion, frustrations, and fears could fall away. Cato Pearce of Rhode Island, who eventually served as a minister to his black community there, said he "used to go into the woods every night," seeking meditation, mental escape, and personal space to practice his sermons (Pearce 1842:18). Sampson might have visited the woods in a more utilitarian capacity as well, though. Piersen (1988:98) states that Africans from the "forest regions" of West Africa (such as the Gold Coast) were "especially artful in the use of snares and traps for capturing small game . . . [and] certain Yankee blacks won local renown for their hunting skills, like Black Nim the deer hunter or Roswell Quash the 'scourge of foxes.'"

Likewise an opening in the brush, invisible to the uninitiated, might in the eyes of the enslaved have led to a clearing that welcomed weary minds, there for a few minutes or hours to think or pray, gather informally with friends or simply "quit the master for awhile" (Upton 1988:367; see also Fitts 1996; Isaac 1982). Perhaps that creek led to a good fishing hole. Down by the marshes, when the tide receded, one could be sure of finding a good oyster bed or a nest of quail eggs. The paths along the fence lines, worn to hard-packed dirt tracks by the long passage of feet, recalled the connectedness of the black community across white boundaries.

I imagine Plato, or whoever the boatman actually was, would have had the most freedom of movement of all. He would have been one of the more important individuals to the success of the estate and implicitly trusted by the Royalls. He might also have achieved particular status in the enslaved community, however, because of the ability to carry news and information all up and down the river from Medford to Boston and all the ports in between that his freedom of movement allowed him. Frederick Douglass (1845:286) said that the boatmen on his master's plantation outside Baltimore, Maryland, were "esteemed very highly by the other slaves, and looked upon as the privileged ones of the plantation; for it was no small affair, in the eyes of the slaves, to be allowed to see Baltimore."

The Royalls' boatman made trips to town that likely lasted more than a day and perhaps kept him for as many as two or three days away from the farm. What is more, unlike the baker's apprentice, he was not passing from one master's hands to another's. There was no one at the other end of his journey to take him in hand and put the boatman to work for his or her own purposes. He was there to deliver the goods and return to Ten Hills Farm, where impatient and eager ears would gather round to hear the latest tales. Plato, whose classical name suggests he was an African by birth, might have found especial pleasure in these temporary escapes. He would have felt the loss of his freedom in a way that little Joseph, son of Diana, or Prine, daughter of Belinda—both born in Medford— could not.

The Boatman

The boatman's brow was furrowed, his lips tucked thinly against his teeth. To an outsider he might have looked fierce, angry even, but he would have been surprised to hear it. The familiar hot tightness in the pit of his stomach, spreading upward, always anticipated one of these river trips. The feeling was, if anything, pleasurable. His frown was one of concentration. There was much to do. The boat was loaded before dawn. Wool, barrels of cider, bales of English and upland hay, bound for Boston and then points unknown. It would take all day just to get to Boston and drop off the shipment. Tonight he would take in the city; drink grog at a waterfront tavern, try his hand at paw paw in the alley outside, see friends he had not seen since his last trip some months before, and—who knows—maybe look for a little trouble.

Out here on the river, the boatman thought he liked the sound of water lapping on the sides of the boat. It shut out all the noise of a troubled mind and let a body think. Or not. To sit and not think at all—a luxury he rarely experienced these days, always worrying about what the old master was going to do or say next. The water held a peculiar solace for him. His ancestors lived beneath its surface. It was said among some of his elders that drowning carried the soul back across the water to Africa. The boatman thought that death by drowning might not be so bad. He imagined the water would cradle him on his journey. And, oh, the blessed silence. One day, he thought . . . maybe . . . but not today.

Not today.

He shook himself from his reverie.

When he reached Boston, the boatman knew he would have to keep his mouth shut and do as he was told. Impatient merchants and brusque ship captains would be waiting on his delivery, quick to anger or to cuff him on the back of the head for some imagined transgression. Sometimes they would even try to instigate an altercation for sheer entertainment—trick him with words into a situation where anything he said would get him in trouble. He knew when that was coming. It made him stiffen in a momentary paralysis. He could hear it in the feigned innocence of their voices and see it in the barely concealed expression of self-amusement in their faces. But all that was in Boston, a day's journey from here, and he would quickly be done with them. Master Royall would be expecting him back in a day or two, but who could tell exactly how long such a trip would take? Who would know if he stopped off along the way to visit a friend or a lover?

All up and down the riverbanks he could see evidence of his people. Invisible except when you knew where to look. Bare patches leading into *the undergrowth. There, a small boat covered with branches. Up ahead, a boy with trousers rolled to the knees, revealing black coltish legs, seemed intent upon catching minnows in the shallows. He saw the boatman and shot one bony arm up above his head, his sleeve falling almost to the shoulder. He let it linger there, wavering in silent greeting. A distant flash of white teeth—joyous and unencumbered—as if the weight of the world were not yet on those frail shoulders. The boatman touched a finger to his forehead in recognition. On these brief river trips, the boatman thought, he did not live by another's leave. Here, on the river, he was captain of his own soul and master of his own fate. As it was in the beginning. As it had always been meant to be.*

Summary

Landscape can be read as a physical map of social relations and realities of the past, for it is "much more than representation—it is rather the site of the construction of meaning" (Hall 2000:50). Planned landscapes often reflect conscious attempts by those who commission them to state an ideal or to force behavior from surroundings. The landscapes of inequality found in various American slave regimes, for example, betray the hope that white spatial and visual dominance in architecture and the landscape would translate into an internalized acceptance of social and political dominance, both by their social inferiors as well as their own peers. Archaeologists have been able to demonstrate, however, the existence of alternative landscapes, as well as multiple levels of involvement and experience of the same landscapes, that would have challenged the power presented in such implicated places.

The Royalls succeeded in creating a landscape that seemed to reflect, and legitimate at least to themselves, their hegemony in the town, but their many slaves experienced these spaces in alternative ways. On the one hand, they must surely have felt the restrictiveness of close living and working conditions with the Royalls that characterized New England slavery. On the other hand, because landscapes become implicated only insofar as they recall how one has experienced them on an individual level, the same landscapes that legitimated the Royalls' power to the Royalls and their peers would have held different implications for the enslaved, whose experience of the landscape was structured by their servitude and ways of adapting to it. The differential use of the work yards surrounding the slave quarters from the courtyard it shares with the main house illustrates how these were "shared but contested" spaces (Garman 1998:134).

The land immediately surrounding the mansion house, from the Royalls' perspective, might have served as a daily reminder of their legitimate mastery over land and men. The neoclassical architectural elements of house, quarters, and gardens implicated the rightful hierarchy of men that stemmed from time immemorial. The trash-strewn work yards emphasized the separation between master and slave, work and leisure, clean and unclean. To the enslaved on the estate, these same work yards might have represented a welcome retreat from constant surveillance, despite their appearance or smell. To them the work yards might have connoted family ties and time away from the master: long smokes on the stoop out back, an impromptu game of checkers or marbles, some quiet time to sew, make beads, or tell stories about Africa, and freedom to the children who had never known it.

Epilogue

An interpretive approach impels us toward the multifac-
eted consideration of all aspects of our sites and their contexts—historical, cultural, and environmental—so that we
can arrive at a point where the lines of evidence begin to
coalesce and point to meaning.
                              —MARY C. BEAUDRY, 1996

It is hardly a surprise to me that I am an archaeologist. As with many of my profession, my career choice seems in retrospect to have the heavy weight of inevitability, the logical outcome of a long-standing fascination with the past. That
I would eventually find nothing so absorbing as the interface between cultures
seems also more than chance.

My father is the number-five child of a Chinese immigrant father and Chinese-
Hispanic mother. My own mother is full-blooded Euroamerican. That makes me
"half brown," as I sometimes say, but "all American." And yet I have a soft spot
for hot foods, jade jewelry, and the glow of a rice-paper lamp, and I have always
felt everywhere and, to some extent, precisely nowhere quite at home. Looking
back at my childhood and upbringing, huddled somewhere in a murky space
between Chinese ghost stories and ballpark franks, I see that the questions that
have occupied me in my work are the very questions that have occupied me in
my life. What is the relationship between the individual, the object, and society
or culture (see Hodder 1986)?

There is a brass gong in my foyer and oolong tea in my cupboard. I speak no
Cantonese, I have been listening to Ozomatli recently, and, with the exception
of a number of lucky bamboo plants and other small accents, my apartment

is outfitted like a Crate and Barrel catalog. My ethnicity as an Asian American therefore is to a certain degree optional—"accidental" (see Liu 1998)—but, in all likelihood, partly "racially motivated" (Orser 2007:81). I see the physical world I have amassed around me and instinctively sense that the same processes of creative negotiation and expression of self and identity that lie at the heart of the interpretations presented here are still at work in my own life, all around me. I believe I am not alone in that, however. The question of the recursive relationship between individual, object, and society may contain emotional resonance for me because of my personal experience with the material world and my own self-conscious ways of using it as a biracial person to navigate cultural boundaries, but it still signifies in the larger, "rational accumulation of knowledge" we call science (Johnson 1999:37).

I have tried to present a wide range of evidence and materials recovered from or relating to the Isaac Royall family and their many slaves. In particular, in bringing an ethnographic approach and analysis to documents, architecture, landscape, and archaeology, I have tried to focus on the diverse experiences of the individuals from that site, black and white, and to offer possible interpretations of how those different experiences were negotiated through material symbols. "Just what did they mean by doing or saying or building that?" "To whom were they addressing themselves?" "What was the reply?" These have been questions I have tried to keep at the forefront of my interpretations of the material evidence at this site. Of course, the answers to those questions depended on the multiple personal identities of the individuals involved, the particular settings and circumstances in which they found themselves, and thus what they chose as appropriate, relevant, or efficient means of communicating about themselves with others. How one constructed the commonsense world, or the *doxa,* and negotiated one's place in it differed vastly between master and slave because of who they were (Bourdieu 1977). The exigencies and realities of their daily lives and interactions with other cultural actors based on their social, economic, and racial backgrounds dictated to some extent what aspects of the material world and what kinds of social action, or *praxis,* they would incorporate into their respective *habitus* (Bourdieu 1977).

This study has sought to reconstruct the "commonsense world" that the Royalls and the people they held as slaves made for themselves and to present a contextual consideration of the discourses of colonialism and the construction of public and private identities that both engaged in—with each other as well as among themselves. It was this statement and response that drew the diversity of individual experiences at Ten Hills Farm together into a discernible pattern. In documents, artifacts, landscape, and architecture, I have seen what I have interpreted to be evidence of these contestations between master and slave as they struggled to define themselves and each other in the violent and shifting world of pre-Revolutionary America.

In reconstructing the *doxa* of master and slave in this study, a variety of lines of evidence have come into play. A historical archaeologist, talking over a plastic cup of wine and a precariously balanced plate of three-layered Mexican dip, six kinds of pasta salad, and some optimistically prepared cocktail wieners in grape jelly and ketchup, might be overheard to say that she spends more time digging through archives than she does through dirt. It is a catch phrase among historical archaeologists (see Schrire 1992) so commonplace that it is sometimes surprising that it can still elicit chortles from nonarchaeologists, who might assume that she is trying to be witty. Perhaps, but even stated in jest, every historical archaeologist who uses the metaphor is implicitly recognizing and accepting what Beaudry (1996:480) has put in print quite matter-of-factly:

> Archaeology is an approach to [the study of culture], and we all know that an archaeological approach can be applied as readily to documents, landscapes, and aboveground material culture as it can to things buried in the ground.

Primary and secondary documentary research has been one of the most essential components of this study, meant to complement and enhance the three seasons of archaeological investigations at the site. This research provided the ethnographic, social, historical, and archaeological contexts for the study of both Anglo- and African American identity and society in 18th-century New England. It also built the historical framework of a specific site in which to place all later investigations and interpretations of other sources of data.

But written sources, both primary and secondary, are not just raw data providing arid facts; they can, and indeed should, be approached etically as well as emically, in order to elicit as much real cultural information as possible from a variety of sources: probate records, censuses, tax valuations, account books, letters, and newspapers, to name a few. While trying to situate the Royalls and their slaves in the broader, global tides of imperial expansion, colonialism, and the birth of a uniquely American culture, I also wanted to leave room for these individuals' own intentionality and to keep in mind that not all social groups underwent, responded to, or were affected by these processes in the same way. Taking lead from Henry Glassie's (1982) sumptuous monograph, *Passing the Time in Ballymenone,* and Beaudry, Cook, and Mrozowski's powerful article, "Artifacts and Active Voices" (1991:163), I have tried to construct a historical ethnography of Ten Hills Farm that portrayed its inhabitants not just "from the top down" or even "from the bottom up" but "from the inside out."

Statements of power, resistance, and accommodation through material objects have been viewed here as at least on some level intentional, personally motivated, and historically derived from specific societal conflict, contradiction, or compromise. While recognizing that the Royalls and their slaves did not act wholly independently from larger economic, social, and political processes, I have tried to avoid portraying them as a passive medium through which, and on which, these processes worked, but instead to recognize them as people who were probably conscious of many of the personal agendas, fears, and desires that drove their actions. Ethnographic analysis of the documentary record has allowed me to construct an explanatory framework for material culture and the use of space recovered archaeologically and to speculate about the motivations for their acquisition and use. Henry (1991:9) has called the internal influences on a person's choices in consumer behavior and the use of, and interaction with, the material world an irretrievable "Black Box," but I find that this is only partly, literally true. A contextually constructed historical ethnography of a site allows us to make at least educated guesses about individual motives that go beyond mere extravagant wishful thinking.

To wit, I believe that in conjunction with the historical ethnography described above, archaeological research at the Royall House has revealed many of the material statements of power the Royalls chose to use on their own behalf. Isaac Royall, Sr., provides an example of how the material world could be manipulated not just to reflect the self, but actually to redefine it. A historical ethnography of his life and times has also hinted at some of the idiosyncratic influences that might have affected his decision-making processes in that, showing how it was possible for an ambitious carpenter's son to use material statements of legitimacy in a shifting and fluid society to achieve access to the highest levels of society, but then for his son to use many of the same material statements to bar others from following the family's lead.

The Royalls' slaves were also communicating with material symbols, negotiating their identities in a liminal space somewhere between how they defined themselves and how they were defined by others. Various documentary sources suggested that the impositions of slavery and enslaved people's physical proximity to the Royalls would have set outer, practical limits to the construction of family, community, and identity. Within those limits, however, there were many ways that private identities could be constructed as well. Traditions in the realm of spirituality, medicine, and kinship have all suggested how the Royalls' slaves might have defined themselves within slavery, while naming practices and artifacts of clothing, leisure, self-adornment, personal presentation, and hygiene have pointed to ways they might have defined themselves in spite of it. The construction and manipulation of these various aspects of personal identity through material symbols would have provided a way for people to survive the violence, oppression, and discrimination of slavery and to maintain a beauty of spirit and a semblance of dignity while doing it. At the same time, I have argued that none of these expressions of identity—material or behavioral—is best interpreted as evidence of African or even African American ethnicity. Rather the artifacts from the ground and the modes of expression and behavior indicated in documents and born in part of slavery were structurally tied to the process of racialization, both arising from as well as giving definition to the constructions of "black" and "white" in Massachusetts at that time.

The fact that food procurement and preparation at Ten Hills Farm does not seem to have factored heavily in these constructions is, in my opinion, one of the most interesting divergences between this site and slave sites from across the South and Caribbean. Although there may have been other opportunities for autonomous development, such as the revelries and celebrations of alley society in nearby cities such as Boston, I cannot help but interpret the apparent curtailment of independent subsistence and economic activities among the enslaved at Ten Hills Farm as a great loss.

Architecture and landscape provided another window into the common-sense interpretation of the world that the Royalls and their slaves made. The concepts of "multilocality" (Rodman 1992), "implication" (St. George 1998), and "experiential" or "processional landscape" (see Barrett 1994; Upton 1988) help to problematize the concept of place and to establish social life at Ten Hills Farm as a kind of performance in motion. In the manipulation of architecture and landscape, the Royalls succeeded in creating a material backdrop to the performative aspects of their social lives that seemed to reflect, and to legitimate at least to themselves, their hegemony in the town and what I called earlier their rightful mastery over land and men.

Enslaved people, however, experienced these spaces in alternative ways because landscapes become implicated only insofar as they recall how one has experienced them on an individual level. On the one hand, the close living and working conditions with the Royalls that characterized New England slavery must surely have been restrictive and burdensome. On the other hand, the same landscapes that seemed to legitimate the Royalls' power to themselves would have held different implications for the people held as slaves, whose experience of the landscape was structured by slavery and their ways of adapting to it. A differential use of space, revealed archaeologically, in the work yards surrounding the slave quarters and the courtyard it shares with the main house has suggested how these might have been what Garman (1998:134) characterizes as "shared but contested" spaces. Through these spaces the Royalls sought to legitimate their claims of dominance, while their slaves sought to assert their own ideas about the world and their place in it by ignoring, circumventing, or creating their own implications for the same spaces. Somewhere in the middle they must have reached a compromise, but it would have been one that needed to be reestablished every day anew with each new setting, circumstance, or interaction.

The archaeology of early African America is one of the most prolific areas of research and publication in the field of historical archaeology. The number of articles and books on the topic coming out in the last decade is astounding, and the trend promises to intensify. The annual meeting of the Society for Historical Archaeology, which took place in Providence, Rhode Island, in 2003, featured no fewer than six symposia dedicated to the African American experience in the Americas, three on that experience in the northern colonies. It is a trend that continues at the annual meetings to this day. These scholars' contributions to the refinement of our understanding of African American slavery and its effect on African American culture, are, as Beaudry (1996:489) has said, "among the best our field has to offer." I hope this study has also made a useful contribution toward understanding American slavery in its colonial New England setting. I hope that in synthesizing a range of documentary, artifactual, architectural, art historical, and landscape evidence into a historical ethnography of a particular site, I have enabled readers to see some of the variations of slavery found in New England but also have encouraged them to refrain from engaging in arguments about comparative "quality of life."

I think the evidence here also underscores the findings of an already large body of literature of recent years on early African America that seems to suggest that there is no such thing as a pan-African American experience or identity in this country and that the experiences of Africans and their African American descendants under slavery varied widely, affected by myriad factors that are often hard to separate and categorize for analysis. Principally because of economic and demographic differences in the region, New England slavery can be said to have been broadly different from plantation slavery, but within New England there were many differences between urban and rural slavery and skilled and unskilled labor. On the individual family level, experience depended on specific, often fickle personal relationships with the master that could change from person to person or even day to day. The Royalls' slaves would have had a range of different social realities as "colonial New England slaves" owned by a single family. The estates in Medford, Stoughton, and Freetown had vastly different slave population sizes, ranging from 30 to two. The individuals enslaved there were involved in all kinds of labor and had varied living arrangements, and some seemed favored over others by their masters. Is there no wider story to be told, though? Does it all come down to individual experience and particular circumstance? Beaudry (1996:496) thinks not: "As novelists and poets know," she says, "it is in the very particularity of individual experience that a broader understanding of the human experience is to be found."

I have found that the particularities of much of the archaeological literature on early African Americans have this to say about a broader human condition: that these people were neither wholly disempowered nor wholly inarticulate in the discourses of colonialism, power, and subjugation that their masters brandished about with such pomp and puffery. If we take a view "from the inside out" of these people and the families and communities they built, we see that they were actively engaging in those discourses with their masters, often in historically silent or invisible or overlooked ways, but no less potently for that.

> Society is not peaked like a pyramid or layered like a cake. It is composed of communities simultaneously occupying space and time at the same human level. . . . All seem reasonable from within, strange from without, silent at a distance. The way to study people is not from the top down or the bottom up, but from the inside out, from the place where people are articulate to the place where they are not, from the place where they are in control of their destinies to the place where they are not. (Glassie 1982:85–86)

New England slaves do not seem to have been any more in control of their destinies than enslaved people under any other regime, but they do seem to have been equally expressive. Using the economic value of their bodies and their labor to negotiate with those who wanted to exploit them (Wilkie 2000:244), enslaved people, North and South, often succeeded in forcing discourses of power and subjugation imposed by masters to be reframed under the rubric of accommodation, acceptance, and grudging compromise.

Even in recognizing the diversity of individual experience represented at Ten Hills Farm, and 18th-century New England society at large, it is still possible, as others have done, to "come to see the commonalities that drew them together" (Wilkie 2000:239). The abandonment of "totalizing frameworks" in favor of a "focus on cultural actors" that has characterized historical archaeologists' attempts of recent years to reinvent themselves and their discipline does not preclude the possibility of contributing to a wider history (Beaudry 1996:496). The Royalls and their slaves led vastly different lives, occupying the very highest and the very lowest strata of the social spectrum, and yet they were inextricably linked, partners in the same dance. By studying them together we come to the richest understanding of who they were on their own, as well as how they all contributed to the forging of a new nation, as indebted to the drama and tragedy and triumphs and individual human episodes of their lives as to those of any other.

Appendix 1
PLANT REMAINS FROM THE ROYALL HOUSE

JULIE HANSEN

Nine samples of sediment were floated from various contexts at the Royall House, yielding a small number of seeds, fruit fragments, and small pieces of charred wood. The species represented by seeds are *Rubus* sp. (raspberry, blackberry, and so on), *Sambucus canadensis* (elderberry), and *Vitis vinifera* (grape). All of the seeds are mineralized rather than carbonized. Phosphatic mineralization typically occurs in the presence of highly organic deposits where human and other species' waste is concentrated (Carruthers 1991; Green 1979). The few remains from the Royall House suggest a context where refuse from the hearth or oven was deposited along with human waste, possibly in an outhouse.

The wood represented is oak (*Quercus robur*), maple (*Acer* sp.), possibly plane tree (*Platanus* sp.), and *Robinia* sp. (locust). Most of the pieces were too small to make a good transverse section for identification.

Rubus sp. There are many species of *Rubus* that can be found in New England, including *R. Allegheniensis* Porter (Allegheny blackberry, *R. chamaemorus* L. (cloudberry), *R. flagellaris* Willd. (northern dewberry), *R. occidentalis* L. (black raspberry), and *R. strigosus* Michx. (American red raspberry). It is not possible to distinguish the seeds of all of these species, however. The plants often form thorny thickets along hedgerows, fences, and openings in forests. Depending on the species, the fruit ripens from June through the summer (Duke 1992:170). The fruits are used for jams, pies, juices, and flavorings.

Sambucus canadensis L. (American elder). This is a small shrub that grows in meadows, clearings, and alluvial forests (Duke 1992:176). The fruit ripens in the summer, late June to July, and is used in preserves, pies, jelly, beverages, and flavorings (Fernald and Kinsey 1943:349).

Vitis vinifera L. (grape). Although there are species of wild grape native to eastern North America (for example, *V. aestivalis, V. labrusca*), it is probable, based on the size and shape of the grape seeds from the Royall House, that these are of the domesticated species. They were probably consumed as fresh fruit or may have been present in raisins from which the seeds had not been removed.

TABLE A1.
Plant remains

Context	Species	Plant Part	Number	Comments
W. Yard EU 41 209	cf. Chenopodium	Seed	1	Modern
W. Yard EU 41 210A	Carbon Frags.	Fruit?		
	Indet.	Wood		Too small
W Yard EU 41 210D	Rubus sp.	Seed	146 (63)	
	Sambucus canadensis	Seed	3	
	Vitis vinifera	Seed	(1)	
	Cf. Platanus	Wood		
	Acer	Wood		
W. Yard EU 41 211	Rubus	Seed	7(1)	
	Vitis vinifera	Seed	1	
	Carbon Frags.	Fruit?	7	
	Quercus robur-type	Wood		
W. Yard EU 30 148	Acer	Wood		
W. Yard EU 35 185	Carbon Frags.	Fruit?		
W. Yard EU 36 173B	Rubus	Seed	50 (11)	
	Carbon Frags.	Fruit?		
W. Yard EU 36 173D	Rubus	Seed	1	
	Chenopodium	Seed	1	Modern
	Carbon frags.	Fruit?		
	Cf. Robinia sp	Wood		
W. Yard EU 36 188B	Rubus	Seed	73(67)	
	Sambucus canadensis	Seed	2	
	Carbon Frags.	Fruit?	28	
	Acer	Wood		
	Quercus	Wood		
EU 47 229C	Rubus	Seed	1 (1)	
	Chenopodium	Seed	4	Modern
	Acer	Wood		
	Quercus	Wood		
S. Yard EU 27 123B	Indet.	Wood		Too small

References Cited

CARRUTHERS, W.

1991   Mineralized plant remains: Some examples from sites in southern England. In
        E. Hajnalová, ed., *Palaeoethnobotany and archaeology,* 75–80. Nitra: Archaeo-
        logical Institute of the Slovak Academy of Sciences.

DUKE, JAMES A.

1992   *Handbook of Edible Weeds.* Boca Raton: CRC Press.

FERNALD, MERRITT L., AND ALFRED C. KINSEY

1943   *Edible Wild Plants of Eastern North America.* Cornwall-on-Hudson: Idlewild Press,.

GREEN, F. J.

1979   Phosphatic mineralization of seeds from archaeological sites. *Journal of Archaeo-
        logical Science* 6: 279–84.

Appendix 2
REPORT ON THE FAUNAL REMAINS FROM THE ISAAC ROYALL HOUSE

Elizabeth Terese Newman and David B. Landon

Methodology

The analysis of the Royall House faunal assemblage was carried out by bagged provenience lot. We removed the bone specimens from each bag, sorted them by class and body part, and recorded our observations on a printed spreadsheet. The spreadsheets were subsequently entered into a Microsoft Access database to create a catalog and assist in analysis.

We made taxonomic identifications using comparative osteological material in the Zooarchaeology Laboratory at the University of Massachusetts, Boston. Mammal bones that could not be identified to specific taxa were grouped by size categories (see below). We recorded skeletal part in a system modified after Gifford and Crader (1977). Whenever possible, we recorded the fusion stages of the ends of the bone and symmetry. Finally, we recorded human modifications to the bones in the form of butchery, weathering, and burning and taphonomic modifications in the form of weathering and rodent and carnivore damage. We examined the *Bos taurus*, *Sus scrofa*, and Caprine teeth and recorded wear stages after Grant (1982).

General Description of Collection

NUMBER OF IDENTIFIED SPECIMENS (NISP)

The faunal collection from the Isaac Royall House contains a total of 4,358 individual bones, bone fragments, and shell. Of those, 3,978 (91.28%) are bone and bone fragments, and 380 (8.72%) are shell. We assigned all but 37 of the bone and bone fragments a broad taxonomic category below the level of vertebrate, and all but 54 of the shell to family level.

Species Representation
Bones

Mammals, birds, fish, and amphibians are all present in this collection. Because of their highly fragmentary nature, we were able to identify 2,410 (60.58%) of the bones only to this taxonomic level. We assigned the remaining 1,568 to more specific categories.

Mammals: Fully 86.97% (3,790) of the collection is mammal (table A2). We did not identify 2,312 below this level. Of the remaining 1,478, we identified the species *Bos Taurus* (cow), *Sus scrofa* (pig), and *Felis catus* (cat). We used slightly broader categories to identify caprine (sheep or goats), *Canis sp.* (dogs), *rattus sp.* (rats), and *Sylvilagus sp.* (rabbits) because of the difficulty in distinguishing these species solely on osteological characteristics. Finally, we assigned 693 of the bones to the still broader categories of small, medium, and large. We defined a small mammal as anything smaller then a pig. A medium mammal is larger then a pig, but smaller then a cow. A large mammal ranges in size from a cow upward. The large percentage of bones categorized as "Medium Mammal" is likely a result of the difficulty in distinguishing many caprine and pig bones, especially when these bones are fragmentary.

TABLE A2.

Remains—mammals

Class	Species	Name	NISP	% of Class	% of Collection	MNI	% of Class	% of Collection
Mammal	*Bos taurus*	Cow	392	10.34	8.99	7	26.92	12.73
Mammal	Large		210	5.54	4.82	0	0.00	0.00
Mammal	Caprine	Sheep/Goat	120	3.17	2.75	6	23.08	10.91
Mammal	*Sus scrofa*	Pig	249	6.57	5.71	6	23.08	10.91
Mammal	Medium		473	12.48	10.85	0	0.00	0.00
Mammal	*Canis sp.*	Dog Family	1	0.03	0.02	1	3.85	1.82
Mammal	*Felis catus*	Cat	12	0.32	0.28	2	7.69	3.64
Mammal	*Rattus sp.*	Rat	9	0.24	0.21	3	11.54	5.45
Mammal	*Sylvilagus sp.*	Rabbit	2	0.05	0.05	1	3.85	1.82
Mammal	Small		10	0.26	0.23	0	0.00	0.00
Mammal	Un-identified		2312	61.00	53.05	0	0.00	0.00
Total			**3790**	**100.00**	**86.97**	**26**	**100.00**	**47.27**

Birds: With 96 identified specimens (2.20%), the birds (table A3) make up the next largest class of bones. Of these we did not identify 57 (59.38%) to a more specific category. We identified only three species, *Branta canadensis* (Canada goose), *Gallus gallus* (chicken), and *Meleagris gallopavo* (turkey) in this collection. We assigned the remaining bones to the broader family categories of Anatidae (swans, ducks, and geese), Columbidae (pigeons and rock doves), and Galliformes (chickens and turkeys).

TABLE A3.
Remains—birds

Class	Species	Name	NISP	% of Class	% of Collection	MNI	% of Class	% of Collection
Bird	Anatidae	Swans, Ducks, Geese	3	3.13	0.07	1	14.29	1.82
Bird	*Branta canadensis*	Canada Goose	3	3.13	0.07	1	14.29	1.82
Bird	Columbidae	Pigeon or Rock Dove	7	7.29	0.16	1	14.29	1.82
Bird	Galliformes	Chicken/ Turkey Family	2	2.08	0.05	1	14.29	1.82
Bird	*Gallus gallus*	Chicken	19	19.79	0.44	2	28.57	3.64
Bird	*Meleagris gallopavo*	Turkey	5	5.21	0.11	1	14.29	1.82
Bird	Unidentified		57	59.38	1.31	0	0.00	0.00
Total			**96**	**100.00**	**2.20**	**7**	**100.00**	**12.73**

Fish: With only 53 bones, fish (table A4) represent only 1.22% of the entire collection. The small size of the fish bones makes them less likely to preserve and more difficult to recover then other bones. As a result the fish are much more likely to be underrepresented then the other classes of animal. Furthermore the fish are largely represented by vertebrae, and so, given the difficulty in identifying fish based only on this bone, we were largely unable to identify them below the level of class. We were, however, able to assign a small number of bones to the species *Melanogrammus aeglefinus.* (Haddock), and a further few bones to one related family, Gadidae (cods, hakes, and haddocks).

TABLE A4.
Remains—fish

Class	Species	Name	NISP	% of Class	% of Collection	MNI	% of Class	% of Collection
Fish	Gadidae	Cods, Hakes, and Haddocks	8	15.09	0.18	1	16.67	1.82
Fish	*Melanogrammus ae.*	Haddock	5	9.43	0.11	3	50.00	5.45
Fish	Unidentified		40	75.47	0.92	2	33.33	3.64
Total			**53**	**100.00**	**1.22**	**6**	**100.00**	**10.91**

Amphibians: The amphibians (table A5) are represented by only two small bones and are likely an accidental addition to the collection. Using the collections at the Museum of Comparative Zoology at Harvard University, we identified one of the two as belonging to the species *Bufo americanus* (American toad). Because of the small size, we were unable to identify the other bone below the level of Anura (frogs and toads). However, given the size and the fact that it was recovered from the same context as the other, it is our belief that the bone is from the same individual.

TABLE A5.
Remains—amphibians

Class	Species	Name	NISP	% of Class	% of Collection	MNI	% of Class	% of Collection
Amphibian	Anura	Frog/Toad	1	50.00	0.02	0	0.00	0.00
Amphibian	*Bufo americanus*	American Toad	1	50.00	0.02	1	100.00	1.82
Total			**2**	**100.00**	**0.05**	**1**	**100.00**	**1.82**

Shell

With 380 identified specimens, the shell (table A6) makes up a significant part of the Royall House collection. We identified the shell as belonging almost exclusively to the *Pelecypod* (bivalves) class, with the exception of a single unidentified Gastropod. Among the *Pelecypods,* three species, *Crassostrea virginica* (eastern oyster), *Mercenaria mercenaria* (northern quahog), and *Mya arenaria* (soft shell clam), were identified. We identified one further specimen to the family level of Mytilidae (the mussels). Finally, we were unable to identify 53 specimens as anything more specific then *Pelecypod* as a result of their extremely poor state of preservation.

TABLE A6.
Remains—shells

Class	Species	Name	NISP	% of Class	% of Collection	MNI	% of Class	% of Collection
Gastropod	Unidentified	Gastropods	1	0.26	0.02	1	6.67	1.82
Pelecypod	*Crassostrea virginica*	Eastern Oyster	302	79.47	6.93	10	66.67	18.18
Pelecypod	*Mercenaria mercenaria*	Northern Quahog	20	5.26	0.46	4	26.67	7.27
Pelecypod	*Mya arenaria*	Soft Shell Clam	3	0.79	0.07	0	0.00	0.00
Pelecypod	Mytilidae	Mussles	1	0.26	0.02	0	0.00	0.00
Pelecypod	Unidentified		53	13.95	1.22	0	0.00	0.00
Total			**380**	**100.00**	**8.72**	**15**	**100.00**	**27.27**

Discussion

The total species composition of the collection is an interesting departure from the profile of faunal assemblages from comparable sites in other parts of the country. In their article on subsistence on coastal plantations, Reitz et al. note that "Evidence from coastal/estuarine plantations indicates that planters, slave, and freedmen all used wild resources extensively," and Theresa Singleton notes, "At every slave site where food remains have been recovered and analyzed, there is evidence that African-Americans consumed at least some wild foods." This is not the case at the Royall House. The composition of the collection is exclusively domestic. Wild mammals have no significant presence beyond the likely accidental inclusions of a very few small mammals. The birds also show very little in the way of possible wild animals. The class is dominated by the chickens. The pigeons, the second largest identified group, could possibly be wild, hunted animals, but documentary and archaeological indications of the presence of a pigeon house on the site indicate that they were likely domestic animals as well. Finally, the haddock, identified among the fish bones, is a deep-water dwelling fish, and would be the sort of animal bought at market.

Minimum Number of Individuals, Weight, and Biomass
Minimum Number of Individuals (MNI)

The MNIs presented in tables A2–6 (see above) are based on calculations that take into account body-part representation, symmetry, portion of the body part, and, when available, fusion stage. As a result these numbers are highly conservative. We calculated the MNI for the shells by counting the number of shells with hinge portions present and dividing by two. We did not identify upper and lower hinges.

Weight

Table A7 presents the total weight, in grams, for each identified taxonomic category, as well as percentages and average weights.

Biomass

The numbers presented below in table A8 present an estimated meat weight in kilograms for species of bird, fish, and mammal. The formula used follows the method proposed by Reitz. The biomass calculations show an alternate way of calculating the relative importance each species contributed to diet. Of the mammals the cow shows an overwhelming predominance, especially when it is, again, combined with the large mammals. This is a point worth noting and possibly bears further investigation.

Total weight for each identified taxonomic category

Class	Species	NISP	Weight	% of Class	% of Collection	Average Weight
Amphibian	Anura	1	0.10	50.00	0.00	0.10
Amphibian	*Bufo americanus*	1	0.10	50.00	0.00	0.10
Total		**2**	**0.2**	**100.00**	**0.00**	**0.10**

Class	Species	NISP	Weight	% of Class	% of Collection	Average Weight
Bird	Anatidae	3	0.70	1.65	0.00	0.23
Bird	*Branta canadensis*	3	5.00	11.79	0.03	1.67
Bird	Columbidae	7	0.90	2.12	0.01	0.13
Bird	Galliformes	2	0.80	1.89	0.01	0.40
Bird	*Gallus gallus*	19	14.50	34.20	0.09	0.76
Bird	*Meleagris gallopavo*	5	5.90	13.92	0.04	1.18
Bird	Unidentified	57	14.60	34.43	0.09	0.26
Total		**96**	**42.4**	**100.00**	**0.27**	**0.44**

Class	Species	NISP	Weight	% of Class	% of Collection	Average Weight
Fish	Gadidae	8	4.40	15.60	0.03	0.55
Fish	*Melanogrammus ae.*	5	12.60	44.68	0.08	2.52
Fish	Unidentified	40	11.20	39.72	0.07	0.28
Total		**53**	**28.2**	**100.00**	**0.18**	**0.53**

Class	Species	NISP	Weight	% of Class	% of Collection	Average Weight
Mammal	*Bos Taurus*	392	8064.40	56.43	51.61	20.57
Mammal	Large	210	1513.30	10.59	9.68	7.21
Mammal	Caprine	120	619.60	4.34	3.97	5.16
Mammal	*Sus scrofa*	249	1452.00	10.16	9.29	5.83
Mammal	Medium	473	828.70	5.80	5.30	1.75
Mammal	*Canis sp.*	1	0.20	0.00	0.00	0.20
Mammal	*Felis catus*	12	4.20	0.03	0.03	0.35
Mammal	*Rattus sp.*	9	1.80	0.01	0.01	0.20
Mammal	*Sylvilagus sp.*	2	0.90	0.01	0.01	0.45
Mammal	Small	10	3.50	0.02	0.02	0.35
Mammal	Unidentified	2312	1801.71	12.61	11.53	0.78
Total		**3790**	**14290.31**	**100.00**	**91.45**	**3.77**

Class	Species	NISP	Weight	% of Class	% of Collection	Average Weight
Vertebrate	Unidentified	37	4.30	100.00	0.03	0.12
Total		**37**	**4.3**	**100.00**	**0.03**	**0.12**

Class	Species	NISP	Weight	% of Class	% of Collection	Average Weight
Gastropod	Unidentified	1	0.00	0.00	0.00	0.00
Pelecypod	*Crassostrea virginica*	302	1171.10	92.93	7.49	3.88
Pelecypod	*Mercenaria mercenaria*	20	43.30	3.44	0.28	2.17
Pelecypod	*Mya arenaria*	3	2.90	0.23	0.02	0.97
Pelecypod	Mytilidae	1	0.40	0.03	0.00	0.40
Pelecypod	Unidentified	53	42.50	3.37	0.27	0.80
Total		**380**	**1260.2**	**100.00**	**8.06**	**3.32**

TABLE A8.

Estimated meat weight for species of bird, fish, and mammal

Class	Species	NISP	BIOMASS (KG)	% BIOMASS
Bird	Anatidae	3	0.01	2.08
Bird	*Branta canadensis*	3	0.09	12.48
Bird	Columbidae	7	0.02	2.62
Bird	Galliformes	2	0.02	2.35
Bird	*Gallus gallus*	19	0.23	32.88
Bird	*Meleagris gallopavo*	5	0.10	14.50
Bird	Unidentified	57	0.23	33.08
Total		**96**	**0.71**	**100.00**
Class	Species	NISP	BIOMASS (KG)	% BIOMASS
Fish	Gadidae	8	0.10	18.26
Fish	*Melanogrammus ae.*	5	0.23	42.82
Fish	Unidentified	40	0.21	38.92
Total		**53**	**0.54**	**100.00**
Class	Species	NISP	BIOMASS (KG)	% BIOMASS
Mammal	*Bos taurus*	392	86.26	51.91
Mammal	Large	210	19.14	11.52
Mammal	Caprine	120	8.57	5.16
Mammal	*Sus scrofa*	249	18.44	11.09
Mammal	Medium	473	11.13	6.70
Mammal	*Canis sp.*	1	0.01	0.00
Mammal	*Felis catus*	12	0.10	0.06
Mammal	*Rattus sp.*	9	0.04	0.03
Mammal	*Sylvilagus sp.*	2	0.02	0.01
Mammal	Small	10	0.08	0.05
Mammal	Unidentified	2312	22.39	13.47
Total		**3790**	**166.17**	**100.00**

Taphonomic History

WEATHERING

In the entire collection, 850 bones and bone fragments exhibit weathering greater then or equal to stage two weathering as defined by Behrensmeyer. This represents 19.57% of the entire collection. In addition large numbers of shell were observed to be in a poor state of preservation, possibly a result of weathering. By far the largest number of weathered bones was from the context comprising units 36, 40, 41, 44–49. While this is the largest context, containing more than half of the total NISP, a disproportional 27.35% of this context's bones exhibit weathering. The majority of the units exhibit considerably less weathering (figure A1).[1] The high degree of weathering seen in context 36, 40, 41, 44–49, a large, filled-in cellar hole, is likely indicative of a gradual depositional process. We believe the bones were deposited into the cellar hole over a long period of time, and that this area was open to the elements throughout that period of deposition.

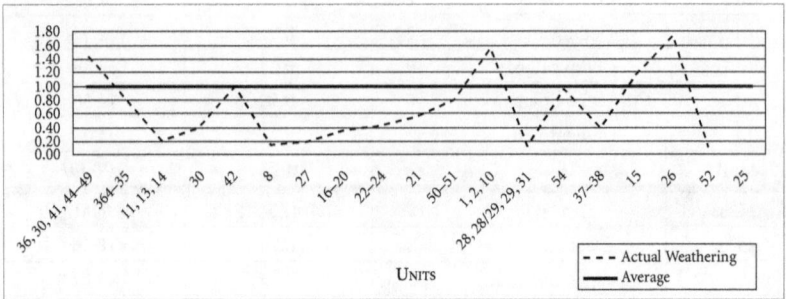

FIG. A1. Weathering distribution.

RODENT/CARNIVORE

Unlike the weathering, rodent and carnivore damage we observed on the bones is minimal. Only 0.83% of bones exhibit rodent gnawing, and 0.64% of bones show evidence of carnivore damage. None of the units displays a particularly extreme concentration of either. This is of particular interest in light of our interpretation of the weathering seen in context 36, 40, 41, 44–49. The high level of weathering and low level of rodent and carnivore damage indicates that the area was relatively free of scavengers and pests.

1. Contexts ordered by NISP in descending order.

Human Modifications

BUTCHERING

We identified butchering marks on 394 of the bones in the Royall House collection, and we recorded four categories of butchering: cuts, chops, shears, and saws. Cuts are fine lines across a bone, like the marks left by a knife. Chops are marks that remove a "v" shaped piece of bone, like the mark left by an ax or cleaver. Shears are cuts that extend through a bone, dividing the bone into multiple pieces. Finally, saws appear similar to shears, but exhibit small striations on the cut surface of the bone from the teeth of a saw. In the Royall House collection, shears are by far the most common type of butchery mark we identified. On the 394 butchered bones, we observed and recorded 410 shear marks. Next most common are the cut marks, appearing 314 times. We recorded chop marks on only 64 of the bones, and saw marks were extremely rare, appearing only 33 times.

BURNING

With only 110 bones (2.53%) in the entire collection exhibiting any sort of burning, this form of human modification appears to be of limited significance.

UTILITY

We calculated actual and expected high and low utility percentages for *Bos taurus*, *Sus scrofa*, and the caprines following the method developed by Walter Klippel. Utility percentages are calculated by dividing the body into the low utility parts, or the head and the feet including the carpals and tarsals, and high utility parts, or the remaining parts of the body. Actual percentages are then calculated for the collection as a whole and compared with expected percentages calculated based on the expected body part representation in a single animal. The calculations for expected body part representation used herein are based on those developed by Crader (1984). This calculation of utility is useful in two ways. First, it provides clues to how the food was obtained. If animals are raised, butchered, and consumed entirely on site, then one would expect that the actual high and low utility percentages of the collection would be fairly close to the expected percentages for a single animal. If, on the other hand, the animal were market bought, one would expect that the higher utility parts would be overrepresented, as a market bought animal rarely includes the lower utility body parts (Klippel:1193). The actual utility percentages for the Royall House are extremely close to the expected percentages for *Bos taurus*, *Sus scrofa*, and Caprines. Therefore it seems reasonable to assume that the members of the Royall household were raising, butchering, and consuming whole animals on site. It is unlikely that they were obtaining a high number of their animals from markets or, conversely, selling off parts of their animals and consuming others.

Second, the calculation of high and low utility provides insight into any potential differential distribution of the carcasses across the site. While Shultz and Gust have developed an excellent economic correlation of body part representation for 19th-century Sacramento, this method is of limited application to the study of mid-18th-century collections. The high/low utility calculations provide insight into similar issues of differential distribution without forcing us to impose the culinary values and market pressures of the 19th century on the 18th. While it is true that throughout the 18th century all parts of an animal were used in cooking by all groups of people, the high utility parts are certainly the meatiest, more highly nutritious, and most easily processed and prepared parts of a carcass (Klippel:1193). The low utility parts, on the other hand, provide less nutritional value and generally require intensive processing. Therefore it is reasonable to expect that *if* there is any differential distribution, the higher utility parts would be associated with higher status contexts.

As mentioned above, the high/low utility calculations for the site showed that the body-part representation found at the site was closely representative of what one would expect to see from the presence of complete animals, so it seems that there was no differential distribution at the site as a whole. In an effort to identify potential areas across the site where this distribution differed, we constructed frequency distributions using the high/low utility categories. This analysis did not reveal any dramatic differences; however, there are some irregularities to be found. When combined with other context information and analyses, the application of this information may prove fruitful.

Frequency Distributions

NISP

Fully 54.88% of the identified bones were found in the context comprising units 36, 40, 41, and 44–49. Units 15, 25, 26, and 52 all contain less then ten bones each. The other units contained a fairly even representation (see table A9).

Taxon/Species Distribution

The distribution of classes of animal over the site is, again, fairly even. Mammal dominates the collection everywhere, though units 42, 28, 28/29, 29, and 31 exhibit a relatively high proportion of shell. Unit 52 contains a somewhat high proportion of bird bone; however, this is possibly insignificant, resulting from the small sample size of the context. Fish bones appear in only eight of the larger contexts, with no fish bones appearing at all in contexts containing fewer then 89 bones. 76% (39) of the fish bones appear in the largest context (units 36, 40, 41, 44–49). Again this is likely influenced by taphonomic processes. The two

Frequency distributions

Excavation Units	NISP	% NISP
36, 40, 41, 44-49	2384	54.88
34-35	390	8.98
11,13,14	376	8.66
30	222	5.11
42	182	4.19
8	160	3.68
27	114	2.62
16-20	108	2.49
22-24	89	2.05
21	78	1.80
50-51	65	1.50
1,2,10	64	1.47
28, 28/29, 29, 31	54	1.24
54	22	0.51
37-38	14	0.32
15	9	0.21
26	6	0.14
52	6	0.14
25	1	0.02
Total	**4344**	**100.00**

amphibian bones found in unit 49 are likely an accidental inclusion. Shell tends to be found in the larger contexts. This is likely a result of sample size.

Mammal Distribution

Bos taurus: No contexts show a particularly high level of *Bos taurus* bones. The contexts associated with units 11, 13, 14, 40, and 42 show relatively low levels of *Bos taurus* bone. However, in all cases except for unit 42, when the NISP of *Bos taurus* and "large mammal" are combined, the numbers become very close to what is expected. Therefore the discrepancy may be either an identification or taphonomic problem.

Caprine: None of the contexts appears to show an absence of caprine bones. Contexts associated with units 11, 13, 14, and 16–20 appear to show high concentrations of caprine. Furthermore both of these contexts also show above average levels of *Sus scrofa* and "medium mammal," indicating that this aberration is real rather then the result of identification or taphonomic issues.

Sus scrofa: As mentioned above, units 11, 13, 14 and 16–20 show an elevated number of *Sus scrofa* bones. The other units show a close to average distribution.

Canis sp.: a single tooth from a dog was found in unit 54. This is likely an accidental inclusion and is unlikely to represent the deposition of an entire animal.

Felis catus: The bones of at least two individual cats (one adult, and one aged 6 to 8 weeks) are found in units 35, 36, 41 (six bones), 42, 44, 49. The diverse skeletal part representation indicates that in both cases the bones represent the deposition of an entire animal.

Rattus sp.: All nine bones assigned to the rat family were found in units 36, 44 (7 of the bones), and 49.

Sylvilagus sp.: The two rabbit bones were found in units 42 and 47.

Bird Distribution

Anatidae: Only three Anatidae bones were found.[2] They were found in units 8, 44, and 48.

Branta canadensis: Three bones identified as belonging to Canada goose were found in units 27, 35, and 41.

Columbidae: One bone from the pigeon family was found in the context associated with unit 35. All others were found in the same context in units 41, 47, and 49.

Galliformes: The two bones identified as belonging to the Galliformes were found in units 27 and 47.

Gallus gallus: The majority of the chicken bones were found in association with the context comprised of units 36, 40, 41, and 44–49. However, none of the units shows a larger then expected percentage of chicken bones.

Meleagris Gallopavo: Few turkey bones were found. Again, the majority were found in the context associated with units 36 , 40, 41, and 44–49, but none of the contexts shows an overabundance of turkey.

---

2. Because of the small number of identified bird bones, the frequency distributions are of limited significance.

Fish Distribution

Gadidae: Bones identified as Gadidae were found in units 27, 36, 41, and 49 (four bones).[3] No context shows a significantly high proportion of Gadidae, though with so few identified bones, this distinction is of limited use.

Melanogrammus aeglefinus: All bones identified as haddock were found in the context associated with units 36, 40, 41, and 44–49. We did not identify haddock anywhere else on the site.

Shell Distribution

Crassostrea virginica: Units 8 and 42 show an extremely high proportion (16.89% and 26.92% respectively) of eastern oyster relative to the expected percentage of 6.78%. Eastern oyster only appears in the larger contexts. This may be a result of taphonomic pressures.

Mercenaria mercenaria: We identified only 20 of these shells. They have a fairly even distribution across the site, with no concentrations appearing anywhere.

Mya arenaria: We identified only one soft shell clam. It is associated with unit 27.

Mytilidae: A single shell from the mussel family was found with context number 8.

Burning and Butchering

The distributions of both burned and butchered bones falls very close to expected numbers across the site. As is shown in fig. A2, butchered and burned bones deviate off of the expected average as the sample size decreases, negating the importance of most of the peaks and valleys on the chart.

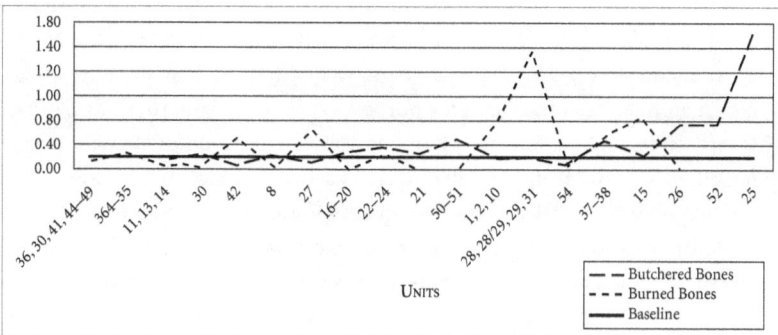

Fig. A2. Distribution of human modifications to bone.

3. As was the case with the birds, the low numbers of identified fish render the significance questionable.

We also calculated frequency distributions for types of butchering across the site. While the patterns are largely the same as for the overall butchering numbers, a few units show some potentially interesting deviations. The high frequency in cut marks seen in unit eight, and the high number of chop marks in unit 42 appear to be somewhat out of proportion to the rest of the site and potentially bear further investigation.

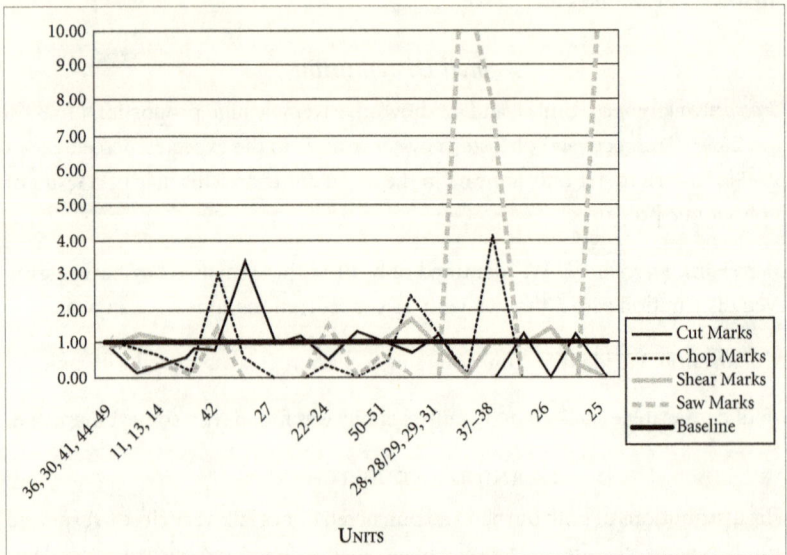

FIG. A3. Butchery types distribution.

Finally, in his study of the Kingsmill Plantation Slave Quarter, Larry McKee cites the intensity processing of the bones of as a potential marker of ethnicity when studying slave assemblages. In the slave quarters, McKee identifies a pattern of high intensity processing for purposes such as making soups and stews. The low percentage of butchering at the Royall House unfortunately makes this method somewhat inapplicable to this particular collection. However, the processing intensity McKee notes is frequently found on the bones that would be categorized as low utility. In an effort to understand the relative intensity of butchering on high and low utility body parts, we analyzed the average number of butchery marks per bone in both high and low utility categories. In every case the low utility bones averaged more butchery marks then the high utility. This is possibly related to high intensity butchering, but it is also possibly a function of the basic mechanics of butchering the lower utility parts, as many of the low utility parts require more work simply to remove them from the carcass.

UTILITY

As discussed above, the frequency distributions of high and low utility provide potential insight into differential distribution across the site. In the case of the Royall House, distribution appears overall to be fairly even (figures A1–A3). While allowing for sample size, the contexts containing units 8, 27, 34–35, and 42 all appear to contain a relatively high number of high utility *Bos taurus* bones. Only the context containing units 16–20 appears to contain an inordinately high number of low utility *Bos taurus* bones. The *Sus scrofa* utilities appear even more level. Contexts associated with unit 21 and units 34–35 show a high percentage of high utility bones, whereas contexts associated with units 8, 11, 13, and 14 display a higher then expected percentage of low utility bones. Finally, the caprines appear to exhibit higher percentages of high utility bones in contexts associated with units 8, 27, and 30, the low utility bones appear in excessive numbers in contexts associated with units 11, 13, 14, 21, and 42. It is interesting that there is very little in the way of a pattern among the species utility, leading us to believe that the differential patterns noted here are most likely accidental. However, it may be useful to correlate this data with other patterns observed in the total assemblage.

Qualitative Impressions

AGE

Little in the collection allowed for determination of age among the animals, and, as a result, the analysis presented herein is somewhat impressionistic. We conducted wear analyses on the teeth identified as *Bos taurus*, *Sus scrofa*, and caprine; however, their small numbers limit the depth of the analysis to some extent. That said, wear patterns do indicate that animals of fairly widely ages were being butchered, an assertion supported by the range in fusion stages observed on the bones. The advanced stages of wear on third molars, as well as the presence of some very "young" teeth not yet in wear, indicate that the husbandry techniques being used were not terribly focused. If, for instance, the husbandry of the pigs had been a directed goal, one would expect to see only fairly young pigs present. The definite presence of older animals indicates that conscious selection was likely not a factor.

SEX

Even less information was obtained about the sex of the animals. We identified one chicken bone (the tarsometatarsus) as belonging to a female animal. Based on fragments of the pelvis, we also identified three caprines as female. Finally, the greatest number of animals sexed were the pigs. All of our determinations were based on the canine teeth, which are, in pigs, sexually dimorphic. Of the *Sus scrofa* canines, we determined that three belonged to female animals, and four were classed as male. Given the relatively small number of animals sexed, little more can be said.

Pathologies

We observed four instances of pathologies on bones in the collection. Two occur on radii from a pig, one on the roots of a tooth, also from a pig, and one on the vertebra of a medium mammal. The pathologies were not caused by injury or malnutrition but were caused by an unidentified disease. Again, given the low level of occurrence, these incidences are likely of little significance, though they do support the idea of unfocused husbandry.

References Cited

Crader, D. C.

1984   *Hunters in Iron Age Malawi: The Zooarchaeology of Chencherere Rockshelter.* Malawi Government Ministry of Education and Culture, Malawi.

1990   Slave Diet at Monticello. *American Antiquity* 55(4): 690–717.

1984   The Zooarchaeology of the Storehouse and the Dry Well at Monticello. *American Antiquity* 49(3): 542–58.

Gifford, D. P., and D. C. Crader

1977   A Computer Coding System for Archaeological Faunal Remains. *American Antiquity* 42(2): 225–38.

Gilbert, B. M., et al

1985   *Avian Osteology.* Flagstaff: B. Miles Gilbert.

Gilbert, G. M.

1980   Mammalian Osteology. Laramie: Modern Printing Company.

Grant, A.

1982   The Use of Tooth Wear as a Guide to the Age of Domestic Ungulates. In *Ageing and Sexing Animal Bones from Archaeological Sites,* edited by B. Wilson, C. Grigson and S. Payne, 91–108. Oxford: British Archaeological Reports.

Hillson, S.

1986   *Teeth.* Cambridge: Cambridge University Press.

McKee, L.

1987   Delineating Ethnicity from the Garbage of Early Virginians: Faunal Remains from the Kingsmill Plantation Slave Quarter. *American Archaeology* 6(1): 31–39.

Olsen, S. J.

1979a   North American Birds: Postcranial Skeleton. In *Osteology for the Archaeologist.* vol. 3. Cambridge: Harvard University Press.

1979b   North American Birds: Skulls and Mandibles. In *Osteology for the Archaeologist*. vol. 3. Cambridge: Harvard University Press.

REITZ, E., ET AL.

1985   Archaeological Evidence for Subsistence on Coastal Plantations. In *The Archeaeology of Slavery and Plantations Life*, edited by T. A. Singleton, 163–91. San Diego: Academic Press.

REITZ, E., AND E. WING

1999   *Zooarchaeology*. Cambridge Manuals in Archaeology. Cambridge: Cambridge University Press.

SCHMID, E.

1972   *Atlas of animal bones. For Prehistorians, Archaeologists and Quaternary geologists / Knochenatlas. Fur Prahistoriker, Archaologen und Quartargeologen*. Amsterdam, New York: Elsevier Pub.

SCHULZ, PETER D., AND SHERRI M. GUST.

1983   Faunal Remains and Social Status in 19th Century Sacramento. *Historical Archaeology* 17(1): 44–53.

SINGLETON, THERESA.

1991   The Archaeology of Slave Life. In *Before Freedom Came: African-American Life in the Antebellum South*, 172, edited by Edward D. C. Campbell, Jr., with Kym S. Rice. Richmond: Museum of the Confederacy.

Glossary

Many of the terms discussed below may be confusing for nonarchaeologists. Even within the archaeological community itself, there is not always agreement about what each of these terms means, because many of them can "mean different things to different people" (Johnson 1999: 188).

This glossary includes only terms that have been discussed in the text, that are of important theoretical relevance, but that may be esoteric or "jargony" in nature for those who are not conversant with the ideas.

AGENCY.

Often cast in opposition to structure (and structuralism, see below), which poses individuals as mindless automatons, acting blindly according to a deep-lying, culturally predetermined course of action. Agency allows for individual human intent, action, and ability to effect an outcome but stops short of total free will, for it recognizes that all people act within the larger framework and/or "logic" of the cultures of which they are a part.

CONTEXT.

The artifacts, features, soil matrices, and residues found in association with each other in the archaeological record. An artifact is virtually meaningless without the context of where it was found and what was found with it to aid in its interpretation.

CULTURAL IMPLICATION.

Robert Blair St. George's (1998) term for the metaphor of place. The physical components of place can be created and used to convey thoughts, ideas, or things without specifically referencing them, just as linguistic implication can.

EMIC.

An understanding of the concepts, distinctions, values, and mores as they are significant to, and classified by, inside participants of a particular culture. See also etic.

ETIC.

An understanding of the concepts, distinctions, values, and mores of a particular culture as they are significant to, and classified by, an outside observer, such as a scientific researcher. See also emic.

DOXA.

Pierre Bourdieu's (1977) term for the "common sense world" within a particular culture, encompassing systems of values and morality, spirituality, social relations, health, nature, and any number of other daily "taken for granteds." The doxa, like habitus, is created through praxis, but is more of a collective phenomenon than an individual one. See habitus and praxis below.

EXPERIENTIAL LANDSCAPE.

The physical landscape as it is experienced socially and culturally by the people who inhabit it, pass through it, work or interact with others within it. Some landscapes are constructed with the express purpose of being experiential, and some are not, but all landscapes are experienced as social entities regardless.

HABITUS.

A subconscious understanding, subject nevertheless to interpretation and alteration, of how one's particular culture works; a set of ideas, created through praxis (see below), that guides the "social 'art' of living," and from which one draws what one believes will be effective and appropriate means of action (Bourdieu 1977: 19). A culture's collective habitus is called the doxa. See also doxa.

PRAXIS.

Another concept developed by the French anthropologist Pierre Bourdieu (1977) and explored further in this text as it is applied by the British archaeologist John Barrett (1994), to refer to the daily "performance" of social life. Praxis refers to the physical actions of people through which a social and cultural environment is created; through which a person comes to know and understand that environment; and ultimately through which that person learns how to act in a given culture. See also habitus and agency.

MULTILOCALITY.

A concept developed by the anthropologist Margaret Rodman (1992) that explores the social constructions of place and the multiple social meanings a single physical space may have for the different people who inhabit it, based on their individual experiences within it.

STRUCTURALISM.

A theory that posits human culture as being governed by deep-lying and unconscious rules (called "deep structures"), analogous to the rules of grammar in language. Structuralism is often treated in opposition to theories of agency. Neostructuralism seeks to reconcile the two by recognizing deep structures as pliable—lending "structure" if you will, but not rigidity, to human culture, which allows for diversity of individual action and intent that still fits within a cultural "pattern." The concepts of habitus, praxis, and the doxa all fit within a neostructuralist framework and leave ample room for human agency.

Terminus Post Quem (TPQ).

The "date after which" a feature or soil layer must have been deposited, usually determined by the artifacts found in association with the feature or soil layer, based on their known dates of production and/or popularity. TPQ dates can be approximate or absolute.

Terminus Ante Quem (TAQ).

The "date before which" a feature or soil layer must have been deposited, usually determined by the artifacts found in association with the feature or soil layer, based on their known dates of production and/or popularity. TAQ dates can be approximate or absolute.

References Cited

Account Book

1724– Photocopied manuscript of the accounts payable and receivable of Isaac Royall,
1749 Sr., and Isaac Royall, Jr. On file at the Royall House Slave Quarters, 15 George St., Medford, MA.

AHS (Antigua Historical Society)

1720– "Miscellaneous Records" on microfilm. Church of Jesus Christ of Latter Day
1729 Saints, Salt Lake City, UT.

Aresty, Esther B.

1970 *The Best Behavior: The Course of Good Manners from Antiquity to the Present.* New York: Simon and Schuster.

Armstrong, Douglas V.

1990 *The Old Village and the Great House.* Chicago: University of Illinois Press.

Ascher, Robert, and Charles Fairbanks

1971 Excavation of a slave cabin: Georgia, USA. *Historical Archaeology* 5: 3–17.

Bailey, Ronald

1992 The slave(ry) trade and the development of capitalism in the US: the textile Industry in New England. *The Atlantic Slave Trade: Effects on Economies, Societies, and Peoples in Africa, the Americas and Europe,* Inikori and Engerman, eds. Durham: Duke University Press, 205–46.

1998 'Those valuable people, the Africans': the economic impact of the slave(ry) trade on textile industrialization in New England. *The Meaning of Slavery in the North,* David Roediger and Martin H. Blatt, eds. New York: Garland Publishing, 1–31.

Babson, David W.

1990 The archaeology of racism and ethnicity on southern plantations. *Historical Archaeology* 24 (4): 20–28.

BAKER, VERNON

1980   Archaeological visibility of Afro-American culture: an example from Black
        Lucy's Garden. *Archaeological Perspectives on Ethnicity in America: Afro-
        American and Asian American Culture History,* Robert L. Schuyler, ed. Baywood
        Monographs in Archaeology 1. Farmingdale, NY: Baywood Publishing, 29–37.

BARRETT, JOHN C.

1994   *Fragments from Antiquity: An Archaeology of Social Life in Britain, 2900–1200 B.C.*
        Oxford: Basil Blackwell.

BARTH, FREDERIK

1969   Introduction. *Ethnic Groups and Boundaries: The Social Organization of Cultural
        Difference,* F. Barth, ed. London: G. Allen and Unwin, 9–38.

BEAUDRY, MARY C.

1996   Reinventing historical archaeology. *Historical Archaeology and the Study of
        American Culture,* Lu Ann De Cunzo and Bernard L. Herman, eds. Knoxville:
        University of Tennessee Press, 473–97.

1999   Foreword. *The Archaeology of Manners: The Polite World of the Merchant Elite
        of Colonial Massachusetts.* By Lorinda Goodwin. New York: Kluwer Academic/
        Plenum Publishers.

BEAUDRY, MARY C., L. J. COOK, AND S. A. MROZOWSKI

1991   Artifacts and active voices: material culture as social discourse. *The Archaeology
        of Inequality,* Randall H. McGuire and Robert Paynter, eds. Cambridge:
        Blackwell, 150–91.

BERLIN, IRA

1998   *Many Thousands Gone: The First Two Centuries of Slavery in North America.*
        Cambridge, MA: Belknap Press of Harvard University Press.

BIBB, HENRY

1849   *Narrative of the Life and Adventures of Henry Bibb, an American Slave.* Reprinted
        in *Slave Narratives,* William L. Andrews and Henry Louis Gates, Jr., eds. (2000).
        New York: American Library: 425–566.

BINFORD, LEWIS

1980   Willow smoke and dogs' tails: hunter-gatherer settlement systems and archae-
        ological site formation. Reprinted in *Contemporary Archaeology in Theory,*
        Robert Preucel and Ian Hodder, eds. (1996). Oxford: Blackwell Publishers, 39–60.

BLAKE, MARNI

1998   An Archaeological Plan and Documentary Survey for the Royall House Site,
        Medford, Massachusetts. Master's thesis completed for Boston University
        Department of Heritage Management, 1998.

BOSTON EVENING POST

1739   June 11. Advertisement for an infant slave a few days old, to be given away.

1743   March 14. Advertisement for the lease of a good farm in the town of Stoughton.

1740   January 14. Report of "Nocturnal Frolicks" in Roxbury, Massachusetts.

1746   December 8. Double suicide of a couple threatened with separation.

1752   February 24. Advertisement by Isaac Royall, Jr., for four "Negroes."

1762   March 22. Advertisement by Isaac Royall, Jr., for a "Negro Wench" and "four of said Wench's children."

BOSTON GAZETTE

1729   May 19–26. Advertisement by Jacob Royall for sale of slaves.

        June 2–9. Advertisement by Jacob Royall for sale of slaves.

        September 8–15. Advertisement by Jacob Royall for Dutch chimney tiles.

1737   July 25–Aug.1. Announcement of the Royalls' arrival from Antigua, July 27.

1739   June 4–11. Announcement of Isaac Royall, Sr.'s death in Charlestown on June 7.

1756   March 15. Advertisement by Isaac Royall, Jr., for the lease of a farm and the sale of slaves in Medford.

BOSTON GAZETTE AND COUNTRY JOURNAL

1759   September 24. Runaway slave advertisement.

1761   June 8. Advertisement by Isaac Royall, Jr., seeking coach horses and a coachman.

1767   November 23. Runaway slave advertisement.

BOSTON GAZETTE AND WEEKLY ADVERTISER

1754   May 14. Runaway slave advertisement.

        May 21. Runaway slave advertisement.

BOSTON GAZETTE OR WEEKLY JOURNAL

1756   March 15. Advertisement by Isaac Royall, Jr., for three "Negroes."

BOSTON NEWS LETTER

1736   November 25–December 2. Letter from Antigua.

1763   June 9. Report of a shocking murder in Taunton, Massachusetts.

BOSTON WEEKLY POST-BOY

1749   September 25. Runaway slave advertisement.

BOURDIEU, PIERRE

1977   *An Outline of a Theory of Practice.* Cambridge: Cambridge University Press.

BOWER, BETH ANNE

1991   Material culture in Boston: the black experience. *The Archaeology of Inequality,* McGuire and Paynter, eds., 55–63.

BRAGDON, KATHLEEN

1988   The material culture of the Christian Indians of New England, 1650–1775. *Documentary Archaeology in the New World,* Mary C. Beaudry, ed. Cambridge: Cambridge University Press, 126–31.

BROOKS, REV. CHARLES, AND JAMES M. USHER

1886   *History of the Town of Medford, Middlesex County, Massachusetts, from Its First Settlement in 1630 to 1855.* Revised, enlarged, and brought down to 1885 by James M. Usher. Boston: Rand, Avery.

CANNON, WALTER B.

1842   "Voodoo" death. Reprinted 1979 in *Reader in Comparative Religion: An Anthropological Approach*, 4th ed., William A. Lessa and Evon Z. Vogt, eds. New York: Harper and Row: 367–73.

CHAN, ALEXANDRA

2003   *The Slaves of Colonial New England: Discourses of Colonialism and Identity at the Isaac Royall House, Medford, Massachusetts, 1732–1775.* Ph.D. dissertation, Boston University. Ann Arbor: UMI.

CHIREAU, YVONNE

1997   Conjure and Christianity in the nineteenth century: religious elements of African American magic. *Religion and American Culture* 7 (2): 225–46.

CLIFFORD, JAMES

1986   Introduction: partial truths. *Writing Culture: The Poetics and Politics of Ethnography*, James Clifford and George E. Marcus, eds. Berkeley: University of California Press, 1–26.

CLIFFORD, JAMES, AND GEORGE E. MARCUS

1986   *Writing Culture: The Poetics and Politics of Ethnography.* Berkeley: University of California Press.

CODY, CHERYLL ANN

1982   *Slave Demography and Family Formation: A Community Study of the Ball Family Plantations, 1720–1896.* Ph.D. dissertation, University of Minnesota.

COLONIAL HOMES

1989   Isaac Royall House. *Colonial Homes* 15 (5): 100ff.

COOK, LAUREN J., REBECCA YAMIN, AND JOHN P. McCARTHY

1996   Shopping as meaningful action: toward a redefinition of consumption in historical archaeology. *Historical Archaeology* 30 (4): 50–65.

COUGHTRY, JAY

1981   *The Notorious Triangle: Rhode Island and the African Slave Trade, 1700–1807.* Philadelphia: Temple University Press.

COWGILL, GEORGE L.

1993   Distinguished lecture in archeology: beyond criticizing New Archeology. *American Anthropologist* 95 (3): 551–73.

CSIKSZENTMIHALYI, MIHALY

1993   Why we need things. *History from Things*, Steven Lubar and W. David Kingery, eds. Washington: Smithsonian Institution Press, 20–29.

CUMMINGS, ABBOT LOWELL

1986   Inside the Massachusetts House. *Common Places*, Dell Upton and Michael Vlach, eds. Athens: University of Georgia Press, 219–39.

DEAGAN, KATHLEEN

1988   Neither history nor prehistory: questions that count in historical archaeology. *Historical Archaeology* 22 (1): 7–12.

DeCorse, Christopher

1999   Oceans apart: Africanist perspectives on diaspora archaeology. *I, Too, Am America.* Theresa Singleton, ed. Charlottesville: University Press of Virginia, 132–58.

2001   *An Archaeology of Elmina: Africans and Europeans on the Gold Coast, 1400–1900.* Washington, DC: Smithsonian Press.

Deetz, James

1988   American historical archaeology: methods and results. *Science* 239: 362–67.

1996   *In Small Things Forgotten: The Archaeology of Early American Life.* New York: Anchor Books.

Delle, James A.

1999   The landscapes of class negotiation on coffee plantations in the Blue Mountains of Jamaica: 1790–1850. *Historical Archaeology* 33 (1): 136–58.

Donnan, Elizabeth

1931   *Documents Illustrative of the History of the Slave Trade to America: The Eighteenth Century,* vol. II (1969). New York: Octagon Books.

1932   *Documents Illustrative of the History of the Slave Trade to America: New England and the Middle Colonies,* vol. III (1969). New York: Octagon Books.

Douglas, Mary, and Baron Isherwood

1979   *The World of Goods.* New York: Basic Books.

Douglass, Frederick

1845   *Narrative of the Life of Frederick Douglass, an American Slave.* Reprinted in *Slave Narratives,* William L. Andrews and Henry Louis Gates, Jr., eds. (2000). New York: American Library: 267–368.

1855   My Bondage and My Freedom. New York: Miller, Orton, and Mulligan. Available as full electronic text as part of the University of North Carolina Chapel Hill digitization project, Documenting the American South. http://www.docsouth.unc.edu/neh

Drake, Samuel Adams

1906   *Historic Mansions and Highways around Boston.* Boston: Little, Brown.

Earl, Riggins R., Jr.

2003   *Dark Symbols, Obscure Signs: God, Self, and Community in the Slave Mind.* Knoxville: University of Tennessee Press.

Emerson, Matthew C.

1999   African inspirations in New World art and artifact: decorated pipes from the Chesapeake. *I, Too, Am America.* Theresa Singleton, ed. Charlottesville: University Press of Virginia, 47–82.

Epperson, Terrence W.

1990   Race and the disciplines of the plantations. *Historical Archaeology* 24 (4): 29–36.

1999a   Constructing difference: the social and spatial order of the Chesapeake Plantation. *I, Too, Am America.* Theresa Singleton, ed. Charlottesville: University Press of Virginia, 159–72.

1999b   The contested commons: archaeologies of race, repression, and resistance in New York City. *Historical Archaeologies of Capitalism,* Mark P. Leone and Parker B. Potter, Jr., eds. New York: Klewer Academic/Plenum Publishers, 81–110.

2001   A separate house for the Christian slaves, one for the Negro slaves: the archaeology of race and identity in the late seventeenth-century Virginia. *Race, Material Culture, and the Archaeology of Identity*, Charles E. Orser, Jr. ed. 71–87.

EQUIANO, OLAUDAH

1789   *The Interesting Narrative of the Life of Olaudah Equiano or Gustavus Vassa, the African, Written by Himself.* Reprinted in *Slave Narratives,* William L. Andrews and Henry Louis Gates, Jr., eds. (2000). New York: American Library: 35–242.

ESCOTT, PAUL D.

1979   *Slavery Remembered: A Record of Twentieth-Century Slave Narratives.* Chapel Hill: University of North Carolina Press.

FERGUSON, LELAND

1979   Afro-American slavery and the 'invisible' archaeological record of South Carolina. *The Conference on Historic Site Archaeological Papers,* vol. XIV. Stanley South, ed. Columbia: USC.

1992   *Uncommon Ground: Archaeology and Early African America, 1650–1800.* Smithsonian Institution Press, Washington, DC.

FINNEY, ARTHUR L.

1974   The Royall House in Medford: a re-evaluation of the structural and documentary evidence. *Architecture in Colonial Massachusetts. Publications of the Colonial Society of Massachusetts* 51. Boston: Colonial Society of Massachusetts, 23–41.

FITTS, ROBERT

1996   Landscapes of northern bondage. *Historical Archaeology* 30 (2): 54–73.

FOX-GENOVESE, ELIZABETH

1988   *Within the Plantation Household: Black and White Women of the Old South.* Chapel Hill: University of North Carolina Press.

FRANKLIN, MARIA, AND LARRY MCKEE

2004   African diaspora archaeologies: present insights and expanding discourses. *Historical Archaeology* 38 (1): 1–9.

FRAZIER, E. FRANKLIN

1939   *The Negro Family in the United States.* Chicago: University of Chicago Press.

GARMAN, JAMES C.

1998   Rethinking "resistant accommodation": toward an archaeology of African-American lives in southern New England, 1638–1800. *International Journal of Historical Archaeology* 2 (2): 133–60.

GASPAR, DAVID BARRY

1985   *Bondsmen and Rebels: A Study of Master-Slave Relations in Antigua.* Baltimore: Johns Hopkins University Press.

GATHERCOLE, PETER W., AND DAVID LOWENTHAL, EDS.

1990   *The Politics of the Past.* New York: Routledge.

GENOVESE, EUGENE D.

1974   *Roll, Jordan, Roll: The World the Slaves Made.* New York: Vintage Books.

GIBB, JAMES G.

2000   Imaginary, but by no means unimaginable: storytelling, science, and historical archaeology. *Historical Archaeology* 34 (2): 1–6.

GIROUARD, MARK

1980   *Life in the English Country House: A Social and Architectural History.* Harmondsworth, Middlesex, England: Penguin Books.

GLASSIE, HENRY

1982   *Passing the Time in Ballymenone: Culture and History of an Ulster Community.* Philadelphia: University of Pennsylvania Press.

GOMEZ, MICHAEL A.

1998   *Exchanging Our Country Marks: The Transformation of African Identities in the Colonial and Antebellum South.* Chapel Hill: University of North Carolina Press.

GOODWIN, LORINDA B. R.

1999   *The Archaeology of Manners: The Polite World of the Merchant Elite of Colonial Massachusetts.* New York: Kluwer Academic/Plenum Publishers.

GOULD, STEPHEN JAY

1996   *The Mismeasure of Man.* New York: W. W. Norton.

GRADY, ANNE

N.d.   The Royall House Slave Quarters. Paper assessing the architectural and historical evidence for slave occupation of the structure, given to the Royall House Association November 19, 1997.

GRADY, ANNE, AND EDWARD CHAPPELL

N.d.   Notes on the Isaac Royall Kitchen, House, and the Presence of Slaves. Written assessment given to the Royall House Association September 30, 1998.

GRAY, THOMAS R.

1832   *The Confessions of Nat Turner, the Leader of the Late Insurrection in Southampton, Virginia, as Fully and Voluntarily Made to Thomas R. Gray.* Richmond: T. W. White.

GREENBLATT, STEPHEN, AND GILES GUNN

1992   Introduction. *Redrawing the Boundaries: The Transformation of English and American Literary Studies.* New York: Modern Language Association of America, 1–11.

GREENE, LORENZO JOHNSTON

1942   *The Negro in Colonial New England 1620–1776.* Reprinted (1966), Port Washington, NY: Kennikat Press.

1944   The New England Negro as seen in advertisements for runaway slaves. *Journal of Negro History* 29 (2): 125–46.

GUTMAN, HERBERT

1976   *The Black Family in Slavery and Freedom, 1750–1925.* New York: Vintage Books.

HANDLER, JEROME S.

1997   An African-type healer/diviner and his grave goods: a burial from a plantation slave cemetery in Barbados, West Indies. *International Journal of Historical Archaeology* 1 (2): 91–127.

HANDSMAN, RUSSELL, AND MARK LEONE

1989   Living history and critical archaeology in the reconstruction of the past. *Critical Traditions in Contemporary Archaeology: Essays in the Philosophy, History, and Sociopolitics of Archaeology,* Valerie Pinsky and Alison Wylie, eds. Cambridge: Cambridge University Press, 117–35.

HANSEN, JULIE

2002   Plant remains from the Royall House, Medford, MA. Unpublished report on nine floated soil samples from various contexts at the Royall House.

HALL, MARTIN

1992   Small things and the mobile conflictual fusion of power, fear, and desire. *The Art and Mystery of Historical Archaeology,* Anne E. Yentsch and Mary C. Beaudry, eds. Boca Raton, FL: CRC Press, 373–99.

1999   Abualtern voices? Finding the spaces between things and words. *Historical Archaeology: Back from the Edge,* Pedro Paulo A. Funari, Martin Hall, and Sîan Jones, eds. London: Routledge, 193 203.

2000   *Archaeology and the Modern World: Colonial Transcripts in South Africa and the Chesapeake.* London: Routledge.

HARDESTY, DONALD L., AND BARBARA J. LITTLE

2000   *Assessing Site Significance: A Guide for Archaeologists and Historians.* Walnut Creek: Alta Mira Press.

HARRISON, FAYE V.

1995   The persistent power of "race" in the cultural and political economy of racism. *Annual Review of Anthropology* 24: 47–74.

HARVARD LAW LIBRARY SPECIAL COLLECTIONS

1778   *Will and Codicils of Isaac Royall, Jr.* Kensington, England, May 26, 1778. Photocopy of original manuscript.

HENRY, SUSAN

1979   Terra-cotta tobacco pipes in 17th-century Maryland and Virginia: a preliminary study. *Historical Archaeology* 13: 14–38.

1991   Consumers, commodities, and choices: a general model of consumer behavior. *Historical Archaeology* 25 (2): 3–14.

HERMAN, BERNARD L.

1999   Slave and servant housing in Charleston, 1770–1820. *Historical Archaeology* 33 (3): 88–101.

HODDER, IAN

1982   Theoretical archaeology: a reactionary view. *Symbolic and Structural Archaeology*, Ian Hodder, ed. Cambridge, UK: Cambridge University Press, 1–16.

1989   Writing archaeology. *Antiquity* 63: 268–74.

1986   *Reading the Past: Current Approaches to Interpretation in Archaeology*, 2nd ed. Cambridge: Cambridge University Press.

HOOPER, JOHN H.

1900   The Royall House and farm. *Medford Historical Register* 3 (4): 133–51. Reprinted in the *Royall House Reporter*, Oct. 1964 and Jan. 1965, n.p. On file at the Royall House Association, 15 George St., Medford, MA.

HOOVER, GLADYS N.

1974   *The Elegant Royalls of New England*. New York: Vantage Press.

HORTON, JAMES OLIVER, AND LOIS E. HORTON

1979   *Black Bostonians: Family Life and Community Struggle in the Antebellum North*. New York: Holmes and Meier.

1997   *In Hope of Liberty: Culture, Community, and Protest among Northern Free Blacks, 1700–1860*. New York: Oxford University Press.

HOUSE OF REPRESENTATIVES

1787   Nov. 23. "The Memorial of Belinda, an African." Original manuscript, Massachusetts Historical Commission (Archives), *Acts and Resolves*, October Session, chapter 142.

HOWSON, JEAN E.

1990   Social relations and material culture: a critique of the archaeology of plantation society. *Historical Archaeology* 24 (4): 79–91.

HUDGINS, CARTER

1989   Robert "King" Carter and the landscape of Tidewater Virginia in the Eighteenth Century. *Earth Patterns*, William Kelso and Rachel Most, eds. Charlottesville: University Press of Virginia, 59–70.

HUME, IVOR NOEL

1969   *A Guide to Artifacts of Colonial America*. New York: Alfred A. Knopf.

HUNTER, PHYLLIS WHITMAN

2001   *Purchasing Identity in the Atlantic World: Massachusetts Merchants, 1670–1780*. Ithaca: Cornell University Press.

ISAAC, RHYS

1982   *The Transformation of Virginia, 1740–1790*. Chapel Hill: University of North Carolina Press.

1992   Imagination and material culture: the Enlightenment on a mid-18th-century Virginia plantation. *The Art and Mystery of Historical Archaeology: Essays in Honor of James Deetz*, Anne Elizabeth Yentsch and Mary Beaudry, eds. Boca Raton: CRC Press, 401–26.

JACKSON, ROBERT TRACY

1907　*History of the Oliver, Vassall and Royall Houses in Dorchester, Cambridge, and Medford.* Boston.

JACOBS, HARRIET A.

1987　*Incidents in the Life of a Slave Girl, Written by Herself.* Jean Fagan Yellin, ed. Cambridge, MA: Harvard University Press.

JARRATT, REVEREND DEVEREUX

1806　*The Life of the Reverend Devereux Jarratt.* Baltimore: Warner and Hannah. Reprinted (1969) New York: Arno Press.

JOHNSON, MATTHEW

1999　*Archaeological Theory: An Introduction.* Oxford: Blackwell Publishing.

JONES, NORRECE T., JR.

1990　*Born a Child of Freedom, Yet a Slave: Mechanisms of Control and Strategies of Resistance in Antebellum South Carolina.* Hanover, NH: Wesleyan University Press.

JONES, SÎAN

1997　*The Archaeology of Ethnicity: Constructing Identities in the Past and Present.* London: Routledge.

1999　Historical categories and the praxis of identity: the interpretation of ethnicity in historical archaeology. *Historical Archaeology: Back from the Edge,* Pedro Paulo A. Funari, Martin Hall, and Sîan Jones, eds. London: Routledge, 219–32.

JOYCE, ROSEMARY

2006　Writing historical archaeology. *The Cambridge Companion to Historical Archaeology,* Dan Hicks and Mary C. Beaudry, eds. Cambridge: Cambridge University Press.

KAPLAN, SIDNEY, AND EMMA NOGRADY KAPLAN

1989　*The Black Presence in the Era of the American Revolution.* Amherst: University of Massachusetts Press.

KEMBLE, FRANCES ANNE

1984　*Journal of a Residence on a Georgian Plantation in 1838–1839.* Edited, with an introduction, by John A. Scott. Athens: University of Georgia Press.

KING, WILMA

1995　*Stolen Childhood: Slave Youth in Nineteenth-Century America.* Bloomington: Indiana University Press.

KLEIN, TERRY H.

1991　Nineteenth-century ceramics and models of consumer behavior. *Historical Archaeology* 25 (2): 77–91.

KLEIN, TERRY H., AND CHARLES LEEDECKER

1991　Models for the study of consumer behavior. *Historical Archaeology* 25 (2): 1–2.

KLINGELHOFER, ERIC

1987　Aspects of early Afro-American material culture: artifacts from the slave quarters at Garrison Plantation, Maryland. *Historical Archaeology* 21 (2): 112–19.

KOLCHIN, PETER

1983   Reevaluating the slave community: a comparative perspective. *The Journal of American History* 70 (3): 579–601.

1993   *American Slavery, 1619–1877.* New York: Hill and Wang.

KULIKOFF, ALLAN

1974   The beginnings of the Afro-American family in Maryland. *Law, Society, and Politics in Early Maryland,* Aubrey C. Land, Lois Green Carr, and Edward D. Papenfuse, eds. Baltimore: Johns Hopkins University Press, 171–96.

1978   The origins of Afro-American society in Tidewater Maryland and Virginia, 1700–1790. *William and Mary Quarterly* 3rd ser. V. 35 (2): 226–59.

1986   Tobacco and Slaves: the Development of Southern Cultures in the Chesapeake, 1680–1800. Chapel Hill: University of North Carolina Press.

LADY OF BOSTON, A

1832   *Memoir of Mrs. Chloe Spear, a Native of Africa, who was Enslaved in Childhood and Died in Boston, January 3, 1815 . . . Aged 65 Years.* Boston: James Long. Available as full electronic text as part of the University of North Carolina–Chapel Hill digitization project, called *Documenting the American South.* http://www.docsouth.unc.edu/neh

LAGUERRE, MICHEL

1987   *Afro-Caribbean Folk Medicine.* South Hadley, MA: Bergin and Garvey Publishers, Inc.

LAMAR, MARJIE

N.d.   Reference material and illustrations. On file at the Royall House Association.

LEE, JEAN BUTENHOFF

1986   The problem of slave community in the 18th-century Chesapeake. *William and Mary Quarterly* 3rd ser. V. 43 (3): 333–61.

LEEDECKER, CHARLES

1991   Historical dimensions of consumer research. *Historical Archaeology* 25 (2): 30–45.

LEONE, MARK P.

1999   Setting some terms for historical archaeologies of capitalism. *Historical Archaeologies of Capitalism,* Mark P. Leone and Parker B. Potter, Jr., eds. New York: Klewer Academic/Plenum Publishers, 3–20.

LEONE, MARK P., AND PAUL A. SCHACKEL

1987   Forks, clocks, and power. *Mirror and Metaphor: Material and Social Constructions of Reality,* Daniel W. Ingersoll, Jr., and Gordon Bonitsky, eds. Lanham, MD: University Press of America, 45–61.

LIU, ERIC

1998   *The Accidental Asian: Notes of a Native Speaker.* New York: Random House.

MAINE HISTORICAL SOCIETY

N.d.   *Genealogy of Royall Family.* Collection 1358. Not paginated.

MARKS, JONATHAN
1994   Black, white, other. *Natural History,* December: 32–35.

MARTIN, SAMUEL, ESQ.
1745   *An Essay Upon Plantership Humbly Inscribed to his Excellency George Thomas,*
        Esq. Chief Governor of all the Leeward Islands, as a Monument to Ancient
        Friendship. Antigua: Samuel Clapham. Reprinted (1765) London: A. Millar.

MASSACHUSETTS SPY
1774   Feb. 10. Letter from an African.
        March 24. Letter from Phyllis Wheatley.

MCEWAN, BONNIE G., AND GREGORY A. WASELKOV
2003   Colonial origins: the archaeology of colonialism in the Americas. *Historical*
        Archaeology 37 (4): 1–3.

MCGUIRE, RANDALL H.
1982   The study of ethnicity in historical archaeology. *Journal of Anthropological*
        Archaeology 1 (2): 159–78.

MCKEE, LARRY
1987   Delineating ethnicity from the garbage of early Virginians: faunal remains from
        the Kingsmill Plantation slave quarter. *American Archaeology* 6 (1): 31–39.
1992   The ideals and realities behind the design and use of 19th-century Virginia slave
        cabins. *The Art and Mystery of Historical Archaeology,* Anne E. Yentsch and Mary C.
        Beaudry, eds. Boca Raton: CRC Press, 195–214.
1994   Is it futile to try and be useful? Historical archaeology and the African-American
        experience. *Northeast Historical Archaeology* 23: 1–7.
1999   Food supply and plantation social order: an archaeological perspective. *I, Too,*
        Am America, Theresa Singleton, ed. Charlottesville: University Press of Virginia,
        218–39.

MCMANUS, EDGAR J.
1973   *Black Bondage in the North.* Syracuse: Syracuse University Press.

MHC (MASSACHUSETTS HISTORICAL COMMISSION)
        Archives Collections. Probate records, court records, town records, etc. on micro-
        film. Cited as listed in the collections' card catalog, by volume number and page
        (e.g., MHC *Archives* 25: 390).
1754   Massachusetts Slave Census. Microfilm.
1771   *Massachusetts Tax Valuation.*

MHS (MASSACHUSETTS HISTORICAL SOCIETY)
1877   African-American petition to Governor Thomas Gage, 1774. *Collections of the*
        Massachusetts Historical Society, volume III, fifth series. Boston: Massachusetts
        Historical Society, 432–33.
N.d.   Medford Town Records through 1830. Microfilm.

MICHAEL, RONALD L., ED.
1998   *Archaeologists as Storytellers. Historical Archaeology* 32 (1). Special edition
        published by the Society for Historical Archaeology.

MIDDLESEX COUNTY PROBATE COURT FILE PAPERS, FIRST SER. 1648–1871

1739   Will, probate inventories, accounts of administration of Isaac Royall, Sr. of
        Charlestown. Case #19545.

1747   Will of Elizabeth Royall of Charlestown. Case #19543.

1750   Probate inventory of Andrew Hall, Esqr. of Medford. Case #10098.

1769   Probate inventory, accounts of administration of Henry Vassal of Cambridge.
        Case #23336.

1778   Probate inventory, accounts of administration of Isaac Royall, Jr., absentee, of
        Medford. Case #19546.

MILLER, GEORGE, WITH CONTRIBUTIONS BY PATRICIA SAMFORD,
ELLEN SHLASKO, AND ANDREW MADSEN

2000   Telling time for archaeologists. *Northeast Historical Archaeology* 29: 1–22.

MINTZ, SYDNEY, AND RICHARD PRICE

1976   *An Anthropological Approach to the Afro-American Past: A Caribbean Perspective.*
        Philadelphia: Institute for the Study of Human Issues.

MOORE, GEORGE H.

1866   *Notes on the History of Slavery in Massachusetts.* Reprinted (1968) New York:
        Negro Universities Press.

MORGAN, PHILIP D.

1998   *Slave Counterpoint: Black Culture in the Eighteenth-Century Chesapeake and
        Lowcountry.* Chapel Hill: University of North Carolina Press.

MORRISON, HUGH

1952   *Early American Architecture from the First Colonial Settlements to the National
        Period.* New York: Oxford University Press.

MOYNIHAN, DANIEL PATRICK

1965   *The Negro Family: A Case for National Action.* United States Dept. of Labor,
        Office of Policy Planning and Research.

MROZOWSKI, STEPHEN A., AND MARY C. BEAUDRY

1990   Archaeology and the landscape of corporate ideology. *Earth Patterns,* William
        Kelso and Rachel Most, eds. Charlottesville: University Press of Virginia, 189–208.

MULLINS, PAUL R.

1999a   Race and the genteel consumer: class and African-American consumption.
        Historical Archaeology 33 (1): 22–38.

1999b   *Race and Affluence: An Archaeology of African America and Consumer Culture.*
        Fairfax: George Mason University.

NEHGS (NEW ENGLAND HISTORIC GENEALOGICAL SOCIETY)

1907   *Vital Records of Medford, MA to the Year 1850.* Boston: New England Historic
        Genealogical Society.

NEWMAN, ELIZABETH TERESE, AND DAVID B. LANDON

2002   *Report on the Faunal Remains from the Isaac Royall House, Medford, MA.* Unpub-
        lished report on the faunal analysis commissioned by Alexandra Chan in 2001.

OGUNDIRAN, AKINWUMI

2002   Of small things remembered: beads, cowries, and cultural translations of the Atlantic experience in Yorubaland. *International Journal of African Historical Studies* 35 (2–3): 427–57.

OLIVER, VERE LANGFORD

1894,   *A History of the Island of Antigua from the First Settlement in 1635 to the Present*
1896,   *Time*, 3 vols. London: Mitchell and Hughes.
1899

ORSER, CHARLES E., JR.

1985   Artifacts, documents, and memories of the black tenant farmer. *Archaeology* 38 (4): 48–53.

1994   Toward a global historical archaeology: an example from Brazil. *Historical Archaeology* 28 (1): 5–22.

1996   Beneath the material surface of things: commodities, artifacts, and slave plantations. *Contemporary Archaeology in Theory*. Robert Preucel and Ian Hodder, eds. Cornwall: Blackwell Publishers, 189–202.

1998   The archaeology of the African diaspora. *Annual Reviews in Anthropology* 27: 63–82.

2007   *The Archaeology of Race and Racialization in Historic America*. Gainesville: University Press of Florida.

PATTERSON, ORLANDO

1982   *Slavery and Social Death: A Comparative Study*. Cambridge, MA: Harvard University Press.

PAYNTER, ROBERT

1990   Afro-Americans in the Massachusetts historical landscape. *The Politics of the Past*. P. Gathercole and D. Lowenthal, eds. London: Unwin Hyman, 49–62.

PEARCE, CATO

1842   *A Brief Memoir of the Life and Religious Experience of Cato Pearce, a Man of Color: Taken Verbatim from His Lips and Published for His Benefit*. Pawtucket, RI.

PENDERY, STEVEN

1987   *Symbols of Community: Status Differences and the Archaeological Record in Charlestown, Massachusetts, 1630–1760*. Ph.D. dissertation, Harvard University.

PENNINGTON, JAMES W. C.

1849   *The Fugitive Blacksmith; or, Events in the History of James W.C. Pennington, Pastor of a Presbyterian Church, New York, Formerly a Slave in the State of Maryland, United States*. London: Charles Gilpin.

PHILLIPS, ULRICH BONNELL

1929   *Life and Labor in the Old South*. Boston: Little, Brown, and Company.

PIERSEN, WILLIAM DILLON

1988   *Black Yankees: The Development of an Afro-American Subculture in Eighteenth-Century New England*. Amherst: University of Massachusetts Press.

PONTOPPIDAN, ERIK

1760   Foreword: To the Reader. *A Reliable Account of the Coast of Guinea,* by Ludewig
        Ferdinand Rømer. Reprinted 2000, translated from the Danish and edited by
        Selena Axelrod Winsnes. New York: Oxford University Press, 5–12.

POTTER, PARKER B., JR.

1991   What is the use of plantation archaeology? *Historical Archaeology* 25 (3): 94–107.

1997   The archaeological site as an interpretive environment. *Presenting Archaeology to
        the Public,* John H. Jameson, Jr., ed. Walnut Creek: Alta Mira Press, 35–44.

PRAETZELLIS, ADRIAN

1998   Introduction: Why every archaeologist should tell stories once in a while.
        Historical Archaeology 32 (1): 1–3.

PRAETZELLIS, ADRIAN, MARY PRAETZELLIS, AND MARLEY BROWN III

1987   Artifacts as symbols of identity: an example from Sacramento's Gold Rush Era
        Chinese community. *Living in Cities: Current Research in Urban Archaeology,*
        Edward Staski, ed. Special Publication Series no. 5. N.p.: Society for Historical
        Archaeology, 38–47.

PROWN, JULES DAVID

1993   The truth of material culture: history or fiction? *History from Things,* Steven Lubar
        and W. David Kingery, eds. Washington: Smithsonian Institution Press, 1–19.

PUCKETT, NEWBELL NILES

1926   *Folk Beliefs of the Southern Negro.* New York: Negro Universities Press.

REBORA, CARRIE, PAUL STAITI, ERICA E. HIRSHLER, THEODORE E. STEBBINS, JR.,
        AND CAROL TROYEN, EDS.

1995   *John Singleton Copley in America.* New York: Metropolitan Museum of Art.

REITZ, ELIZABETH J., TYSON GIBBS, AND TED A. RATHBUN

1985   Archaeological evidence for subsistence on coastal plantations. *The Archaeology
        of Slavery and Plantation Life,* Theresa A. Singleton, ed. San Diego: Academic
        Press, 163–91.

RENSBERGER, BOYCE

1981   Racial odyssey. *Science Digest,* January/February.

RHA (ROYALL HOUSE ASSOCIATION)

1724–   Royall Family Papers. Filed at the Royall House Slave Quarters.
1779

RHS (RHODE ISLAND HISTORICAL SOCIETY)

1743   Last will and testament of Samuel Royall, a house carpenter, Dec. 10, 1739. Tenth
        Book of Wills 025: 326.

RODMAN, MARGARET C.

1992   Empowering place: multilocality and multivocality. *American Anthropologist* 94
        (3): 640–56.

ROYALL CORRESPONDENCE

Sept. 4, Gov. Jonathan Belcher to Isaac Royall, Sr., thanking him for the Negro boy, com-
1731   miserating over drought conditions. Handwritten transcript at Royall House Association.

Jan. 18, Gov. Jonathan Belcher to Isaac Royall, Sr., asking for another Negro boy as ap-
1732   prentice to his coachman. Handwritten transcript at Royall House Association.

June 12, Gov. Jonathan Belcher to Isaac Royall, Sr., asking again for another Negro boy,
1732   informing him on progress of the purchase of the Medford estate. Handwritten transcript at Royall House Association.

Aug. 15, Gov. Jonathan Belcher to Isaac Royall, Sr., about meeting with Jacob Royall
1732   on purchasing Medford estate, giving estimate of additional costs for repairs and beautification, advising him to spend his money elsewhere. Handwritten transcript at Royall House Association.

Jan. 29, Gov. Jonathan Belcher to Isaac Royall, Sr., encouraging his move to Massa-
1732/33 chusetts, teasing Madam Royall about her fear of northern winters. Handwritten transcript at Royall House Association.

Aug. 15, Isaac Royall, Sr. to Edmund Quincy, about family life, life as merchant, Medford
1736   estate. Typed transcript at Royall House Association.

Nov. 16, Gov. Jonathan Belcher to Isaac Royall, Sr., about young Isaac's tutor and suita-
1736   bility after all of Medford property, once finished, for a "Gentleman's seat." Handwritten transcript at Royall House Association.

Jan.   Isaac Royall, Jr., to Lord Dartmouth, about his political views on the relation-
1774   ship between Great Britain and the colonies. Typed transcript at Royall House Association.

May 31, Isaac Royall, Jr., to Lord North, from his exile in Kensington, requesting financial
1777   aid. Typed transcript at Royall House Association.

Aug. 6, Isaac Royall, Jr., to Lord North, repeating request for financial aid. Typed tran-
1777   script at Royall House Association.

May 29, Isaac Royall, Jr., to Edmund Quincy, about American property and life in exile.
1779   Original manuscript, Massachusetts Historical Society.

ST. GEORGE, ROBERT BLAIR

1998   *Conversing by Signs: Poetics of Implication in New England Culture.* Chapel Hill: University of North Carolina Press.

SAMMARCO, ANTHONY MITCHELL

1999   *Images of America: Medford.* Charleston: Arcadia Publishing.

SARNA, JONATHAN

1978   From immigrants to ethnics: toward a new theory of "ethnicization." *Ethnicity* 5: 370–78.

SAVITT, TODD

1978   *Medicine and Slavery: The Diseases and Health Care of Blacks in Antebellum Virginia.* Urbana: University of Illinois Press.

SCHACKEL, PAUL A.

1992   Probate inventories in historical archaeology: a review and alternatives. *Text-Aided Archaeology*, Barbara Little, ed. Boca Raton: CRC Press, 205–15.

SCHMIDT, PETER, AND STEPHEN A. MROZOWSKI

1983   History, smugglers, change, and shipwrecks. *Shipwreck Anthropology*. Richard A. Gould, ed. Albuquerque: University of New Mexico Press, 143–71.

SCHRIRE, CARMEL

1992   Digging archives at Oudepost I, Cape South Africa. *The Art and Mystery of Historical Archaeology: Essays in Honor of James Deetz*, Anne E. Yentsch and Mary C. Beaudry, eds. Boca Raton: CRC Press, 361–72.

1995   *Digging through Darkness: Chronicles of an Archaeologist.* Charlottesville: University Press of Virginia.

SEABURG, CARL, AND ALAN SEABURG

1980   *Medford on the Mystic.* U.S.A.: Camera Stat Associates.

SINGLETON, THERESA A.

1991   The archaeology of slave life. *Before Freedom Came: African-American Life in the Antebellum South.* The Museum of the Confederacy and the University Press of Virginia.

1999   Introduction. *I, Too, Am America: Archaeological Studies of African-American Life*, Theresa A. Singleton ed. Charlottesville: University Press of Virginia.

SOBEL, MECHAL

1987   *The World They Made Together: Black and White Values in Eighteenth-Century Virginia.* Princeton: Princeton University Press.

SODERLUND, JEAN R.

1985   *Quakers and Slavery: A Divided Spirit.* Princeton, NJ: Princeton University Press.

SOUTH CAROLINA GAZETTE

1736   No. 4. Extract of two letters from two gentlemen in Antigua, dated Aug. 4.

SPECTOR, JANET D.

1991   What this awl means: toward a feminist archaeology. *Engendering Archaeology: Women and Prehistory.* Oxford: Basil Blackwell, 388–406.

STAHL, ANN, ROB MANN, AND DIANA DIPAOLO LOREN

2004   Writing for many: interdisciplinary communication, constructionism, and the practices of writing. *Historical Archaeology* 38 (2): 83–102.

STERN, STEPHEN

1991   Introduction. *Creative Ethnicity: Symbols and Strategies of Contemporary Ethnic Life*, Stephen Stern and John Allen Cicala, eds. Logan: Utah State University Press, xi–xx.

STEVENSON, BRENDA E.

1996   *Life in Black and White: Family and Community in the Slave South.* New York: Oxford University Press.

STEWART-ABERNATHY, LESLIE

1992   Industrial goods in the service of tradition: consumption and cognition on an Ozark farmstead before the Great War. *The Art and Mystery of Historical Archaeology,* Anne E. Yentsch and Mary C. Beaudry, eds. Boca Raton, FL: CRC Press, 101–26.

STONE, PETER G.

1997   Presenting the past: a framework for discussion. *Presenting Archaeology to the Public,* John H. Jameson, Jr., ed. Walnut Creek: Alta Mira Press, 23–34.

STYRON, WILLIAM

1992   *The Confessions of Nat Turner,* Vintage edition. New York: Vintage International.

SUFFOLK COUNTY PROBATE FILE RECORDS

1749   Probate inventory of the widow Grace Knight of Boston. Case # 9457.

SWEENEY, KEVIN M.

1984   Mansion people: kinship, class, and architecture in western Massachusetts in the mid–eighteenth century. *Winterthur Portfolio* 19 (4): 231–55.

TATE, THAD, JR.

1965   *The Negro in Eighteenth-Century Williamsburg.* Williamsburg: Colonial Williamsburg Foundation, distributed by the University Press of Virginia, Charlottesville.

THOMAS, HUGH

1997   *The Slave Trade: The Story of the Atlantic Slave Trade 1440–1870.* New York: Simon and Schuster.

THOMPSON, ROBERT FARRIS

1983   *Flash of the Spirit: African and Afro-American Art and Philosophy.* New York: Random House.

TRUTH, SOJOURNER

1850   *Narrative of Sojourner Truth.* Reprinted in *Slave Narratives,* eds. William L. Andrews and Henry Louis Gates, Jr. (2000). New York: American Library: 567–676.

TWOMBLY, ROBERT C.

1973   Black resistance to slavery in Massachusetts. *Insights and Parallels,* William L. O'Neill, ed. Minneapolis: Burgess Publishing, 11–56.

TWOMBLY, ROBERT C., AND ROBERT H. MOORE

1967   Black Puritan: the Negro in seventeenth-century Massachusetts. *Race Relations in British North America 1607–1783,* Bruce Glasrud and Alan Smith, eds. (1982) Chicago: Nelson-Hall, 145–63.

UPTON, DELL

1986   Vernacular domestic architecture in eighteenth-century Virginia. *Common Places,* Dell Upton and Michael Vlach, eds. Athens: University of Georgia Press, 315–35.

1988   White and black landscapes in eighteenth-century Virginia. *Material Life in America 1600–1860.* Robert Blair St. George, ed. Boston: Oxford University Press, 357–69.

VITELLI, KAREN, ED.

1996   *Archaeological Ethics*. Walnut Creek: Alta Mira Press.

VLACH, JOHN MICHAEL

1991   Plantation landscapes of the antebellum South. *Before Freedom Came: African-American Life in the Antebellum South*. Museum of the Confederacy, ed. Richmond: Carter Printing Company, 21–47.

WALL, DIANA DI ZEREGA

1991   Sacred dinners and secular teas. *Historical Archaeology* 25 (4): 69–81.

1999   Examine gender, class, and ethnicity in 19th-century New York City. *Historical Archaeology* 33 (1): 102–17.

WARD, W. E. F.

1958   *A History of Ghana* (revised second edition). London: George Allen and Unwin, Ltd.

WEBBER, THOMAS L.

1978   *Deep like the Rivers: Education in the Slave Quarter Community 1831–1865*. New York: W. W. Norton.

WEIK, TERRENCE

2004   Archaeology of the African diaspora in Latin America. *Historical Archaeology* 38 (1): 32–49.

WHITE, SHANE, AND GRAHAM WHITE

1998   *Stylin': African American Expressive Culture from Its Beginnings to the Zoot Suit*. Ithaca: Cornell University Press.

WILD, HELEN TILDEN

1908   The old Royall House. *Massachusetts Magazine* 1 (3): 168–73.

WILKIE, LAURIE

1995   Magic and empowerment on the plantation: an archaeological consideration of African-American worldview. *Southeastern Archaeology* 14 (2): 136–48.

1996   Medicinal teas and patent medicines: African-American women's consumer choices and ethnomedical traditions at a Louisiana plantation. *Southeastern Archaeology* 15 (2): 119–31.

1997   Secret and sacred: contextualizing the artifacts of African-American magic and religion. *Historical Archaeology* 31 (4): 81–106.

2000   *Creating Freedom: Material Culture and African American Identity at Oakley Plantation, Louisiana, 1840–1950*. Baton Rouge: Louisiana State University Press.

2004   Considering the future of African American archaeology. *Historical Archaeology* 38 (1): 109–23.

WOLF, ERIC

1982   *Europe and the People without History*. Berkeley: University of California Press.

WOOD, PETER H.

1974   *Black Majority: Negroes in Colonial South Carolina from 1670 through the Stono Rebellion.* New York: Alfred A. Knopf.

WYLIE, ALISON

1989   The interpretive dilemma. *Critical Traditions in Contemporary Archaeology: Essays in the Philosophy, History, and Sociopolitics of Archaeology,* Valerie Pinsky and Alison Wylie, eds. Cambridge: Cambridge University Press, 18–27.

YELLIN, JEAN FAGAN, ED.

1987   *Incidents in the Life of a Slave Girl, Written by Herself.* Cambridge, MA: Harvard University Press.

YENTSCH, ANNE E.

1992   Gudgeons, mullet, and proud pigs: historicity, black fishing, and southern myth. *The Art and Mystery of Historical Archaeology,* Anne E. Yentsch and Mary C. Beaudry, eds. Boca Raton, FL: CRC Press, 373–99.

1994   *A Chesapeake Family and Their Slaves: A Study in Historical Archaeology.* Cambridge: Cambridge University Press.

1995   Beads as silent witness of an African-American past: social identity and the artifacts of slavery in Annapolis, MD. *The Written and the Wrought: Complementary Sources in Historical Anthropology,* Kroeber Anthropological Society Papers no. 79, Mary Ellen D'Agostino, Elizabeth Prine, Eleanor Casella, Margot Winer, eds., 44–60.

Index

racialization, process of, 9, 11, 12, 13, 38, 151, 174, 178, 231

recreation. *See* leisure time

Royall, Elizabeth McIntosh, **62**, **115**, 146, 149

Royall, Isaac, Jr. *See* Royalls, the: family

Royall, Isaac, Sr. *See* Royalls, the: family

Royall, Mary ("Polly") & Elizabeth, **116**

Royall, Penelope, 49, 86, 105, **115**, 131, 145, 146, 149

Royalls, the

—family: in Antigua, 47–57; estates at Stoughton & Freetown, 52, 62, 77, 84, 85, 139, 140, 147, 150, 232; in Maine/ New England, 47, 108; portraits of, **62**, **115**, **116**; probate inventories of (*see* probate inventories: relations to slaves) 43, 135, 219, 155–74; as slave traders, 19, 20, 23, 47–50, 108; at Ten Hills Farm, 57–63; and tenants, 203–211, 212, 233

—House: archaeology at, 25, 27, **28–30**, **36–39**, **41**, 57–59, 110–22, **112**, **119**, **121**, **124**, **140–42**, 155, **157**, 158, **159**, **169–70**, **171**, 174–94, **178**, **181–82**, **184–88**, 213–17; description of, **28–30**, **34**, 36–41; history of, 33, 36, 40–42; historical interpretations of, 20–21; slave quarters, 42, **43**, 44, 140. *See also* animal remains; plant remains

—slaves: children & childhood, 74–75, 85, 86, 142, 144, 145, 147, 148–49, 166, 167, 173, 179, 195; conjuration & belief systems, 129, 155, 157–60, 195; ethnic background of, 1, 85–87, 157, 158, 206; demographic profile of, 44, 138–52, **148**; exploitation of environment (*see* animal remains; plant remains); freedom of movement, 194, 196, 221, 223; healthcare & medical self-help, 129, 168–72, **169**, **171**, 195;

leisure time activities, 129, 174–89, **178**, **181**, **182**, **184**, **185**, 195; naming practices, 146–52; relations to Royall family, 43, 135, 219, 155–74; self-presentation & adornment, 129, **140–142**, 186–89, **187**, **188**, 195; tenure at Ten Hills Farm, 145

S

slave community. *See* black family under slavery

slave family. *See* black family under slavery

slave trade in New England: economic role of, 8, 66, 68, 94; importance of West Indian connection to, 68, 71–73, 94; slave ports of, 68

slavery/slave life in Massachusetts: alley society, 91, 92, 137, 220, 231; black assimilation, 81–89; black resistance to, 89–94; close living/working conditions of, 43–44, 194, 196, 211, 213, 219, 221, 225, 230, 231; compared with American South & Caribbean, 14, 27–28, 56, 66, 69, 72, 74, 77, 81, 86, 88, 95, 138, 160, 192–93, 217, 231; conjuration & use of magic, 92–93, 162–64; dispersed task system of, 76–77, 193–94, 220–22; generalists, 76–77; history of, 7, 67–71; laws governing black behavior, 70, 77–80, 92, 95; legal rights of blacks, 66, 78–80; legal status of blacks, 77; Cotton Mather's description of, 65; personal presentation, 86–88, 93–94, 205–6; population statistics, 73, 81–82, 94, 136; sex ratios, 81, 95, 133, 135, 194; slave census of 1754, 76, 82–84, 137, 138, 142, 180, 205; social conditions, 73–80, 94–95, 135–38, 194; specialists, 73–75

social discourse. *See* material culture

www.ingramcontent.com/pod-product-compliance
Lightning Source LLC
Chambersburg PA
CBHW021852020426
42334CB00013B/302